Therapeutic Games and Guided Imagery

Volume 2

Tools for Professionals Working with Children and Adolescents with Specific Needs and in Multicultural Settings

Monit Cheung
Graduate College of Social Work
University of Houston

LYCEUM
BOOKS, INC.
Chicago, Illinois

© 2014 by Lyceum Books, Inc.

Published by

LYCEUM BOOKS, INC.
5758 S. Blackstone Avenue
Chicago, Illinois 60637
773-643-1903 fax
773-643-1902 phone
lyceum@lyceumbooks.com
www.lyceumbooks.com

All rights reserved under International and Pan-American Copyright Conventions. No part of this publication may be reproduced, stored in a retrieval system, copied, or transmitted, in any form or by any means without written permission from the publisher.

6 5 4 3 2 1   14 15 16 17 18

ISBN 978-1-935871-44-6

Printed in the United States of America.

Library of Congress Cataloging-in-Publication Data

Cheung, Monit.
  Therapeutic games and guided imagery : tools for mental health and school professionals : working with children, adolescents, and their families / Monit Cheung. — 1st ed.
    p. cm.
  Includes bibliographical references and index.
  ISBN 978-1-935871-44-6 (alk. paper)
  1. Play therapy. 2. Child psychotherapy. 3. Psychotherapy. 4. Games—Therapeutic use. I. Title.
  RJ505.P6C54   2006
  615.8¢5153—dc22
                                                        2005037274

To download recordings of the guided imagery techniques in this book, please visit www.lyceumbooks.com/guidedimagery.

Therapeutic Games and Guided Imagery, Volume 2

Advisory Editor
Thomas M. Meenaghan, *New York University*

Related books of interest

Therapeutic Games and Guided Imagery, Volume 1: Tools for Mental Health and School Professionals Working with Children, Adolescents, and Their Families
Monit Cheung

Child Sexual Abuse
Monit Cheung

Child and Family Practice: A Relational Perspective
Shelley Cohen Konrad

Social Work Practice with Families: A Resiliency-Based Approach, Second Edition
Mary Patricia Van Hook

Secondary Traumatic Stress and the Child Welfare Professional with Training Guide
Josephine G. Pryce, Kimberly K. Shackelford, and David H. Pryce

Children and Loss
Elizabeth C. Pomeroy and Renée Bradford Garcia

School Social Work: Practice, Policy, and Research
Carol Rippey Massat, Robert Constable, Shirley McDonald, and John P. Flynn

Interviewing for the Helping Professions: A Relational Approach
Fred R. McKenzie

Best Practices in Community Mental Health: A Pocket Guide
Vikki L. Vandiver

Contents

List of Therapeutic Exercises vii
Table of Functions xi
Acknowledgments xii
Preface xiii
Introduction: Evidence-Based Therapeutic Practice xxi
        Trends in Therapeutic Use of Creative Modalities xxi
        Evidence-Based Therapeutic Practice xxiv
Therapeutic Exercises
    Part A Therapeutic Games and Activities 1
    Part B Guided Imagery 291
Final Words: Solution-Focused Interventions 387
        Portable Therapeutic Toolbox: An Example 405
References 407
Contributors 413
Index 425

Therapeutic Exercises

Part A: Therapeutic Games and Activities

A1.	3 in 1 ADHD Games	Chau Nguyen Todd
A2.	A Simple Start	Monit Cheung
A3.	Active Feelings	Shaneka Postell
A4.	Arbol de familia (Immigrant Family Tree)	John Betancourt
A5.	Back-Off Bingo	Laura Welch
A6.	Be Positive	Cornesia L. Russell
A7.	Bi- or Multicultural Identity	Tuan Nguyen
A8.	Body Speaks	Benjamin Pratt
A9.	Body Works	Kayla Cooper
A10.	Breaking the Ice	Monit Cheung
A11.	Building Cultural Pride	Venus Tsui
A12.	Building Diverse Communications	Micki Washburn
A13.	Bye-Bye Bullies	Carol A. Leung
A14.	Choose Your Own Adventure	Rachel Barajas
A15.	Cleaning the Dirty Laundry	Monit Cheung
A16.	Compliments	Monit Cheung
A17.	Connecting Latino Families	Maria Cano
A18.	Connections and Relationships	Monit Cheung
A19.	Dealing with Divorce	Chloe Walker
A20.	Divominos	Karen R. Greenberg
A21.	Dot Exercise	Jennifer Edwards
A22.	Environmental Mindfulness	Misty Miller
A23.	Family Time	Ada Cheung
A24.	Feeling Beads	Sandra L. Williams
A25.	Feeling Faces	Karen Mei-Lin Lau, Monit Cheung, Rachel Wai-Yee Cheung
A26.	Focus	Juan C. Macias
A27.	Following Hands and Focusing	Caroline Hendrix
A28.	Forum Theater	Mark Trahan
A29.	Gender Identity Game: Who Am I?	Micki Washburn
A30.	Giver and Receiver	Alicia Michele Thomas
A31.	Grandfather's Parcel	Ruprekha Baruah
A32.	Graph My Feelings	Kim Ba
A33.	Group Drawing	Monit Cheung
A34.	Hands Connection	Monit Cheung
A35.	Hospital Visit	Monit Cheung, Ashleigh Scinta

A36.	How I See Myself	Ophelia Mok
A37.	How to Tame Your Temper	Ivy E. Crank
A38.	Imitated for Self-Control	Yuliana Medina
A39.	King's "Rule-ette" Game	Nicole Willis
A40.	Let's Rebuild: A Game about Life	Victoria Reyes
A41.	Make Believe or Truth	Regenia G. Kerr
A42.	My Fantastic Family	Connie Villasmil
A43.	My Favorite Things	Marilyn Hotchko-Scott
A44.	Name It . . . Word It . . . Style It!	Jasmine Walls
A45.	Overcoming Shame Game	Allison Marek
A46.	Peer Influence Exercise	Sergio Cruz
A47.	Power List	Anny Ma
A48.	Practice Your Limits	Susan Kulbeth
A49.	Puppet Communication	Monit Cheung
A50.	Puzzle Pieces	Antonella Lazzaro
A51.	Rainbow Questions	Diana Scroggins
A52.	Safe House, Safe Space	Ashleigh Scinta
A53.	Sharing Your Heart	Casey Williams Hedges
A54.	SimCircle	Agnes Ho
A55.	Smiling Face	Lai-man Ada Yip
A56.	Snapshots for Moods	Ada Cheung
A57.	Strength Flower	Ada Cheung
A58.	Visualizing	Kelly Holmes
A59.	Where Is the Bird	Monit Cheung
A60.	Working Through Secrets	Noa Ben Yehuda

Part B: Guided Imagery

B1.	A Walk in Someone Else's Shoes	Chloe Walker
B2.	Bullying Role Reversal	Jolanna Jenae' Watson
B3.	Children in Military Families	Monique McWilliams Wall, Monit Cheung
B4.	Coping with the Aftereffects of Physical Abuse	Debbie Kumar-Misir
B5.	Everyone Is Important	Maria Cano
B6.	Fighting the Feeling of Anger	Marilyn Hotchko-Scott
B7.	Finding Hope	Laura Welch
B8.	Float Away	Kayla Cooper
B9.	Freeing Feelings	Jenna Halseth
B10.	From Yellow School Bus to White City Bus	Elizabeth Owsley
B11.	Go to My Country	Cristal Atilano
B12.	Glistening Stream and Body Image	Ivy E. Crank

B13.	Healing Parent-Teen Conflict	Ruprekha Baruah
B14.	Helping Children Sleep after a Parent Has Been Incarcerated	Nicole Willis
B15.	I Am Strong, Confident, and Powerful!	Jenaia Leffel
B16.	Laughing Yoga	Monit Cheung
B17.	My Family Tree	Joy Welch
B18.	My Favorite Thing	Juan C. Macias
B19.	Pain Management	Ashleigh Scinta
B20.	Petals Overcoming Trauma	Monica Ortiz-Holtkamp
B21.	Practice Makes Perfect	Patrick Leung
B22.	Release Angry Feelings	Lai-man Ada Yip
B23.	Releasing the Emotional Burden of Trauma	Rachel Barajas
B24.	Rice Therapy	Monit Cheung
B25.	Safe Driving for Teens	Monit Cheung
B26.	Sandbox Play	Ashante Montero
B27.	Secret Password	Monit Cheung
B28.	Sleep Tight	Karen R. Greenberg
B29.	Stay Focused	Patrick Leung
B30.	The Journey Home	Allison Marek
B31.	Trilingual Relaxation Journey	Monit Cheung, Elena Delavega, Wenjun June Zhu
B32.	Under the Sea	Sandra L. Williams
B33.	Willing to Seek Help	Carol A. Leung
B34.	Working through Trauma	Noa Ben Yehuda
B35.	Yes or No	Monit Cheung
B36.	Yoga Body Scan	Tira Burford

Table of Functions

Therapeutic Games and Activities

Ice-Breaker	A2 A10 A18 A21 A32 A34 A44 A54 A59
Rapport/Relationship Building	A3 A8 A12 A16 A18 A26 A27 A32 A34 A40 A41 A42 A43 A47 A49 A51
Assessment of Functioning	A1 A9 A10 A14 A15 A19 A20 A22 A23 A29 A31 A36 A37 A38 A40 A41 A42 A45 A46 A48 A50 A52 A53 A54 A56 A57 A58 A60
Feeling Expression	A1 A3 A4 A5 A6 A7 A9 A10 A12 A13 A15 A17 A20 A21 A23 A24 A25 A28 A29 A30 A32 A33 A35 A37 A39 A40 A41 A42 A47 A49 A55 A60
Cultural Awareness	A4 A7 A8 A11 A17

Guided Imagery

Concentration/Awareness	B1 B3 B11 B18 B21 B22 B24 B25 B27 B29
Visualization of Success	B5 B7 B8 B10 B11 B16 B21 B25 B34
Controlling Anxiety	B4 B6 B8 B11 B13 B14 B19 B20 B22 B23 B26 B28 B30 B32 B33
Gaining Insight	B1 B2 B5 B7 B9 B12 B16 B17 B21 B22 B34 B36
Self-Care	B16 B28 B36
Indigenous Practice	B11 B21 B24 B29 B31

Acknowledgments

I would like to first thank David Follmer, publisher of Lyceum Books, for believing in the use of creative modalities in clinical social work and counseling. Thanks must also go to my contributors, whose short bios are included in the back, for allowing me to include their work with children and adolescents who have difficulties expressing their mental health and/or life challenges due to special needs or cultural differences. I would also like to thank my research assistants—Denise Greenwood, Anna Maria Tepedino, Ada Yip, and Wenjun Zhu—for providing editorial support and preparing most of the guided imagery soundtracks available for download with this book. My appreciation goes to my copy editor, Paul Mendelson, and Siobhan Drummond, managing editor, and to all the Lyceum staff behind the scenes for making this book a viable means for communicating mindfulness, healing, and recovery. And finally, thank you, readers, for using this book as your clinical tool.

Preface

Monit Cheung's book *Therapeutic Games and Guided Imagery: Tools for Mental Health and School Professionals Working with Children, Adolescents, and Their Families* was published in 2006 focusing on general tools for therapeutic use. Reviewers found the book beneficial for understanding the theoretical base of play therapy and for creative practice with children and adolescents and families in a variety of settings (Mazza, 2007; "Review of," 2006; Russell, 2009; Saice, 2007). This second volume delves deeper into the use of games and guided imagery exercises by focusing specifically on therapeutic effects with children and adolescents who have specific needs related to medical issues, traumatic issues such as sexual abuse, grief and bereavement, physical disabilities, and behavioral problems. Furthermore, it contains games and guided imagery exercises that are technology-based and culture-specific for use by mental health and school professionals when working with children and adolescents from a variety of ethnic and cultural backgrounds.

Current research confirms the effectiveness of utilizing games and guided imagery tools with children and adolescents. Therapeutic play and computer games have been used with children who were hospitalized with cancer (Li, Chung, & Ho, 2011), and McLean (2008) discussed the usefulness of guided imagery for decreasing anxiety and stress among children undergoing painful medical procedures. Similarly, a 2008 case study by Robson details a nine-year-old's use of play therapy and computer games during bereavement therapy after the death of his fifteen-year-old brother. Game-based cognitive-behavioral therapy has been utilized in group settings with children who have been sexually abused (Misurell, Springer, & Tryon, 2011; Springer & Misurell, 2010). In addition, multimedia games have been used for work with children and adolescents with a variety of disorders, including autism spectrum disorders (Khandaker, 2009; Stokes, 2008), attention deficit hyperactivity disorders (Wilkinson, Ang, & Goh, 2008), and Down syndrome (Wuang, Chiang, Su, & Wang, 2011). Additionally, La Roche, Batista, and D'Angelo (2011) conducted content analyses on guided imagery scripts and determined that cultural differences often require that scripts be adapted for use with specific client populations.

The literature supporting the use of games and guided imagery tools among children with special needs warrants the development of this second volume of *Therapeutic Games and Guided Imagery*. Like in the first volume, this book contains an introduction followed by two parts: Part A—"Therapeutic Games and Activities" and Part B—"Guided Imagery." Additionally, this volume also includes evidence-based literature to inform multicultural applications. It also includes eleven sets of solution-focused therapeutic questions focusing on the various stages of a counseling and therapeutic process. These stages are (1) identify assessment areas, (2) focus on differences in solutions, (3) seek formal and informal support, (4) express feelings, (5) set up goals, (6) find possible solutions, (7) compare with resolved issues, (8) imagine resolved scenes, (9) evaluate with scaling questions, (10) look into strengths and positivity, and (11) use solution-focused closure techniques. Furthermore, a portable toolbox of miniatures is suggested to be useful for home visits and other simple therapeutic functions.

Recordings of the various guided imagery techniques described in this book can be downloaded at www.lyceumbooks.com/guidedimagery for teaching and practice purposes. Therapists can select a piece with the theme suitable for the client to test if it is helpful to achieve a desirable outcome, and then work with the client to change the wording, length, or pace to enhance effectiveness. In addition, similar to the feeling faces illustrated in the first volume, the cultural adaptation of the feeling therapeutic tool has included translated feeling words in Spanish (See figure 1 and figure 2) and Chinese (see A25). These bilingual feeling charts—along with a trilingual exercise (see B32) and a variety of other cultural and indigenous exercises (such as B38)—aim to inspire practitioners to generate additional ideas for therapeutic use. Two additional sets of feeling charts—with English words and without wording—are also provided after figure 2 for designing a feeling matching game or "guess the feeling" game, as well as for inserting specific language(s) for indigenous practice. With creativity and flexibility, this book provides many therapeutic tools to help engage children, adolescents and their families from various ethnic and cultural backgrounds, in different settings, focusing on diverse needs and solutions.

Figure 1 Positive Feelings—English and Spanish

Cheerful Alegre	Confident Confiado	Calm Calmado
Ecstatic Dichosa	Excited Emocionada	Great Venturosa
Happy Feliz	Hilarious Divertido	Hopeful Esperanzada
Rejoicing Con gran gozo	Lovestruck Enamorada	Okay Conforme
Relaxed Relajada	Satisfied Satisfecho	Silly Tonto

Figure 2 Negative Feelings—English and Spanish

Angry Enojado	Anxious Ansiosa	Ashamed Avergonzada
Bored Aburrido	Confused Confundido	Depressed Deprimida
Disgusted Asqueada	Embarrassed Abochornada	Enraged Encolerizado
Exhausted Agotada	Frightened Aterrorizado	Lonely Solitaria
Mad Enojado	Sad Triste	Shocked Aturdido

Figure 3 Positive Feelings—English only

Cheerful	Confident	Calm
Ecstatic	Excited	Great
Happy	Hilarious	Hopeful
Rejoicing	Lovestruck	Okay
Relaxed	Satisfied	Silly

Figure 4 Negative Feelings—English only

Angry	Anxious	Ashamed
Bored	Confused	Depressed
Disgusted	Embarassed	Enraged
Exhausted	Frightened	Lonely
Mad	Sad	Shocked

Figure 5 Positive Feelings—no labels

Figure 6 Negative Feeings—no labels

Introduction
Evidence-Based Therapeutic Practice

Trends in Therapeutic Use of Creative Modalities

The process of breaking the persistent silence is a crucial step during psychotherapy and clinical practice with children and adolescents. More often than not, these young clients are coming in involuntarily for counseling out of compliance with an authority figure. From their perspective, counseling is viewed as a source of punishment. As a creative counseling professional, it is essential to discover the most effective techniques when trying to draw their attention. Utilizing creative technology or visual means may establish a more flexible and fun environment where even the resistant or reticent clients feel more comfortable to relate their message or express their feelings with you. This book is a collection of creative techniques that have been tested to help children and adolescents feel more at ease when sharing their concerns. The trend of using creative modalities is clearly illustrated through the examples tested in the field with three themes—variety, diversity, and context.

Variety is exhibited through a combination of techniques. Although the term *techniques* is used to represent actual therapeutic procedures, it is also stressed that the idea of applicability and adaptability plays a major role in the development of all these creative ideas. Furthermore, it is through applicability and adaptability that you may discover your own set of creative ideas to meet the needs of your specific client. Therefore, based on the experience gained from utilizing various given tools from this book, professionals have the flexibility to also choose components that aim to produce specific therapeutic outcomes. Among the therapeutic games, techniques include paper-pencil to draw or color, cut-and-paste artwork, card creation, collage building, and game designs. Among the guided imagery exercises, the book introduces ideas to use praise, repeat strengths, and highlight solutions and to also engage the clients with all sorts of approaches such as touching, speaking, creating ideas, and identifying self-care strategies. This book acts as a source for creative techniques, and each technique is a stepping-stone for professionals to develop their own creative skills.

Diversity is the recognition of the need for respect. We know the basic essential steps of being an effective clinician include examining client history, assessing their current feelings and functions, and then providing guidance towards a solution while testing and reexamining the application of our tools and methods. Unfortunately, the clients we serve come to us from various backgrounds; therefore we cannot apply the same steps for each client. Accordingly, it should be our intention to meet them wherever they are when brought to our office out of respect for their specific needs. Some clients may be victims of trauma causing them to lack the ability to trust others due to losing the sense of safety or social cohesion. In those cases, the clinician's first step should be about building a trusting relationship with the client and establishing a safe environment. Some clients may be victims of abuse, and the first step may be to determine if the client understands the meaning of telling the truth in a non-threatening manner before providing any type of treatment. Some clients may be from a family of military background and are experiencing adjustment difficulty due to the possibility of lacking attention of a parent or experiencing emotional changes when another parent returns or leaves. They are in need of identifying, understanding, and coping with these emotions; therefore, clinicians may begin with educating them about the emotion they are expressing. Diversity is not only about respecting the specific needs of the clients but also developing expertise to help clients deal with their problems. Problem areas illustrated in this book include foster care transition or kinship care, incarcerated parents, drugs, alcohol, mental illness, and homelessness or housing issues. In order to create a culturally relevant atmosphere for the clients to feel their existential self with a meaning in life, cultural integration techniques, such as yoga, qigong, use of Taoist stories, origami, and acupressure were used in both the therapeutic games and guided imagery exercises as a therapeutic ritual before going deeper into therapeutic moments. These exercises help children process their reaction to trauma or secondary trauma. They can be adapted based on Latino, Asian, African American, Native American, and other indigenous practices that value clients' own contributions in the healing process.

Context means environmental and cultural support. By means of active involvement in a dynamic environment, clients in psychotherapy do not need to be fluent in English to participate. We call this type of involvement "translinguistic application"—without the boundary of using a specific language—because these exercises are considered kinetic communications that apply to all five senses to help clients process their thoughts, feelings, ideas, and solutions. Even in a guided imagery mode, concrete tools could be used to help clients think about what is in front of them that may act as obstacles or generate energy. The idea of connecting between our mind and our environment when thinking about solutions is a way of linking clients' basic needs (school, health, food, emotion, self-care, physical remedies) to their psychological well-being. It would be easier for clients to detect and utilize their ability to cope with or solve problems when they are able to relate something meaningful to them (through thinking, touching, seeing, feeling, and even smelling) before processing something abstract, such as stress reduction, bullying, discrimination, safety, and so on.

Contextualized practice integrates a variety of techniques and includes diversity as the target goal for encouraging client involvement. In social work education, the Council on Social Work Education (CSWE) publishes an educational policy that aims to address or infuse the teaching of contextualized practice in all curricula:

> Social workers are informed, resourceful, and proactive in responding to evolving organizational, community, and societal contexts at all levels of practice. Social workers recognize that the context of practice is dynamic, and use knowledge and skill to respond proactively. Social workers 1) continuously discover, appraise, and attend to changing locales, populations, scientific and technological developments, and emerging societal trends to provide relevant services; and 2) provide leadership in promoting sustainable changes in service delivery and practice to improve the quality of social services. (Educational Policy 2.1.9, CSWE, 2008).

This educational standard responds to the context that shapes practice to prevent us from jumping to conclusions by encouraging the use of careful assessments. "Practice gaps" can be averted if we take the time to express our appreciation for client participation while recognizing that time is required for knowledge to be digested and transferred into reality. It is suggested that these exercises should not be used rigidly because practitioners are collectively a role model from whom our clients learn how to live life with flexibility and creativity.

Professional help-seeking is not an expectation and thus not usually initiated by children and adolescents themselves. Therefore, when these clients are brought to your office, it is crucial to take the time to understand their feelings and also share the importance of spending time in a stress-free environment while dealing with life stressors. Ask them what relaxation means to them and what they do for relaxation. For example, use a weight (such as holding a water bottle for a few minutes and noticing your arm is gradually drifting) to represent a life metaphor, addressing the idea that simple matters can be accumulated into a problem if we ignore the significance of measuring the effect of a specific feeling experienced over time. Use song lyrics to process thoughts and ideas. Use self-care methods to identify how to release tension. Use story books to discuss wants, beliefs, and solutions, as alternative endings based on justice and child perspective can be incorporated in the discussion. It would be useful to get a feel of what the client finds joy in doing and attempt to apply it during the session to establish a better connection and an open environment.

Evidence-Based Therapeutic Practice

Therapeutic games and guided imagery are effective tools when treating children and adolescents in both individual and group settings. The variability, creativity, and contextualized practice theme in these exercises provide facilitators with the ability to tailor the therapeutic session with contents that integrate possible solutions distinguished by the client or definition on a specific issue, impact, life task, or a combination of the three. The creative use of a "concrete means" to help clients stay in touch with their abilities and wishes is productive because young people need a youth-oriented channel to express their concerns, particularly when it is related to peers connections. Interpersonal relations are important determinants of mental well-being and the achievement of a healthy self-identity (Leversen, Danielsen, Birkeland, & Samdal, 2012). Among various client populations, perceived life-satisfaction is indicative of psychological well-being achieved through the development of competence, relatedness, and autonomy (Leversen et al., 2012). If these needs are not clearly met or are conflicting with the client's perceived goal, the client's behavior will move away from being productive (Harvey & Retter, 2002). Through therapeutic games and guided imagery, facilitators will have the ability to create an environment that can support clients' need for autonomy, while helping them realize they are capable of setting goals to satisfy their needs (Eryilmaz, 2012; Leversen et al., 2012). Individuals are encouraged to develop greater motivation to strive for outcomes when they first-handedly experience these achievements in a non-threatening environment.

Literature has provided various forms of support (practice wisdom and evidence-based data) to address how therapeutic exercises have been applied in counseling and mental health treatment. Table 1 summarizes systematic review results in eight categories of practice with supporting evidence to encourage the use of therapeutic games and guided imagery. Although many related research studies were tested on adult subjects and across categories of practice, this summary identifies the importance of these creative approaches when handling crisis situations, traumatic responses, self-care, and sharing practice experiences with creative modalities. These categories include assessment and intervention, diverse cultures, developmental needs, special needs, immigrants, kinetic communications, secondary trauma, and applicability of guided imagery.

Table 1 Systematic Review to Support the Use of Therapeutic Games and Guided Imagery

1. Assessment and Intervention

Research	Theme	Method	Measures	Subjects	Findings or Practice Recommendations
Apóstolo & Kolcaba, 2009	Use of guided imagery (GI) to decrease depression, anxiety, and stress among psychiatric inpatients with depressive disorders	Two group, quasi-experimental. Measured stress, anxiety, depression and comfort of a control group and a usual care group 21 min GI, once a day, 10 days	Psychiatric Inpatients Comfort Scale (PICS) Depression, Anxiety, and Stress Scales (DASS-21)	60 depressive patients hospitalized short-term	Results indicated the use of GI subsequently reduces symptoms of depression, anxiety, and stress while also increasing comfort. It is recommended that guided imagery be used in psychiatric settings with depressive patients.
Baile, De Panfilis, Tanzi, Moroni, Walters, & Biasco, 2012	Use of drama to help caregivers release emotional burden of caregiving	Teaching graduate students how to use sociodrama and psychodrama to understand the emotional aspects of end-of-life caregiving		26 master's students in palliative medicine	Various techniques were used (warm-up, role creation, doubling, role reversal) to identify hidden emotions and communication dilemmas related to end-of-life care.
Cohen, 2000	Using therapeutic-restorative biographies (TR-Bios) and a non-competitive board game to provide intervention to Alzheimer patients	Pre-pilot test, actual intervention	Communications	Alzheimer's disease patients, family members, and volunteers	Results indicated the effectiveness of improved communication between family caregivers, patients, and staff in care settings.
Eryilmaz, 2012	Development of a model for subjective well-being among adolescents	Data collection	Satisfaction with Life Scale (SWL); Positive and Negative Affect Scale (PANAS); Scale for Basic Need Satisfaction in General; Reasons for Living Inventory	227 adolescents (107 male, 120 female)	Adolescent well-being was found to be directly affected by reasons for living and level of needed satisfaction. Reasons for living also had a mediating effect between subjective well-being and need satisfaction.

Table 1 Systematic Review to Support the Use of Therapeutic Games and Guided Imagery—(continued)

Gibbons & Jones, 2003	Health profiles of grandparents parenting their grandchildren	Data collection (via survey) and analysis	Medical Outcomes Trust SF-36 TM Health Survey; Grandparent Assessment Tool (GAT)	65 grandparents (65 completed GAT, 61 completed both SF 36 and GAT); majority female, Caucasian, married	Majority of grandparents' health were affected by the caregiving experience; some were considered "at risk." Many grandparents reported an improvement in their physical and emotional health due to caregiving responsibility despite experiencing health burden.
Harvey & Retter, 2002	Comparison of girls and boys in relation to Glasser's four psychological needs (fun, freedom, power and control, and love and belonging)	Data collection and analysis	Basic Needs Survey	1,200 students K–12 in a midsized New England city near Boston	Findings supported greater need for autonomy and freedom with age for both genders. Power and control as a variable was expressed by both genders but at younger ages. Females expressed higher need for love and belonging than boys at both latency age and adolescence.
Leversen, Danielsen, Birkeland, & Samdal, 2012	Need satisfaction for adolescents through leisure activities	Data collection and descriptive analysis	Huebner's Student Life Satisfaction Scale (SLSS); Basic Need Satisfaction at Work Scale (subscales used: competence, relatedness, autonomy); Participation in leisure activities (self report); Family Affluence Scale (FAS)	3,273 Norwegian students 15–16 years old	Findings were in conjunction with previous support of importance of need satisfaction among adolescents through school, family, and peers.

Lin, Hsu, Chang, Hsu, Chou, & Crawford, 2010	Examine pivotal moments and changes during the Bonny Method of Guided Imagery and Music of patients with depression	A qualitative research design and discovery-oriented approach were used	NA	Interview 5 patients with depression after each of the 8 sessions of the Bonny Method of Guided Imagery	Results supported the feasibility of incorporating the Bonny Method of Guided Imagery and Music into treatment when working with patients suffering from depression.
Mooradian, Cross, & Stutzky, 2006	Kinship care among American Indian families	Qualitative data collection and analysis	NA	31 American Indian grandparents with sole caregiving responsibility	Confirmed cultural values of elders' role in family. Relations between this population and mainstream culture remain strained due to "historical trauma."
Peck, Bray, & Kehle, 2003	Relaxation and guided imagery as an intervention for children with asthma	Multiple-baseline design	State-Trait Anxiety Inventory for Children (STAIC); T-Anxiety Scale; Pediatric Asthma Quality of Life Questionnaire; Asthma Self-Efficacy Scale; Asthma Problem Behavior Checklist; Daily Asthma Diary	4 middle-school students aged 12–13 with history of asthma diagnosed, a recorded diminishment in lung function, and emotional precipitants to the child's asthma and/or emotional consequences of living with asthma	RGI was observed as a beneficial treatment in combination with standard medical treatment and was more effective for some students than others. Future research should examine differential responses to treatment.
Rabin, Blechman, & Milton, 1984	Marriage contract game for adulthood	Multiple-baseline design	Behavior checklist	4 pairs of relatively untroubled couples	Increase problem-solving behavior, mood, and affective behavior.
Short, 1991	Use of guided imagery and music with problems of physical illness and trauma	3 case studies	Bonny Method of Guided Imagery and Music (GIM)	NA	Results indicated evidence of linkage between the mind and the body. The GIM is not merely a mental activity, but also related to the physical health.

Table 1 Systematic Review to Support the Use of Therapeutic Games and Guided Imagery—(continued)

Sklare, Sabella, & Petrosko, 2003	Explore the effectiveness of group solution-focused guided imagery on recurring individual problems	Repeated ANOVA, and qualitative analysis of the data	Pre-test, midsession, and post-test were measures with 15 questions each	44 participants took part in the activity and were divided into 4 different group settings	Positive results were obtained from the pre-test condition to midsession and from midsession to post-test. Evidence showed efficacy of the guided imagery intervention based on quantitative analysis of self-reported progress toward solutions.
Weigensberg, Lane, Winners, Wright, Rodriguez, Goran, & Spruijt-Metz, 2009	Pilot study: Use of Interactive GI to reduce stress and salivary cortisol in overweight Latino adolescents	Two group, randomized 45 min. stress-reduction IGI, once a week for four consecutive weeks	Perceived Stress Scale (17 item) Salivette System (to measure salivary cortisol levels prior to IGI)	12 patients (6 male, 6 female) age 14–17 with body-mass index greater than 95th percentile	Results showed moderate to large decrease in salivary cortisol levels across group, and was well received and enjoyed by the experiment group. Results suggested that interactive GI can be an effective tool to reduce stress and subsequently lower salivary cortisol levels. Future research should assess the long-term effects of IGI on stress.
Wiener, Battles, Mamalian, & Zadeh, 2011	Use of board game with cancer patients	Qualitative feedback from professionals	NA	110 professionals	Games were found instrumental for helping youths with cancer to share their feelings throughout the process from diagnosis to end of life preparation, including coping and adjustment to related issues such as depression, prognosis, peer-relationships, and self-esteem. It is suggested to apply therapeutic games to build rapport and increase comfort when sharing concerns.

2. Diverse Cultures

Research	Theme	Method	Measures	Subjects	Findings or Practice Recommendations
La Roche, Batista, & D'Angelo, 2011	Culturally competent relaxation	Multiple baseline across individuals	Beck Anxiety Inventory (BAI); Center for Epidemiological Studies Depression Scale (CES-D); Individualism/Colle Scale (INDCOL); Self-report weekly log	66 adults who identified themselves as Latino	Results confirmed the relationship between Latinos' allocentrism and treatment adherence.
Menzies & Kim, 2008	A pilot study on examining the effectiveness of relaxation and guided imagery in Hispanic persons who were diagnosed with fibromyalgia	Repeated measures pre-test and post-test design	Short-Form McGill Pain Questionnaire (SF-MPQ); Arthritis Self-Efficacy Scale (ASES); Mental Health Inventory (MHI)	10 participants were recruited through regional hospital clinics and Hispanic community newspaper (18 years or older) with a diagnosis of fibromyalgia, MMSE score higher than 25, and a Fibromyalgia Impact Questionnaire score higher than 20	Study showed improvement in self-efficacy for managing pain and other symptoms and functional status.
Tsai, 2004	Audiovisual Relaxation Training for anxiety, sleep, and relaxation among Chinese adults with cardiac disease	Quasi-experimental design, using pre-test and post-test study	NA	A convenience sample of 100 cardiology patients was involved in the study. (Treatment: N=41; Control: N=59)	Studied reflected the beneficial possibility of Audiovisual Relaxation Training for patients specifically with cardiac disease.

3. Developmental Needs (Physical and Mental)

Research	Theme	Method	Measures	Subjects	Findings or Practice Recommendations
Andersson & Moss, 2011	Investigate pre-conscious processes in exercise behavior change by comparing the efficiency of guided imagery and manipulation of implementation intention	A randomized control was used. One-way MANCOVA and univariate tests were used	Pre- and post-interventions were carried out to measure outcome variables	50 sedentary participants (34 female; 16 male) aged 19–56 were being monitored for their physical activity for 2 weeks	Study suggested the direct connection between guided imagery and implementation intention interventions with increase in exercise behaviors.

Table 1 Systematic Review to Support the Use of Therapeutic Games and Guided Imagery—(continued)

Duncan, Hall, Wilson, & Rodgers, 2012	Enhancing integrated regulation for exercise by using mental imagery intervention	Single-system design, compare with baseline	BREQ-2; Exercise Imagery Questionnaire (EIQ)	102 women between 22 and 50, who exercised less than once a week for at least 6 months prior to the study	Participants in the imagery group experienced greater changes compared to the control group. The use of imagery interventions is supported.
Hernández-Guzmán, González, & López, 2002	The effect of guided imagery on children's social performance	Compare treatment group and control group by using baseline study and follow-up	NA	40 withdrawn and rejected 1st graders (aged 6–8 years)	Study reflected the use of guided imagery to cause an increase and also aid in maintaining positive socialization behaviors and coping skills.
Kwekkeboom, Huseby-Moore, & Ward, 1998	Imaging ability and effective use of guided imagery	Correlational design was used to explore the relationship between scores on selected measures of image generation and absorption with the ability to use guided imagery successfully	D. F. Marks' (1973) Vividness of Visual Imagery Questionnaire; G. H. Betts' (1909) shortened Questionnaire upon Mental Imagery (P. W. Sheehan, 1967); and one measure of absorption, Tellegen's Absorption scale (TAS)	60 graduate students aged between 22 and 49	The successful group had higher TAS scores while there were no differences in image generation scores. Finding may be applied towards the development of a clinically useful instrument to predict the likelihood of success when utilizing guided imagery to relieve cancer pain and related distress.

4. Clients with Special Needs

Bell, Skinner, & Halbrook, 2011	Examine the effect of solution-focused guided imagery on golfers with the yips	Multiple-baseline across participant design was used	5 interventions of the solution-focused guided imagery (SFGI) protocol	4 experienced golfers with Type I yips participate in the study	SFGI protocol was effective with multiple facilitators present. Data showed the effect maintained 12–14 weeks after intervention. It is suggested to examine the effects of individuals experiencing task-specific focal hand dystonia across tasks (e.g., musicians, tennis players).

Fisher, 2007	Investigate the effect of guided mental imagery on intrinsic reading motivation of 4th and 5th grade students	Convenience sampling techniques were used	Motivation to Read Profile (MRP)	88 fourth and fifth grade children from 1 elementary school in a suburban district in central New Jersey	Both mental imagery and prediction training were observed to increase reading motivation. No relationship was found between the amount of time spent reading and vividness of imagery.
Louie, 2004	Explore the effects of guided imagery relaxation in people with chronic obstructive pulmonary disease (COPD)	Randomized controlled design, independent t-test was used to compare the difference in age, lung function, and smoking history between the groups	An oxygen saturation monitor; Pro-comp biofeedback; a modified Bozrg Scale for Breathlessness	26 participants aged 52 to 83 years were used in data analysis (24 male; 2 female). Half in treatment group and half in control group	Guided imagery relaxation was observed as a technique for reduction in anxiety while undergoing a significant increase in level of oxygen saturation.
Kim, Newton, Sachs, Giacobbi, & Glutting, 2011	Examine the effects of guided imagery and exercise imagery (GREI) to increase self-reported leisure-time exercise behavior among older adults	T-test and repeated-measures ANOVA were completed for data analysis	Leisure-Time Exercise Questionnaire (LTEQ); Exercise Imagery Inventory (EII)	93 community-dwelling healthy older adults with average age of 70.38 were involved in control group or treatment group with 6 weeks intervention	Guided imagery and exercise imagery were both recognized as effective tools when wanting to increase self-reported leisure-time exercise behavior.
Streng, 2008	Promoting child mental health with therapeutic board games	Review of "Lifegames" board games for therapeutic use	N/A	N/A	The review indicated the need for evidence-based research on group work with children and the "Lifegames" toolbox as well.

Table 1 Systematic Review to Support the Use of Therapeutic Games and Guided Imagery—(continued)

5. Immigrants

La Roche, D'Angelo, Gualdron, & Leavell, 2006	Culturally Competent Relaxation Intervention (CCRI): Allocentric Imagery (AIE) rather than Idocentric Imagery (IIE) for use with Latinos to reduce anxiety	6 groups of 3–4 patients completed 8 one-hour, weekly sessions using IIE and then AIE	Beck Anxiety Inventory (BAI); Individualism-Collectivism Scale (INDCOL)	25 adults who identified themselves as Latinos	Relationship was observed between increased AIE practice and reduction in anxiety levels. Relationship was also identified between individual levels of allocentrism and AIE, but no relationship was distinguished between idiocentrism and AIE. Increased knowledge of cultural characteristics of Latinos is suggested for increased effectiveness.
Mooradian et al., 2006	See #1. Assessment and Intervention				
Weigensberg et al., 2009	See #1. Assessment and Intervention				

6. Kinetic Communications

Bell et al., 2011	See #4. Clients with Special Needs				
Jain, McMahon, Hasen, Kozub, Porter, King, & Guarneri, 2012	Healing touch with guided imagery for PTSD in returning active duty military	Repeated measures analysis of covariance (RMANCOVA)	Gold-standard PTSD Checklist (PCL)—Military; Beck Depression Inventory (BDI-II); gold-standard SF-36 measure; Cook-Medley Hostility Inventory	123 active duty military were randomized to 6 sessions in 3-week period	Study indicated a direct connection between healing touch with guided imagery and the reduction of PTSD-related symptoms in a returning, combat-exposed active duty military population.
Lin et al., 2010	See #1. Assessment and Intervention				

7. Secondary Trauma

Staples, Abdel Atti, & Gordon, 2011	Mind-body skills group sessions with children and adolescents experiencing PTSD in Gaza	Data collection: 571 children and adolescents who attended a mind-body skills group in Gaza. Group sessions: 2 hours, twice a week, 10 weeks	CPSS Likert Scale 27-item Children's Depression Inventory (CDI); Hopelessness Scale for Children (HSC)	129 of 500 participants experiencing PTSD with matching baseline post-data	Results indicated that mind-body skills sessions may be more effective with older children experiencing PTSD, but it appears this treatment is effective for all ages experiencing depression. Hopelessness scores improved as well. All areas revealed continuous improvement at the 7-month follow-up. Limitations included the lack of a control group. Study indicated that mind-body skills groups can result in sustenance with decreased PTSD symptoms and depression during continuous experience of political violence.

8. Applications of Guided Imagery

Abdoli, Rahzani, Safaie, & Sattari, 2012	Guided imagery with perceived happy memory	Randomized experimental treatment provided 3 times per week for 3 weeks		20 GI with tape 20 GI with happy memory 20 control	Results indicated a reduction of chronic tension-type headache in terms of frequency, intensity and duration in both GI groups but not in the control group. It is suggested to use GI for reducing chronic headache.
Apóstolo & Kolcaba, 2009	See #1. Assessment and Intervention				
Cohen, 2000	See #1. Assessment and Intervention				

Table 1 Systematic Review to Support the Use of Therapeutic Games and Guided Imagery—(continued)

Cohen, Firth, Biddle, Lewis, & Simmens, 2009	The first therapeutic game for Alzheimer's disease	Observed Emotion Rating Scale, questionnaire	NA	Single group, within participants design, and 2 control conditions	The game presented results of reduction in signs of depression/sadness with an increase of pleasure from the patient.
Gonzales, Ledesma, McAllister, Perry, & Dyer, 2010	GI and effects on preoperative anxiety and postoperative outcomes	Randomized, single-blind 28-min. GI in private setting prior to operation on head or neck	Amsterdam Preoperative Anxiety and Information Scale (APAIS); Vertical Visual Analog Scale (vVAS)	44 patients undergoing same-day, outpatient surgery on head or neck	Results showed decrease in preoperative anxiety and postoperative pain at the 2-hour and 1-hour measurement period, therefore indicating the potential benefit of GI on same-day surgery. Further research on same-day surgical settings should be conducted before this practice can be recommended.
Jaffe, 2003	Create a therapeutic board game for children in psychotherapy (storyteller and the sacred stones)	Using storytelling and therapeutic ritual, tenets of narrative and systemic family therapy	Sessions were audiotaped and transcribed. Participants and their parents were given post-play interviews to examine the experience of the game	5 children between ages of 4 and 12 were recruited from the community to play the game	Older participants (9–12) needed less aid to complete game tasks. Younger participants (4–8) appeared to function better with direct parent involvement.
Kramer, 2010	Healing factors of Guided Affective Imagery (GAI)	Compare and contrast European and American approaches to Guided Affective Imagery (GAI)	Qualitative meta-analysis	NA	While GAI in the United States is not perceived by most practitioners as a method of deep psychotherapeutic intervention for neurotic disorders, it is considered as one of the more prevalent intervention techniques reportedly found effective during treatments of various disorders in Europe.

La Roche et al., 2006	See #5. Immigrants			
Li, Chung, & Ho, 2011	Virtual reality games for cancer patient treatment	Compare two groups of cancer patients ages 8–16, regarding the use of therapeutic VR games vs. regular nursing care for a 14-month treatment program	Chinese version of the State Anxiety Scale for Children (CSAS-C); Center for Epidemiologic Studies Depression Scale for Children (CES-DC)	52 treatment 70 control	Participants were observed to present fewer depressive symptoms but significance was not distinguished from anxiety scores. It is suggested to not only apply holistic and quality care for the patients but also include games as part of treatment.
Meadows, 2000	Examine the validity and reliability of the guided imagery and music responsiveness scale	2 types of data analysis were completed by SPSS. Ratings and correlation coefficients are calculated in each session	Sense of Coherence Scale (SOC); Defense Mechanisms Inventory (DMI); Guided Imagery and Music Responsiveness Scale (GIMR)	30 participants aged 19–57 years were rated on their responsiveness to a single GIM session using GIMR	Results showed satisfactory level for both the measurement of validity and reliability.
Muller, 2011	Explore the current practices of guided imagery and music	Anonymous electronic survey was designed for data collection by basic demographics of GIM fellows and characteristics of the clients and the delivery of GIM treatment. T-tests and ANOVAs were used to compute data analysis	Original Bonny Method and modified practices version	107 out of 207 GIM fellows participated in the survey, with 17 male and 88 female	Significant results were found between Bonny Method and subsequently modified practices of GIM fellows' frequency ratings.

Table 1 Systematic Review to Support the Use of Therapeutic Games and Guided Imagery—(continued)

Omizo, Omizo, & Kitaoka, 1998	Guided affective and cognitive imagery to enhance self-esteem	10 weekly guided affective and cognitive imagery sessions	Culture Free Self-Esteem inventory; General Self-Esteem; Social/Peer-Related Self-Esteem; Academic/School-Related Self-Esteem; and Parents'/Home-Related Self-Esteem	60 children ages 8–12 who are at least 25 percent Hawaiian, 34 girls and 26 boys	Guided imagery positively impacted some aspects of self-esteem among Hawaiian children; further research is needed.
Peck et al., 2003	See #1. Assessment and Intervention				
Rabin et al., 1984	See #1. Assessment and Intervention				
Staples et al., 2011	See #7. Secondary Trauma				
Streng, 2008	See #4. Clients with Special Needs				
Swank, 2008	Therapeutic tool with children and families	Literature		NA	Finding provided evidence of games to have the potential of enhancing the therapeutic process and relationships with clients, and to also yield success when addressing identified treatment issues.
Wiener et al., 2011	See #1. Assessment and Intervention				

Part A
Therapeutic Games and Activities

A1
3 in 1 ADHD Games
Chau Nguyen Todd

Items Needed

Wood blocks and/or plastic dominoes set; 35 small index cards (3" × 5"); timer/stopwatch; five poker chips per participant; list of "Sentence Starters" (see attached); small gifts

Target Population

Children ages five and up with attention deficit hyperactivity disorder (ADHD)

Purpose

To teach children skills that will help them control impulses

To help children learn how to focus

To break the ice and build rapport

To help children express feelings related to their illness

To identify strengths and encourage persistence in goal-directed activities

Procedure

Game #1

Cut and paste each sentence starter on an index card. Make up additional sentence starters to fit the behavioral issue being addressed in the session. During individual sessions, pick a card from the deck and give it to the child, and have the child complete the sentence as a starter of the session. Take turns with the child to answer each of the incomplete sentences on the card drawn. Play this game for five to ten minutes. If the game is being used in a group session, each participant selects a card and then completes the sentence on the selected card until everyone has had at least two turns. Discuss with each participant what he or she has learned from the sentence.

Game #2

Ask the child to stay still for one minute. Tell him or her that you will provide five chips as an incentive for completing the task. Repeat the game, adding one additional minute each time for up to five minutes. Ask the child to save the chips to trade in for a small gift or his or her choice of a fun activity during subsequent sessions. A chart indicating the token system may be developed with the child.

Game #3

Ask the child to build a tower with the wood blocks or neatly place each domino in a row. As with game #2, inform the child of the incentive system and tell the child to continue building for one minute. Explain to the child that if he or she focuses on completing the game each time, he or she will receive a poker chip, which may be "cashed in" at a later time or later session for a gift. Repeat the game, adding one additional minute each time, for up to five minutes for a five-year-old and ten minutes for a ten-year-old.

Function in Assessment and Treatment

Assessment

The index cards provide a form of free association that allows children to identify feelings and problems that may be related to their illness or impulse control issues. These three games allow the therapist to assess the intensity of the client's inattention or hyperactivity.

Treatment

The combination of these games allows the therapist to address the symptoms related to ADHD, including impulse control and distractibility. Through participating in these games, clients are given the opportunity to practice concentration skills and self-control. Clients are also allowed to express feelings about their behaviors through the sentence starters. Playing games with the children will help the clinician observe their ability to concentrate, while the poker chips/pennies reward system will encourage them to follow through with delayed gratification or rewards. The reinforcement system should focus on helping the children develop a positive attitude toward the development of appropriate behaviors.

Modifications

These games can be modified for use with children with impulse control problems who may not have ADHD but have a difficult time with self-regulation. You may, for example, skip the first two games and go directly to game #3 to address impulses and concentration.

Sentence Starters

I don't enjoy. . . .
My favorite thing is. . . .
Grownups think. . . .
I consider myself. . . .
I was punished when. . . .
I get in trouble when. . . .
When I do my homework, I. . . .
My best friends tell me. . . .
I feel happiest when. . . .
When I feel scared, I. . . .
I get angry when. . . .
I really care about. . . .

I don't like it when. . . .
I really enjoy. . . .
I cannot stand it when. . . .
Kids tease me about. . . .
I wish people would. . . .
It makes me sad when. . . .
When I daydream. . . .
I feel happy when. . . .
My teachers told me. . . .
I can focus when. . . .
I am confused about. . . .
My parents. . . .

A2
A Simple Start
Monit Cheung

Items Needed

One sheet of white paper for each person (or use the attached "My Dot" sheet in figure A2.1); a ballpoint pen; colored markers; crayons; masking tape (or glue)

Target Population

Clients with concentration problems or diagnosed with anxiety disorder

Appropriate for use during individual or group sessions with clients of all ethnic backgrounds

Purpose

To provide an ice breaker

To help clients achieve emotional stability before processing issues

To help clients concentrate

To deal with negative feelings

Procedure

Ask the client to use a marker (preferably black color) to draw a big dot in the middle of a blank sheet, or start with the "My Dot" sheet.

Alternatively, prepare and cut several round dots in different bright colors—black, red, green, blue, orange, and purple, each representing a part of the client's situations, surroundings, problems, or solutions. Give these dots to the client and ask him or her to put a double-sided masking tape at the back of each dot and then paste it on a piece of blank paper (see an example in figure A2.2). If you want to use the predetermined figure, ask the client to fill each dot with a different color.

Concentrate on the dot and use a ballpoint pen or color markers to draw lines extending from or close to the dot until the entire paper is filled with lines. Next, ask the client to use crayons to color any spaces formed by the lines until the entire paper is filled with various colors.

Function in Assessment and Treatment

Assessment

This exercise is a simple starting point to assess the concentration power of the client. It also allows the client to relax while thinking about the problem or issue to be addressed. The structure of the lines extended may disclose certain thinking patterns such as anxiety, distress, anger, or lack of motivation. The choice of colors may also provide some insights about the client's feelings at the current moment.

Treatment

Clients can use this quick exercise to free associate any issues and transfer them into lines. Lines can be organized or disorganized, long or short, heavy or light, solid or broken, one color or multiple colors. All of these descriptors may present some symbolic meanings to the clients as they may connect to their life issues.

Therapeutic questions may include:

1. When you first focused on the dot, what thought came to your mind?
2. After the first line was drawn, what came to your mind?
3. Which lines represent your current feelings? Past feelings that have been resolved? Past feelings that have not been resolved?
4. If you were to draw one more line on this sheet, where would it be? Now that you drew it, how did it make the drawing different?
5. Quickly in the next few seconds, think of one word that describes this drawing. What is it? Think of another word to go with this first word. Think of another word that is separate from this first word. How about naming a title for this drawing?
6. Different colors mean different things to different people. What do these colors mean to you? How about starting with orange (red, blue, green, purple, black, etc.)?
7. What is the meaning of the spaces without any color?
8. [If the client uses only one or two colors]: How does using one color make you feel? What does it mean if this color connects to a problem (or a solution)?

Concentrate on the dot and draw whatever comes to your mind that connects to this dot. Draw and color continuously until this entire page is filled.

Concentrate on each dot and draw whatever comes to your mind that connects to these dots. Draw and color continuously until this entire page is filled.

The client was asked to use color markers to draw lines and then encouraged to fill the spaces with crayon colors. When discussing the meanings of the lines, colors, and feelings in the drawing process, the client was asked if she would like to use crayons to continue the drawing (because there were still spaces without any colors). The client added solid yellow to some spaces and discussed the symbolic representations of these spaces in relation to the entire drawing. Spaces that were left uncolored had significant meanings to the client as well. The title of this drawing was "I am watching."

Figure A2.1 "My Dot"

10 *Therapeutic Games and Guided Imagery*

Figure A2.2 "My Dots"

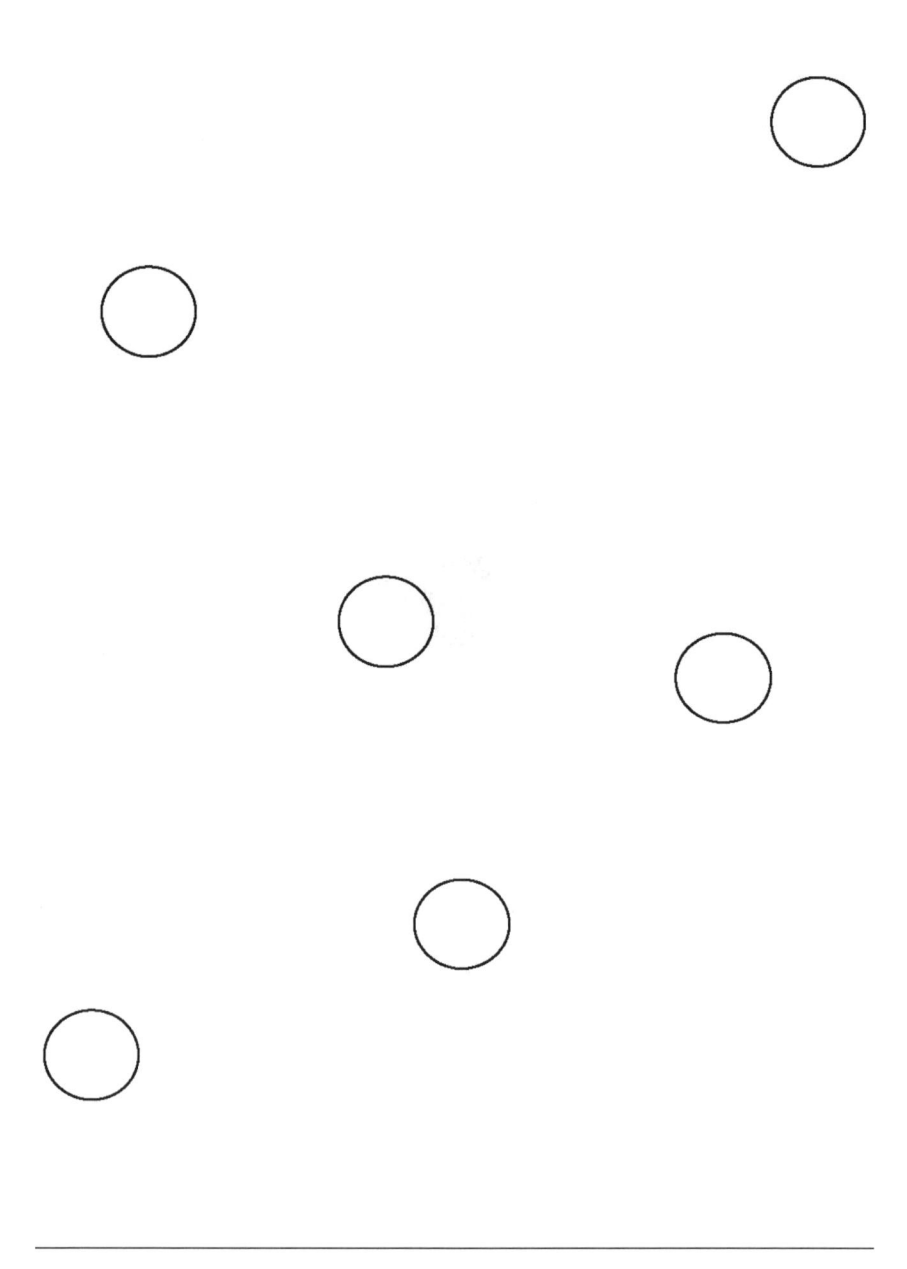

Figure A2.3 An Example (Female/10)

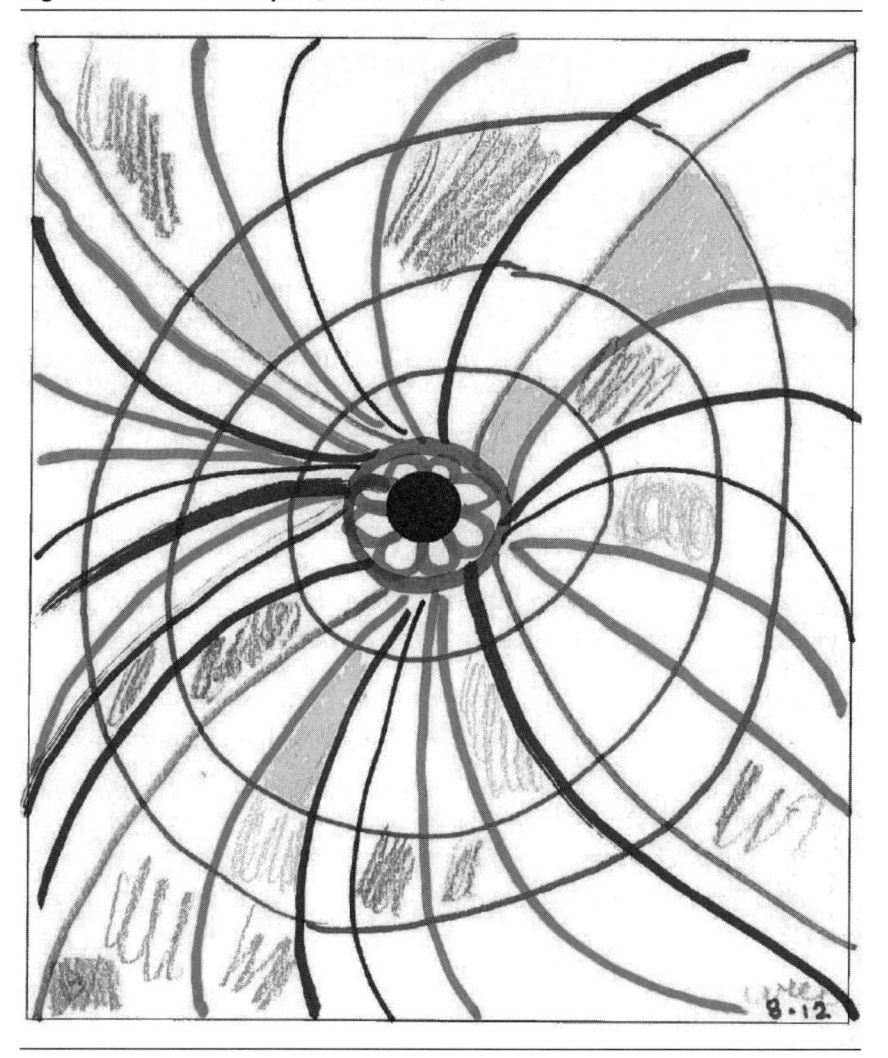

A3
Active Feelings
Shaneka Postell

Items Needed

Three to four pieces of card stock; construction paper or plain white paper; scissors; tape; role-playing scenarios; markers and other drawing materials; three dice: one with numbers (see figure A3.1), one with situations (see figure A3.2) and the other with actions (see figure A3.3); variation of game pieces (cars, doll figures, shapes)

Target Population

Children and adolescents ages six to fifteen experiencing emotional problems in their home environments

Intended for a group setting; children should be grouped with others in a similar age range, such as 6–9, 10–12 and 13–15

Purpose

To explore a range of feelings towards a child's home situation

To help children and adolescents express their feelings with others who may have similar experiences

To promote group interaction and trust

To encourage creativity and uniqueness

To build a positive self-image

Procedure

Creating the Game Board

Make three dice by first cutting cardstock or paper along the edges to create a cross shape (follow instructions given prior to figures). You may divide clients into small groups to design their game boards before connecting them (see figure A3.4). You may use a board with no beginning or ending (see figure A3.5); or tape the pieces together for a continuous board. Make sure to assign each of your key words or focus areas to one or more spaces across the board. For example: Role play a situation; Tell a story about me; Tell about my parents; Write a letter; Set future goals; Describe my family;

How will I help others. With a marker, color or assign a feeling to each empty space; or mark "situation" in some of the spaces.

Playing the Game

Each participant selects a game piece and places it anywhere on the game board to start. Explain to participants that they can move in any direction as long as they move the game piece in order, forward or backward, but not skipping any spaces. Participants will then take turns rolling the number die first and moving the corresponding number of spaces. Once a game piece has landed, the player will read the content in the space and then roll the "action" die to determine how to answer it. If die landed on "situation," roll the situation die first before the action die. For example, if a player's game piece lands on "HAPPY" and the action die is "Sing," then this player will sing a part of a song that has a happy tone. Save a few minutes at the end to process the activity.

Function in Assessment and Treatment

Assessment

This game helps participants understand that they are not alone and that there are other children who may be experiencing the same situation or feelings that they are. It also allows the facilitator to assess positive and negative feelings and attitudes towards personal problems or family values.

Treatment

Children and adolescents can use this exercise to not only effectively practice their communication of feelings with their peers, but also possibly with their parents or primary caregivers. This exercise also helps to build empathic skills and assist participants in bonding with one another. Therapeutic questions may include:

1. Pretend that you are talking to your friends about families. What would you say or how would you describe your family?
2. Tell your father or mother how you really feel about your family's situation.
3. Pretend that you are your father or mother; how would you show that you as a parent are concerned and interested in your children's feelings?
4. Act out how you would show "I understand" to your sibling.
5. You see some children teasing a little boy because his parents are going through a divorce. What would you do or say to these children?

How to Make Dice:

1. Fold each die along each of the six sides (along the dotted lines).
2. With pieces of clear tape, tape each edge to another edge.

14 *Therapeutic Games and Guided Imagery*

Figure A3.1 Die #1: Numbers

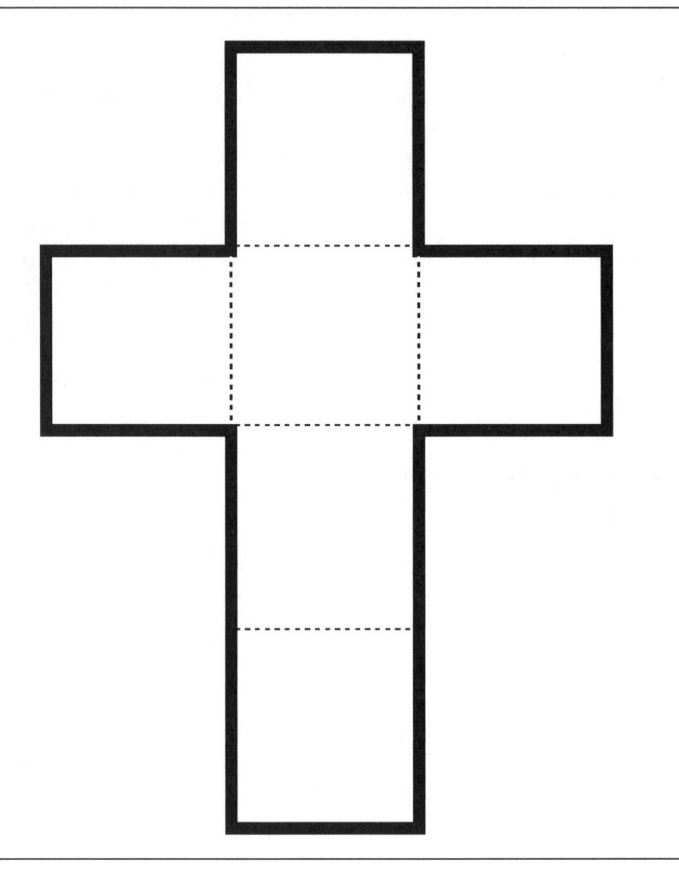

Figure A3.2 Die #2: Situations

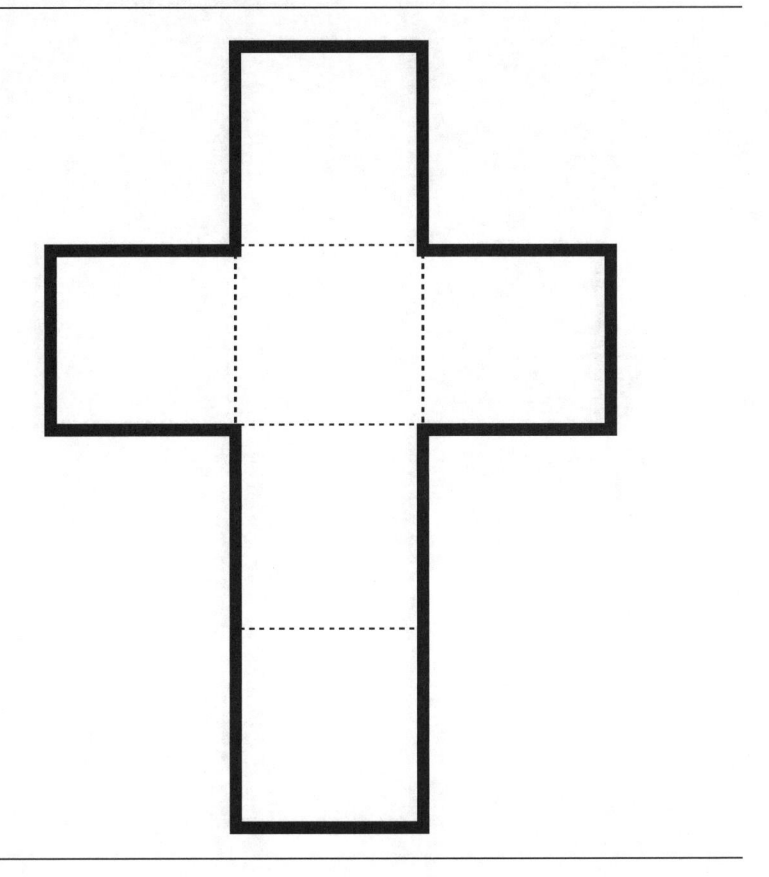

16 *Therapeutic Games and Guided Imagery*

Figure A3.3 Die #3: Actions

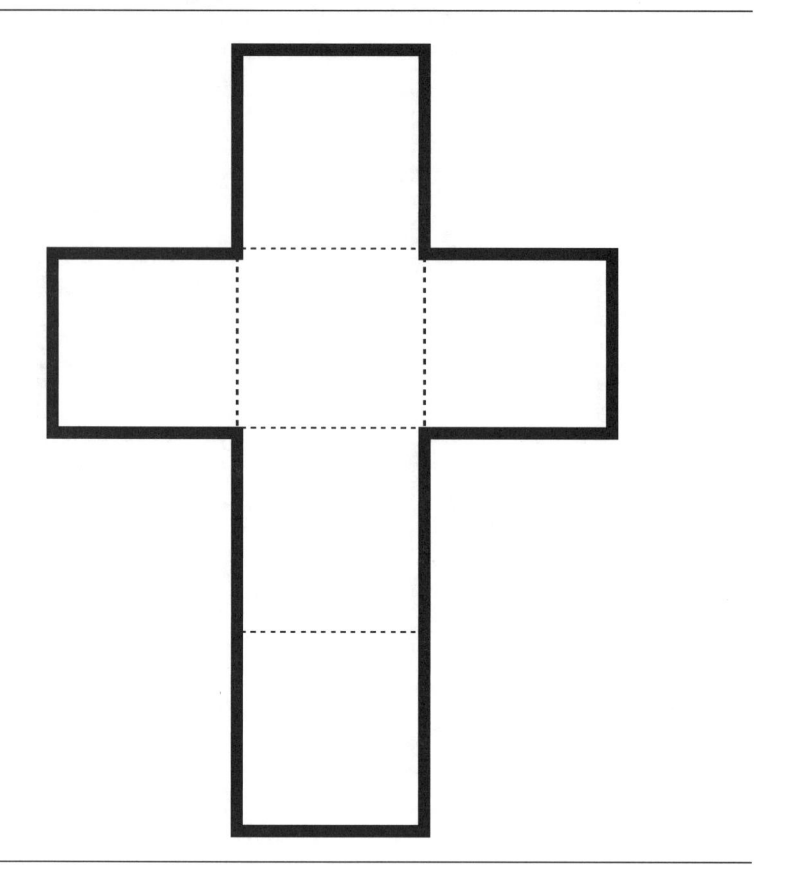

A3 – Active Feelings **17**

Figure A3.4 Game Board

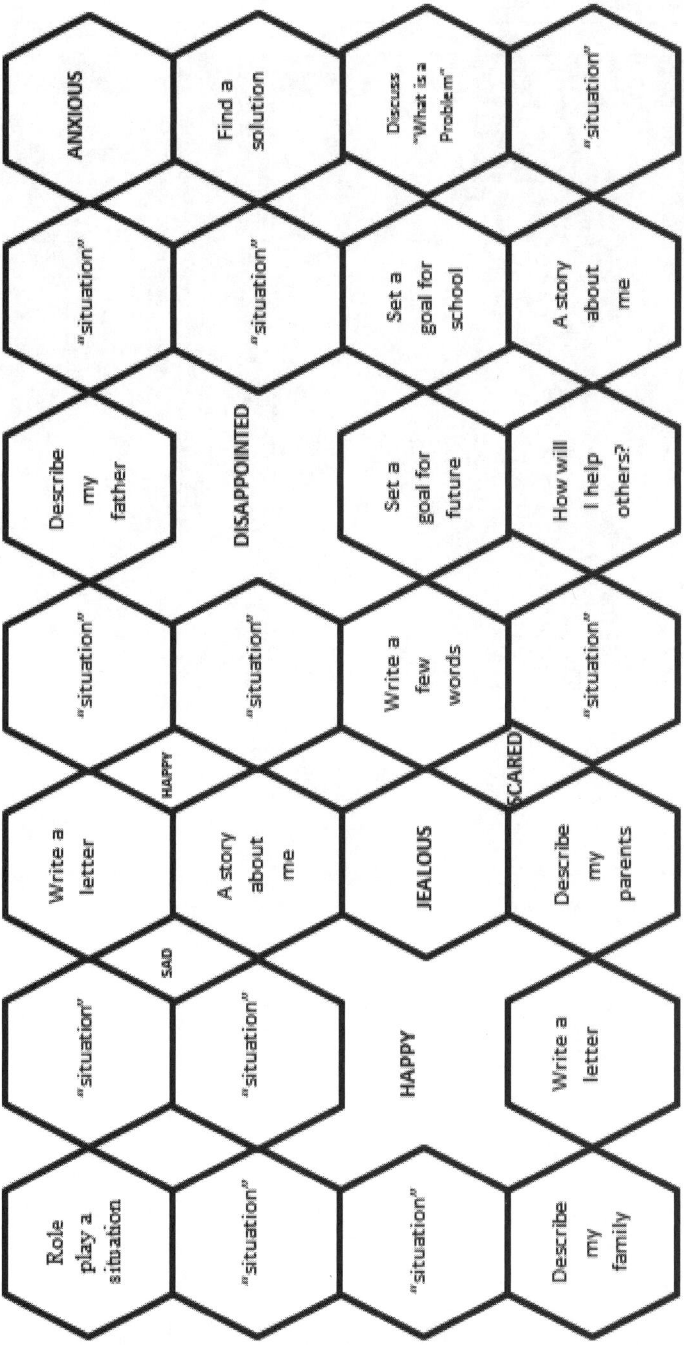

18 *Therapeutic Games and Guided Imagery*

Figure A3.5 Game Board

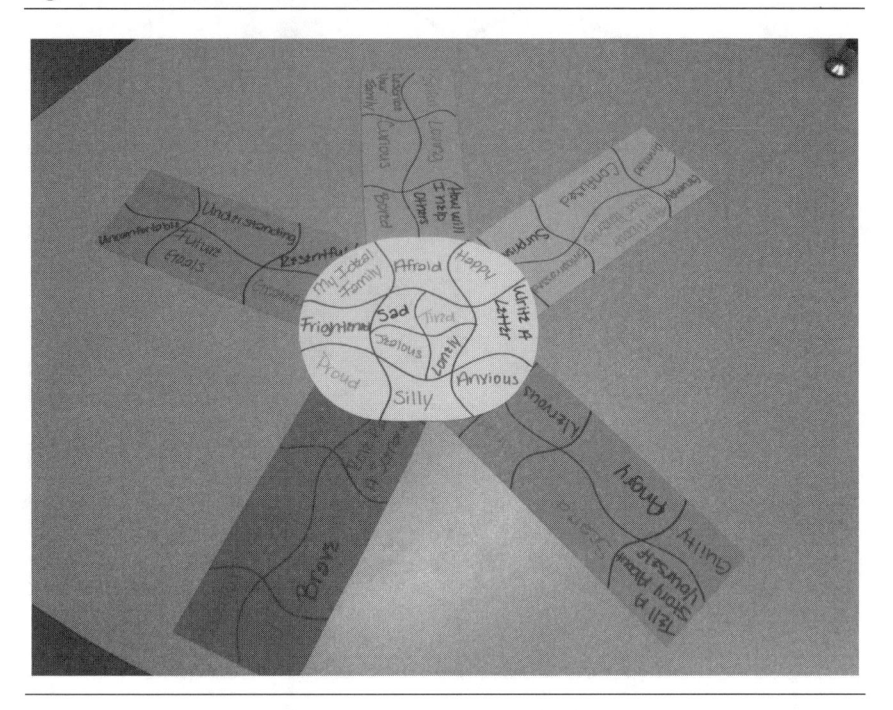

A4
Arbol de familia (Immigrant Family Tree)
John Betancourt

Items Needed

Poster board, leaves drawing (figure A4.1), emotion stems (may start with various emotions pre-written) (figure A4.2), construction paper with earth colors for tree drawing (see figure A4.3), scissors, color pencils or markers, scotch tape, small index cards for flags (see examples in Figure A4.4)

Target Population

Children of Latino immigrants, ages five to nine; children in immigration detention centers; bicultural or bilingual children; children who have had family member(s) recently detained or deported

Purpose

To encourage children who have had family members detained or deported to express feelings or problems related to parents' deportation

To assess children in a detained setting through exploring family options in their residing country

Procedure

Assist the client with drawing and coloring the trunk of the tree. Then allow the client to choose from one to eight pre-cut emotion stems to place on the trunk. Some stems may be prepared with emotion words on them; others may be blank. Next ask the client to fill out the names of family members related to these feelings on the leaves. Have the client tell you stories about the people written on the leaves and the feelings associated with these people. Place the leaves in bundles to represent the closeness of family members. Flags of the country of origin and the residence country can also be posted next to each significant family member. If a member has been or is soon to be deported, ask the client to design a special place on the tree to write special messages for this member.

Function in Assessment and Treatment

Assessment

Individual functioning can be assessed through the child's feelings towards family members who will serve as caregivers when the client's parents are absent. This game encourages the client to tell stories and express difficulties associated with deportation. It also assesses if the child is functioning appropriately in response to the current situation. Through the use of creativity and imagination, the child can think about what constitutes a safe environment, particularly when disclosing feelings about possible caretakers. Be sure to assess adjustment difficulties after a parent has been deported.

Treatment

Use this game to allow the client to tell stories about family members. By picking emotions to build the tree, the child explores options of fulfillment from possible caretakers and identifies support systems reflected through the building of the family tree. The child can explore feelings of loss due to deportation by designing a special space or spot on the tree. The country of origin and reunification issues can be discussed further. Possible questions may include:

What feeling does this family member make you think of?

Who would you feel comfortable enough with to share your tree with?

How do you feel about your mother or father living in another country away from you?

Looking back at the tree you built, was there anything new you learned about your family?

Make two copies for each child. You may prepare some stems with emotion words for younger children to choose from: fearful, frustrated, worried, relieved, shocked, angry, sleepless, emotional

Show the client's country of origin (see http://www.mapsofworld.com/flags for additional flags to use)

A4 – Arbol de familia (Immigrant Family Tree) **21**

Figure A4.1 Leaves

Use this to connect with family members, then place on stems

Figure A4.2 Emotional Stems

A4 – Arbol de familia (Immigrant Family Tree) **23**

Figure A4.3 Tree

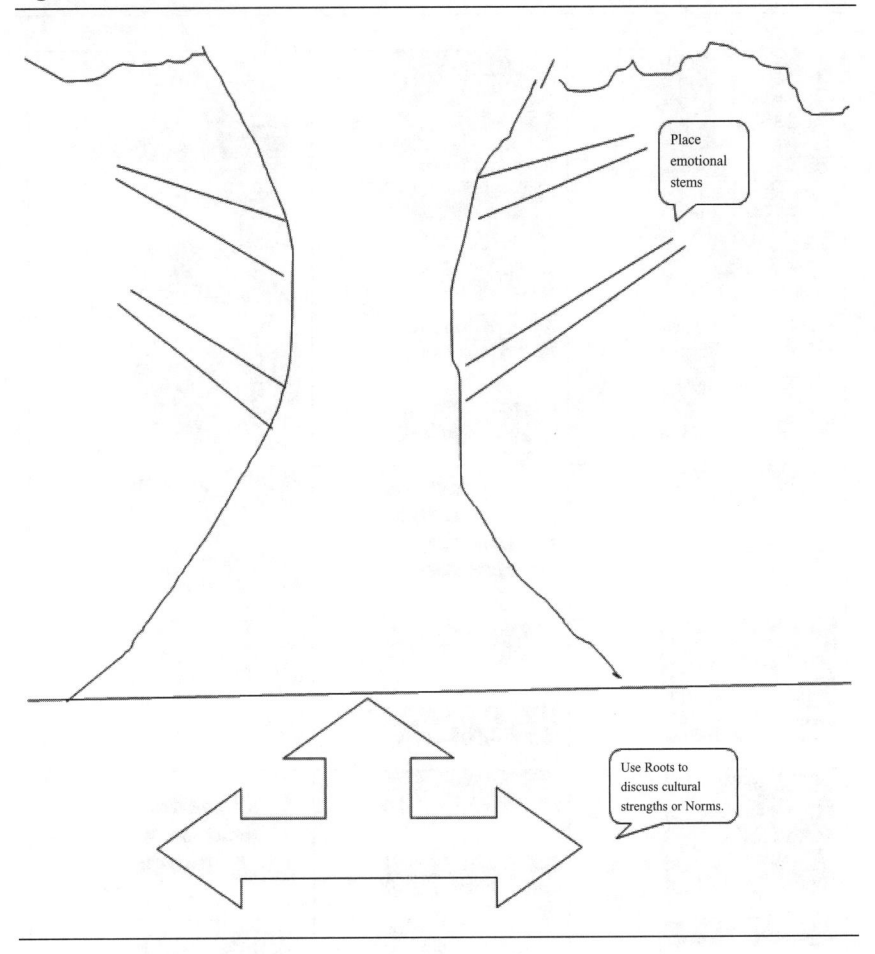

24 *Therapeutic Games and Guided Imagery*

Figure A4.4 Examples of Flags

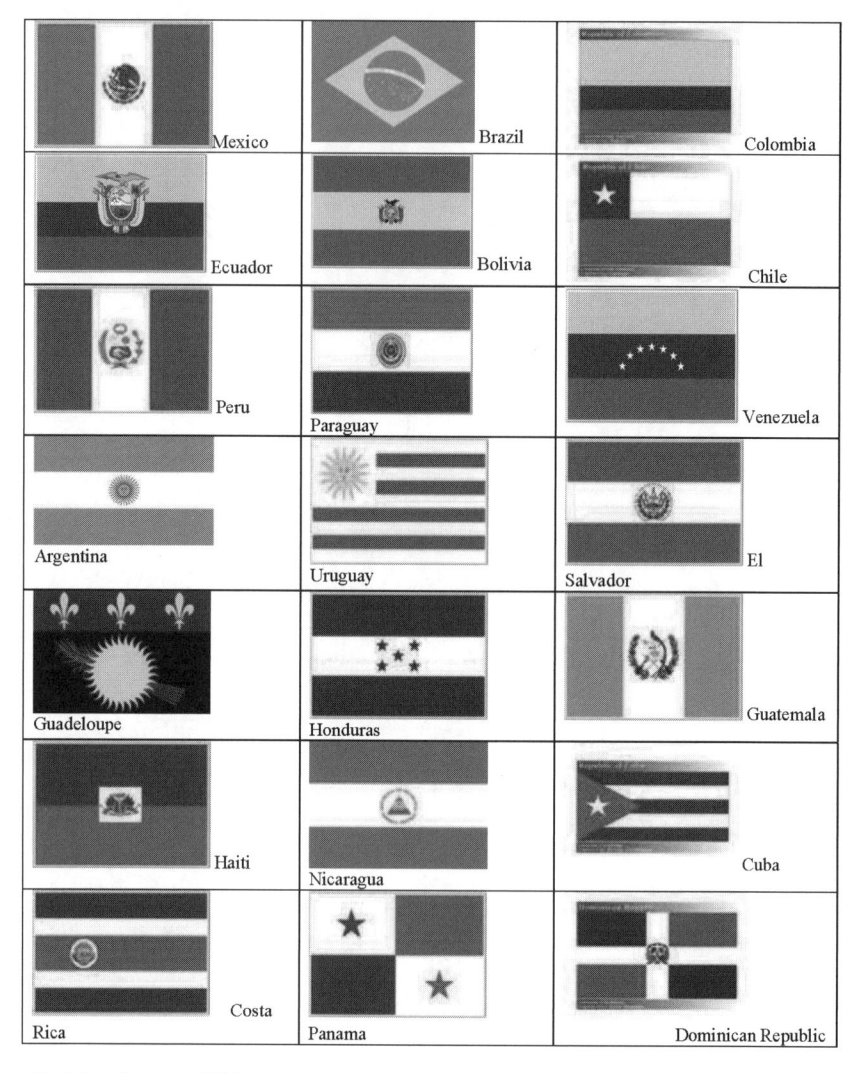

Mexico	Brazil	Colombia
Ecuador	Bolivia	Chile
Peru	Paraguay	Venezuela
Argentina	Uruguay	El Salvador
Guadeloupe	Honduras	Guatemala
Haiti	Nicaragua	Cuba
Costa Rica	Panama	Dominican Republic

Residing Country: USA

A5
Back-Off Bingo
Laura Welch

Items Needed

4" × 4" numbered bingo cards containing actions, words, or phrases that can be used to offset anger (see figure A5.1); set of numbered cards, from 1 to 30, which should include written scenarios that may trigger anger (see figure A5.2); bingo card markers; tokens to be awarded for individual participation; prizes for the bingo winners and for the players with the most tokens

Target Population

Detained children and adolescents ages 10+ who struggle with anger management

Intended for use with groups

Purpose

To establish rapport

To encourage participation

To help participants learn new coping skills such as diverting anger through active participation

To provide an outlet for feelings of anger and frustration

Procedure

Pass out bingo cards and card markers to each player. Inform the players of the rules of bingo (they must cover a full row horizontally, diagonally, or vertically).

Before you begin playing, go through each of the actions on the cards and have the players act them out with you. This shows everyone the appropriate way of performing the action and will encourage participation as the players become more comfortable.

To begin the game, take a numbered card and read the number on the card and the scenario aloud to the players. Bingo cards vary and the numbers on the card do not necessarily correspond to the same action; therefore different players with the same number on their cards may be acting out the same or different actions. For example "The next number is 21. Someone called you a name." The players who have the number on their bingo card should place a card marker over the square containing that number, and act out the action stated on the square.

If the players participate and complete the action, they are given a token for their participation. Play at least two rounds and award a prize to one or two bingo winners of each round. In addition, ask each participant to add up all tokens at the end of the entire game and award another prize to the player(s) with the highest number of tokens. Players who choose not to complete the actions during the game are still allowed to mark their squares when their numbers are called, but have to share the prize with the group if getting bingo.

Once the game has been completed, ask two to three open-ended, reflective discussion questions to close the session. Examples: (1) Can you share a specific emotion or feeling you had at some point during the game? (2) When you saw different people acting out different actions to the same scenario, what was your first reaction or thinking? (3) If you feel angry next time, which expression played in this session can be used to offset your angry feeling?

Function in Assessment and Treatment

Assessment

This game can be used in a group setting with youth who have been detained. Anger management problems are often the cause or result of the youth's detention, and these feelings can become overwhelming, magnified, and unmanageable when youth are confined to a detention setting. This game acts as a great ice-breaker because it not only gives the facilitator the opportunity to assess each individual's levels of anger, but also provides the individuals an outlet to express feelings. Active participation allows the clients to learn anger management techniques in a comfortable and relaxed environment. Participants' responses to the scenarios may also provide relevant insight into their habitual ways of expressing anger and handling difficult situations. Blank spaces on the cards give the clients the freedom to think of their own anger management technique, or proactively assign one of the predetermined actions found on the bingo cards. Clients can choose how much, or how little, they would like to participate and are given incentives to endorse participation even at the most minimal level.

Treatment

This game provides participants with quick and easy anger management techniques that can be used in daily interactions. These can be especially useful due to the heightened stress and emotion experienced during the initial period of detention, and has the potential to decrease the conflict that often arises among detained youth. Reflective discussion questions help the clients verbalize feelings they have experienced while playing the game, and allows them to compare experiences in daily life to those represented on the cards called out. These responses may help to identify specific triggers for individuals, underlying problems that may contribute to their anger, willingness to incorporate anger management techniques into their daily life, and so on. These findings will facilitate further in-depth discussion with the individual or the group in future sessions. Follow-up therapeutic questions may include:

1. What kinds of things or people could make you angry?
2. Do you think you would be able to use some of these actions in your personal life when you feel yourself becoming angry?
3. What would you see yourself doing to control your emotions when you become angry?
4. Did any of the situations read aloud remind you of something in the past? Name a situation and think about how you handled it then. How would you handle this type of situation from now on?
5. If you had to choose one anger management action to use while you are in detention, which would it be?

Figure A5.1 Bingo Cards

1 Count to 5	**16** Clap Hands Twice	**4** Take a Deep Breath	**11** Clench Fists Open and Closed
7 Snap Your Fingers	**5** Say, "I'm Sorry"	**30** Close Your Eyes	**15** Say Something Funny
2 Combine Any Two	**26** Three Jumping Jacks	**10** Walk Away	**17** Say, "Woosah"
20 Say, "I Forgive You"	**8** How Do You Feel? (one word)	**23** Choose Your Own!	**3** Say Something Positive

Figure A5.1 Bingo Cards—(continued)

6 Count to 5	22 Clap Hands Twice	13 Take a Deep Breath	25 Clench Fists Open and Closed
29 Snap Your Fingers	9 Say, "I'm Sorry"	18 Close Your Eyes	27 Say Something Funny
12 Combine Any Two	14 Three Jumping Jacks	28 Walk Away	19 Say, "Woosah"
24 Say, "I Forgive You"	17 How Do You Feel? (one word)	20 Choose Your Own!	21 Say Something Positive

Figure A5.1 Bingo Cards—(continued)

7 Count to 5	**12** Clap Hands Twice	**16** Take a Deep Breath	**2** Clench Fists Open and Closed
30 Snap Your Fingers	**4** Say, "I'm Sorry"	**26** Close Your Eyes	**18** Say Something Funny
1 Combine Any Two	**9** Three Jumping Jacks	**13** Walk Away	**11** Say, "Woosah"
17 Say, "I Forgive You"	**23** How Do You Feel? (one word)	**28** Choose Your Own!	**26** Say Something Positive

Figure A5.1 Bingo Cards—(continued)

8 Count to 5	**7** Clap Hands Twice	**29** Take a Deep Breath	**18** Clench Fists Open and Closed
6 Snap Your Fingers	**24** Say, "I'm Sorry"	**12** Close Your Eyes	**9** Say Something Funny
11 Combine Any Two	**3** Three Jumping Jacks	**10** Walk Away	**5** Say, "Woosah"
15 Say, "I Forgive You"	**22** How Do You Feel? (one word)	**17** Choose Your Own!	**13** Say Something Positive

Figure A5.1 Bingo Cards—(continued)

15 Count to 5	**22** Clap Hands Twice	**3** Take a Deep Breath	**1** Clench Fists Open and Closed
19 Snap Your Fingers	**5** Say, "I'm Sorry"	**21** Close Your Eyes	**28** Say Something Funny
16 Combine Any Two	**7** Three Jumping Jacks	**29** Walk Away	**6** Say, "Woosah"
13 Say, "I Forgive You"	**25** How Do You Feel? (one word)	**17** Choose Your Own!	**11** Say Something Positive

A5 – Back-Off Bingo

Figure A5.2 Scenario Cards

1	2	3	4	5
You feel yourself getting ready to fight	A staff person found illegal drugs in your locker but didn't believe you were framed	A classmate makes fun of you	You physically hurt someone	A classmate is talking in class but the teacher blames you
6	7	8	9	10
You get in an argument with your parents	Your mother blames you for problems at home	You get angry and then say something you regret	Your parents are hitting each other	You were made fun of for getting a good grade or helping the teacher
11	12	13	14	15
Your friend was murdered	Your best friend hooked up with your boyfriend/girlfriend	You feel angry or sad but no one seems to listen or understand	Your brother/sister just hit you	You feel that you are getting angry
16	17	18	19	20
A peer at school challenges you to a fight	You hear a friend gossiping about you or your family	Someone cuts you in line for lunch	You are sad or upset because your father is not around	You have to take care of your sibling(s) all of the time
21	22	23	24	25
Someone calls you a name	Your teacher sends you to the office	You were sent to the juvenile detention center for something you didn't do	You get in trouble at school for misbehaviors	Someone makes a negative comment about your skin color
26	27	28	29	30
Your parent kicks you out of the house	Your siblings gang up on you	A classmate pushes you in the hallway	You apologize to a friend but this friend won't accept your apology	Someone steals something from you

A6
Be Positive
Cornesia L. Russell

Items Needed

One long sheet of white construction paper; cutouts of speech bubbles (see figure A6.1); a poster board/frame; color markers or pencils; music player (CD player, iPod, or small radio); glue

Target Population

Children suffering from a terminal illness

Appropriate for children of all races, ethnicities, and cultures

Purpose

To help children express how they feel about their hospitalization

To help children illustrate what they would like their visitors to do or say

To provide a topic to share with visitors

To give children an opportunity to express their independence and confidence

Procedures

Prior to the exercise, engage the child in conversations to ice-break by asking questions such as:

- How do you feel today?
- Can you name two persons who are special to you?
- What would you say or do to make your visitors smile?
- How does it make you feel when people visit you but they look sad?
- What would you like to hear from your visitors?

To begin this exercise, give the child thirty minutes to draw a picture of his or her visitors (background music may be played if desired). Start with the most frequent visitor or the most important visitor. Emphasize the importance of drawing happy, smiling faces to encourage positivity from the visitors. When the drawing is done, ask the child to talk about a special characteristic of each visitor.

Next, ask the child to use the speech bubbles to show what he or she would like each of the visitors to say or do when they come to visit the child. Have the child write these words in a speech bubble, and glue the bubble next to the person in the drawing. Some children may feel unsure about what they may want people to say. In this case, ask the child to remember things his or her visitors have said or done that made them feel good, happy, and hopeful. When the child has completed the picture, follow up with open-ended questions about the picture such as "What do you see yourself saying to your visitors [e.g., your parents] to make them feel relaxed?"

Function in Assessment and Treatment

Assessment

Assess the patients to see where they are in the process of adjusting to the illness. This allows for rapport building as the patient becomes comfortable in the environment. This therapeutic exercise serves as a means to assess what the patients want others to say to them. It will also provide insight to the therapist on how others may have influenced the patient's mood. This will help the therapist to design some words that the patient can say to create a relaxing atmosphere for the visitors. This exercise can serve as an alternative way to express feelings for the next visit, especially if the therapist feels that a patient is uncomfortable in directly expressing feelings to his or her visitors.

Treatment

It is often very difficult for children who are facing terminal illness to express how they feel to others, even those closest to them. This therapeutic exercise allows the patients to feel unique about themselves through drawing or painting that displays positivity. This can promote a parallel effect for the visitors to think about using positive responses and feelings toward the patients during a hospital visit. This exercise helps patients to emotionally prepare for visitors. Positive images created through drawing and bubble creations can be displayed in the room as a constant reminder for positivity. Therapeutic questions may include:

1. How do you feel about being positive toward yourself and your visitors?
2. Someone says, "Having an illness does not mean that you cannot be positive"; what do you think about this saying? (Then ask the child to complete the statement, "Having an illness means that. . .

(e.g., . . . I now understand what caring means). When you feel positive, smile. How do you think your visitors may feel when you smile?
3. What would you say when your parents visit next time to make them feel at ease?
4. What would you like your parents to say during their next visit to make you feel at ease?

A6 – Be Positive **37**

Figure A6.1 Speech Bubbles

A7
Bi- or Multicultural Identity
Tuan Nguyen

Items Needed

One sheet of white paper for each person; colored markers

Target Population

Adolescents or adults who are experiencing stress navigating their values, beliefs, expectations, and customs of two or more different cultures

Suitable for individual or group sessions with participants of all ethnicities

Purpose

To facilitate clients in identifying various aspects of their cultures

To encourage clients to share their feelings about the various aspects of their cultures

To encourage clients to discuss difficulties they are experiencing related to being bi- or multicultural

To encourage clients to discuss ways of coping

Procedures

Give each client one piece of paper. Have the clients turn the paper in a landscape orientation, fold it into three equal sections, and then unfold it.

Ask the client to choose two cultures he or she is navigating and write down the name of that culture at the top of the first and third column. Next, have the client think of positive and negative words or images that come to mind when thinking about each specific culture, and then have him or her draw or write them in the respective column. Clients may also draw themselves according to the values and expectations of that culture. When the client is finished, give him or her an opportunity to share what he or she chose to use and why. Discuss ways clients have been able to adjust to different cultures and what solutions might be helpful in the future.

Last, ask the client to write down his or her name in the middle section, and draw a picture of himself or herself incorporating positive aspects of both cultures that he or she would like to adopt or keep. Clients can draw themselves in the way that they would like to look, dress, or appear as bi- or multicultural individuals. Underneath the drawing, have the client list ways that he or she can incorporate the positive aspects of each culture into his or her life, as well as remove the negative aspects from his or her life.

Function in Assessment and Treatment

Assessment

Based on what the clients write, draw, and disclose, clinicians can assess clients' degree of insight into the impact of their cultures on their self-identity, emotions, relationships, educational and career goals, religious affiliation, and other areas of their lives. Clinicians can also discover and address the problems or difficulties clients are facing as related to having multiple cultures.

Treatment

Clients may use the colors to further express their feelings in what they write or draw. Clinicians can ask what those colors mean to the clients. After completing the three sections, clients can refold the paper into three parts and tape, glue, or staple the ends so that the paper can stand upright. Clients can recognize that they have the power to thrive and stand proud as bi- or multicultural individuals.

For bi- or multicultural children or young adolescents who are having conflicts with their parents as a result of a clash of cultures, the clinician can conduct the following exercise to assist those individuals in expressing their thoughts and feelings. Divide the paper into three parts. In the middle part, they can draw a picture of one of their parents. Then in the first section (to the left of the picture), they can list positive aspects of that parent and the parent's culture. In the section to the right, they can list negative aspects of that parent and the parent's culture. They can then refold each page, tape the ends together, and make the paper stand upright. They can then discuss their thoughts and feelings about their parent and their parent's culture. This will help them better understand how multifaceted their parent is, and the degree to which their parent's culture has influenced who he or she is and what he or she does. The picture can then be used to encourage the young client to think of what he or she would like to say to the parent.

Possible therapeutic questions to ask:

1. What aspects of this culture do you like? What don't you like about this culture?
2. What difficulties have you experienced as a bi-or multicultural person?

3. What is one thing common to both cultures that you like?
4. What aspects of both cultures would you like to embrace, incorporate, or keep in your life? Which aspects would you like to remove?
5. What would the changes look like if you were to adopt or reject certain aspects of the culture?

Figure A7.1 Example

A8
Body Speaks
Benjamin Pratt

Items Needed

30–60 second movie clip that meets the criteria listed below; appropriate equipment to play the clip

Target Population

Adolescents between the ages of 11 and 19

Intended for use with groups or families (may be modified for groups larger than 12)

Purpose

Help participants gain awareness of body language

Highlight the effectiveness of body language as a tool for communication

Demonstrate differing interpretations of body language among group members

Procedures

The pre-selected movie clip must:

1. Be non-animated
2. Be unfamiliar to the participants
3. Show a conversation between characters displaying distinguishable emotions
4. Employ camera angles that sufficiently exhibit the desired type of body language
5. Meet group context (groups of adolescents should see an adolescent in the clip)
6. Be culturally relevant to the group (minimize gender or cultural biases)

Prior to playing the clip, inform the participants that James Borg (2011) states that human communication consists of 93 percent body language and paralinguistic cues, and only 7 percent words. Be sure to define both "body language" and "paralinguistic cues"

> Body language—The gestures, movements, and mannerisms by which a person or animal communicates with others. (*Merriam-Webster Online*, 2012)
>
> Paralinguistic cues—Nonverbal elements, such as intonation, body posture, gestures, and facial expression that modify the meaning of verbal communication. (*Mosby's Medical Dictionary*, 8th edition, 2009)

Play the clip with the volume muted. Invite participants to watch the movie clip and observe what is happening by focusing on the mood of the conversation (happy, sad, angry, flirtatious, etc.). When the clip is finished, ask participants to discuss their observations by giving specific evidence for that observation. For example, if a participant feels someone in the clip is angry, engage that participant to explain an observable cue such as, "The vein in his forehead was popping out." If the responses vary during discussion, you may play the clip again, to give participants an opportunity to modify their opinions after hearing other participants' points of view.

Next, divide participants into smaller groups of two or three people. Ask them to create a dialogue for the clip to see which group will have the most accurate understanding and perception of the interaction in the clip. After 10–15 minutes, ask each group to perform a dialogue for the clip. If further discussion is needed, ask participants how certain changes in body language may have affected the tone of the message that the actors were conveying to one another.

[If the content of the original dialogue is not related to the therapeutic theme, the following steps can be skipped.] Once each group has given a dialogue, play the clip again with full volume and see which group's dialogue was closest to the actual message being conveyed. As facilitator, decide which group was closest to the dialogue of the movie. Ask that group to explain the cues that helped them figure out what was going on in the movie clip. If the movie clip differs dramatically from all of the dialogues created by the groups, ask participants what could have been done to more clearly demonstrate the purpose of communication between the actors in the movie.

End the exercise by discussing participants' personalized forms of body language, as well as the messages they might be knowingly, or unknowingly, conveying. Ask questions such as, "How do you normally sit in class?" "What kinds of hand gestures or body movements do you use when you talk to someone in your family?" "What message do you think you are sending when you _____ (input body language referenced by the participant)?"

Function in Assessment and Treatment

Assessment

This activity facilitates rapport-building and familiarity among group members through communication between the participants. It also allows participants to express their capacity for reading communicative cues from other people. The facilitator also gains insight into the social and cultural aspects of communication used among participants.

Treatment

This activity increases participants' awareness of body language and clearly demonstrates the critical role that body language plays in communication. It provides participants with the opportunity to observe and to interpret body language. Through discussion, participants will become aware of differing interpretations of body language and may gain appreciation for accepting others' perspectives. In conjunction with other activities, this may also serve as a cornerstone for groups or participants in need of enhanced communication skills.

Through careful selection of the movie clip, the exercise can be modified for use with specific client populations such as divorce, bullying, and parent-child conflict.

A9
Body Works
Kayla Cooper

Items Needed

A sheet of paper pasted with a "My Self" picture (see figure A9.1); emotions cards; therapeutic question cards; art media (crayons, markers, pens/pencils, colored pencils, paint, etc.); optional: stickers (emotions, medical) and cards with physical assistance (e.g., wheelchair, walker, braces) or other related aspects (e.g., pain, ache, hurt)

Target Population

Ages 4+ with a physical disability

Purpose

To help children identify and understand their physical disability

To assess the child's perception of his or her physical and emotional self

To help children express their feelings about having a disability

Procedure

Use a sheet of paper to paste the body picture on it. Ask the child to use this to show what his or her face may look like when thinking about him or herself. The child can use any color and writing or drawing medium. The child can even use the white space to add in the environment, family or friends, and other items to define "self."

Once the child has defined disability with a picture, you will spread out the emotion cards with the faces up. Tell the child to look at all the faces and to pick one card up. Help the child express what that chosen emotion is.

Ask the child if the person in the picture feels that way, for example, "Is the person in your picture *happy* like the face on this card?" "What made this person *happy*?"

Ask the child more questions about feelings (from the perspectives of self or others).

If the child added people or items to the picture, ask how important these people/items are to the child.

Using the therapeutic question cards, ask the child a question. Allow the child to verbally respond or draw it on the "My Self" picture.

Function in Assessment and Treatment

Assessment

This activity can be used as an assessment tool to determine how much the child knows about the medical aspects of his or her disability, how the child perceives the physical aspects of disability, and also how the child feels emotionally about a disability. The child may be too young to understand what a disability is, thus it is best to avoid using the term *disability*. Instead, identify the child's own word when defining disability, for example, "How does using a wheelchair make you feel?"

This activity can help assess the factors within the child's environment. Is the child being teased at home or in school or day care? Is the child feeling left out? Is the child frustrated and acting out at home or school because he or she feels frustration about the limitation(s)?

Treatment

Using this activity will allow the child to express any feelings he or she may have about the disability. The child may be too young to understand and verbally express these feelings. The use of art and coloring would provide insight into the child's world and the child's perspective about the disability. After the assessment, work with the child and caregivers to identify environmental accommodations, stress reduction methods, education materials for other family members, and referrals for occupational and physical therapy. Treatment can also include activities that will help build the child's confidence and increase self-worth and self-esteem. This can also be done with siblings, friends, or peers of the client. Follow-up therapeutic questions may include:

1. If you could choose any activity to do (without thinking about your limitations), what would it be?
2. If you could go to any place you wanted, where would you go?
3. Who has helped you the most?
4. How do you feel when you can't do something?
5. When you need help with something, who do you ask for help?
6. What can make you sad? What would you do when you feel sad?

7. Name something or someone that can make you change from sad to happy.
8. When do you feel big and strong?
9. What do you like about yourself? About your caregiver (mom, dad, nurse/doctor, etc.)?
10. When you look in the mirror, what do you see? (If negative: How do you change a negative image to a positive one? If positive: How do you maintain this positive image?)
11. At termination or discharge: What would you tell another patient about your recovery?

48 *Therapeutic Games and Guided Imagery*

Figure A9.1 Example

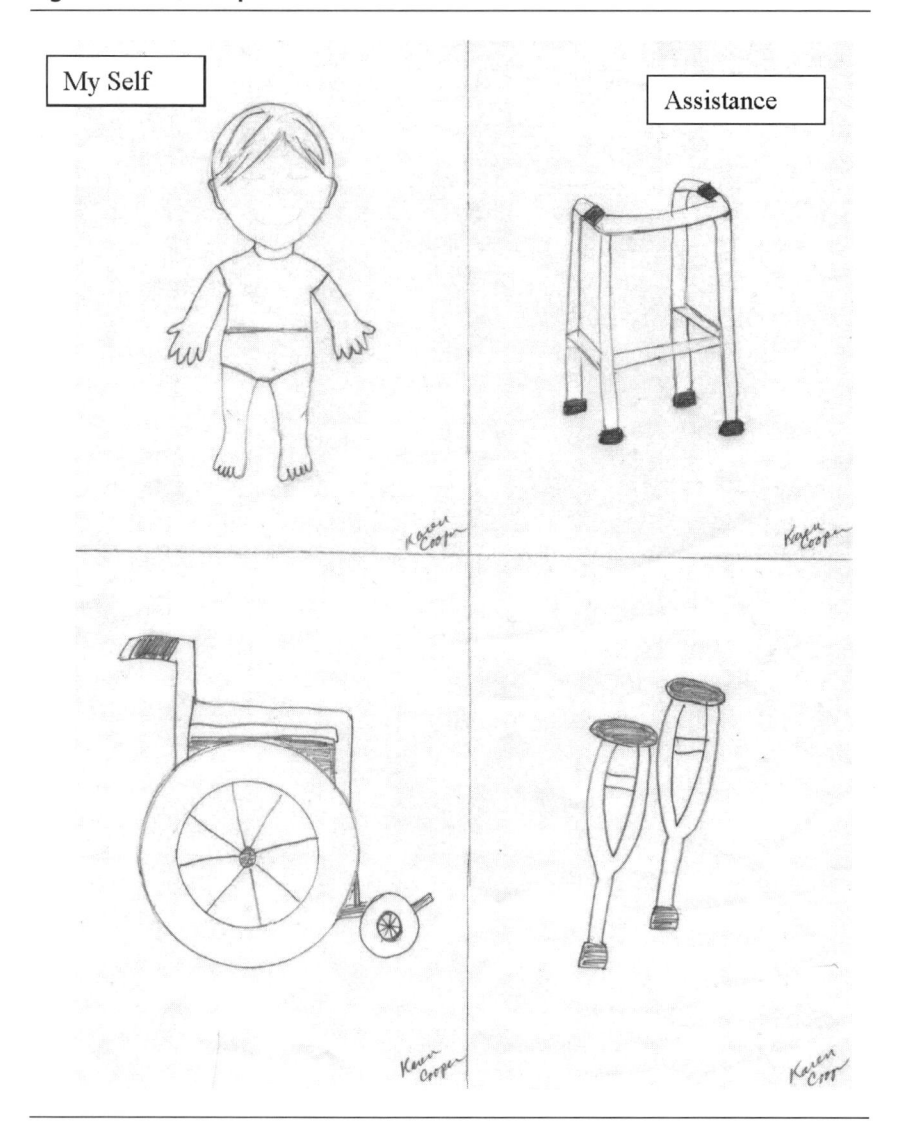

A10
Breaking the Ice
Monit Cheung

Items Needed

Three question/response sheets (see figure A10.1): Sheet 1: Questions to Break Silence, Sheet 2: Breaking Resistance, and Sheet 3: Interviewing an Adolescent (each on a different color paper); three different colored index cards (25 for each color)

Target Population

Children or adolescents who are silent or not actively participating in an individual session

Suitable for all ethnic backgrounds

Purpose

To address a young client's emotional reaction to therapy

To help resistant children understand the intent of therapy

To encourage children to share their feelings

To help children deal with anxiety, fear, grief, or trauma

Procedure

Prior to the session, print out the three question sets. Cut them apart and paste them onto the index cards, one question per card. Use the same color card for each set of questions.

At the start of the exercise, introduce yourself and your function. Ask if the child knows the purpose of this meeting. Also ask if the child wants to tell you something, for example, "Tell me one reason you are here today," or "Tell me what happened." If the child remains silent, use the following game as an ice-breaking activity using the cards from sheet #1 (for children) or sheets #2 or 3 (for adolescents). Suggestions for transitioning to the activity are:

49

Sheet #1

1. Self-determination: "Some children or teens come to therapy but have concerns about therapy. I understand that I am a stranger; it's okay not to say anything now. I just want you to know that I am here to help you and listen to you. Whenever you are ready, you can tell me what I can do to help. Let's start with a game."
2. Universalization: "In my practice, I have worked with children and teens. Here are some of the questions (or responses) my clients had when we first met. Take a card and let the card ask a question (or express) for you."
3. Response: "You will read the question and I will try to answer it for you. If this is not a question that you would like me to respond to, draw another card."

Sheet #2

1. Reflection of feelings: "These are responses from teenagers. Please take one and read it." "Is this feeling similar to or different from yours?"
2. Understanding: "Take another card. How would you respond to a friend who expressed this feeling?"
3. Help: "Take another card. What would you think this person wants from me?"

Sheet #3

1. Explain that these cards are the most common counseling questions. Since the client does not want to talk, you may say, "How about if you choose a question card and I'll answer it?" (Prepare your answers in advance, which should be helpful to teens.)
2. After answering, draw a question, read it, and encourage the client to take his or her turn to answer. If the client refuses, you can continue to provide your answer and check the client's response.

Function in Assessment and Treatment

Assessment

This ice-breaking tool incorporates transference techniques that help resistant children and adolescents disclose their feelings. It helps the therapist understand and define "the problem" with a client-centered approach. You may add more cards based on your client's age and background.

Treatment

Use of additional techniques to respond to the client's initial answers may help the client understand the importance of counseling. Be supportive and discuss how silence can be used as a defense mechanism to guard one's self, and how constant use of silence can become a barrier to communication and problem solving.

Use the following strategies to respond to the client's responses and body language.

- Be positive: Respond to the client with a positive answer, for example, "It is nice." "I understand."
- Reframe: Respond by asking a question: "What do you think?" "If you were your parents, what would you do?"
- Solicit the client's response: "I don't know the answer either." "I'm here to listen to you." "I can only guess." "It's up to you to make this decision."
- Reflect feelings: "This question seems to reflect that you are not very happy about coming here." "This response has a few feelings associated with it. I sense anger, frustration, and at the same time confusion. Tell me more about your feelings."
- Reflect meanings: "It seems that you want to go home. Is this true?"
- Address fear or concern: "Tell me one of the uncertainties behind this question/response." "I sense concern. Tell me more."

Figure A10.1 Sheet 1: Questions to Break Silence

What is counseling?
What is social work?
Who are the kids you see?
What is a social worker?
Why do I have to come here?
Did I do something wrong?
Am I being punished?
Is something wrong with me?
Do Mom and Dad think something is wrong with me?
Do my parents still love me?
Do my parents care?
Will my friends think something is wrong with me?
Will my friends make fun of me if they find out?
Will it hurt?
Is it like going to the doctor?
How long does it take?
When will I get to go home?
If I don't like it, will I have to come back?
What am I supposed to say and do?
What if I say something wrong?
Should I tell bad things about my family?
Will you tell anybody what I say?
Can I just stay here and not do or say anything?
I saw a counselor before, but it wasn't helpful. Will you be able to help me?
Why must I see you?
What do you want from me?

Figure A10.2 Sheet 2: Breaking Resistance

My folks don't even care; exactly what do you want?
Why do you want to help?
Can I go now?
What do you want to hear?
My feelings? None!
Whatever you said is OK for my parents.
I don't know who you are.
What do you want from me?
I have a bad mood, and I don't want to say anything!
I'll give you five minutes.
Hurry up!
Nothing!!
Get lost!
Boring!
Nobody wants me.
My parents have the answers.
Go ask them.
Get lost!
I don't want to talk.
I don't want any help.
I just don't like it.
That's all!
Everybody just wants to criticize me.
We can say anything here?
I just want to say "shit."
I just don't want your help.
You act just like my mom!
Don't ask, OK?
I don't know why I am here. You tell me.
What do you want from me?
I don't even know what's going on.
Tell me why I must be here.
What's going on with my mom and dad?
Don't make me say anything.

Figure A10.3 Sheet 3: Interviewing an Adolescent

How are you getting along with others?
What are your future plans?
When you look back at your past, what do you remember?
Tell me your earliest memory—that is, the first thing that you can remember.
What kinds of things make you happy?
What kinds of things make you sad?
How do you feel about being here (agency)?
Tell me about your family.
What are your current interests and hobbies?
Tell me about your closest friend.
How would you describe yourself?
Tell me about somebody you like.
Tell me about somebody you don't like.
How is your health?
What kind of work experiences have you had?
What worries you the most?
What do you think you can get when you come to counseling?
How do you define depression?
What is love?
What do you enjoy the most with your family?
Tell me three words to describe life.
What is (was) your favorable subject in school?
What can make you upset or mad?
Who can make you upset or mad?
If you had three wishes, what is your first wish?

A11
Building Cultural Pride
Venus Tsui

Items Needed

"Cultural Heritage and Pride" worksheet; writing utensil for each participant

Target Population

Adolescents and adults exploring cultural identities and building multicultural cohesiveness

Suitable for cultural sensitivity training

Intended for use with groups, particularly in a multicultural setting

Purpose

To explore and build a cultural identity

To help participants understand and respect unique characteristics of each individual in different ethnic groups

To build group cohesion among people with different cultural backgrounds.

To appreciate cultural differences and diversity

Procedure

Form groups of three or four participants based on their ethnic or cultural identities; or assign each group with an ethnic or cultural identity. Give each participant a copy of the "Cultural Heritage and Pride" worksheet based on the assigned identity. Ask each member to first complete the worksheet and use the extra space at the bottom of the workshee to brainstorm words, phrases, images, symbols, and so on that are connected to the assigned culture. Allow ten minutes to complete the form.

Next, have the group members take turns sharing their responses and encourage group members to ask each other questions or comment on similarities they share. Emphasize the importance of respectful communication and appreciation of cultural differences. Last, ask each group to come up with a group definition of *culture* to share with the larger group. Allow 20 to 25 minutes for group discussion.

56 *Therapeutic Games and Guided Imagery*

Finally, facilitate a large group discussion where participants can share and discuss differences, similarities, and new information they found through their small group discussion. Ask open-ended questions to allow particpants to express their reactions to the exercise and the different feelings and emotions they may have experienced. Discussion questions may include:

- Was there anything you expected to learn about someone else's culture that you did or didn't learn?
- Did you learn anything from people who share the same cultural background?
- How can you relate this experience to other experiences in which you built, or will build, relationships with people from other cultures?

At the end of the discussion, have each group read their finalized definition of *culture*. Then discuss the differences and similarities present in the definitions, and the unique aspects of these definitions. Combining all ideas, the larger group will come up with a definition that they feel best represents the definition of culture or present a formal defintion of culture: "Culture is a shared set of practices and traditions that characterize a group of people or society. Culture can include language, music, arts, food, clothing, traditions, ceremonies, spiritual beliefs and practices, family structure, communication, patterns, and values."

Function in Assessment and Treatment

Assessment

This activity can help participants increase their cultural awareness and connect or reconnect with their cultural identity. By assessing the participants' awareness of and ability to appreciate different cultural heritages, the facilitator can gain insight into the individual's level of comfort, understanding of his or her own culture, and acceptance of other cultures.

Treatment

In a group session with a multicultural setting, this activity encourages each member to explore and build her or his cultural identity while gaining exposure to cultural traditions that differ from his or her own. You can use this activity to build group cohesion among group members of different cultural or ethnic backgrounds. This activity will allow participants who share the same cultural background to recognize the cultural nuances (such as language, cultural beliefs, and values) present within the same ethnic group, and learn how to appreciate and embrace the uniqueness present within these cultural differences.

Worksheet: Cultural Heritage and Pride

Race and/or ethnicity: _____

Name at least three unique aspects of this culture and/or heritage of which a member of this culture feels proud.

1)

2)

3)

Others:

What makes you proud of this culture and/or heritage? Why?

_____
_____
_____
_____

What is a uniqueness of this culture that is important to you? To the entire cultural group, what is one thing that is important to this culture and/or heritage as a whole?

_____
_____
_____
_____
_____

Brainstorm: What comes to your mind when you think about this culture and/or heritage? What is your definition of "culture"?

A12
Building Diverse Communications
Micki Washburn

Items Needed

Ten to 20 unlined colored index cards; one set of stackable blocks (for building a tower); colored markers or a label maker and colored tape; discussion topics (figure A12.1)

Target Population

Families or siblings of a member(s) who self-identifies as lesbian, gay, bisexual, or transgender/gender nonconforming

Only include children who are nine and older

Groups of three to six participants

Purpose

To break the ice and build rapport among group members

To normalize open discussion about LGBT issues

To allow participants to express both positive and negative feelings associated with having an LGBT family member

To process secondary traumatization which may occur from having a family member who is part of an oppressed or marginalized group

Procedure

Prior to the session, write specific topics related to the group on the colored index cards. It may be beneficial to laminate the cards for frequent usage. Topics commonly associated with working with the LGBT populations are included in figure A12.1. Once the index cards are completed, put 18 blocks aside. On the large side of the remaining blocks, paste different feelings or emotions (use feeling figures in the introduction of this book). On the 18 blocks initially set aside, label 6 with "my choice," 6 with "left choice," and 6 with "right choice."

Prior to playing the game, ask for three volunteers (one to shuffle the topic cards, and two to construct the tower). Explain the rules of removing and stacking blocks: (1) you cannot remove a block from the top row of the tower; (2) you may touch only the block you are trying to remove; (3) when you remove the block, you must place it on the top level of the tower. Next, inform the players that each round will have a pre-selected topic, and each block has one of four labels: an emotion, "my choice," "left choice," and "right choice." For each block a player selects, he or she must read the label and then complete a sentence to identify either the emotion or the choice: (1) I feel _____ when _____; (2) I made this choice, so _____.

To demonstrate how the game works, pick a topic card such as "therapy." Then select a block in the middle of a tower. If the block's emotion is "scared," then you might say, "I feel scared when I don't know what to say in therapy," or "I made my choice, so I just take a deep breath even though I am unsure of what to say in therapy," or "I made the left choice, so I am here to tell you my experience," or "I made the right choice, so I am happy." Then add the block to the top of the tower.

Once you have demonstrated how to play the game, ask the youngest member of the group to select a topic card. This is the topic that will be used during the game. The player to the left of the youngest player will go first and game play will proceed in a clockwise fashion until the tower falls. When the tower falls, the players must rebuild the blocks and a new topic should be selected from the deck of topic cards. Repeat as time allows, making sure to leave 10 to 15 minutes at the end of the session to recap what have been said and to process feelings about the experience.

Function in Assessment and Treatment

Assessment

This activity allows each participant to practice identification of feelings and the actions he or she usually associates with these feelings. It allows the facilitator to observe which feelings are discussed easily and which ones are avoided, and will help the facilitator gain a better understanding of the feelings and emotions that may go unaddressed during family discussion. The facilitator may also gain insight into each member's current strengths and coping skills, as well as those of the family as a whole.

Treatment

This game is useful because it helps families talk about subjects that are often taboo. It provides participants with a safe place to talk about subjects they may not be encouraged to talk about at home or at school. It is also useful to help group members address feelings of social isolation and feel a sense of connectedness with others struggling with the same family issues. Participants get the opportunity to see how others feel about the topics and how they deal with those feelings, thus learning from each other. This activity can be especially helpful for participants who struggle to identify some, or most, of their feelings and can help provide them with the words and opportunities to learn new coping skills. Through the expression and discussion of different feelings and emotions, family members can build on their strengths by gaining a new perspective and learning to develop connections through shared emotions.

Modifications for the game may include continuing topic discussion in between rounds if the players or the facilitator feel it may be beneficial, and allowing members to select specific topics that directly affect them. The game can also be modified for use with groups of other marginalized populations such as recent immigrants, underrepresented ethnic or minority groups, families with a member who has mental retardation or a pervasive developmental disorder, and so on.

Add or subtract topics from this list to suit your therapeutic goal

Figure A12.1 Topics for Discussion with Families or Groups

Church/Spirituality	Discrimination	Living Two Lives	Separation	Bullying
Keeping Secrets	Transitioning	Coming Out	Dating	Pretending
Safety	Gay	Lesbian	Gender Nonconforming	Divorce
Gossip	Teachers/Coaches	Friends' Parents	Friends	Parents
Grandparents	Aunts, Uncles, Cousins	School	Clothes Dress Code	Showers or Bathrooms
Mental Health	Family Issues	Personal Identity	Physical Disabilities	Therapy

A13
Bye-Bye Bullies
Carol A. Leung

Items Needed

Two sheets of paper per client; trashcan; blank note cards; crayons or colored markers

Target Population

Children dealing with bullies

Children experiencing fear

Suitable in family or group sessions to address emotions

Purpose

To help clients share their emotions about being bullied

To teach children ways to communicate with bullies

To encourage children to think positively about self-image

Procedure

Build rapport with children (e.g., introduce themselves: name, school attending, home-teacher's name and grade level). Ask them to fold one sheet of paper into a shape that represents their school (see figure A13.1). Demonstrate by placing the paper in portrait orientation, folding in both sides of the top section of the paper to form a triangle, and then folding the bottom part of the paper up so that it touches the triangular base.

Ask each child to decorate the outside of the school and write the school name on it. Have each client share what he or she likes and dislikes about school. Then ask each child to unfold the lower part of the school and draw pictures of his or her friends and favorite teachers on the inside of this school. On a second sheet of paper, have the clients draw the bullies and color their feelings toward these bullies. Ask each child to talk about any bullies who have been mean to him or her. Explore what these bullies have said or what actions the bullies have done to make the client upset, scared, or have other feelings or thoughts (see figure A13.2 for example of procedure).

Next, educate the children about ways to talk to a bully. First, ignore the bully. Second, say "Leave me alone." Third, stand up and leave. Fourth, inform a teacher (counselor, social worker) and parents about what happened. Normalize the clients' feelings by stating that when facing this kind of bullying situation, many children ask for help and talk about their feelings. Ask the children to write down the four methods on the back of the "school" to reinforce these skills (plus new ideas generated in discussion.) See figure A13.3 for finished examples.

Ask the children to write the words *teachers* and *parents* (or others) on each side of the triangle flips on the outside of the school to represent trustable adults, and then open the flips and write a few words representing each child's personal strengths (such as positive and firm) and ways to deal with bullying (such as "Be strong" and "Stand up for myself"). Take out the blank note cards for them to write down each encouraging word or phrase. Teach them a deep-breathing technique to feel empowered. In a family session, ask parents to verbalize these strengths to their children to help them build self-esteem.

Last, gather all of the note cards and shuffle them. Have each child take three cards from the pile of note cards and select one to read aloud after taking a deep breath. Empower the clients by saying, "Say it now. Say it again. Say it again, louder this time."

Before the end of the session, ask the clients to say goodbye to the bullies and bullying problem by tearing up the second sheet of paper with bullies or negative feelings, and throw this paper into a trashcan. Explain the symbolic meaning of the paper-tearing action (i.e., feeling powerful because you are in control). Allow the clients to take home the "school" and note cards as reminders of their strength and ability to deal with bullies.

Function in Assessment and Treatment

Assessment

This exercise can be an assessment tool to evaluate the self-esteem level of a child. The actions designed in this exercise help children visualize their ability to solve problems and self-evaluate their ability to say positive things about themselves. It empowers children to use their inner strengths and learn how to be brave and resilient to stand up against bullies. When a client is able to talk about the bullying situation, he or she will be able to stand firm and not be viewed as a victim. When the client knows that he or she can voice his or her concerns freely, he or she will no longer be an easy target.

Treatment

This exercise provides a safe environment for children to share their fears of bullies with teachers, counselors, social workers, and parents. It uses kinetic senses (listening, writing, coloring, verbalizing, thinking, and connecting ideas) to help children develop a sense of self-support and appreciate their own strengths. During the exercise, do not help them to write because it may make them feel powerless or useless. If a child is too young to write (or cannot think of any words to write), replace writing with using random, or selected, colors or images to represent words. These social events can build up the child's own emotional support so he or she can increase self-esteem and sense of belonging, and can thrive in a smaller-knit, accepting environment. Possible therapeutic discussion questions should include:

1. I see/hear that you do not want to go to school. What happened in school?
2. What are three things you like about yourself?
3. Tell me about your friends in school.
4. What are three things you would like in a friend?
5. What can you say next time when someone is teasing you (or beating you)?
6. How do you feel when someone teases you?
7. Can you tell me a time when you had conflict with someone at school? How did you resolve this conflict?
8. How do you feel if someone says you are a bully? What can you do to make that person feel comfortable to talk with you?

This exercise can be used again in a follow-up session, group or individual. Ask the child to make another school (same or different as the previous one) and picture that as a bully-free zone and decorate it whatever way the child wishes to without any specific procedure. This additional procedure helps the child understand more about the meaning of gaining control. It ultimately guides the child to put at least three strengths in his or her mind, such as being courageous, maintaining a positive attitude, and knowing how to seek help.

Other ways to fold a house-shape building:

http://www.origami-make.com/howto-origami-house.php

A13 – Bye-Bye Bullies **65**

Figure A13.1 How to Fold a School

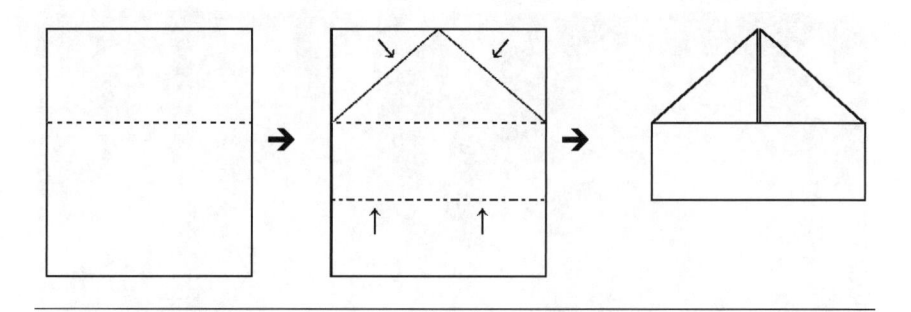

66 *Therapeutic Games and Guided Imagery*

Figure A13.2 Procedures to Complete the School Drawing

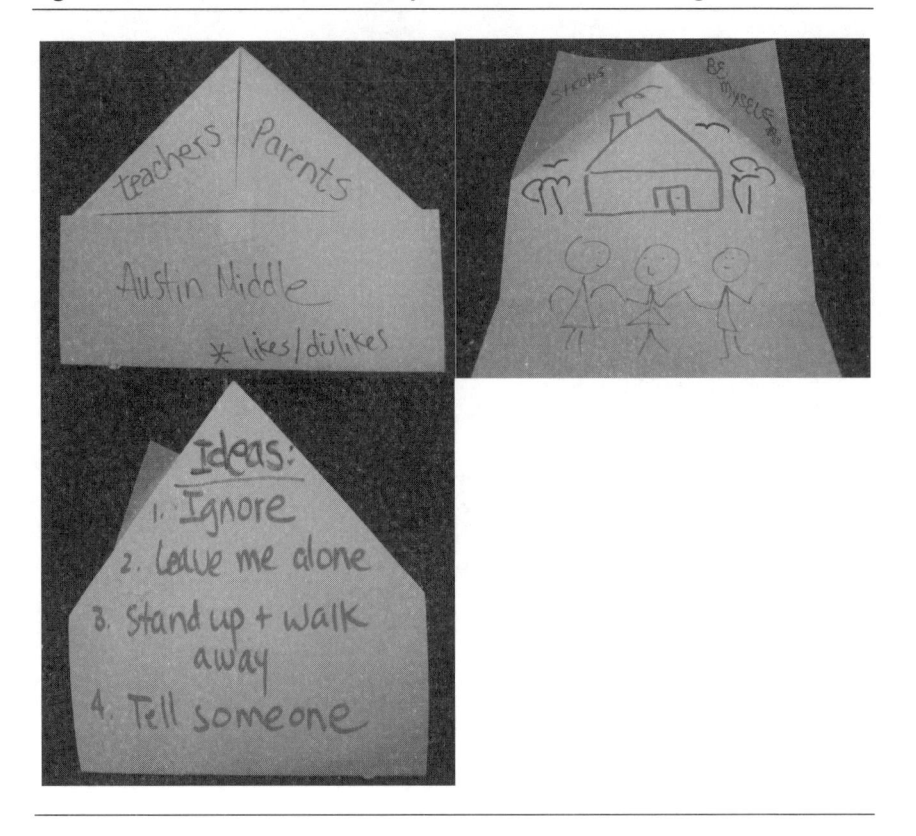

A13 – Bye-Bye Bullies **67**

Figure A13.3 Clinical Examples: The School and the "Bullying" Drawing

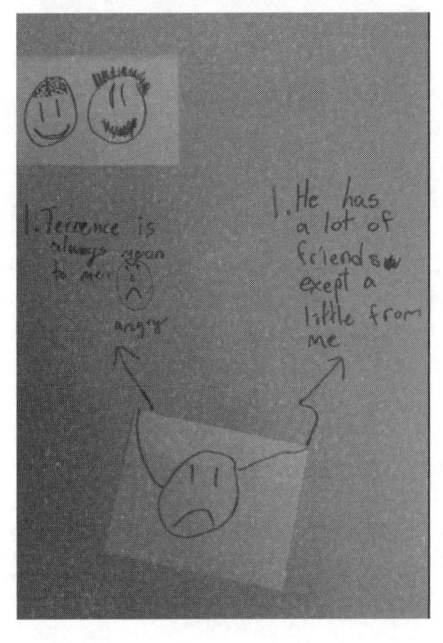

A14
Choose Your Own Adventure
Rachel Barajas

Items Needed

Adventure cards and results cards (see figures A14.1 and A14.2); six pieces of colored construction paper (red, orange, blue, yellow, purple, and black)

Target Population

Adolescents with bipolar disorder or ADHD disorder

Intended for use with individuals, groups, or families

Purpose

To build decision-making and critical thinking skills

To aid in impulse control

To enhance group decision-making skills

Procedure

Cut the adventure cards out and group them together by similar color groups. You may write "Adventure Card" on the back of each one or glue a patterned piece of paper to the back. Tape each piece of colored construction paper to a different area of the room; each piece of paper will be a station. Place each stack of adventure cards at *different* stations than the decision color choices indicated on the card. For example, put yellow cards at the black station or blue cards at the purple station, but make sure each station has some cards of each color. Cut the results cards out and divide them equally among each station. You may write "Results" on the back or glue a different patterned piece of paper to the back of each card.

If using it with a group, divide the participants into two to four groups with an equal number of members in each group. Assign each group to a particular station, designated by a colored piece of construction paper. Each group is to take one adventure card from their assigned station, read it out loud, and come to an agreement on one of the decision options indicated on the card. After the decision has been made, the group will follow the decision's instructions to move to another colored station. At the new station, the group will then select one results card and read it out loud. Continue this process until each group has gone to at least three stations.

If using it with an individual, assign the participant a station to begin with and have him or her pick an adventure card, read it out loud, and choose one of the decision options from the adventure card. The participant will then move to the next station, draw a results card, and proceed by choosing a new adventure card at the new station. Have the participant repeat this procedure for as long as desired.

If using it within a family, have the child and parent(s) complete the procedure, with the parent reading the card to the child and discussing the decision options together. Proceed in the same manner explained above.

At the end of the game, have each group designate a "leader" to explain how the group members made their choices and how they felt about their decision after they read their results card.

If using it with an individual or family, have each individual talk about a decision, the decision process, and how each individual felt about the results.

You may alter the scenarios provided in order to accommodate the needs of younger participants.

Function in Assessment and Treatment

Assessment

The activity allows children to think critically about a situation and then make a decision on how they would react. You may use this game to assess a client's decision-making skills by observing the thought process involved in choosing one option over the other. Since clients with ADHD or bipolar disorder usually have difficulty getting along with others, the game also serves as a way to assess children's functioning within peer groups, and can be especially helpful in identifying specific struggles they face during interactions within a group setting.

Treatment

Many children with ADHD or bipolar disorder have a difficult time making rational and informed decisions. Often, their decision-making processes are emotionally driven and impulsive, and they later regret their actions. Children with ADHD or bipolar disorder benefit greatly from learning to stop, think, and then react. This game allows children to think about successes through each results card because it congratulates the children on making their decision. Since there are no right or wrong answers, children learn how to apply rational and informed decisions that can be applied to their social interactions in a variety of situations.

Figure A14.1 Adventure Cards

You are walking home from school and find a pack of cigarettes on the ground. What do you do? A. Throw it away—Proceed to Orange station B. Keep walking—Proceed to Red station	While you are walking home from school, a stranger in a car rolls down the window and asks you to look at a map to help him. What do you do? A. Tell him you can't—Proceed to Orange station B. Keep walking and ignore him—Proceed to Red station
A friend asks to cheat off your test in school. What do you do? A. Tell this friend "no"—Proceed to Blue station B. Ask the teacher to sit you away from your friend—Proceed to Yellow station	Your friend tells you that her dad has been hitting her. She asks you to keep it a secret and not tell anyone. What do you do? A. Encourage her to tell a teacher—Proceed to Blue station B. Keep it a secret—Proceed to Yellow station
You witness a friend stealing something while at the store together. What do you do? A. Confront this friend—Proceed to Purple station B. Say nothing—Proceed to Black station	You are playing with your neighbor and he/she asks to see your privates. What do you do? A. Tell him/her "no"—Proceed to Purple station B. Go home and tell your parents—Proceed to Black station
You witness a person walking down the street drop $5. What do you do? A. Pick up the money and give it to the person—Proceed to Orange Station B. Keep walking—Proceed to Red station	A classmate passes you a note in class even though your teacher has made it very clear that passing notes is against the rules. What do you do? A. Throw the note away—Proceed to Orange station B. Tell the classmate "no"—Proceed to Red station
You accidentally break a lamp at your home when your parents are outside talking to a neighbor. When they come inside and see it broken on the floor, what do you do or say? A. Apologize and tell your parents it was an accident—Proceed to Blue station B. Wait for your parents to ask you about it and then tell the truth—Proceed to Yellow station	After school, your friend says they are going to smoke pot in the woods. They ask you to join them. What do you do or say? A. Tell them "no thanks"—Proceed to Blue station B. Go with them but do not smoke—Proceed to Yellow station

A14 – Choose Your Own Adventure **71**

You are buying some candies at the convenience store by your house and the cashier forgets to ring up the soda in your hand. What do you do or say?

A. Tell the cashier that she forgot to ring your soda up—Proceed to Purple station
B. Put it back before you leave since the cashier forgot and you don't want to bother her—Proceed to Black station

Your friend just got a new toy. You ask your friend if you can play with it and he says no. What do you do?

A. Accept the answer—Proceed to Purple Station
B. Ask your friend why—Proceed to Black station

Create your own scenarios!

Figure A14.2 Results Cards

Great Job! That's a good decision!	Way to go, you made a successful decision!
High five! Great decision!	You are a decision-making master!
Good job on making that decision!	Awesome decision!

Add and create your own positive results!

A15
Cleaning the Dirty Laundry
Monit Cheung

Items Needed

One sheet of white paper for each person (or use the attached laundry drawing); color markers; three-foot piece of yarn for each person (any color); stapler (or paper clips that look like laundry clips); a board or a hanger; masking tape

Target Population

Child abuse victims

Individual or group sessions

All ethnic backgrounds

Purpose

To help clients address emotions after disclosing abuse

To help clients walk through the healing process

Procedures

Explain to the clients the purpose of this activity: to help them identify and express their feelings.

Ask the clients to pick four colors and to associate a feeling with each color. Next, have the clients draw or trace at least four different types of clothing on the paper and then color them with the chosen colors, singly or mixed. Ask the clients how they feel about the clothes and the colors they used and which feelings are difficult to express. Discuss how feelings can be mixed and why some feelings are more difficult to understand and discuss. When this is done, ask the clients to staple the clothing onto the yarn and connect all the yarns (see figure A15.2 for example). Hang up the string of clothing to represent laundry that has been cleaned (on the blackboard or with a hanger). Ask the clients to express that the clothing being hung is cleaned.

Function in Assessment and Treatment

Assessment

This is an assessment tool that aims to assist young clients in expressing feelings and thoughts in conjunction with "dirty" and "clean." If clients draw the clothing with holes or damaged parts, do not make assumptions but ask how the clients relate the drawing to their current feelings. The hanging action can be used to assess how the clients feel about the process of disclosing the problem (e.g., being abused).

Treatment

After the clients have colored one side of the laundry, you may ask them to draw the other side of the laundry to represent something positive. This activity helps the clients identify their strengths and encourages their participation in the healing process.

Therapeutic questions may include:

- Identify a positive feeling generated from this exercise.
- When you think that the laundry is now cleaned, how do you feel about your self (effort, energy)?
- How does this exercise help you deal with your ____ feeling (choose from the color representation)?
- What advice would you give to other children who have been or were abused by their parents?
- Now we are done with "cleaning," could you choose two other colors to represent your current feelings? Tell me the meaning of each color.
- What suggestions do you have about protecting children?

A15 – Cleaning the Dirty Laundry   75

Figure A15.1 Laundry Pieces

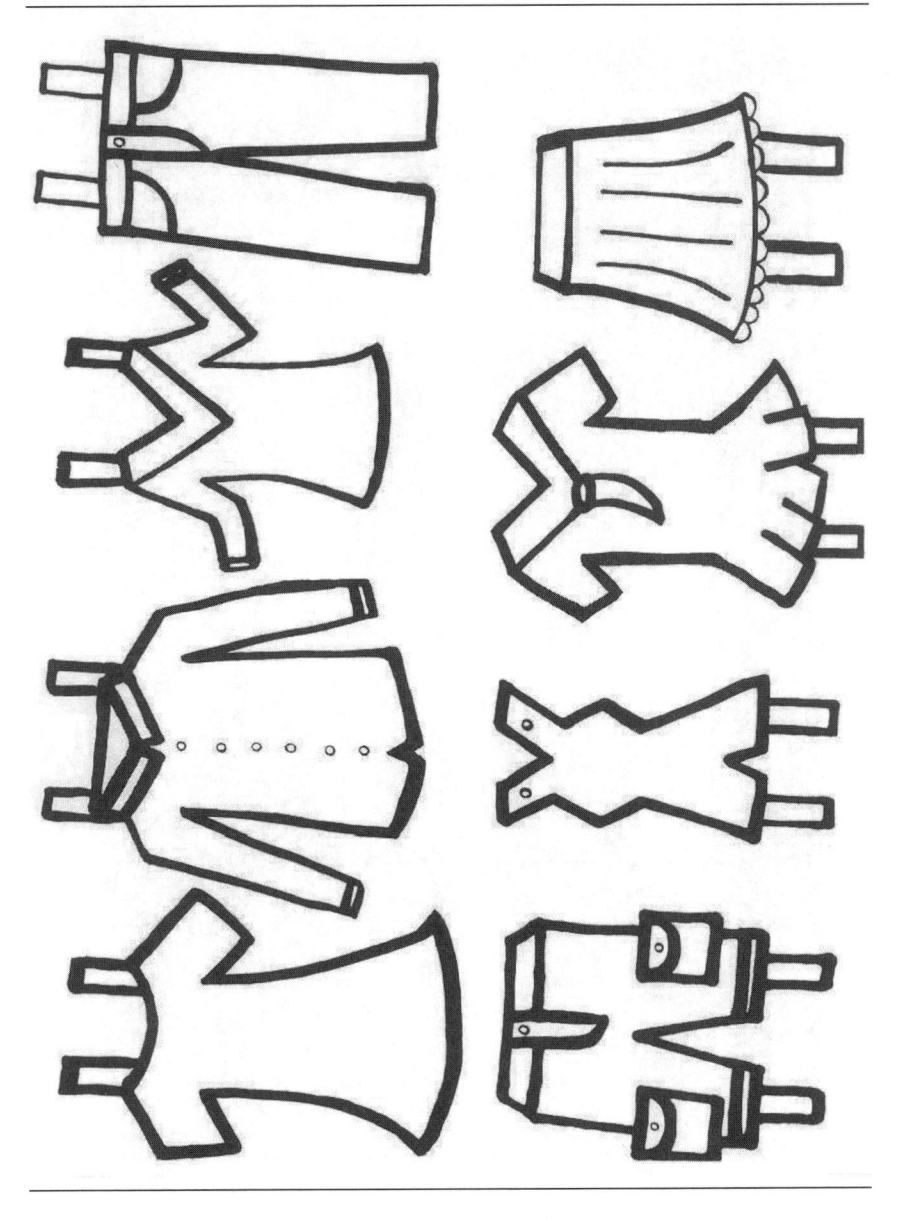

Figure A15.2 Example

A16
Compliments
Monit Cheung

Items Needed

Deck: Two sets of matching "Compliment Cards" on a variety of colored note cards (see figure A16.1)

Target Population

Children 6+ and their parents

For families having family relationship or peer problems

Suitable for children of all cultures and socioeconomic backgrounds

Purpose

To stimulate positive thoughts about family members, practice how to verbalize positive thoughts, and promote communication among family members.

Procedure

Shuffle and deal the entire deck of cards out to the family members (total 48 pairs or choose fewer pairs of cards for fewer participants). The first family member to your right will pick a card from his or her hand and ask which family member has the matching card. The person with the matching card will look at this family member and say something positive about this person, for example, "You are a good person." The complimented person will say something positive in return, for example, "I like your hair." Do not repeat what has been said. Once the cards have been matched, they will place the pair on the table. If the player cannot think of anything to say, he or she can read from any card on the table. Play passes to the right until each player takes at least three to four turns.

Function in Assessment and Treatment

Assessment

This game is designed to promote positive communication and enhance relationship building between children and their parents. It can be used during the first session with the family to assess the relationships between children and their families. It can also be used to measure progress in familial relationships at various points during the therapeutic process.

Treatment

Encourage the clients to write down more compliments on blank note cards. Ask them to use positive and complimentary language with each other at home. If they find a family member using a negative comment in a conversation, they should counter it with a positive comment and then ask for a compliment. Remind the clients that if they use a negative comment to a family member, they must remember to give at least three compliments to that person during the same day.

Make two copies of these cards and paste each statement on a note card

Figure A16.1 Compliment Cards

You are beautiful (handsome).	You are smart.	You are nice.	You go out of your way to make my life special.
You do so much for me.	You are the best.	I know you love me.	You are good at _____ (basketball, art work, cooking).
You always say nice things.	You are good at almost anything.	You have a warm heart.	You are fair.
You are great.	You are a good cook.	You always dress nicely.	Your friends think you are nice.
You friends told me you are cool.	Without you, I would not be able to do this.	When something needs to be done, you always help.	I have confidence in you.
I appreciate your help.	You have done a great job.	You are always there when I need you.	I enjoy your company.
You are a wonderful helper (caregiver).	You are the best in the world.	You are patient.	You are kind.
You have a lovely voice.	You sing well.	You are a good listener.	You have done great work!
You are super!	I respect you.	You made me proud.	I love you.
You are a super mom/dad/child.	I like you a lot.	Your friends told me you are the best.	You are a great story-teller.
You are wonderful.	You make me happy.	I like the way you talk to me.	I like the way you care about me.
You are extraordinary!	You are excellent!	Your effort is appreciated.	Thank you very much!

A17
Connecting Latino Families
Maria Cano

Items Needed

Pretend play family figures (preferably a set of grandparents, parents, and children; may be ordered from www.childrentherapytoys.com); bag to hold the pretend family figures; music and music player; a ball; game cards (can be made using construction paper, colored paper, scissors, and glue; see figures A17.1 and A17.2)

Target Population

Latino children age eight to fourteen whose parents are divorced or separated

Intended for use in a group setting

Purpose

To help children understand that they are not responsible for their parents' divorce or separation

To establish the idea that parents divorce each other, not their family

To emphasize the importance of maintaining relationships with the extended family based on family culture and values, despite divorce or separation

To help children express their feelings and understand those of their family members

Procedure

Prior to the session, create the game cards with some culturally relevant questions. This can include various statements, questions, and symbols for addressing divorce or separation issues (see figure A17.3 for example).

To begin, ask clients to form a circle and place the game cards and the bag with the family in the center of the circle. When the music starts, the players will pass the ball around, "Hot Potato" style. When the music stops, the player holding the ball must blindly select a figure from the bag. Once a figure has been chosen, the player will state which family member the figure represents and select a game card. Last, the player will follow the instructions on the card as if he or she is the family member that was selected from the bag. For example, if a player identifies the selected figure as "grandmother," he or she must respond to the card in the way that he or she thinks the grandmother would. This projection game will help the players understand more from the other person's perspective, with attention on the cultural value behind each response.

After the player takes his or her turn, the card is placed in the discard pile and the figure is returned back to the bag. "Hot potato" will begin again when the music starts and the game will continue this way until each player has had a turn.

End the game with discussion questions addressing any feelings that arose during the game such as, "How does the value or culture within your extended family affect your thinking?" "How do you feel about your current situation with your parents?" "How do your parents show you they love you even after the divorce?" "How do you celebrate special holidays with your family?" "How do your parents let you know you are special?" "How does your family show you they love you?" Also, ask the clients if it was easy or hard to respond to the game card from another family member's point of view, and if it changed their perspective on their parents' separation or divorce.

Function in Assessment and Treatment

Assessment

This game will help children express their feelings about their parents' divorce and understand feelings that other family members may be experiencing as well. The clients' responses to the game cards will give insight into their ability to understand the situation broadly, and will help them to understand that their relationships with extended family members does not have to change because of what their parents did.

Treatment

Through this interactive projective exercise, children begin feeling comfortable to communicate their feelings about how separation and divorce has affected them. Using the family figures and game cards to project different family members' points of view, clients are able to critically think about the perspective of their family members. This reflection also helps the clients to understand that their parents' separation or divorce is not their fault. Additional symbols representing the Latino culture can be used to help children make more game cards. This exercise will help children identify the views from their family members and find solutions to their inner conflict. This exercise can be modified to work with children of other cultures or ethnic backgrounds.

82 *Therapeutic Games and Guided Imagery*

Figure A17.1 One Side of Game Card

> This doll reminds me of my _____ who would answer the question at the back of this card.

Figure A17.2 Other Side of Game Card

What is the most relaxing part after the separation/divorce?	Name one thing that triggered the separation/divorce.	Are things better or worse after the separation/divorce?	What would you change about the way things are now?
This person's answer would be:	This person's answer would be:	This person's answer would be:	This person's answer would be:
Who is there for you when you feel upset or sad?	What do you remember most about the separation/divorce?	How did you find out about the separation/divorce?	When did you realize that things will change? What things have changed?
This person's answer would be:	This person's answer would be:	This person's answer would be:	This person's answer would be:
Share one favorite family memory.	What is one thing about this divorce that you are too afraid or embarrassed to ask?	Name a time when you were particularly upset about the separation/divorce. What happened?	Choose one word to describe the way you feel about the separation/divorce.
This person's answer would be:	This person's answer would be:	This person's answer would be:	This person's answer would be:
If you could have one thing going back to the way it used to be, what would that be?	If you could change your relationship after the separation/divorce, how would you change it?	Who do you miss the most? What is it about him/her that you miss?	What kinds of emotions did you experience during the separation/divorce? Give one example.
This person's answer would be:	This person's answer would be:	This person's answer would be:	This person's answer would be:
How does this symbol relate to the separation/divorce?	How does this symbol relate to your family value or culture?	When you see this symbol, what part about the divorce comes to your mind?	When you see this symbol, what family value comes to your mind?
This person's answer would be:	This person's answer would be:	This person's answer would be:	This person's answer would be:
♥	☺	💧	🚫

A17 – Connecting Latino Families   **83**

Figure A17.3 Examples

A18
Connections and Relationships
Monit Cheung

Items Needed

Two sheets of paper for each person (or use the attached "My Hands and Feet" sheet in figure A18.1); a pen; colored markers or crayons; adhesive tape

Target Population

Clients experiencing social anxiety, parent-child conflicts, overwhelming feelings or low self-esteem

For group ice-breaking

Appropriate for use during individual or group sessions with clients of all ethnic backgrounds

Purpose

To provide an ice breaker

To help clients think about how a problem may be connected to them

To help clients talk about a personal issue with someone in the family

To build parent-child relationships

Procedure

In a group setting, ask the child to trace his or her non-dominant hand on the corresponding side of a sheet of paper (in the "landscape" position). He or she must then have a participant trace his or her other hand on the corresponding side of the paper. If the child is left-handed, he or she should trace his or her right hand first, on the right side of the paper, and vice-versa. If this is an individual session, you will start by tracing the child's dominant hand and let the child complete the other hand. The purpose of this step is to assess the child's hand-eye coordination and to allow an opportunity for the child to work on a project with his or her parent or another member in the session.

Repeat this "drawing" procedure, but this time the child will draw his or her own feet on another piece of paper (also in the "landscape" position). If the child's feet are very large, just draw the front part with toes only.

Then connect the two pieces of paper by taping the backs of them together. Ask the child to draw a circle in the middle between the hands and the feet (see figure A18.2) and decorate this circle to make it look like a head (e.g., with hair, eyes, ears, glasses, etc.) (see figure A18.3). Since this is a free association exercise, no suggestion should be provided as to how to express feelings through the drawing of the "head." Then ask the child to draw a body below the head and make the hands and feet a part of this entire drawing (see figure A18.4).

Function in Assessment and Treatment

Assessment

This exercise aims to find connections, which can be parent-child relationships, peer influences, feeling associations, and other kinds of linkage that can be expressed through the exaggeration of the hands and feet. If the client refuses to draw the feet, it may indicate that something should be further explored—avoid guessing from a third-person interpretation. Drawing is subjective and it should be used with care and patience.

Treatment

You can help the client identify missing components in the drawing, such as adding a ring to the hand, putting more people in the background, or coloring the drawing. While talking about something serious or emotional, the client can continue with the drawing while avoiding uncomfortable eye contact. This will help the client feel more at ease when disclosing a secret or something uncomfortable. Once the client has voiced a concern, you can then encourage the child to talk to you directly. If you detect that the client has a very low esteem or a depressive mood, you may want to draw this person with the client and use the drawing as a means to ask additional questions, such as:

- The hands and feet are very large. They help the person in this drawing to express something important. What would it be?
- If you were this person (in this drawing), what would you be telling me?
- How would this person feel if he or she is talking to me about a secret?
- What kind of secret is it? What would telling a secret feel like?

- What is missing in this drawing? Tell me more about it.
- If the facial expression of this person changed to an upset emotion, who made this person feel this way? How would you talk to this person? Who is this person in reality? How could we help this person?
- What would you do to help this person feel better?

Figure A18.1 Hands-Feet

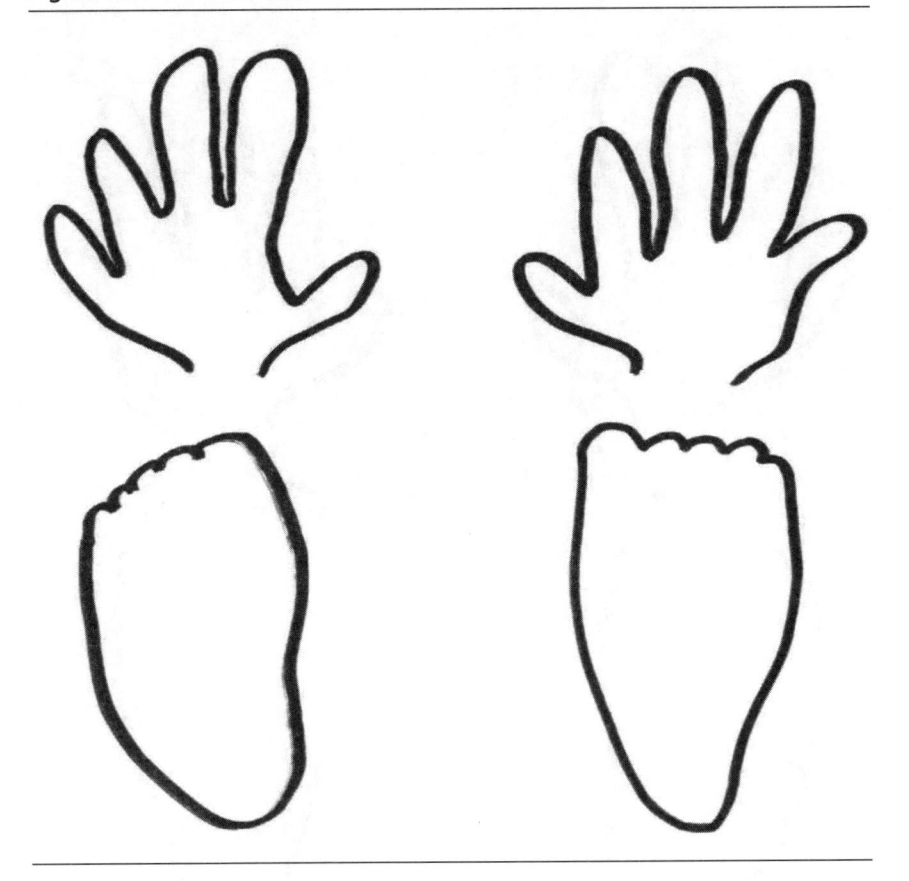

Figure A18.2 Put a Head in the Middle

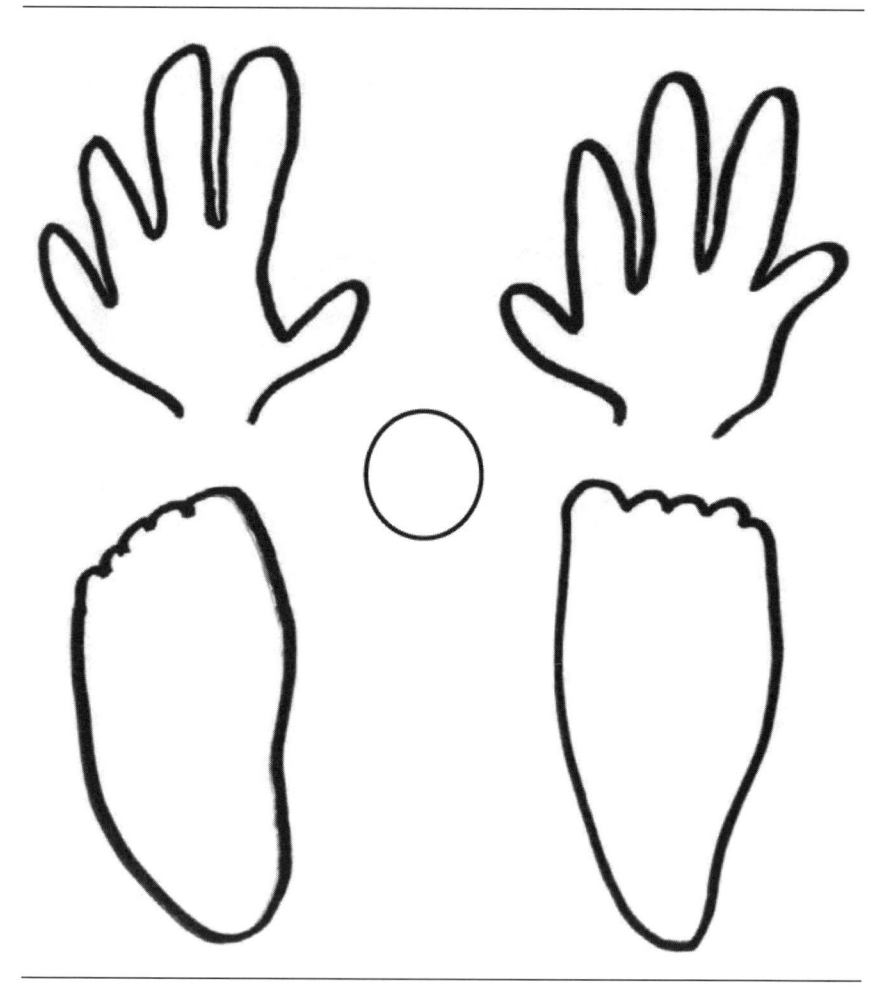

Figure A18.3 A Complete Drawing Example

90 *Therapeutic Games and Guided Imagery*

Figure A18.4 Examples

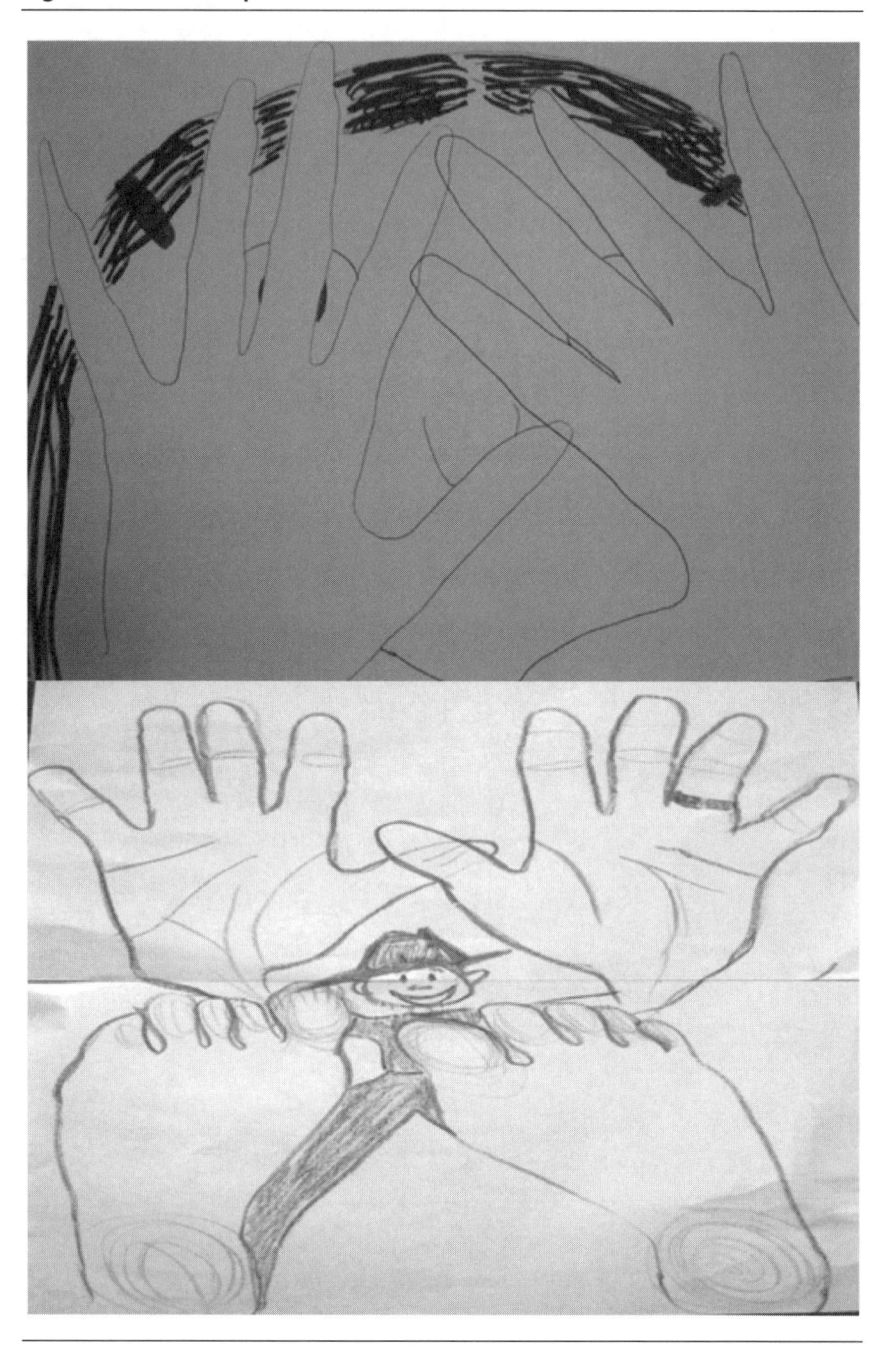

A19
Dealing with Divorce
Chloe Walker

Items Needed

Full deck of 52 playing cards (you and the child may also create a deck, making sure that you maintain four different "suits"); pen and markers

Target Population

Children seven and older dealing with the divorce of their parents, individually or in groups

All cultures and socioeconomic backgrounds

Purpose

To help children dealing with divorce understand the divorce process both from a social perspective and a legal perspective.

To help children identify the different aspects of the divorce process, and which ones they have no control over, some control over, and absolute control over.

To assist children in identification of their expectations of the divorce process and increase their ability to share their voice in the divorce process in a meaningful way.

To assist children in becoming self-advocates.

Procedure

The use of traditional playing cards may be more appropriate with older children and teens. If not using traditional playing cards, ask the child to make a deck of cards using index cards. Note: creation of the cards may take more than one session and can be a part of the therapeutic process.

Divide the cards into four piles and explain that each "suit" represents one of the four different categories: "no control," "some control," "absolute control," and "aspirations." On one card from each of the first three suits, write an example of something over which the child has no control, some control, or absolute control during the divorce process (see figure A19.1). If you are using traditional playing cards, write these categories on a piece of paper instead of the cards. The child will complete the rest of the cards with examples from his or her own experience. After the first three categories are complete, the child can then fill in the aspiration cards, as the final suit, with his or her hopes and dreams. For example, "I want to live with my siblings," "I want to be able to stay on the basketball team even if I move between the two houses of my parents" or "I want to be happy again." Additional examples are included below if the child has difficulty coming up with ideas.

Use the deck as a platform for discussing the child's feelings about control, and for creating an action plan for reaching aspirations that are in the child's control. Draw one card from each category to create the first scenario. Use the control cards to begin discussing a feasible solution (if one exists) to complete the aspiration card. Be cognizant of the fact that only some goals may have a feasible solution. Some possible follow-up questions may include:

1. How will you go about achieving your goal?
2. If you could change one thing about this scenario, what would it be?
3. What did you learn from this process that could help you cope with your problem?
4. How can your parents and siblings help you with your goal?

Function in Assessment and Treatment

Assessment

This game is appropriate for the middle stages of counseling after rapport has been established, as emotionally challenging topics will be discussed. This game can be used to assess children's knowledge of the divorce process. It can also serve as a tool to help children identify the difference between what they can and cannot control during the divorce process. Through use of this exercise, children can learn more about the legal system and the factors that affect the outcome of the divorce.

Treatment

This game enables children to take control over a situation which they may have initially felt they had no control over. It provides an atmosphere where they can openly share any feelings about the divorce and the decisions being made by other parties. It also empowers the children to create their own realistic goals and action plans for attaining these goals. This game can also be modified to work with parents experiencing divorce because it can help them understand the situation from the child's perspective.

A19 – Dealing with Divorce **93**

Figure A19.1 Examples

Figure A19.2 Control in Divorce

No Control	Some Control	Absolute Control
Parents' decision to divorce	Discussion about divorce with mom	My own attitude about divorce
Final custody judgment made by judge	Relationship with dad	My opinion expressed to my amicus attorney
Siblings' attitudes about the divorce	My performance at school	Expression of my feelings about divorce

A20
Divominos
Karen R. Greenberg

Items Needed

A deck of 55 pre-designed playing cards (see figure A20.3)

Target Population

Children and adolescents ages six and older who have experienced parental separation or divorce

Designed for two to six players

Purpose

To encourage children and adolescents to participate in direct discussion about divorce

To help children and adolescents express their feelings

To help participants gain acceptance of parental separation or divorce

To address issues of self-blame

To assist children and adolescents in developing coping skills

Procedure

The object of the game is to play all of the cards in your hand. To begin the game, shuffle the deck of cards and spread them out, face down. To determine the first player, each player chooses one card and the player whose card has the most dots will be the first player; game play will continue in a clockwise rotation. The cards previously drawn should be mixed back into the pile, face down. Next, players will draw cards based on the following standards:
- For 2–4 players, each player draws 10 cards.
- For 5 players, each player draws 8 cards.
- For 6 players, each player draws 7 cards.

Once the players have drawn their cards, they may look at those cards in their hands only, just as in a regular card game.

The first player begins by choosing one card in his or her hand and answering either question on the card. After the question is answered, the player may then place the card down with the question and dots facing up. The next player must choose a card from his or her hand that matches the number of dots on either end of the card that was previously played, and answer the corresponding question. The player can then place the card down, connecting the cards by their numbers (see figure A20.1). Once an answer has been given, it cannot be repeated for the duration of the game. If a player cannot make a match on a turn, he or she must draw from the pile and it will then be the next player's turn.

When a card contains a double (the same number of dots on each end of the card), the player has the option of either playing the card in the same "line of play" or placing it sideways so as to allow a new "line of play." A "line of play" is defined as the layout of played cards that typically will start with a single card and may extend into two opposite directions as players add their matching cards.

The game ends when a player plays all of the cards in his or her hand or when no player can make a play.

Function in Assessment and Treatment

Assessment

This game can be used to assess a youth's ability to cope with problems relating to separation or divorce. It can help participants identify feelings which they would normally find difficult to discuss or adequately express. Through the player's responses throughout the game, the facilitator may gain insight into troubling thoughts, feelings, and attitudes facing the participant; these issues may be addressed in future discussions.

Treatment

This game can enable children and adolescents of divorced parents to adapt positive coping skills in a difficult situation. As part of the treatment plan, future sessions should include follow-up questions and discussion to facilitate the identification of potential solutions to problems and issues that may arise from the divorce. The use of solution-focused therapy or strengths perspective therapy may be incorporated to help the client deal with family conflicts.

A20 – Divominos   **97**

Figure A20.1 Game Example

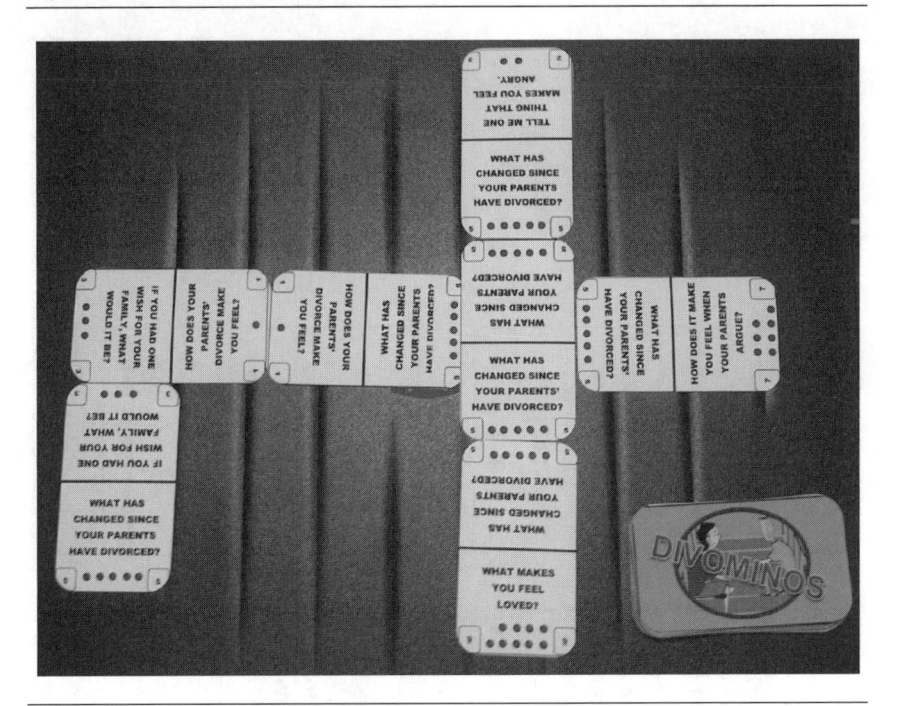

Figure A20.2 Therapeutic Questions

# of Dots	Therapeutic Questions
1	How does your parents' divorce make you feel?
2	Tell me one thing that makes you feel angry.
3	If you had one wish for your family, what would it be?
4	Name something good that has come from the divorce.
5	What has changed since your parents' divorce?
6	What is something you like about your dad? Your mom?
7	How does it make you feel when your parents argue?
8	What would you like your parents to know about your feelings?
9	What makes you feel loved?
10	What do you feel you need from each parent?

98 *Therapeutic Games and Guided Imagery*

Figure A20.3 Predesigned Game Cards

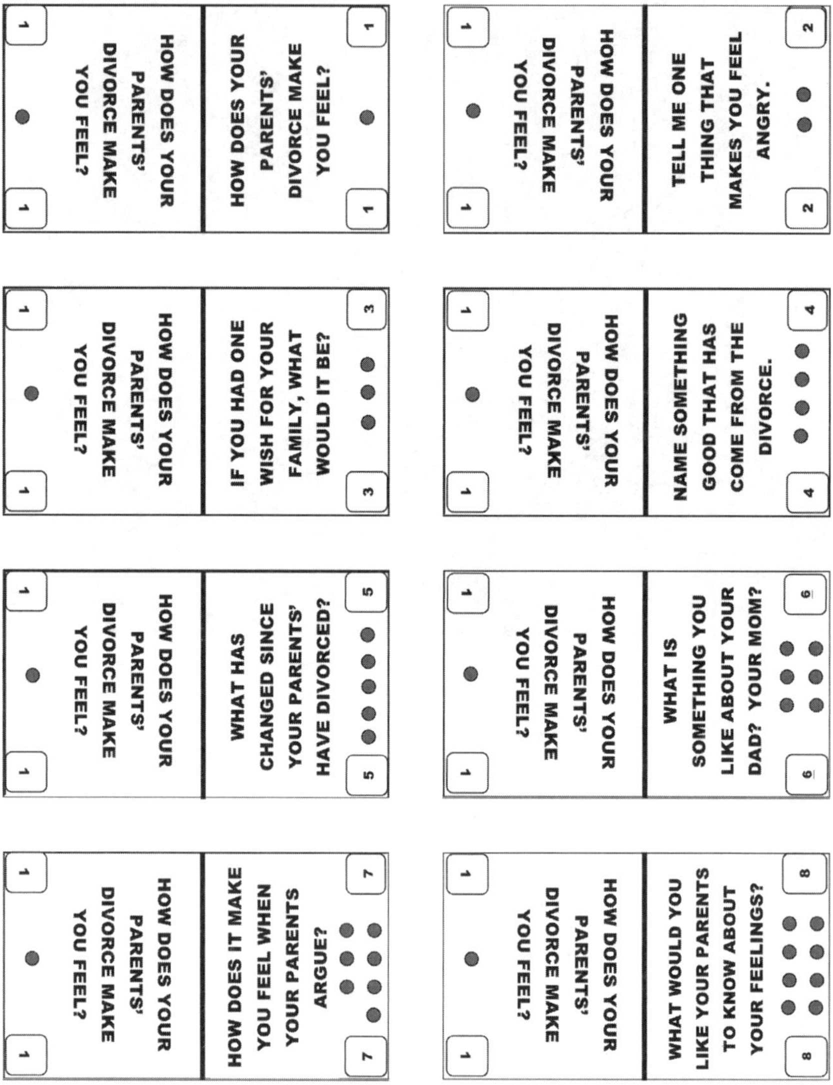

1	HOW DOES YOUR PARENTS' DIVORCE MAKE YOU FEEL?
1	HOW DOES YOUR PARENTS' DIVORCE MAKE YOU FEEL?
1	HOW DOES YOUR PARENTS' DIVORCE MAKE YOU FEEL?
2	TELL ME ONE THING THAT MAKES YOU FEEL ANGRY.
1	HOW DOES YOUR PARENTS' DIVORCE MAKE YOU FEEL?
3	IF YOU HAD ONE WISH FOR YOUR FAMILY, WHAT WOULD IT BE?
1	HOW DOES YOUR PARENTS' DIVORCE MAKE YOU FEEL?
4	NAME SOMETHING GOOD THAT HAS COME FROM THE DIVORCE.
1	HOW DOES YOUR PARENTS' DIVORCE MAKE YOU FEEL?
5	WHAT HAS CHANGED SINCE YOUR PARENTS' HAVE DIVORCED?
1	HOW DOES YOUR PARENTS' DIVORCE MAKE YOU FEEL?
6	WHAT IS SOMETHING YOU LIKE ABOUT YOUR DAD? YOUR MOM?
1	HOW DOES YOUR PARENTS' DIVORCE MAKE YOU FEEL?
7	HOW DOES IT MAKE YOU FEEL WHEN YOUR PARENTS ARGUE?
1	HOW DOES YOUR PARENTS' DIVORCE MAKE YOU FEEL?
8	WHAT WOULD YOU LIKE YOUR PARENTS TO KNOW ABOUT YOUR FEELINGS?

Figure A20.3 Predesigned Game Cards—(continued)

1 — HOW DOES YOUR PARENTS' DIVORCE MAKE YOU FEEL?	9 — WHAT MAKES YOU FEEL LOVED?
1 — HOW DOES YOUR PARENTS' DIVORCE MAKE YOU FEEL?	10 — WHAT DO YOU FEEL YOU NEED FROM EACH PARENT?
2 — TELL ME ONE THING THAT MAKES YOU FEEL ANGRY.	2 — TELL ME ONE THING THAT MAKES YOU FEEL ANGRY.
2 — TELL ME ONE THING THAT MAKES YOU FEEL ANGRY.	3 — IF YOU HAD ONE WISH FOR YOUR FAMILY, WHAT WOULD IT BE?
2 — TELL ME ONE THING THAT MAKES YOU FEEL ANGRY.	4 — NAME SOMETHING GOOD THAT HAS COME FROM THE DIVORCE.
2 — TELL ME ONE THING THAT MAKES YOU FEEL ANGRY.	5 — WHAT HAS CHANGED SINCE YOUR PARENTS' HAVE DIVORCED?
2 — TELL ME ONE THING THAT MAKES YOU FEEL ANGRY.	6 — WHAT IS SOMETHING YOU LIKE ABOUT YOUR DAD? YOUR MOM?
2 — TELL ME ONE THING THAT MAKES YOU FEEL ANGRY.	7 — HOW DOES IT MAKE YOU FEEL WHEN YOUR PARENTS ARGUE?

100 *Therapeutic Games and Guided Imagery*

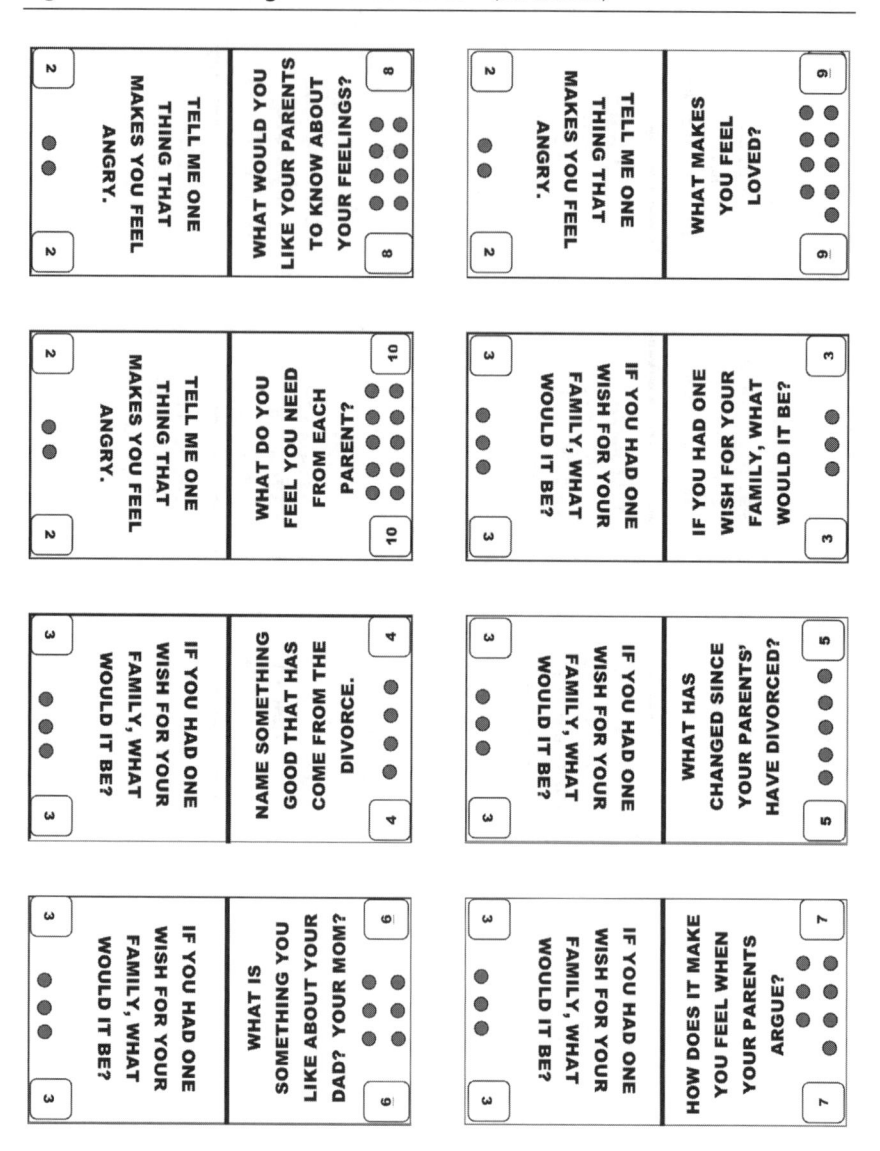

Figure A20.3 Predesigned Game Cards—(continued)

TELL ME ONE THING THAT MAKES YOU FEEL ANGRY. (2)	TELL ME ONE THING THAT MAKES YOU FEEL ANGRY. (2)
WHAT WOULD YOU LIKE YOUR PARENTS TO KNOW ABOUT YOUR FEELINGS? (8)	WHAT MAKES YOU FEEL LOVED? (9)
TELL ME ONE THING THAT MAKES YOU FEEL ANGRY. (2)	IF YOU HAD ONE WISH FOR YOUR FAMILY, WHAT WOULD IT BE? (3)
WHAT DO YOU FEEL YOU NEED FROM EACH PARENT? (10)	IF YOU HAD ONE WISH FOR YOUR FAMILY, WHAT WOULD IT BE? (3)
IF YOU HAD ONE WISH FOR YOUR FAMILY, WHAT WOULD IT BE? (3)	IF YOU HAD ONE WISH FOR YOUR FAMILY, WHAT WOULD IT BE? (3)
NAME SOMETHING GOOD THAT HAS COME FROM THE DIVORCE. (4)	WHAT HAS CHANGED SINCE YOUR PARENTS' HAVE DIVORCED? (5)
IF YOU HAD ONE WISH FOR YOUR FAMILY, WHAT WOULD IT BE? (3)	IF YOU HAD ONE WISH FOR YOUR FAMILY, WHAT WOULD IT BE? (3)
WHAT IS SOMETHING YOU LIKE ABOUT YOUR DAD? YOUR MOM? (6)	HOW DOES IT MAKE YOU FEEL WHEN YOUR PARENTS ARGUE? (7)

Figure A20.3 Predesigned Game Cards—(continued)

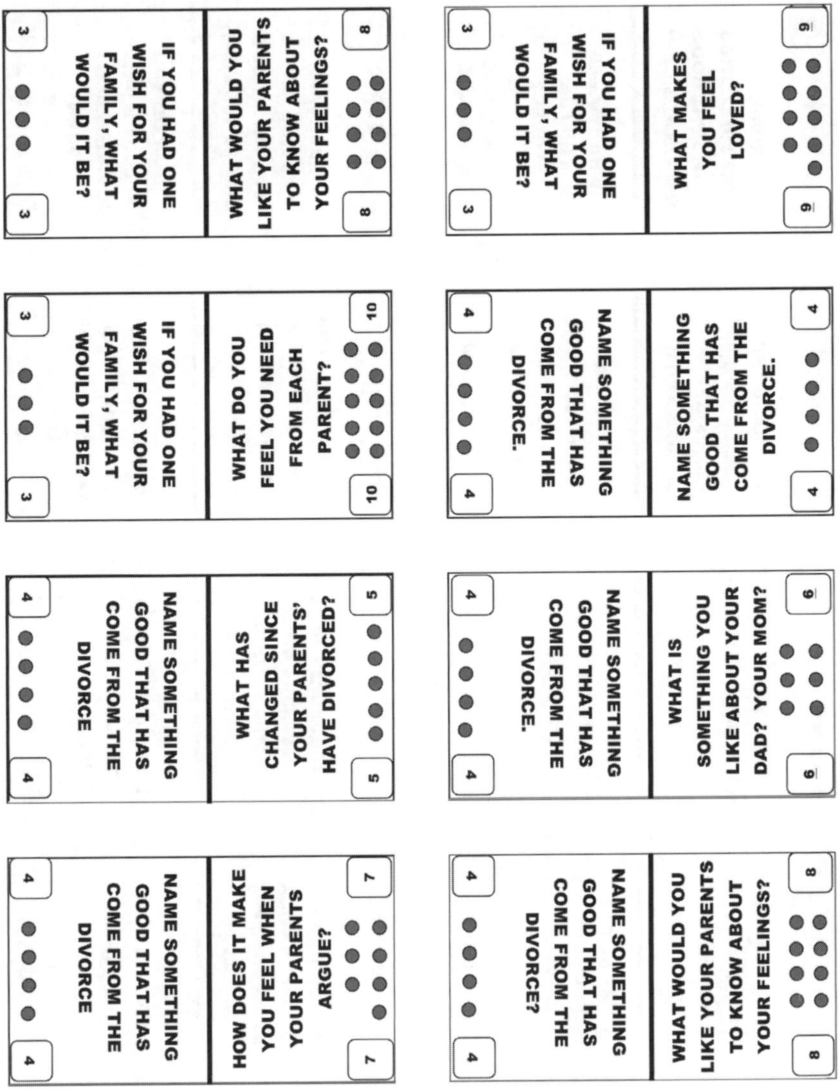

102 *Therapeutic Games and Guided Imagery*

Figure A20.3 Predesigned Game Cards—(continued)

4	NAME SOMETHING GOOD THAT HAS COME FROM THE DIVORCE.
6	WHAT MAKES YOU FEEL LOVED?
4	NAME SOMETHING GOOD THAT HAS COME FROM THE DIVORCE.
10	WHAT DO YOU FEEL YOU NEED FROM EACH PARENT?
5	WHAT HAS CHANGED SINCE YOUR PARENTS' HAVE DIVORCED?
5	WHAT HAS CHANGED SINCE YOUR PARENTS' HAVE DIVORCED?
5	WHAT HAS CHANGED SINCE YOUR PARENTS' HAVE DIVORCED?
6	WHAT IS SOMETHING YOU LIKE ABOUT YOUR DAD? YOUR MOM?
5	WHAT HAS CHANGED SINCE YOUR PARENTS' HAVE DIVORCED?
7	HOW DOES IT MAKE YOU FEEL WHEN YOUR PARENTS ARGUE?
5	WHAT HAS CHANGED SINCE YOUR PARENTS' HAVE DIVORCED?
8	WHAT WOULD YOU LIKE YOUR PARENTS TO KNOW ABOUT YOUR FEELINGS?
5	WHAT HAS CHANGED SINCE YOUR PARENTS' HAVE DIVORCED?
9	WHAT MAKES YOU FEEL LOVED?
5	WHAT HAS CHANGED SINCE YOUR PARENTS' HAVE DIVORCED?
10	WHAT DO YOU FEEL YOU NEED FROM EACH PARENT?

Figure A20.3 Predesigned Game Cards—(continued)

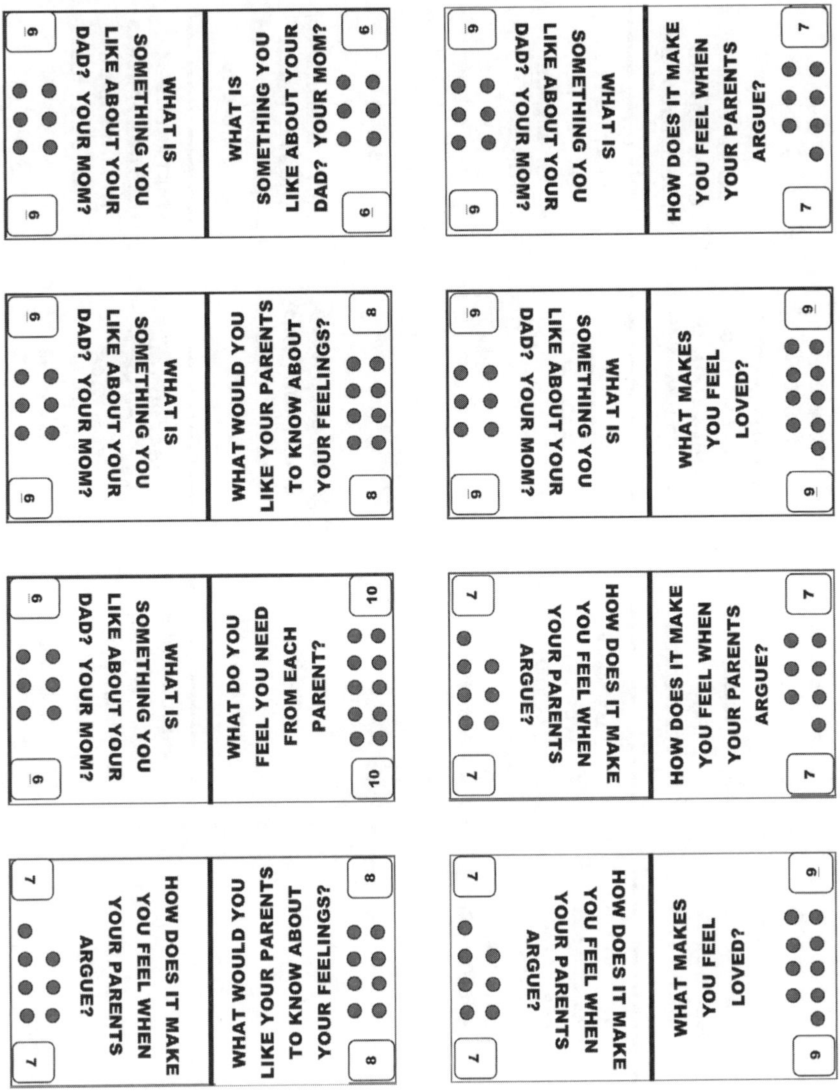

104 *Therapeutic Games and Guided Imagery*

Figure A20.3 Predesigned Game Cards—(continued)

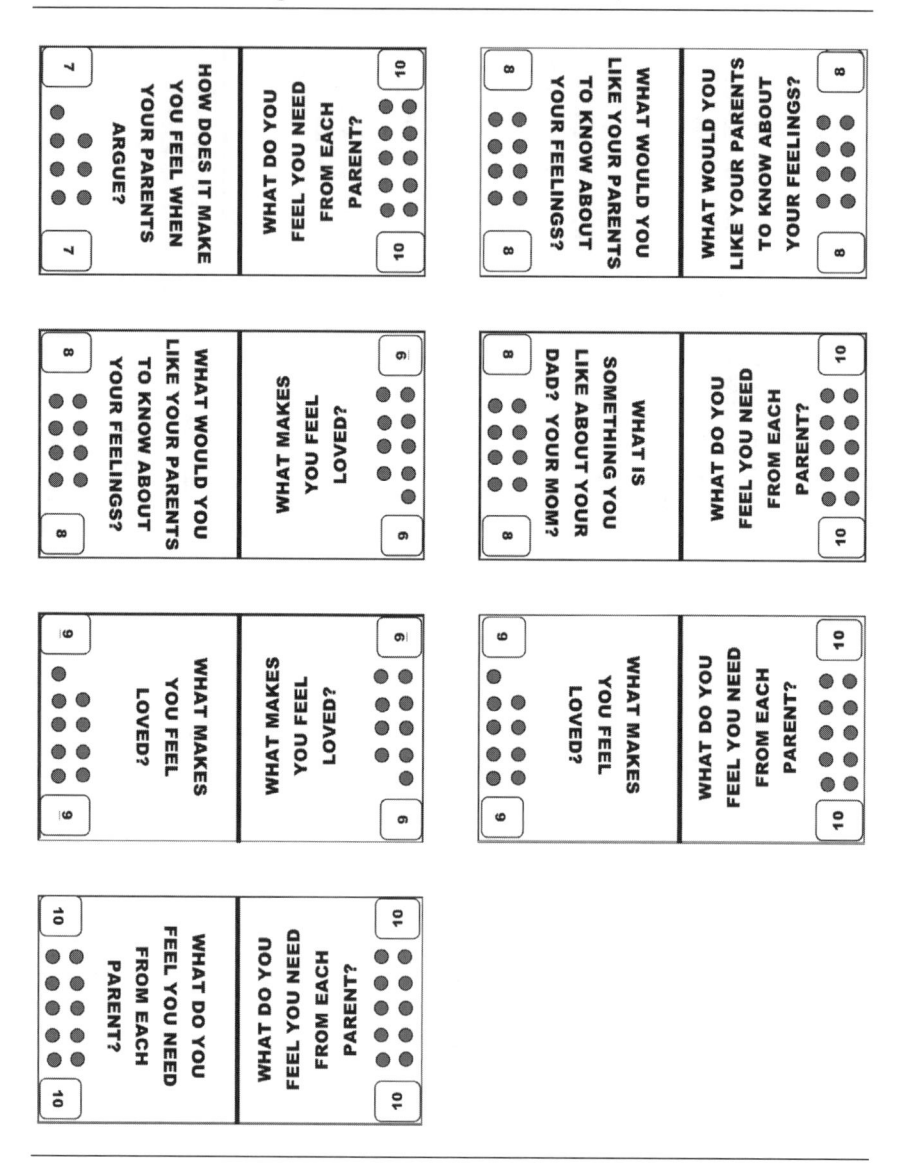

7	HOW DOES IT MAKE YOU FEEL WHEN YOUR PARENTS ARGUE?
10	WHAT DO YOU FEEL YOU NEED FROM EACH PARENT?
8	WHAT WOULD YOU LIKE YOUR PARENTS TO KNOW ABOUT YOUR FEELINGS?
8	WHAT WOULD YOU LIKE YOUR PARENTS TO KNOW ABOUT YOUR FEELINGS?
8	WHAT WOULD YOU LIKE YOUR PARENTS TO KNOW ABOUT YOUR FEELINGS?
9	WHAT MAKES YOU FEEL LOVED?
8	WHAT IS SOMETHING YOU LIKE ABOUT YOUR DAD? YOUR MOM?
10	WHAT DO YOU FEEL YOU NEED FROM EACH PARENT?
9	WHAT MAKES YOU FEEL LOVED?
9	WHAT MAKES YOU FEEL LOVED?
9	WHAT MAKES YOU FEEL LOVED?
10	WHAT DO YOU FEEL YOU NEED FROM EACH PARENT?
10	WHAT DO YOU FEEL YOU NEED FROM EACH PARENT?
10	WHAT DO YOU FEEL YOU NEED FROM EACH PARENT?

A21
The Dot Exercise
Jennifer Edwards

Items Needed

Eight different colors of colored dot stickers (four of each color) and the attached worksheet (figure A21.1)

Target Population

Children eight to twelve who need help controlling negative emotions; individual or group sessions

Purpose

To break the ice with a child who does not want to talk

To help the child understand the meaning of each emotion expressed

To teach a coping skill for handling negative emotions

Procedure

Take the worksheet and ask the children to pick an emotion that they often have difficulty experiencing. Tell them to pick an emotion that they often have right before they get in trouble. Have them put a colored dot on the paper next to that emotion. Next have them think about what it feels like when they have that emotion, and what parts of their body in which the emotion is expressed. Then ask them to put a sticker of the same color on the different body parts such as face, cheek, arm, fingers. Ask what that part of the body feels like when they have that emotion. Then have them tighten or tense up that part of their body. When holding the tightness they count to five and then release the tension. Talk to them about how their body feels once they have released the tension. Pick another emotion and repeat the procedures so that the body has many colored dots to the point of exaggeration. When they look at each other in a group or look at a mirror in an individual session they will share how tension can be released with this exercise. Finally, explain that the next time they feel frustrated, they could think about this tension-relief practice to avoid reacting negatively to the situation they are facing.

Function in Assessment and Treatment

Assessment

You will participate in the game with the kids, either individually or in groups. You may check whether the children will show resistance when being asked to place dots on their body. Children often feel uncomfortable putting dots on the face, fearing that people may judge them by their look. You may encourage them to focus their attention on themselves, particularly their facial expression when they have certain feelings or thoughts, rather than on how others may judge them. You may also ask them to try feeling the dots being connected with their physical body and emotional status.

Treatment

Children are asked to put each of their dots on a piece of paper. As each dot is peeled from the body, they are reminded to connect and write down their feelings next to the dot pasted on the paper. This not only assesses children's ability to connect the dots with their physical body but also, through writing down feeling words, they will be able to transform abstract feelings into concrete words. In addition, if children have negative feelings, they can think about removing these feelings by taking away the dots. If children have positive feelings, they can express them by telling something or someone related to these feelings.

Figure A21.1 Emotions for the Dot Exercise

Emotion	Dot
Angry	
Anxious	
Ashamed	
Bored	
Confused	
Depressed	
Disgusted	
Embarrassed	
Enraged	
Exhausted	
Frightened	
Frustrated	
Irritated	
Lonely	
Mad	
Sad	

A22
Environmental Mindfulness
Misty Miller

Items Needed

Two worksheets (figure A22.1—Environmental Mindfulness and Figure A22.2—Environmental Observations); pencil, markers or colored pencils

Target Population

Children and adolescents who struggle with concentration and self-expression

Purpose

To help clients increase their awareness of the environment

To facilitate discussions about how to develop a greater sense of self-control

To broaden the clients' view of how they can change and regulate their emotions

Procedure

This activity is intended to take place outside. If conducted indoors, the facilitator should use a computer or other tools to project a natural environment. Allow the client to find a calm and peaceful space where he or she can foster self-awareness of the environment. Briefly discuss the five senses and how we use them daily without really realizing it. Ask the client to read the "Mindfulness" handout before beginning the activity. Allow the client as much time as needed to complete the activity. After processing the first activity, use the "Observations" handout to stimulate additional discussions. Encourage the client to draw or write a story reflecting his or her experience in an environment while being present and reflective in the moment. Ask the client what other thoughts came to mind while he or she was still and reflective. Empower the client to think about what he or she could do if the environment was to be modified according to his or her wish and how this change may affect his or her emotions.

Function and Assessment in Treatment

Assessment

This activity allows the client to center thoughts and feelings about the environment through the senses, which promotes regulation and self-control. Reflection and discussion help the client develop awareness about his or her reactions and what he or she focuses on in the environment. This assessment procedure allows the practitioner to gain insight into the client's reaction and reflection process, which may help gain a better understanding of the client's behavior in other complex situations.

Treatment

This activity helps clients focus on the here and now, being present, and understanding the environment around them. This gives clients a sense of control about their feelings, senses, environment, and how they view the world. Focusing on being still and present in the moment gives clients the opportunity to reflect about what lies beneath the surface, which enables clients to feel calm and ready for discussion. Suggested therapeutic questions include:

1. What is self-control?
2. How do you use your senses to gain self-control when the environment is not presented with a positive tone?
3. What would you change about your surroundings (may include people, places, things, or feelings)? How would these changes affect you and the people in your life?

110 *Therapeutic Games and Guided Imagery*

Figure A22.1 Worksheet 1—Environmental Mindfulness

Environmental Mindfulness

Using your senses to be aware of your environment; being present in the moment.

You have five senses you can use to explore your environment: *sight, hearing, smell, touch* and *taste*. You will use four senses today. We recommend you do not taste what you do not know. Find a calm and peaceful spot to sit down. Use your sight, hearing, smell and touch to help you complete the following sentences.

When I look around I see...

_____

_____

When I am calm and quiet, I hear...

_____

_____

When I close my eyes and inhale, I smell...

_____

_____

When I touch _____ it feels...

_____

_____

Figure A22.2 Worksheet 2—Environmental Observations

Environmental Observations

Using your senses to be aware of your environment; being present in the moment

Find a spot to sit quietly by yourself. Try sit very still without saying anything for ten minutes. Record your experience. What do you hear? What do you see? How do you feel? You may draw a picture of your surroundings or write a short story that reflects your feelings about the outdoors.

A23
Family Time
Ada Cheung

Items Needed

A print out of an empty house (see figure A23.1); pens, pencils, crayons or markers

Target Population

Children five and older

Adolescents experiencing emotional distress at home

Clients who have difficulty directly expressing their feelings and thoughts

Individuals, groups with six or fewer members, or families

Purpose

To assess family functioning from the participant's perspective

To help the client express feelings and thoughts

To describe family dynamics and family rituals

To identify coping strategies

Procedure

Clinician explains the significant impact that family has on our mental health and well-being. Highlight the ways in which family can influence the way we feel about ourselves, how we identify ourselves, and how we react with other people in school, the community, and at work. Therefore, it is important for clients to understand family dynamics and explore interactions among family members.

Present the client with a piece of drawing paper with an empty house printed on it (figure A23.1). Encourage the client to complete the picture by adding family members. Ask the client to include family activities, or draw out feelings or anything about the home environment (see figure A23.2.). Additional papers can be used to add other thoughts and ideas about the family. If the client draws out family members, ask the client to write down the names of each person and draw a symbol next to each person about his or her favorite activities. Inform the client that there is no right or wrong feeling or answer, and every family is unique.

Function in Assessment and Treatment

Assessment

This exercise assesses the family structure and functioning. Topics for assessment may include whether the family has group activities or gatherings, whether there is domestic violence or other types of abuse, who spends time with each other and who spends time alone, and how members communicate or fail to communicate with one another. This activity builds rapport and provides opportunities for the client to discuss hidden family issues.

Treatment

This exercise helps clients express feelings about family structure and dynamics and recognize that every family is uniquely different. They will have a better understanding of how their family background and family interaction affects their emotions and behaviors. It also helps clients realize that they can make choices to change family dynamics and encourages clients to seek help when the family is not functioning properly.

This is a clinical example from a five-year-old child. He described his baby sister as crying all the time, mom has to feed her milk, daddy just sits on the couch watching television, older brother is playing guitar loudly, he is always by himself but he likes to play with his pet hamster, and his mom always gets him pepperoni pizza. Reprinted with consent.

114 *Therapeutic Games and Guided Imagery*

Figure A23.1 Empty House

Figure A23.2 Full House

A24
Feeling Beads
Sandra L. Williams

Items Needed

Multiple colored beads; multiple color elastic strings; chart of feelings for each participant (figure A24.1); scissors; Ziploc bags; plastic bowls

Target Population

Children ages 8 to 15 in foster care homes

Intended for use with individuals or groups (four members per group) from all cultural and socioeconomic backgrounds

Purpose

To encourage children to express feelings surrounding the foster home

To encourage discussion of past and current events regarding the birth and foster families

To explore ambivalent or contradictory feelings related to foster care and the birth family

Procedure

Ask the clients to assign a colored bead to each feeling on the chart, then tape the beads on the chart. Add more feelings to the chart if needed. Then discuss their choices (e.g., red = angry, blue = sad, yellow = happy, green = attached, gold dotted = hopeful, white = frustrated, black = confused, orange = loved, and purple = anxious) and how the colors remind them of their feelings at the birth home. Tell a story based on these beads about their current feelings toward the foster home.

Next, have each client place beads into his or her plastic bowl to represent his or her feelings as identified in the chart. Share with the clients that feelings can be mixed and intensified. Ask the clients to add beads to their bowl if a feeling is more prevalent or intense. After several rounds of adding beads, empower the clients to share that the colorful beads represent the different feelings they experience.

Ask the clients to connect selected beads on a piece of string and ask them to discuss when certain beads are kept but not others. The clients can keep the stringed beads with them or wear the beads as a bracelet.

Function in Assessment and Treatment

Assessment

Use this activity to assess the client's ability to express feelings concerning foster care placement. It also gives the clients an opportunity to share present and past feelings concerning their family of origin. In a group setting, this activity builds rapport and enhances group communication. Follow-up therapeutic questions may include:

1. What aspects of your foster home are you most excited about?
2. How has being in your foster home changed your life?
3. What feelings do you have about your foster care family?
4. What parts of being in your foster home do you like and not like?

At the end of the discussion, ask participants to share what they have learned while participating in this activity.

Treatment

This activity enables clients to express current feelings about the foster home, share past feelings of the family of origin, and express how they want to feel in the future. In a group setting, clients are given the opportunity to experience a sense of kinship with other individuals who are not part of the family of origin and to discuss similar and different feelings about foster care and the changes in their immediate environment. Therapeutic questions should focus on change and their feelings about adjusting to a new foster home. The activity aims to assist clients with moving forward from ambivalence to acceptance. More feeling words and beads may be added to the chart in subsequent sessions.

Figure A24.1 Chart of Feelings

Sad	Hopeful	Angry
Happy	Anxious	Frustrated
Loved	Attached	Confused

A25
Feeling Faces
Karen Mei-Lin Lau, Monit Cheung, Rachel Wai-Yee Cheung

Items Needed

Note cards; feelings cards (figure A25.1); sentence completion cards (figure A25.2); sharing heart (figure A25.3); positive feeling faces (figure A25.4); negative feeling faces (figure A25.5); Spiritual House (e.g., tissue box or toy house); small gifts or awards

Target Population

Elementary school children who are orphans or survivors of disasters

Chinese children or other ethnicities

Intended for use with groups

Purpose

To encourage children to express and accept their feelings

To facilitate discussions about mutual support

To assess which children may need further professional help or referrals

Procedure

Warm-up Game: Feeling Charade

Cut cards (choose either from figure A25.1 or figures A25.4 and A25.5) and shuffle them. Randomly select the first child to choose a feeling card without showing it to others. The child then acts out (charades) that feeling. Invite the other members to guess the charade feeling. Try at least two rounds of charade and guessing for each group member. Describe how we may have different feelings at different times and feelings can be mixed at any given time. Discuss the normality of having mixed feelings. Although there is no right or wrong with feelings, the way a feeling is expressed may be perceived as positive or negative. Encourage the group members to share feelings and hold on to a positive attitude of learning from each other. If the feelings cards from figure A25.1 are used, members can also design a face on this selected feeling card to represent a positive feeling. If figure A25.4 and figure A25.5 cards are used, encourage the members to color the faces and talk about the symbolic meanings of each color used.

Main Game: Feeling Association

Cut and paste figure A25.2 into cards. All members randomly select three sentence completion cards and complete each statement within the allotted time. Each member takes a turn reading one completed statement at a time to the group. Pay attention to the content and reaction of the group members. Give words of encouragement such as "You are brave" or give a small gift to show support. Continue this exercise for two to three rounds. Facilitate the group so that members will express their feelings, stressing that understanding feelings is a normal, positive, and brave way to accept oneself, which allows others to offer help and encouragement.

Alternatively, figure A25.2 can be used as a worksheet instead of cutting it into cards. Give 15 minutes for the group to complete at least five statements selected by each member. If assigning this task to small groups, each group can select a few statements to complete within the allotted time and then each member reads one selected completed statement to the entire group.

Next, distribute the "sharing heart" paper to each group member. Encourage the members to write down anything that they want to share with the therapist. Ask them to put it into the "spiritual house" without putting their name on the paper. After each member has a chance to discuss the writing individually with the therapist, these anonymous papers may be drawn and read by other members during the next group session as a group sharing mechanism.

Encourage group members to take a few deep breaths to end the session. Inhale the mutual support from others and exhale all the negative feelings expressed during the activity.

Function in Assessment and Treatment

Assessment

This game aims to provide information about mixed feelings when we experience a traumatic event or problem. Expressing feelings can help in the recovery process if we understand the meaning behind each feeling and the function of expression. It is helpful to encourage clients to use their own language or vocabularies to express and explain life difficulties. Chinese translations are provided in this game, but another language can be added as a means to discuss cultural differences in feeling expressions.

Treatment

This game can help clients identify coping strategies. If you find that any group member has encountered emotional problems on an intensive level, please refer them to individual interventions. Therapeutic questions can be used in responding to the completion statements, for example, "Who may respond strongly when you said . . .?" "What would you do next if this statement is true?" "Tell me a word or another statement that can represent your feelings right now."

Figure A25.1 Feeling Cards (感受卡)

生氣 Angry	焦慮 Anxious	慚愧 Ashamed
厭煩 Bored	困惑 Confused	抑鬱 Depressed
惡心 Disgusted	尷尬 Embarrassed	憤怒 Enraged
筋疲力盡 Exhausted	恐懼 Frightened	孤單 Lonely
惱怒 Mad	傷心 Sad	震驚 Shocked
高興 Cheerful	自信 Confident	冷靜 Calm
欣喜若狂 Ecstatic	興奮 Excited	很好 Great
快樂 Happy	開心大笑 Hilarious	期盼 Hopeful
喜樂 Rejoicing	熱戀 Lovestruck	還好 Okay
輕鬆 Relaxed	滿意 Satisfied	傻氣 Silly

Figure A25.2 Sentence Completion Cards (續句卡)

當我感到哀傷時，我會…… When I feel frightened, I will …	當我感覺驚嚇時，我會…… When I feel sad, I will …
人們總是喜歡…… People always like to …	人們告訴我是一個…… People tell me I am …
我希望放棄…… I hope to give up …	我的母親是…… My mother is …
我的優點是…… The best part of me is …	我是…… I am …
我最關注的是…… I am most concerned about …	當我感到愉快，我會…… When I feel joyful, I will …
我會變得瘋狂憤怒，因為…… I can become very angry when …	我覺得困難的是…… It is very difficult to …
我需要…… I need …	我的朋友經常…… My friends always …
我最想…… I want to …	我無法忍受的是…… What I cannot tolerate is …
我被懲罰，因為…… I was punished because …	我感受到樂趣時，我正在…… I have fun when I …
我的父親是…… My father is …	我的好朋友經常…… My best friend always …
我感到自己是…… I feel I am …	我總是害怕…… I am always scared of …
我會感覺到舒適，因為…… I feel comfortable because …	我的生命中最好的一天是…… The best day of my life is …
我最大的弱點是…… My greatest weakness is …	當憤怒時，一個人會變得…… When angry, a person would become …
我曾經有一個惡夢，是關於…… I had a nightmare and it was about …	我很關心…… I care …
我喜歡…… I like …	我感到很迷茫是因為…… I feel uncertain because …
我其中一個願望是…… One of my wishes is …	我確信…… I believe …
如果我是一個男/女人，我會…… If I were a man (woman), I would …	我想…… I think …

124 *Therapeutic Games and Guided Imagery*

Figure A25.3 Sharing Heart

Name: _____ Date: _____

Title of this drawing: _____

A25 – Feeling Faces **125**

Figure A25.4 Positive Feeling Faces—Chinese/English Version

高興 Cheerful	自信 Confident	冷靜 Calm
欣喜若狂 Ecstatic	興奮 Excited	很好 Great
快樂 Happy	開心大笑 Hilarious	期盼 Hopeful
喜樂 Rejoicing	熱戀 Lovestruck	還好 Okay
輕鬆 Relaxed	滿意 Satisfied	傻氣 Silly

文字：張錦芳博士 （Dr. Monit Cheung） 繪圖：張慧儀 (Rachel Cheung) 2008

126 *Therapeutic Games and Guided Imagery*

Figure A25.5 Negative Feeling Faces—Chinese/English Version

生氣 Angry	焦慮 Anxious	慚愧 Ashamed
厭煩 Bored	困惑 Confused	抑鬱 Depressed
惡心 Disgusted	尷尬 Embarassed	憤怒 Enraged
筋疲力盡 Exhausted	恐懼 Frightened	孤單 Lonely
憤怒 Mad	傷心 Sad	震驚 Shocked

文字：張錦芳博士 (Dr. Monit Cheung)　繪圖：張慧儀 (Rachel Cheung) 2008

A26
Focus
Juan C. Macias

Items Needed

Game board (see figure A26.1); game pieces; two dice; game cards; paper boat; marker

Target Population

ADHD children and adolescents

Groups of children or juveniles with learning difficulties

Purpose

To engage clients in learning from real-life situations

To build rapport and establish relationships

To help clients concentrate

Procedure

Using the instructions in figure A26.2, demonstrate the process of making a paper boat to the players. Have each player make and decorate a boat to be used as a game piece. Players should decorate the paper boat with at least one or two concentration words such as "Concentrate," "Focus," "Attention," "Look," "Listen," "Relax," or "Be good."

Ask the players to pass the paper boats around the group. Instruct the players to briefly look at the word(s) on each boat before passing it to the next person. Each boat is passed around the group one time. The facilitator can stop the game at any time and "invite" a boat to be passed around when one or more children are not focused on the game.

To begin the game, arrange clients into small groups. Place the game board in the center where it is equally accessible to all players and place the two sets of game cards in the middle of the board. Instruct players to place their boat game piece on the start position. The first player rolls the dice and moves the piece forward according to the added number on the dice. If a player lands on a question card, he or she must draw a question card and answer the question on the card. If a player lands on a lightning card, he or she must draw a lightning card and complete the action stated on the card. No action is required if a player lands on a blank space. The game may continue past the start space until the facilitator chooses to end the game or the cards have run out.

Function in Assessment and Treatment

Assessment

This game can be helpful in assessing the client's current attention span and concentration ability. In addition, the paper boat allows the practitioner to assess how each individual client deals with a distractor. The different forms of stimulation (the passing of the boat, completing the turn, responding to the question and lighting cards, and engaging with the other members of the game) also allow for observation of specific distractors for each client participating in the game. These observations may be addressed at the end of the game or in future individual or group sessions.

Treatment

The game can be used to help clients identify and understand factors that inhibit their concentration. The game allows the clients to discuss possible techniques to increase attention and concentration. It also enables clients to hear what others do or have done to help with attention and concentration in real-life situations. By holding the paper boat and looking at the words written on it, they can learn to experience distraction and develop the ability to redirect their focus to the main activity. Through a fun exercise, the clients can also share their ideas about what concentration really means to them and their families. Additional cards may be developed and added to the game as related to the theme of the therapeutic session.

Card Questions

Lightning cards

- Close your eyes and take a deep breath.
- Clap your hands 3 times
- Blink 5 times
- Name a sport
- Gently tap your head with your hand 4 times
- Face someone and smile
- Make a funny face
- Pose like a dancing chicken

- Close your eyes and slowly count from 1 to 5
- Name an animal
- Raise both arms in the air slowly and bring them back down
- Name something green

Question Cards

- Think of a situation where you can't concentrate well; what is the situation?
- What distracts you the most?
- If you are trying to do your homework and something distracts you, what can you do to make this "distraction" go away?
- If you go to your teacher and say, "I can't concentrate; could you help me?" what might your teacher say?
- What could happen if your classmates don't pay attention during a fire drill?
- What helps you focus the most?
- What have you done in the past that has helped you focus?
- What can you do to help you maintain focus when you have to read?
- Where were you the last time you were able to concentrate?
- How do you feel when you can't concentrate?
- What does "concentration" ("focus") mean to you?

(Instructions retrieved from http://underbellyarts.com.au/2011/about/fold-your-own-boat/)

130 *Therapeutic Games and Guided Imagery*

Figure 26.1 The Game Board

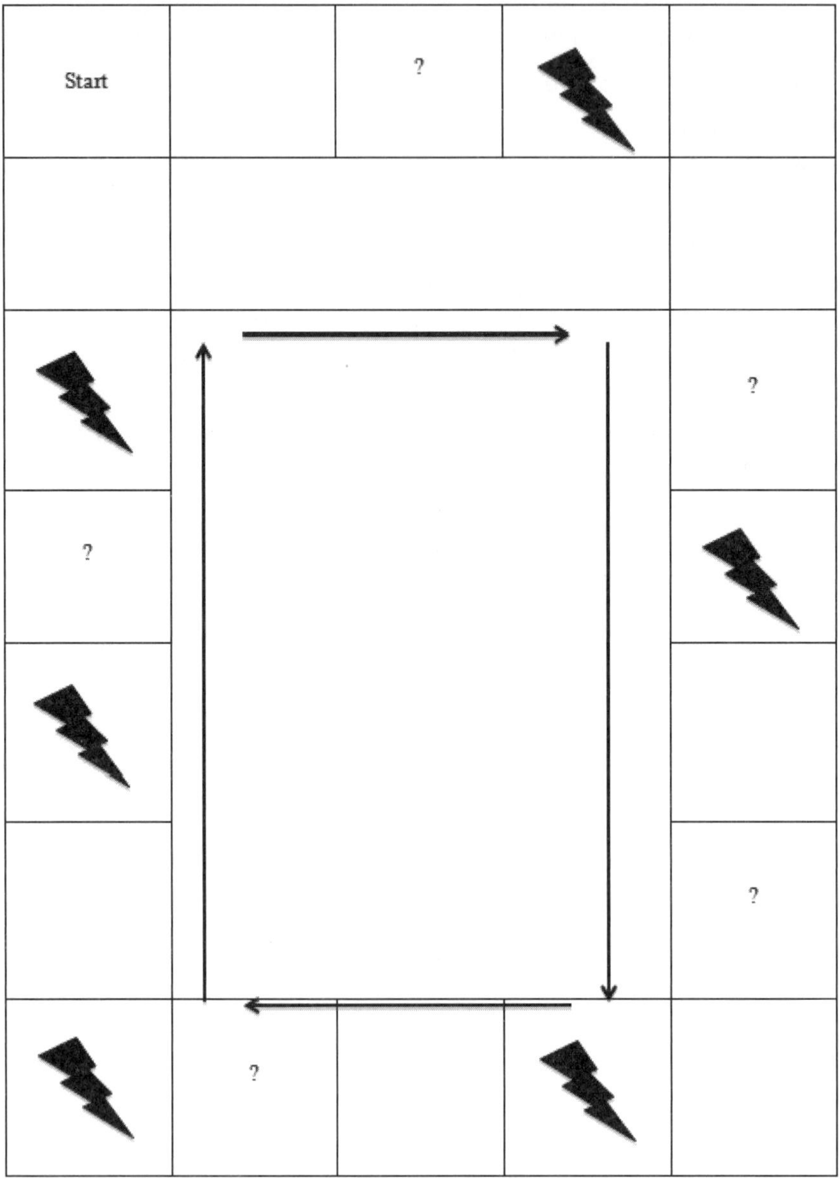

Figure 26.2 Paper Boat Instructions

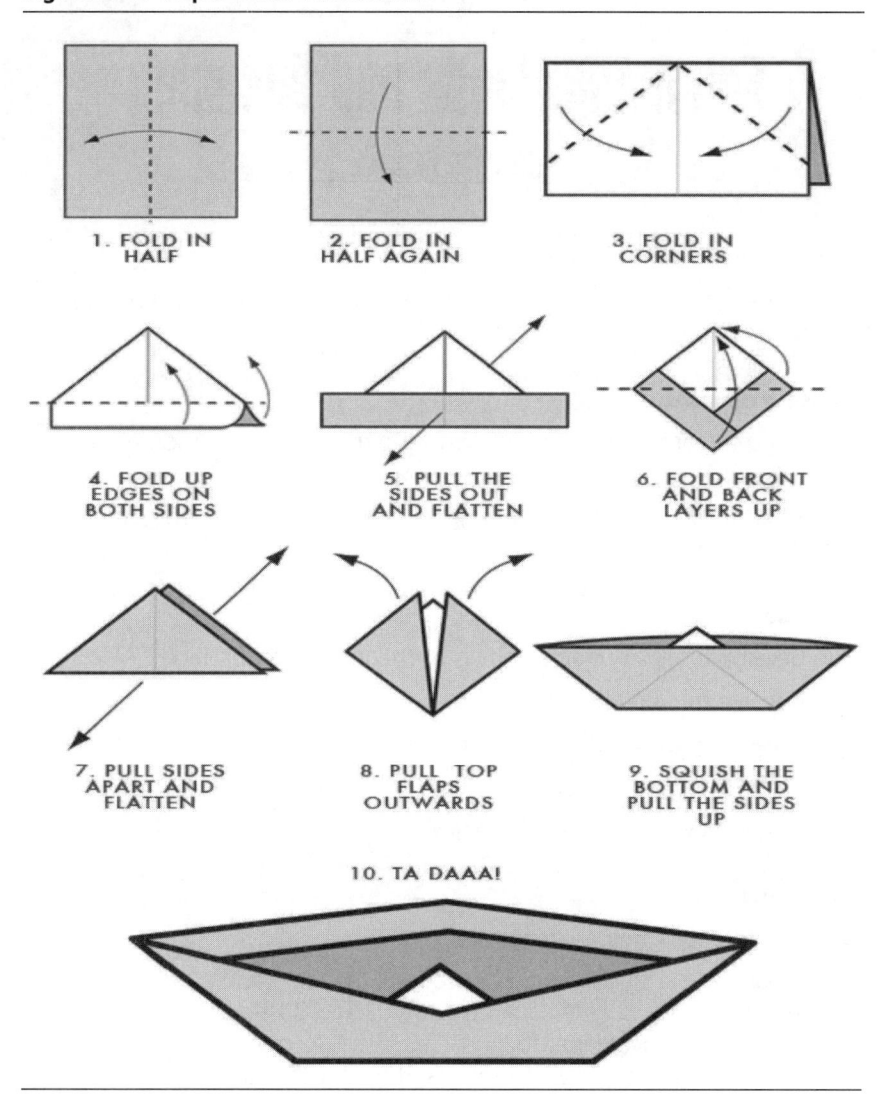

A27
Following Hands and Focusing
Caroline Hendrix

Items Needed

Blank pieces of small or medium-sized paper for each client; writing utensils of the same color

Target Population

Adolescents or other individuals who suffer from eating disorders or impulse control issues

This activity should be used in a group setting, with an even number of participants.

Purpose

To develop a better understanding of the presenting problem

To practice mindfulness skills

To enhance group dynamics and cooperation

To promote introspection of emotions and conflict

To increase awareness of universality

Procedure

Part 1: Mindfulness Guided Imagery

Pair off participants and have them choose a "leader" and a "follower" and ask the participants to face each other. For 15 to 30 seconds, the "leader" will create hand movements for the "follower" to mirror. After the time is up, have the participants switch roles and repeat the same exercise. Follow the exercise with a debriefing discussion, in which you address any observation of giggling, humor, or uncomfortable interaction. Follow-up therapeutic questions may include:

1. What was it like to be the leader or the follower?
2. Which role did you feel most comfortable with?
3. How hard or easy was it to focus on mirroring the other person's movements?

Part 2: Focusing on Concepts

Pass out the blank pieces of paper and writing utensils to each participant. Have each person write a word that elicits a negative emotional response for the client (facilitator may provide minimal examples, such as "family" or "school," for clarification). Gather the pieces of paper and fold them in half so you cannot see what is written on them.

Have each participant select one of the pieces of folded paper. Instruct the participants to perform the "follower" and "leader" exercise again (for 15 to 30 seconds) while thinking about the word written on the piece of paper they selected. Once the first round is complete, have the participants select a new piece of paper and switch roles. Complete the exercise again. Follow-up questions may include:

What was it like to follow the leader's hands while thinking about the topic?

Did your hand movements change?

Function in Assessment and Treatment

Assessment

Mindfulness activities assist clients to tolerate distress via distraction and focus on external stimuli. Mindfulness activities may also aid individuals with high levels of anxiety, depression, or fluctuating moods by calming their thoughts through focus on external stimuli and thus regulating physiological responses.

This activity encourages a client to intentionally concentrate on one specific topic. However, this intervention is client-centered as the clients generate their own topics.

Treatment

Use of this activity promotes the elements of mindfulness. The participants may report feeling "silly" or worried that they will make a mistake when giggling and humor occurs during the activity. Engage the group members about this phenomenon. Discuss how it's ok to make mistakes. Having the client choose a personal concept and randomly selecting topics for consideration enhances the adolescents' autonomy.

A28
Forum Theater
Mark Trahan

Items Needed

Chairs

Target Population

Adolescents 12 to 18 years of age concerning decision-making and life choices

Intended for use with groups of at least five participants

Purpose

To teach adolescents how to discuss their experiences and feelings

To provide a forum to review life choices, teach personal responsibility for decision making, and provide adolescents with helpful suggestions about future life choices

To relate to others through shared vulnerability concerning their personal choices and behaviors

To learn about others in a safe, secure, and relaxed environment

To educate adolescents without directive communication about the choices they face and alternatives to current behaviors that may be detrimental to their development.

To provide a channel for adolescents to identify their own capacity to self-regulate and change behaviors instead of relying upon an adult or family member to tell them what to do

To create a support system among peers

Procedure

To begin, present an introduction to the exercise for group members. Based on assessment of the group members' personalities, select a member from the group to share a problem, dilemma, or challenging or difficult situation experienced at school, home, or with friends. After the participant has shared, identify the different roles in the story and ask for the adolescent to choose group members to play the different roles from the story while they become observers. Make sure to choose someone to portray the role of the storyteller in the enactment. Members of the group are allowed to decline participation if they do not feel comfortable. Roles may include actual people, objects, or themes such as "bullying" or "the school system." Those chosen to play roles will then take three to five minutes to privately discuss the details of the story. You will be the director of the enactment while these chosen group members will present the story by acting it out in a respectful manner within a ten-minute time frame.

After the group has acted out the scene, ask the storyteller and other group members (those not played in the scene) to identify decision moments in which the person might have made an alternative choice or exhibited a different behavior. Each suggested alternative decision choice or behavior will be reenacted by the selected actors (or newly designated actors) to provide the original storyteller with an alternative outcome to the scene. After all of the possible outcomes have been presented, ask the group to consider the benefits and drawbacks of each decision by using the discussion to provide the storyteller with feedback about alternative ways of considering the problem. Have the storyteller identify the best choice among the enactments and ask the actors to reenact some part of the story with the new choice, behavior, and outcome. Conclude with a group debriefing of the entire process through group discussion. Encourage the group members to identify whether they could relate the original dilemma and the alternative choices to their own life.

Function in Assessment and Treatment

Assessment

Drama-based education interventions with adolescents have been found to be effective in health education, drug and alcohol use, and HIV prevention (Blakely & Pullen, 1991; Denman, Davis, Pearson, & Madeley, 1996; Denman, Pearson, Moody, Davis, & Madeley, 1995) among immigrant populations facing problems with emotional expression and behavioral difficulties (Moneta & Rousseau, 2008), and working in schools to teach children interpersonal skills and bullying prevention (Gourd & Gourd, 2011).

There are adolescents that may be limited in their capacity to participate, including:

1. Those who are developmentally delayed and may not be able to participate in role-playing because of distractibility, lack of insight, or problems with motor skills.
2. Those who have a history of conduct disorder and may not maintain attention or may disturb the process of the role play by acting inappropriately due to lack of empathy for others.

Note: This type of intervention is not appropriate for situations such as physical, sexual, emotional, verbal, or spiritual abuse. Due to the nature of abuse, role play can stimulate memories which may re-traumatize the participant, resulting in heightened levels of post-traumatic stress symptoms.

Treatment

Adolescents are encouraged to bring up issues that are socially relevant. Adolescents will feel more comfortable speaking about personal situations when they know it is a safe place to address these issues. During the exercise, it is important to leave plenty of time to debrief the experiences of the enactment. While facilitating these debriefing sessions, the facilitator may repeat back a synopsis of what the group members said, without judgment. This helps clients feel that they have been heard and validated.

A29
Gender Identity Game: Who Am I?
Micki Washburn

Items Needed

Magazines featuring men, women, and children of various racial backgrounds and in a variety of situations; magazines that feature animals, famous landmarks, and historical figures; scissors; poster board; glue sticks; magic markers; glitter glue

Target Population

Children and adolescents ages five years and older who identify as transgender, gender independent or gender nonconforming

Purpose

To identify how the child conceptualizes the self and what characteristics are "like," and "not like"

To help the child express ideas about gender identity in a way that may not require a binary

To identify and evaluate the child's perspective of the gender spectrum

To facilitate the expression of both positive and negative feelings associated with one's assigned sex and one's gender expression

To assess the child's expectations for the future in terms of gender and gender roles

To help the child process traumatization inherent among members of an oppressed or marginalized group

*Note: The use of gendered pronouns is intentionally omitted from this exercise.

Procedure

Invite the child to select a piece of poster board and five to six magazines. Have the child divide the poster board into four sections with either the markers or glitter glue. Ask the child to cut out pictures of things that "are a lot like you," that are "sometimes like you," and that "are not like you."

Have the child paste these pictures in three of the sections of the poster board, creating a title to suit each section (or mark as "are a lot like me," "sometimes like me," or "are not like me") and leaving the fourth section empty. Discuss the pictures chosen for each section and ask the child to elaborate on why the child chose certain pictures for each category. Ask what the child liked or disliked about the selected pictures. Finally, in the remaining empty space, make a collage of images that the child hopes to see for the future. Have the child sign and date the poster.

Function in Assessment and Treatment

Assessment

This activity provides children an opportunity to verbally and nonverbally express the way they conceptualize "the self," how they perceive characteristics similar and dissimilar to them, and discuss feelings about their current physical characteristics. Using emphasis on the future, the activity provides a hopeful outlook for the clients and allows for creativity in visualizing the future "self," This exercise also allows the therapist to assess for current strengths and coping skills, as well as levels of gender dysphoria.

Treatment

This exercise helps the participants initiate dialogue about self-identity, including personal, familial, and societal perceptions. It provides the participants with a safe environment to address issues that may be discouraged at home or in school. The use of the "sometimes like you" categorization helps to convey the idea that gender roles are not rigid and can be fluid. With older children, this exercise helps to deconstruct the gender binary and open discussion about gender as a continuum. It also allows for children to go through the "normal" identity development processes, which includes determining their preferred gender expression and gender roles. This activity can be especially helpful for participants who currently identify with both or neither genders, or are confused with GLBTQ issues.

Modifications

This exercise can also be done in a group setting with other children in the same age range, or used to facilitate discussion with family members who are having difficulties dealing with the child's gender expression.

A30
Giver and Receiver
Alicia Michele Thomas

Items Needed

Paper, pens, pencils, colored pencils, crayons, and markers; gift box (figures A30.1 and A30.2)

Target Population

Children or adolescents dealing with grief, death or loss, or secondary trauma

Individuals dealing with anger or low self-esteem

Appropriate for use with individuals and can be used in groups of six children or adolescents of similar age

Purpose

To help clients see the importance of mutual exchange through thoughtful gifts

To assist clients in the expression of feelings through positive interaction

To promote the importance of giving

To help clients learn to understand others

Procedures

Provide the client with a gift box and ask him or her to think of someone they would want to give their gift to. You may also choose someone for the client if specific relationship problems have been previously identified. Remind the client that this is an opportunity to share something he or she has not had the opportunity to.

Next, ask each participant to complete the statements on the gift box as part of a gift to the selected person (see figure A30.2).

1. "I feel ____ when I'm thinking of you." This statement defines the current status of the relationship and can be completed using words such as "sad," "happy," "mad," "scared," "confused," "anxious," and so on.

139

2. "I would like to tell you ____." This statement allows the client to directly express something specific to the recipient and can be completed with statements such as, "I miss you"; "I am sad that you don't love me"; "I pray for you," and so on.
3. "I would like to give you ____." This statement allows the client to show love through the act of thoughtful giving and can be completed with gifts such as "a hug," "a kiss," "a stuffed animal," "a card," and so on.

Using the words, phrases, or statements the client chose, ask him or her to write, draw, color, or symbolize each on the blank side of their gift box. Other thoughtful expressions may be included such as "courage to face life difficulties," "sharing your problems," or "a season pass to go skiing any time you want."

Ask the client to talk about the three responses he or she gave, and any additional expression that may have been added later. Ask the client questions such as, "How do you think he or she may feel or react when you give the gift?" "What do you want him or her to feel when you give the gift?" "What is it about this gift that this person may like it?"

Next, pretend that the person who received the gift gives a similar one back in return. Ask the client to think about what he or she would like that person to do:

1. "I would like this person to share a feeling with me, such as _____."
2. "I would like this person to tell me _____."
3. "I would like this person to give me _____."

Ask the client what is the reason for choosing these responses and discuss the corresponding feelings, and any new feelings that may arise. Discuss how the client would react if he or she actually received the gift and how he or she would feel. The second part of this exercise may be repeated again, but this time having the client complete the statements in the way he or she believes the gift recipient would respond. Follow-up discussion questions may include (1) How did you decide what gifts to give? (2) Is there anything else you wish could have given? (3) Is there anything else you want to say to this person but haven't? Allow the client to take the picture home as a reminder of his or her ability to express feelings and understand the feelings of others.

Function in Assessment and Treatment

Assessment

This exercise provides an opportunity for the client to uncover and understand feelings he or she has about a specific person. It allows the client to address grief, angry feelings, amorous feelings, and so on through an art medium. You may help the client also address personal questions such as "What do I miss?" "What do I want?" or "How do I want things to be?" Through discussion of the gifts, the client is able to identify the symbolic meaning of what is included and how it may impact the recipient. This exercise can also provide insight into the client's emotional maturity by observing his or her ability to understand, identify, and express feelings and emotions.

Treatment

Giving and receiving gifts is a very special and magical event for children. Through this exercise, the client is able to process and express feelings about the selected recipient through a form of personal appreciation. Feelings that the client may find difficult to express can become easier since these feelings are part of a gift. This game helps the client to learn how to express feelings now and in future interactions. Furthermore, understanding and reflecting on the recipient's potential reactions and responses will help the client understand that feeling expression is a two-way process. Even in the situation that the recipient is no longer living, the client can feel released that he or she has been engaged in this two-way communication in a therapeutic setting. This exercise can become a formal closure to say good-bye to the deceased.

142 *Therapeutic Games and Guided Imagery*

Figure A30.1 Gift Box Template (Side 1)

The giver's name is _____ Date: _____

The recipient is _____

"I feel _____
(sad, happy, mad, scared, confused, anxious, etc.) when I'm thinking of you."

"I would like to tell you _____
(I miss you; I am sad that you don't love me; I pray for you, etc.)."

"I would like to give you _____
(a hug, kiss, stuffed animal, card, etc.)."

Figure A30.2 Gift Box Template (Side 2)

A31
Grandfather's Parcel
Ruprekha Baruah

Items Needed

One empty cardboard box about 12 square inches; three different sheets of wrapping papers; 30 index cards; pen; tape; scissors; CD player and music

Target Population

Adolescents ages 13 to 17 who have run away from home

Appropriate for clients of all ethnic groups and socioeconomic backgrounds who suffer from low self-esteem

For a group setting with a minimum of five participants

Purpose

To enhance self-esteem and improve social skills

To communicate about the importance of positive attitudes

To help participants learn from criticism and develop a sense of self-concept

Procedure

Preparation: In a group session, create additional activity cards (see figure A31.1) with group members after each topic has been presented and discussed—self-concept, self-development, and learning from criticism. Choose a song with lyrics about social skills or self-concept (e.g., Doctors and Dealers' "Social Skills") and encourage the group to analyze or sing this chosen song. Prerecord different pieces and various lengths of a chosen work of music (or the song just sung by this group) for about a total of 20 minutes.

Wrap the empty cardboard box with a wrapping paper chosen by the group. Ask the group members to name the wrapped box based on a symbol or meaning about self-concept or a loving person, and so on, for example, "Grandfather's parcel." Design this name and mark it on the box.

To start the game, have the participants sit in a circle and place the stack of index cards (words faced down) in the center of the circle for participants to draw from. As music plays, the "Grandfather's parcel" will be passed clockwise from the facilitator around the circle until the music stops. When a piece of music stops, the participant holding the box must pick out an index card, read the instructions and follow the directions. Once the individual has completed the activity, place the used index card in a separate pile and repeat the exercise until everyone has a chance to participate or all the index cards have been used.

Function in Assessment and Treatment

Assessment

This game may be played at the halfway mark of a six- to eight-week session. By this time, the group members have become familiar with one another and feel comfortable enough to share their feelings about self-concept. The use of music and the interaction of passing the parcel keeps the game interactive as members share pertinent issues relating to their self-concept and a person they missed. This activity will provide information about the members' levels of social skills and their definition of self-concept.

Treatment

Self-esteem is not an innate human quality; it is developed through our daily experiences and interactions with significant persons in our lives. Adolescent runaways are likely to have self-esteem problems, and this lack of self-worth is often a key issue among children and adolescents who act out or misbehave. Due to this deficit, they generally fall behind in social and academic development, and they tend to receive more criticism, derision, and harsh methods of discipline due to their inappropriate behavior and lack of self-awareness. Intervention strategies must aim at creating, fostering, and maintaining self-esteem through group interactions.

Figure A31.1 Examples for the Index Cards

Self-Valuing	Sense of Self-Development	Learning from Criticism
Mention one thing in you that you like the most.	Mention something you are good at.	Jessica's father called her a loser because she failed her math test, and Jessica is feeling down in the dumps. What would you say to Jessica to make her feel that she is a good person?
Describe one thing about you that has meaning to you.	Mention one thing you did in school that is a big accomplishment.	Rita makes fun of your old fashioned tennis shoes. What would be the best way to react to her criticism?
Mention something a family member had said about you that is very nice.	Close your eyes and recall a time when you were able to put your views across to your family without screaming or yelling.	You want to surprise Mom by taking out the garbage, but the bag breaks, creating a big mess, and your mother yells at you. How would you best handle this situation?
Describe a characteristic within you that came from your hard work.	Recall a time when a person made you feel valuable; what did this person say to you?	You have worked all night to complete a school project. Your dad came in and started criticizing it. What would you say to Dad to appreciate his comment (even though you are not going to change any part of it)?

A32
Graph My Feelings
Kim Ba

Items Needed

Five numbered feeling faces (angry, sad, neutral, happy, very happy); item response sheet; graph handout (8.5" × 11"); four different colored markers or crayons

Target Population

Adolescents age 11 and older

Adolescents who find it difficult to talk about their emotions

Suitable for work with individuals or groups

Purpose

To break the ice

To build rapport

To encourage open expression of feelings

Procedure

Set out the numbered feelings faces (one through five) which the client will use to identify their response to each item you read aloud. For each item read aloud, the client will record their response on the item response sheet (see figure A32.1) by using the five feelings and their corresponding numbers. For example, if the first item read aloud is "rules" and the client feels angry when he or she thinks of this word, they would write the number "1" next to the item.

If the client does not have a specific reaction to the item, he or she may choose the "neutral" feeling face (number 3).

Once the child has responded to each item on the list, he or she will graph each group according to the groupings shown in figure A32.1 (family, school, social group, activities). The client should graph one group at a time, and each group should be assigned a different color. When the client finishes graphing the responses for the group, he or she should connect the dots and label the group accordingly. There should be four separate lines of different colors and each with four points on the graph.

Function in Assessment and Treatment

Assessment

This activity can help assess the client's emotions and feelings in reference to family, school, social group, and basic physical habits. By graphing their responses, clients have a visual aid that demonstrates their general mood and attitude towards specific aspects of their life. The game can also indicate relevant areas that should be addressed. This activity can help build rapport and may also be done silently with clients who are not comfortable verbally sharing their feelings.

Treatment

After receiving a visual depiction of the client's feelings, invite the client to explain his or her feelings about each item. This can help facilitate discussion about resolving negative feelings that the client may have towards a specific aspect of his or her life. It may also encourage discussion about items or people who were not on the list, and their feelings towards them. In advanced levels, the client may be allowed to change the faces or add more items to the list. This exercise is most beneficial when followed by therapeutic discussion questions such as:

1. Looking at your graph, which of the four groups makes you feel the happiest? Is the graph accurate?
2. Looking at your graph, which of the four groups makes you feel the most angry? Is the graph accurate?
3. Were there any items for which you had difficulty selecting an emotion? If so, tell me what made it difficult for you.
4. Think of someone close to you who was not mentioned in the list. Describe this person and what he or she means to you.
5. Are there any feelings that you would like to change, add, or remove from the graph? What are they?
6. Looking at the lines on your graph, what do they share in common?
7. What do you think will help some of your negative feelings become more positive?

Worksheet

Read the following items in order:

1. Boy/Girlfriend _____
2. Brother _____
3. Class _____
4. Counselor _____
5. Dad/Step-Dad _____
6. Teacher _____
7. Eating _____
8. Friend _____
9. Going Out _____
10. Homework _____
11. Mom/Step-Mom _____
12. Neighbors _____
13. Sister _____
14. Exercise _____
15. Test _____
16. Waking Up _____

Groups

Family (A)

2. Brother
5. Dad (or Step-Dad)
11. Mom (or Step-Mom)
13. Sister

School (B)

3. Class
6. Teacher
10. Homework
15. Test

Social Group (C)

1. Boy/Girlfriend
4. Counselor
8. Friend
12. Neighbor

Activities (D)

7. Eating
9. Going Out
14. Exercise
16. Waking Up

150 *Therapeutic Games and Guided Imagery*

Figure A32.1 Feelings Connected with Who Chart

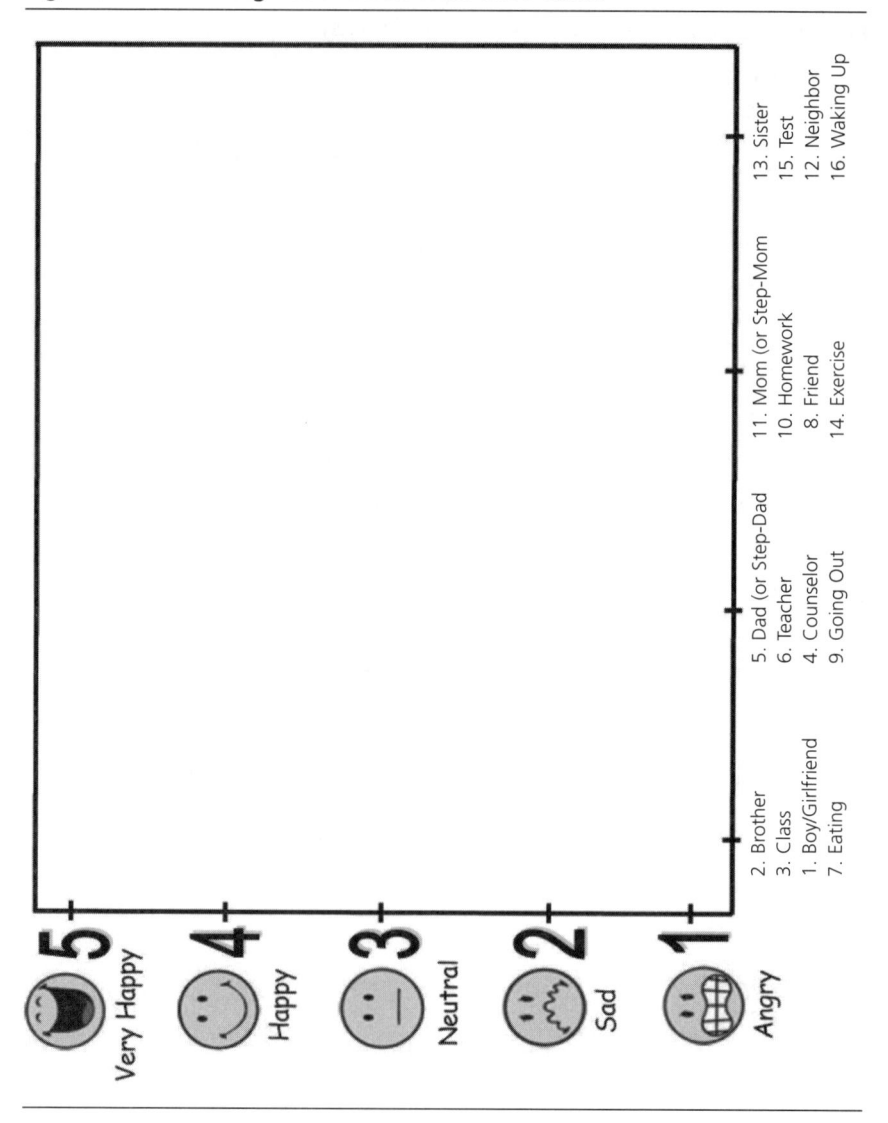

Feelings	
5 Very Happy	
4 Happy	
3 Neutral	
2 Sad	
1 Angry	

1. Boy/Girlfriend
2. Brother
3. Class
4. Counselor
5. Dad (or Step-Dad)
6. Teacher
7. Eating
8. Friend
9. Going Out
10. Homework
11. Mom (or Step-Mom)
12. Neighbor
13. Sister
14. Exercise
15. Test
16. Waking Up

A33
Group Drawing
Monit Cheung

Items Needed

Two sheets of construction paper; one sheet of white paper for each person; color markers

Target Population

Families dealing with loss

Suitable in a group session to address emotions

Suitable for all ethnic backgrounds

Purpose

To help clients address emotions

To encourage children to share feelings with their family members

To help children deal with grief or trauma

Procedure

Introduce yourself and your role. Ask the most senior person (in the group or family) to say his or her name first and introduce the youngest person; the youngest person then tells the group one thing about himself or herself, then introduces the person of his or her choice. After introductions, each person should write, draw, or symbolize something on their sheet of white paper, to represent his or her feelings toward the person who has just passed away (or was hospitalized, has experienced trauma, or left the family) (see figure A33.1).

Next, circulate the construction paper and ask each person to put one item from the earlier drawing or writing on this piece of paper to represent the family's reaction to the death, trauma, or loss. Ask each member to share how he or she feels about the project, and about what he or she contributed to it. Remind the group that feelings and thoughts are subjective and no judgment about their expression will be made. If time allows, circulate the construction paper twice and encourage the clients to write or draw additional thoughts or feelings and discuss them as well.

Possible variation: A theme can be chosen by the group before starting the group drawing. Start by writing the theme (e.g., stress, pain, etc.—see examples) on top or at a corner of the construction paper. After two to three rounds of drawings, take a photo of the drawing, ask the group to determine a title, cut out each component from the drawing, and then ask the group to rearrange them on another piece of construction paper. They can choose to paste the drawing down or talk about the contents first before finalizing it. Ask the group to share additional thoughts about this process and about the revised drawing.

Function in Assessment and Treatment

Assessment

This is an assessment tool incorporating free association techniques that aim to help children and adolescents disclose their feelings to people in the family or others close to them. It also assists the young clients to build upon feelings and thoughts generated from other family members. It provides an opportunity for the family or groups to openly address any unresolved feelings.

Treatment

This exercise encourages open communication among family or group members. Instead of (or in addition to) doing the cut-and-paste step, invite each child to choose a color (or two) and tell the group about the meaning of the chosen color. Ask the child to color one part of the drawing with this color. Incorporation of these additional steps can help children understand the importance of their participation. Feelings and thoughts are subjective and no judgment about their expression will be made.

Therapeutic questions to bring about discussion may include:

- Name this drawing (and the rearranged drawing).
- Identify your own feeling and then a feeling identified by someone else who participated in this drawing.
- Recall a time you spent with ____. Tell me one thing from this memory that is also connected to this collective drawing.
- If you were to say something to ____, what would you say now?
- How does this drawing help you deal with the trauma or loss of ____?

Figure A33.1 Example 1—Pain

154 *Therapeutic Games and Guided Imagery*

Figure A33.2 Example 2—Stress

Figure A33.3 Example 3—My Family

A34
Hands Connection
Monit Cheung

Items Needed

Make copies of the hands (see figure A34.1) on different colored paper (one hand per participant); a single-hole puncher; one piece of ribbon or yarn per participant (about five inches long, in various colors); colored markers or crayons; stickers (optional); a digital camera

Target Population

Clients who are nonverbal

Suitable for all age groups

Purpose

To provide an ice-breaker in group work

To introduce each other in a group setting

To determine the goal of the session(s)

To identify each person's uniqueness and strengths

To build group cohesiveness

Procedure

First, ask the participants to trace one of their hands onto a piece of colored paper and cut out the drawing (or use the pre-cut "hand" provided). Punch one hole on both sides of the "hand"—on the thumb and the little finger. Ask them to write their name on the palm (as large as possible as a means to introduce themselves). Then instruct them to write down one thing about themselves on each finger on the "hand," such as a unique characteristic, a strength, a hobby, the name of their best friend, a favorite toy, book, or game, or a word that is associated with their future or something they would like to accomplish. Decorate the "hand" with markers and stickers. Ask each participant to take turn to share their hand with the group.

After completion, tie a string (ribbon or yarn) around one hole; make sure one side of the string is longer than the other side. Ask them to tie the longer side of the string to another "hand." The goal is to tie all the decorated hands and place them together so that a digital photo can be taken (see example). The visualization of the "togetherness" of these hands can be a tool to educate the group about the meaning and process of forming group cohesiveness. In an individual session, this exercise can be used to identify the process of healing. Each "hand" represents a part of this process so the client can gain perspective about things that have yet to be done. At closure, tie all the hands together to represent a task completed (see figure A34.2.)

Function in Assessment and Treatment

Assessment

This exercise can also be done in individual therapy as a routine in each session. Allow time for the client to write down ideas and thoughts, and then put them together as a final closure. In group sessions, this exercise provides a means to connect the participants and allows them to visualize the impact the result has when they connect with one another. You can use each hand completed in a session to summarize the client's progress, discuss how much a client invests his or her time into the therapeutic process, or compare with previous "hands" to address how much the client has gained over time.

For young children, this exercise can assess their eye-hand coordination while observing how they tie the string into the small hole. It also provides an opportunity to observe their patience and creativity.

Treatment

This is a therapeutic tool for the discussion about diversity. Since colors and themes can be incorporated in the art-making process, you can lead the clients to learn about different ideas to draw a conclusion about how they can resolve a difficulty or make a decision.

Therapeutic questions after the hands are connected:

- If you were to move these hands, how would you like it to change? Try it.
- What words among these hands can give you insight about a solution (to your problem)?
- Which special characteristic (or strength) would you like to have?
- Look at all these hands—now close your eyes. What would you say to your parents (teachers) about your completion (or creation)?

158 *Therapeutic Games and Guided Imagery*

Figure A34.1 Hand

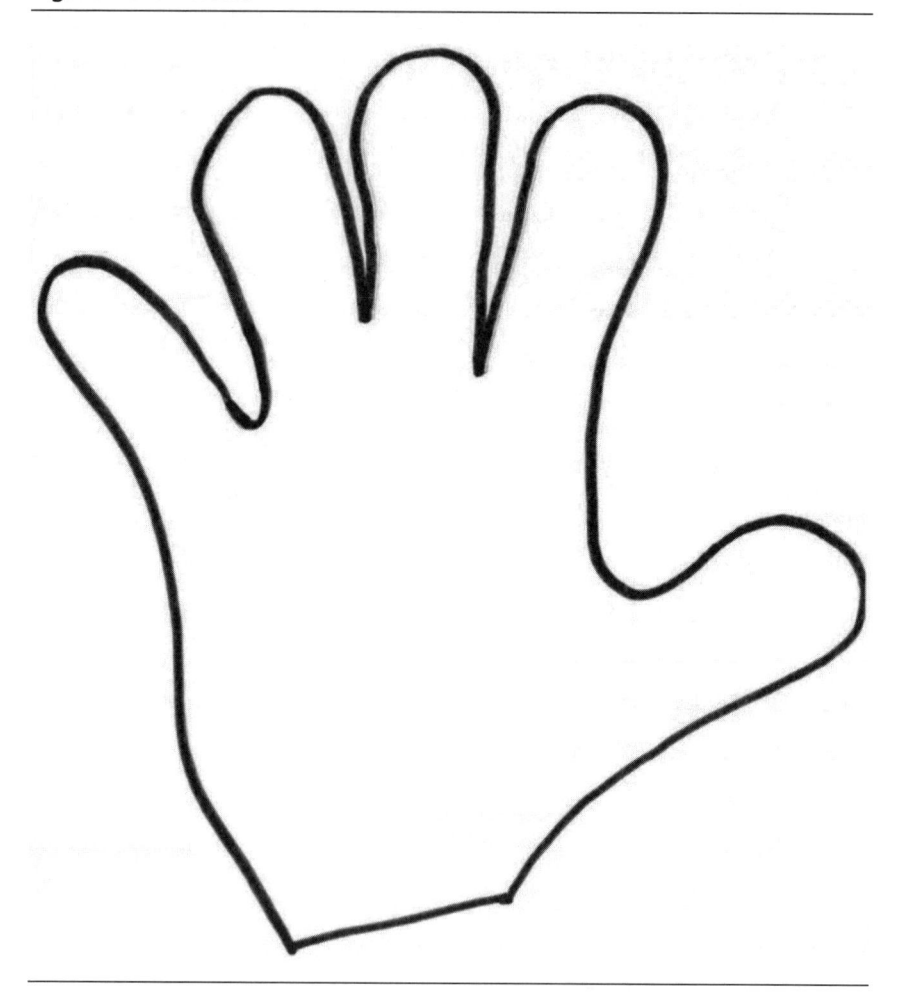

Figure A34.2 Example

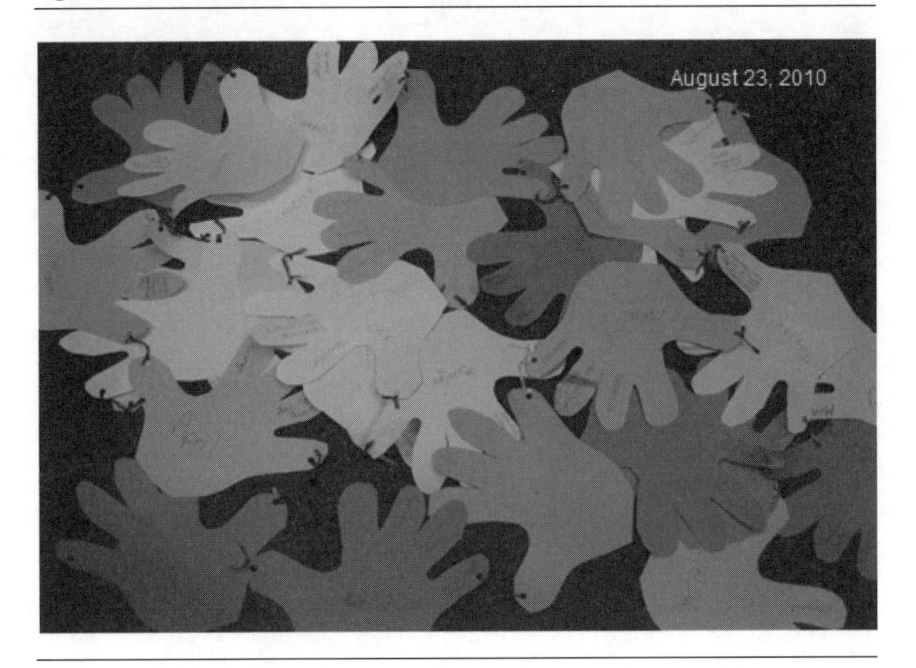

A35
Hospital Visit
Monit Cheung and Ashleigh Scinta

Items Required

A stack of about 40 cards that relate to hospital visits: medical personnel, facility and equipment, feelings, illnesses, people, etc. (make two copies of figure A35.1 and cut them out and paste onto index cards); small gifts or prizes (such as coloring books and crayons, small stuffed animals, deck of playing cards, etc.)

Target Population

Young children visiting someone in a hospital, such as a veteran, grandparent, parent, or sibling

Siblings of children diagnosed with cancer or other chronic or terminal illnesses

Group work in a medical setting

For those who are unable to express their anxiety about hospitalization

Purpose

Process children's fears and anxieties about their illness

Address feelings related to the hospitalization or ongoing hospital visits of a loved one or friend with a chronic illness

Reduce feelings of uncertainty or anxiety about a hospital visit (either before or after the visit)

Procedure

Deal six to eight cards to each participant. Ask participants to flip all matched pairs of cards in their hand and place them face up on the table. Each participant takes a turn to briefly share something about the pictures on the matching cards, in relation to an expected hospital visit (e.g., relationship with the patient visited, expectations, or any concern about the visit). Participants then place the remaining unmatched cards face down in the middle of the table along with other unmatched cards from the deck.

Each participant then takes a turn to flip two cards to try to get a pair of matched cards. If there is a matched pair, the participant will take the cards, state one thing about the matched image, and flip again. If there is no match, the person to the right will flip two cards next to try to get a matched pair. The goal is to share concerns and facilitate discussions about the hospital visit. The player with the most matched cards wins a prize. Each player will also receive a small gift for the patient to be visited.

Function in Assessment and Treatment

Assessment

This game aims to reduce fear and anxiety about illnesses, particularly for children visiting the hospital for the first time or children with a chronic illness. The game also educates children about medical procedures and personnel. It can be used to address the terms used in a medical setting. Additionally, it can assess children's level of understanding about the situation and feelings about facing a new situation.

Treatment

This game helps children process their feelings and develop coping methods about a new situation (such as someone being hospitalized). It provides them with an opportunity to share their fears or experiences. It can be used as a communication tool between a patient and his or her young siblings or for a parent to use when explaining hospitalization to his or her children in a child-friendly manner. Therapeutic questions may include:

1. Who can help a patient reduce pain?
2. What can you do to help this patient to feel comfortable?
3. How can you explain ___'s illness to your teacher or friend?
4. How do you feel about this particular illness?
5. Name something that is not in these cards that you want to talk about.
6. If you would add another word or thing to this game, what would it be? How does it relate to your hospital experience (the hospital visit or the person you will be visiting)?

162 *Therapeutic Games and Guided Imagery*

Figure A35.1 Game Cards

Hospital	Waiting Room	Operating Room	Pharmacy
Wound	Medicine	Stethoscope	Bandage
Medicine Cup/Spoon	Needle/Injection	Surgical Mask	Crutches
Doctor	Nurse	Social Worker	Sibling
Father	Mother	Friend	Baby

A35 – Hospital Visit 163

Figure A35.1 Game Cards—(continued)

Pain	Headache	Scared	Dizzy
Blood	Wash Hands	Cancer	Anesthesia
Wheelchairs	Hospital Bed	Illness	Concern
Sad	Patient	Grandparent	Tired
I.V.	Hospital Gown	Stitches	Cast

A36
How I See Myself
Ophelia Mok

Items Needed

Activity card for every person (see figure A36.1); writing utensils or markers

Target Population

Individuals with body image concerns

Reticent clients

Suitable for group or individual sessions

Purpose

To verbalize thoughts about self-image

To explore the impact of eating disorders on self-perception

To guide development of treatment goals

Procedures

Provide each client with the activity card and ask him or her to respond to all eight sections of the card. Next, the client must cut the sections into eight individual cards and place the cards in order of importance to him or her. Ask the client to discuss his or her thoughts and feelings connected to each card and concerning the order in which he or she placed the cards.

Next, ask the client to select two cards to give up and then reorder the remaining cards as needed. Discuss any changes in order and the corresponding thoughts and feelings.

Again, ask the client to give up two more cards and reorder as needed, discussing any relevant changes and important thoughts or emotions.

With the remaining four cards (writing facing the client), the client must turn to the facilitator (individual session) or a group member (group session) and allow the other person to take two cards at random. Then the client must examine the final two cards and share any thoughts or feelings about the process.

Function in Assessment and Treatment

Assessment

This activity is a way to begin a conversation with clients. Based on what clients choose to write about their internal and external characteristics, you can begin to understand each client's self-perception and worldview of what is important to him or her. When played in a group, the activity can be a source of building group cohesion through an increased sense of universality with other group members.

Treatment

This activity is a way to help clients examine actual qualities they have and those they wish to have. It also provides a way to discuss the impact of eating disorders on their lives and the possibility of what they may be giving up or have already lost. It can act as a starting place to explore clients' strengths and goals.

Therapeutic questions may include:

1. What was the difference between giving up cards and having them taken away?
2. Recall a time when you felt like something was being taken from you.
3. How does the prioritizing of these characteristics connect with your life?
4. If you could add another actual characteristic you possess and a wishful characteristic, what would they be?

Figure A36.1 Activity Cards

Internal characteristic I have	Internal characteristic I wish for
Internal characteristic I have	Internal characteristic I wish for
External characteristic I have	External characteristic I wish for
External characteristic I have	External characteristic I wish for

A37
How to Tame Your Temper
Ivy E. Crank

Items Needed

Poster with pictures and photos representing each step in the temper taming process (see figure A37.1); scenarios (see figure A37.2); 8" × 11" sheets of paper divided into three horizontal parts for comic strip (see figure A37.3); scissors; tape or glue; markers, crayons or colored pencils; rewards (optional)

Target Population

Elementary school students struggling with anger management and who have difficulty accepting "no"

Intended for use with groups

Purpose

To assist children in recognizing situations that may trigger their anger

To help children pay attention to physical warning signs that might indicate anger

To encourage children to process situations and their corresponding feelings

To empower children to take control of their anger and to make good choices

To help children apply the anger steps to a real-life scenario in guided and independent practice

Procedure

Tape posters with anger steps to wall where all students can refer to them.

Clients should be seated:

"Today we're going to learn how to know your anger and calm yourself down. Raise your hand if you've ever been angry (pause). We've all been angry at some point. To help us learn about what might make us angry, I'd like to tell you a story about my friend Alexander. Please listen carefully."

Read *Alexander and the terrible, horrible, no good, very bad day*.

Ask clients to stand up.

"Alexander really did have a rotten day! Now we're going to learn four steps that can help us deal with our bad days or times when we feel angry. Okay, the first step is. . ." (Refer to poster illustrated in figure A37.1 as necessary to assist students in learning steps).

1. *Buttons* (demonstrate pushing button in palm of hand and point to step on poster): First we need to know what makes us angry. You might get angry when someone tells you 'no' when you ask to do something, when a classmate pushes you on the playground, or when someone doesn't ask you to play a game and you feel left out. (Practice "button" symbol.)

2. *Warning* (demonstrate time-out symbol with hands and point to step on poster): Then we need to learn what happens to our bodies when we feel angry. You might feel your face get hot, your hands might get shaky, your stomach or head might start hurting, you may squeeze your hands into fists, feel jumpy or helpless, or you may feel like you want to yell or cry. (Practice "warning" symbol.)

3. *Stop* (demonstrate symbol by pushing both arms forward with palms out): Next we need to know that anger can be tricky. Sometimes we may think that we're angry, but we may just be feeling sad, guilty, or disappointed. We can stop and think (demonstrate symbol again) to ask ourselves, "What happened?" and "What else did I feel when I got angry?" (Practice "stop" symbol.)

4. *Choices* (demonstrate symbol by putting both index fingers to sides of forehead): The last step in learning how to tame our tempers is called choices. *You* are the boss of your anger and you have the strength to overpower it. Instead of getting angry, try talking it out, standing up for yourself, or sharing your feelings. It's *your* choice. (Practice "choices" symbol.)

Once each step has been explained, the clients will play "Simon Says." Explain the rules of the game and try a practice round. For example: "Simon says button!" and players should show the "button" symbol. After a couple of rounds, speed up the pace of the game. Game play should continue for ten minutes.

After completion of the game, ask the clients to sit down again. In this portion of the activity, several scenarios will be given and each player must show the symbol they would use in each situation. At the end of the exercise ask each player to give a "thumbs up" if he or she has ever tried _____ (fill in the blank with a choice a child stated or one of the options that you listed).

The final exercise utilizes a comic strip to apply these strategies to an easily relatable situation. The clients will practice matching steps from a grocery store scenario with the four anger management strategies: Buttons, Warning, Stop, and Choices. Clients will cut out each of the motions from the third row of the comic strip and tape or glue them to the empty row, below the matching step from the scenario. If clients finish early, they may color in the pictures on the comic strip.

When all children have completed their comic strips, review each step in the scenario and explain the answers. Rewards may be given to those who completed their comic strip correctly (optional).

End the session with *Anger Management—How to Squeeze Your Angries Out* (http://www.youtube.com/watch?v=WkKLz61RHXo), which shows another way to calm down through a progressive muscle relaxation exercise.

Function in Assessment and Treatment

Assessment

This game can be used in a school social work setting for an entire classroom, for a small group of students that have been struggling with anger management, or in individual practice. In individual therapy sessions, students can choose their own anger scenarios to work through using each step.

Treatment

This exercise allows children to recognize their anger and to develop healthy strategies for dealing with anger in the future. Children can learn to increase their awareness of specific situations that trigger their anger, use simple biofeedback to notice physical warning signs, stop and think about the situation prior to reacting, and choose from healthy or "good" choices to avoid having negative reactions. Through discussion, children can consider various feelings associated with anger and learn a wide range of coping strategies from the facilitator and their peers.

Resources

Namka, L. [Lynne Namka]. (2010). *Anger Management—Squeeze Your Angries Out* (video file). Retrieved from http://www.youtube.com/watch?v=WkKLz61RHXo.

Verdick, E., & Lisovskis, M. (2003). *How to take the grrrr out of anger*. Minneapolis, MN: Free Spirit Publishing Inc.

Viorst, Judith. (1972). *Alexander and the terrible, horrible, no good, very bad day*. New York: Aladdin Paperbacks.

Special thanks to teacher Lindsay M. Clement for her feedback in the development and administration of this exercise.

Figure A37.1 Example Posters

Example of poster illustrating anger management strategies and each stage in the temper-taming process: Buttons, Warning, Stop, and Choices.

Figure A37.2 Scenarios

Scenario	Questions (After posing question, pause so that all students have time to demonstrate the symbol.)
So you're in the grocery store with your mom, and you spot the coolest toy you've ever seen on the shelf. Your eyes get really big when you look at it and you're feeling very excited because you want the toy so much. Then you look over at your mom . . .	What step might you use? Show me the symbol. Why did you choose that symbol? <u>Answer:</u> Buttons <u>Why:</u> You know that you will feel angry if your mom says you cannot have the toy.
Your mom says no and you notice that your face is starting to get red and hot, your arms are shaking, and you start stomping your feet.	What step might you use now? Show me the symbol. Why did you choose that symbol? <u>Answer:</u> Warning <u>Why:</u> You notice your body's anger signs.
So now your mom has said no and you're feeling angry. At first you felt shaky, and then in the next moment you wanted to cry in the aisle or run away and hide from her. So you start to wonder . . . "What happened that made me feel angry? What else did I feel when it happened?"	What step would you be using now? Show me the symbol. Why did you choose that symbol? <u>Answer:</u> Stop <u>Why:</u> You stopped and thought about how you felt while you were angry.
You've thought about how you felt now and you're thinking to yourself, "Hmm, how can I make this problem smaller instead of bigger?" You think, "If I throw a fit in the grocery store, it will be worse because I won't get the toy and my mom will probably take away my favorite toy at home." Instead, you decide that you want to make your problem smaller.	What step would you be using now? Show me the symbol. <u>Answer:</u> Stop <u>Why:</u> You thought about the different ways you can handle your anger and better the situation. You asked yourself, "What can I do to make the problem smaller?" or you accepted "no" and moved on.

A37 – How to Tame Your Temper   173

Figure A37.3 Comic Strip Example

Comic strip illustrating anger management scenario (row one: four pictures for each step in grocery store scenario; row two: four blank spaces; row three: four symbols taught during the "Simon Says" game)

To complete the exercise, students cut out each anger management step from the bottom strip and glue steps below each corresponding scene from the grocery store.

A38
Imitated for Self-Control
Yuliana Medina

Items Needed

One set of plastic bowling pins with ball, or ten empty water bottles, labeled with numbers 1–10 (figure A38.1); one set of red cards (see figure A38.2); one set of blue cards (see figure A38.3); score chart (see figure A38.4); feelings faces

Target Population

Children ages three to eight with behavioral and self-control issues

This can be played with an individual or in a group (maximum five players)

Purpose

To communicate the concept of behavior modification in a variety of settings

Procedure

Set the pins or bottles like in a bowling game (see figure A38.1) and draw a line as the starting point. Each player will start by rolling the ball to knock down the pins. The numbers written on each pin will be added up to determine which set of cards the player will choose from. Players with an even sum will pick a blue card, and players with an odd sum will pick a red card. Each red card has a word and each blue card has a sentence.

Each player takes a turn, marks down the total pin score on the score chart, selects a card, and then reads and acts out the word or sentence on the chosen card, imitating how a person may have used the word or sentence to a child and get one ACT point by circling "1" on the chart. Then the player will ask another player (who just completed a turn) to choose a facial expression on the chart to represent a feeling when this player said and acted that word or sentence. This may be a point where you may either ask the player to explore what could have been said differently in order to feel better to get two "ACT" points by circling "2." You may also ask the player what may change his or her own behavior in the future. The game may continue for five or more rounds, lasting about ten to fifteen minutes depending on the number of players.

Function in Assessment and Treatment

Assessment

This game will help determine how the client perceives his or her environment and how other people interact with him or her. It also allows the therapist to assess how well the client is functioning in a variety of environments.

Treatment

This game gives the client an opportunity to modify behavior throughout the game. It helps the client understand the importance of self-control and following rules. It also allows the client to understand the consequences related to rules, and helps him or her to formulate plans to modify behavior accordingly. This game enables the client to "plan ahead" for future situations similar to those described on the cards. In a group setting, it empowers the clients to testify that they are able to control their behaviors, and thus have more control over outcomes in future situations.

176 *Therapeutic Games and Guided Imagery*

Figure A38.1 Bowling Pins Setup

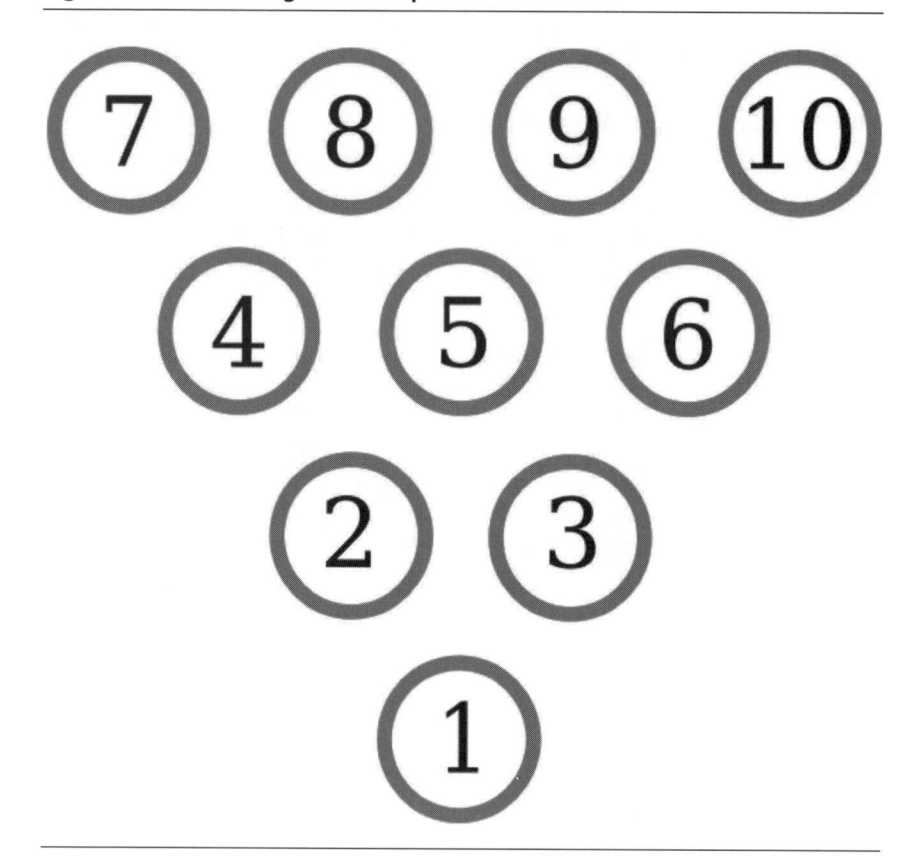

Figure A38.2 Red Cards

O.K.	GOOD
SIT DOWN	GET OUT
DO IT	DONE
STAY STILL	CALM
RULES	SILLY
OBEDIENT	PROUD
BE QUIET	FUNNY
STOP IT	BAD
LOOK	NOISY
LAZY	STAND STAIGHT

Figure A38.3 Blue Cards

DO YOUR HOMEWORK	CLEAN UP THE MESS
YOU ARE RUDE	WASH YOUR HANDS
YOU ARE DISRESPECTFUL	YOU SHOULD KNOW BETTER
I AM GETTING CRAZY	YOU ARE ACTING LIKE A BABY
GO TO BED	YOU NEED TO LEARN SOME MANNERS
GET OUT	I KNEW YOU COULD DO IT
GO TO YOUR ROOM	LOOK AT ME
STAY INSIDE	YOU ARE NOT COMING BACK
SHOW ME YOUR WORK	NOW YOU HAVE THE HANG OF IT
THAT IS THE BEST YOU HAVE EVER DONE	HOW COME?

Figure A38.4 Score Chart

Name	Score 1		Score 2		Score 3		Score 4		Score 5		Total
	PIN	ACT	PIN	ACT	PIN	ACT	PIN	ACT	PIN	ACT	
		1 2		1 2		1 2		1 2		1 2	
		1 2		1 2		1 2		1 2		1 2	
		1 2		1 2		1 2		1 2		1 2	
		1 2		1 2		1 2		1 2		1 2	
		1 2		1 2		1 2		1 2		1 2	
		1 2		1 2		1 2		1 2		1 2	

A39
King's "Rule-ette" Game
Nicole Willis

Items Needed

Full deck of standard playing cards; plastic cups or bowls; fun-sized bags of candies or snacks (M&M's, Gummi Bears, peanuts, etc.); 25 blue note cards, 25 orange note cards, and 6 white note cards; 2 poster boards or large sheets of construction paper; finger paint

Target Population

Youth ages 10 to 16 who have difficulty with anger management, lack appropriate social skills, and have a low frustration tolerance

Intended for subsequent sessions with groups of three to five members

Purpose

To learn how to control angry feelings and improve social skills

Procedure

Prior to the session, create two poster boards: one with a chart of the players' names and session numbers and one displaying the playing cards and their corresponding meanings (see figure A39.1). The blue "Category" cards and the orange "What Happens Next" cards should also be made prior to the session (see figures A39.2 and A39.3).

During the first session, each player should decorate his or her bowl, or cup, using the finger paint. The facilitator should also decorate a bowl, which will later be used to hold the "king's gold." Afterwards, the facilitator will explain the rules of a game for the next session. The purpose of the first session is to develop rapport and give the members an orientation to the group and its purpose. The game can be started in subsequent sessions.

To play the game, fill each player's bowl with 10 to 15 pieces of candy or snack, and have them sit in a circle with their bowls in front of them. Spread out the deck of cards, face down, in a ring shape in the middle of the circle. Put five pieces of candy or snack in the "king's gold" bowl and place that in the center of the circle, along with the "Category" and the "What Happens Next?" cards.

Going clockwise around the circle, each player will draw one card at a time, following the rules displayed on the poster (shown in figure A39.1). So if a player draws a "2," he or she must create a new, simple rule for the game and anyone who breaks the rule must place one of their pieces of candy or snack into the "king's gold." This continues until the last King is drawn, and the player who draws the last King wins the "king's gold." Then all players must count their leftover pieces of candy or snack, writing down their total for that round. The object of the game is to try to keep as many pieces of candy or snack as possible, and any partially or fully eaten pieces will not be counted towards the final score, which helps the children learn self-control and tolerance.

Function in Assessment and Treatment

Assessment

This game is designed for group treatment consisting of four to six sessions. During each session, the facilitator will be able to assess each child's social skills, ability to self-report what the child would do in hypothetical situations, and the approach used when creating new "rules" for the game. An assessment of anger management skills can be achieved through the child's response to hypothetical social situations and by observing the child's reactions to losing a piece of his or her candy or snack as a result of breaking a rule or being the last to follow a rule. The facilitator can track behavioral improvements by observing dynamics and interactions throughout the game, and by the number of weekly points players receive during the course of the sessions.

Therapeutic questions can be used to address behaviors and choices in social situations to help children understand how their anger-control mechanisms work for them and to help develop or reinforce appropriate social skills. Therapeutic questions may include:

1. How did you feel when you had to give up your last piece of candy?

2. What are some other choices _____ could have made in that situation? How are those choices good or bad?

3. How does your body tell you that you are angry?

4. Has anyone in the group ever been in this situation? What did you do?

5. What did you do well during the game? What area(s) are you going to work on in the next game? How?

6. On a scale of 1 to 10, 10 being the best, how well do you think we played together as a group? What did we do that you like the most?

Treatment

Through the use of rewards, appropriate social skills and productive anger management skills can be positively reinforced or shaped. The facilitator can process any inappropriate behavior or responses given during the game with both individuals and with the group. Open discussion can be used as teaching moments concerning issues such as alternative behaviors, coping skills, anger management skills, or other issues that arise during the group. At the end of the fourth or sixth week, the facilitator may process and address individual and group progress with the group, and provide individual feedback by informing members of areas in which they may need to improve. Participants should be given the opportunity to express what they have learned from the experience.

Draw a "2": The player must create a simple rule for the game. Any player who breaks that rule, or is the last to follow the rule must place a candy or snack in the "king's gold." The facilitator should create a few rule cards in advance for those who cannot create appropriate rules (see figure A39.4, "Examples").

Draw a "5": The player must draw from the "What Happens Next" cards, read the card aloud, and state what he or she would do next. If a player gives an inappropriate response, as determined by the leader, he or she must put a piece of their candy or snack into the "king's gold."

Draw a "10": The player must draw from the "Category" cards, read the card aloud, and give an applicable response. Continuing clockwise around the circle, each player will have five seconds to give an applicable response. The first player who cannot do so must place a piece of their candy or snack into the "king's gold."

Draw a "Jack": All players must put their hands on their heads. The last player to put their hands on their head must put a piece of their candy into the "king's gold."

Figure A39.1 Suggestions for "Simple Rules" Cards

Everyone must keep a cup (upside down) on top of their head	Whenever I say "smile," everyone must say "smile"
Whenever I touch my forehead and say "Hmmm . . . ," everyone else must do the same	No one can say names (of players in the game)
Whenever I touch my nose, everyone must touch their noses	Anyone who draws an "ace" must stand up and cheer

Figure A39.2 Suggestions for "What Happens Next?" Cards

You are at the mall with your friends and you find a wallet on the ground with $200 inside of it. What do you do next?	You are in math class working on a hard math problem. You are frustrated because you don't understand it. What do you do next?
You are playing kickball and push another student because you think she is cheating. The coach tells you to sit out of the game. The girl you pushed starts laughing at you. What do you do next?	You are getting tired of someone who is provoking you every day. When no one is looking you smack him. The next day at school, you see him coming towards you in the hall. What do you do next?
You find a blue yo-yo in the parking lot and pick it up and keep it. The next day in class, you overhear someone saying they lost a blue yo-yo. What do you do next?	You are at home and want to go outside with your friends. You ask your mom and she says, "No, you must do your homework first." You are angry because your friends will only be outside for another hour. What do you do next?
You are sitting in class and your best friend tells you to throw a spitball at the "new kid." You shake your head "no," and your friend calls you a "chicken." The teacher has her back turned. What do you do?	You are busy playing your video game and have almost reached the last level on the game. Your grandmother asks you to come downstairs and take out the trash. What do you do next?
You are waiting at the bus stop and another boy walks up and starts talking negatively about your mother. You are angry and embarrassed. What do you do next?	It is computer time in class. There are six students who want to use the computers, but there are only four computers. What do you do next?

Figure A39.3 Suggestions for "Category" Cards

Ice cream flavors	Famous singers or bands	Types of emotions	Things you see at a playground	Knock-knock jokes
Types of candy bars	Places that are unsafe	Movies	Things you can do to calm down when you are angry	People you can go to for help

A40
Let's Rebuild: A Game about Life
Victoria Reyes

Items Needed
Jumbling Tower (48 color-coded wooden pieces already designed with therapeutic questions/words—see figure A40.3)

Target Population
Adolescent girls ages 13 to 16 who are survivors of child sexual abuse.

Intended for use with groups but may also be used with a client and her family

Purpose
To build rapport

To encourage the expression of feelings

To assess client's skills through the use of free association

Procedure
Note: The three concepts represented by the content on the blocks are family, friends, and self

The clinician will build the tower, preparing each level with three blocks, one from each theme, and continue building in a crisscross pattern until the tower is complete (see figure A40.1, figure A40.2). If the group is not familiar with "free association," give members a brief explanation and chance to practice prior to beginning the exercise.

The youngest player will begin and the game will continue in a clockwise direction. Each player will take a turn removing one block from the tower, but cannot remove a block from the top level. Once the player has removed the block, she must either answer the question on the block or use free association for the word on the opposite side.

Sample Questions for Blocks

SELF: If your mirror could talk, what would it say about you?

FRIENDS: How would a close friend describe a unique characteristic of you?

FAMILY: How would someone in your family describe you?

Figure A40.1 Example—Front

> Imagine yourself in a movie; what movie would it be and what character would you play?

Figure A40.2 Example—Back

> SELF-IMAGE

Once the player has completed the task, she will place the block on the top of the tower, and follow the same crisscross pattern as it was built. If a player has drawn the same block twice, the alternate side may be used or another block may be removed. If a player makes the tower fall on a turn, the player must say, "Let's rebuild" and the participants will together rebuild the tower.

Function in Assessment and Treatment

Assessment

This game is useful in the initial assessment of a client. The game assesses how the client perceives herself and those closest to her, and how she believes others may perceive her.

Treatment

Through this exercise, clients can express their feelings in a safe, non-threatening environment. Through the exchanging of feelings and experiences, they begin to realize that they are not alone. The game can promote a sense of connectedness between players and allow the building of healthy relationships. Rebuilding the tower together creates a feeling of synergy and support among the members.

Figure A40.3 Block Examples

If your mirror could talk, what would it say about you?	How would a close friend describe you?	How would someone in your family describe you?
SELF-ESTEEM	SELF-ESTEEM	SELF-ESTEEM
Imagine yourself in a movie; what movie would it be and what character would you play?	Imagine your closest friend in a movie; what movie would it be and what character would they play?	Imagine someone in your family in a movie; what movie would it be and what character would they play?
SELF-IMAGE	SELF-IMAGE	SELF-IMAGE
Imagine you just received really good news; how would you celebrate?	Imagine you just received really good news; which friend do you tell first?	Imagine you just received really good news; who in your family do you tell first?
HAPPINESS	HAPPINESS	HAPPINESS
Think of a time when someone broke their promise to you, how did that make you feel?	Have you ever broken a promise to a friend? How do you think that made this friend feel?	Have you ever broken a promise to a family member? How do you think that made them feel?
TRUST	TRUST	TRUST
Choose a song that describes your life.	Choose a song that best describes you and your close friend's relationship.	Choose a song that describes your relationship with your family.
FEELINGS	FEELINGS	FEELINGS
If you could be anybody in the world, who would you be and why?	Which one of your friends do you look up to and why?	Who in your family do you look up to and why?
ROLE-MODEL	ROLE-MODEL	ROLE-MODEL
If you were a color in the rainbow, which one would you like to be?	Choose a color to represent your closest friend; what color would you choose?	Choose a color to represent someone in your family; what color would you choose?
CREATIVITY	CREATIVITY	CREATIVITY
What is something you are really good at that others may find it hard to do?	What is something your closest friend is good at that you find it hard to do?	What is something that someone in your family is good at that you find it hard to do?
CHALLENGES	CHALLENGES	CHALLENGES
If you won the lottery tomorrow, what would be the first thing that you would buy?	If you won the lottery tomorrow, what would you buy for your closest friend?	If you won the lottery tomorrow, what would you buy for your family?

Figure A40.3 Block Examples—(continued)

VALUE	VALUE	VALUE
If you woke up tomorrow and everything was "perfect," how would things be different?	If you woke up tomorrow and everything was "perfect," what would your friends be like?	If you woke up tomorrow and everything was "perfect," what would your family be like?
PERFECTION	**PERFECTION**	**PERFECTION**
Think of someone that you do not get along with; name one good thing about this person.	If someone said something negative about you to one of your closest friends, what good thing would you want your friend to say about you?	If someone said something negative about you to your family, what good thing would you want your family to say about you?
POSITIVITY	**POSITIVITY**	**POSITIVITY**
If you could change one thing about yourself, what would it be?	If you could change one thing about your closest friend, what would it be?	If you could change one thing about a family member, what would it be?
ACCEPTANCE	**ACCEPTANCE**	**ACCEPTANCE**
What is one thing that brings you comfort and why?	What is one thing that your closest friend can give you to bring you comfort?	What is one thing that your family can give you to bring you comfort?
SUPPORT	**SUPPORT**	**SUPPORT**
Think of a favorite memory; share one good thing about this memory.	Think of your favorite memory with your closest friend; share one good thing about this memory.	Think of your favorite memory with your family; share one good thing about this memory.
EMOTIONS	**EMOTIONS**	**EMOTIONS**
If you would turn into an animal for one day, what animal would you be and why?	If your closest friend was turned into an animal for one day, what animal would this friend be and why?	If a family member was turned into an animal for one day, what animal would this person be and why?
EXPRESSION	**EXPRESSION**	**EXPRESSION**
FREE BLOCK: Share anything you like about yourself.	FREE BLOCK: Share anything you like about your closest friend.	FREE BLOCK: Share anything you like about your family.

A41
Make Believe or Truth
Regenia G. Kerr

Items Required

Game board (refer to figure A41.1); 4 different colored game pieces; 1 rolling die; 3 sets of cards (Make Believe—figure A41.2; Truth—figure A41.3; and blanks for Asking Your Own Questions); stickers; and small prizes.

Target Population

Game can be used for children between the ages of five and ten

Encourage children who struggle with answering questions or refuse to talk to strangers

Game may be used before or after a forensic interview

Appropriate for both genders with various cultural and ethnic backgrounds

Purpose

Assist children in building rapport with others

Help to achieve open communication and promote interaction with others

Encourage children's expressions of their own feelings

Identify underlying problems in the environment that may contribute to nonverbal opposition

Observe the child's degree of playfulness and cooperation

Procedures

Ask the child to choose his or her game piece and decide if he or she wants to start on the "Bee" side of the board or the "Lady Bug" side of the board. The child rolls the die and moves the game piece according to the corresponding number.

If the player lands on the "Make Believe" space, he or she selects a card from the stack of "Make Believe" cards, reads the card and provides a yes-or-no answer. If the player lands on the "Truth" space, he or she selects a card from the stack of "Truth" cards and finishes the statement. If landing on a dot or flower, the player says something that is good or beautiful. If landing on the "Ask Your Own Question" space, the player may choose to ask someone a question (or write down the question on a blank card and ask that question in the next round) and get a prize, or just take a sticker without saying anything at all.

The game is over when the game piece of one of the players lands on "Home" or gets to the other side of the game board (i.e., landing on the "Bee" or the "Lady Bug").

Function in Assessment and Treatment

Assessment

This game helps young children differentiate between truth and make-believe, and understand when it is appropriate to talk about reality or fantasy. It also serves as a bridge to provide educational materials about the meaning of telling the truth and the consequences of lying. In forensic interviews, children who have been sexually abused must show competence if they can differentiate truth from lies. This exercise will help them understand why this procedure is important and what their role is in problem disclosure.

Treatment

For children who are quiet or unwilling to participate, this exercise is a simple way to get them involved. Once a child is able to participate in the game, he or she may be at ease to share additional information. You may ask about the sound of the animal, the name of the pet the child has, or other related questions to build rapport. For children who are fearful of strangers or have separation anxiety from their accompanying adult, you may start this game with both the child and this adult by asking them to take turns to pick up a "Make Believe" card and provide an answer. Once the child is comfortable, you may then say that this adult will be playing the game in the next room with a coworker while you will play this game in this room with the child.

Therapeutic questions may include:

1. When someone lies to you, how does that make you feel?
2. When someone lies to you, what do you think that person is trying to do?
3. What would you like to say to the person that lied to you?
4. How much do you know about_____? Make up two or three questions you would like to ask_____. Then if you land on the space "Ask Your Own Questions" you can use your questions.

Figure A41.1 Example of Game Board (Game board 24" long and 12" wide)

 "BEE"	1 Make Believe	2 Truth	3	4 Make Believe
9	8 Ask Your Own Question	7 Make Believe	6 Ask Your Own Question	5 Truth
10	11 Truth	12 Truth	13 Make Believe	14
19	18 Ask Your Own Question	17	16 Truth	15 Ask Your Own Question
	"HOME"				
15 Ask Your Own Question	16 Truth	17	18 Ask Your Own Question	19
14	13 Make Believe	12 Truth	11 Truth	10
5 Truth	6 Ask Your Own Question	7 Make Believe	8 Ask Your Own Question	9
4 Make Believe	3	2 Truth	1 Make Believe	 LADY BUG

Figure A41.2 "Make Believe" Questions

I have a dog	I have a cat	I have a fish
I have a bird	I have a horse	I have a pig
I like to catch butterflies	I have a pet chicken	I have a pet frog
I have a pet flea	I have a cow in my back yard	I have a duck in my car
I have a pet hamster in a cup	My brother has a pet mouse	I have a goat that lives on my roof
I have a rabbit that lives in my flowers	I have a lizard on a string	I like to go to my grandmother's house
The sky is pink	I have a green snake	I am nice
I do not talk to strangers	I never fuss with my brothers and sisters	I like ice cream
I like to eat mud	I have a pet monkey under my bed	I eat cabbage
I eat prunes	I like spinach	I like hamburgers
I eat bananas	I am a good friend	I am happy

Figure A41.3 "Truth" Questions

I like to be alone when _____	I do not like it when _____	The most hurtful thing that ever happened to me was _____
My favorite thing to do is _____	I want to be a _____ when I grow up	I am happy when _____
I get upset when _____ is happening	It makes me unhappy when _____	I make my parents mad when _____
I know my parents are happy when _____	When my parents get mad at me they _____	I have _____ (number) friends
I worry about my family when they are _____	When I am mad I _____	When I make a mistake I _____
When something good happens to me I _____	I talk to _____ when I am sad or lonely	I am _____
I wish _____	I am excited when _____	I feel better when _____
Good things are _____	Bad things are _____	I smile when I see _____
I like _____	I do not like to _____	I feel sad when _____

A42
My Fantastic Family
Connie Villasmil

Items Needed
Pre-made picture cards; figures sheet (see figure A42.1); characteristics cards (see figures A42.2 to A42.4); blank paper and magazines (for participants to make their own creative choices outside of the options provided); scissors; tape or glue; colored pencils, colored markers, crayons, pens

Target Population
Children age 5+

Suitable for all cultures and socioeconomic backgrounds

Children and adults who do not feel represented by traditional family structures

Appropriate for use with individuals and groups

Purpose
To build rapport

To encourage the understanding of different family structures present in today's society

To assess family relationships and roles as perceived by the client

To encourage the expression of feelings about members of the family unit

To promote understanding and appreciation of different family structures

Procedure
Using the picture cards, present an example of a made-up family, introduce each member of the family, and express a special quality or attribute they contribute to the family dynamics. Explain how each member is an important part of the family. Next, ask the client to create his or her own family by cutting out the appropriate people and characteristics from the figures sheet and the characteristics cards. The client may also draw pieces or cut out pieces from a magazine to better represent the members of the family. The

client should use the coloring utensils to color, write, draw, or design the different characteristics of the family members.

When the family is complete, ask the client to explain who each member is, what their roles are within the family unit, and why he or she chose certain colors, characteristics, and so on for each member. After discussing the family, have the client name something special or unique about each member. Follow-up discussion should address the differences in behaviors and characteristics between his or her family and the example family, and how these may affect the family dynamics.

Remind the client that these differences are neither good nor bad—they are simply unique. This will utilize the strengths perspective to encourage the client in recognizing the best qualities of his or her own family members. It is important to offer corrections to incorrect assumptions when necessary to endorse cultural sensitivity.

In a group setting, have each client share his or her family with the group and give a short description of the family unit, identify some unique characteristics of the family or specific family members, and identify one unique aspect about his or her family. Once everyone has taken a turn, have an open discussion about the differences among the family units portrayed. Follow-up discussion should encourage the clients to share any observations they had and any qualities they saw in other families that they would like for their family, and vice-versa.

*Note: Figures A42.1 and A42.2 can be copied as enlarged or downsized versions in order to appropriately fit the differing sizes of the family members (infant, child, adolescent, and adult).

Function in Assessment and Treatment

Assessment

This game helps to assess the client's understanding of his or her family's strengths, individual roles, and differences from other family structures. By allowing participants the freedom to define their family units, as well as others, they are able to critically process the differences among families. The facilitator may gain insight into the client's biases and negative perspectives towards certain family structures and may use this insight to address issues of cultural sensitivity.

Treatment

Understanding and identifying a family structure is not always easy, especially if the family structure does not conform to societal norms. This activity provides the freedom and adaptability necessary to explore new structures of the American family and encourages participants to recognize their family's individuality and uniqueness. It promotes communication, encourages sharing personal details, and fosters a healthy understanding of single-parent families, LGBT families, grandparents raising children, blended families, and other options not normally represented in standard family structures. This activity also helps build rapport and promote the sharing of personal information in a fun and unstructured manner.

A42 – My Fantastic Family **199**

Figure A42.1 Infant, Child, Adolescent, Adult Figures

200 *Therapeutic Games and Guided Imagery*

Figure A42.2 Female Hairstyles

Figure A42.3 Male Hairstyles

Figure A42.4 Clothes and Accessories

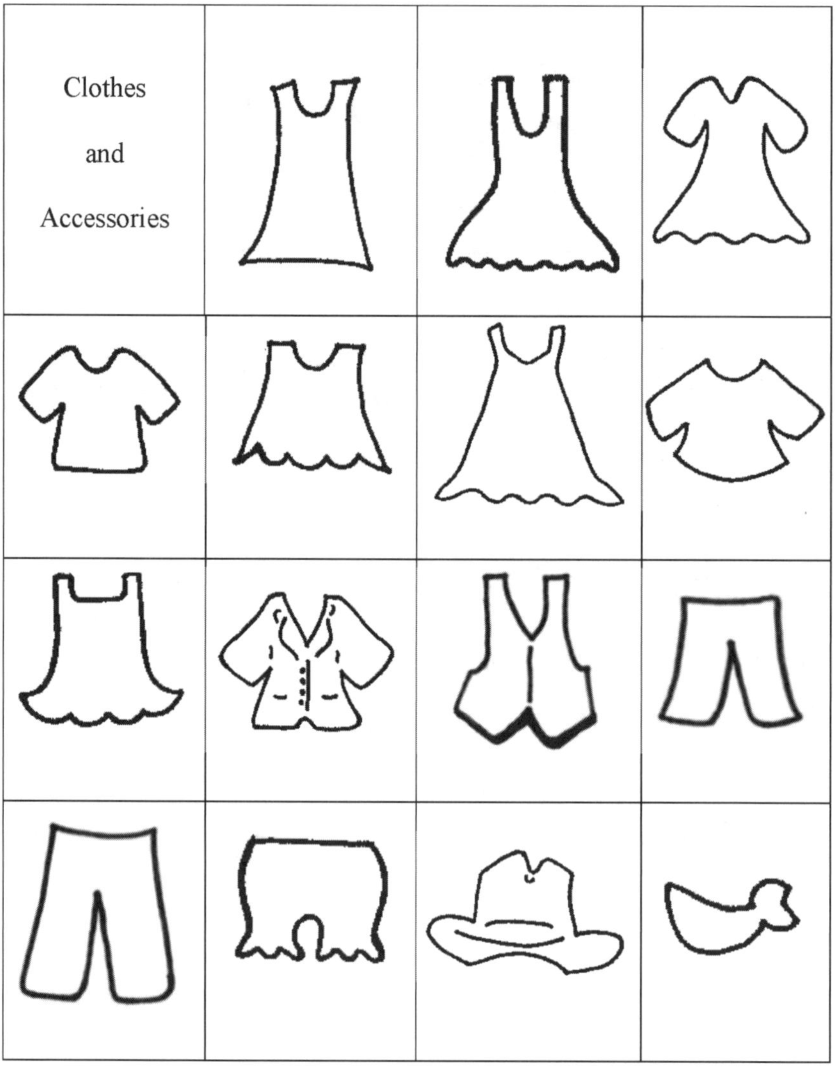

Figure A42.4 Clothes and Accessories—(continued)

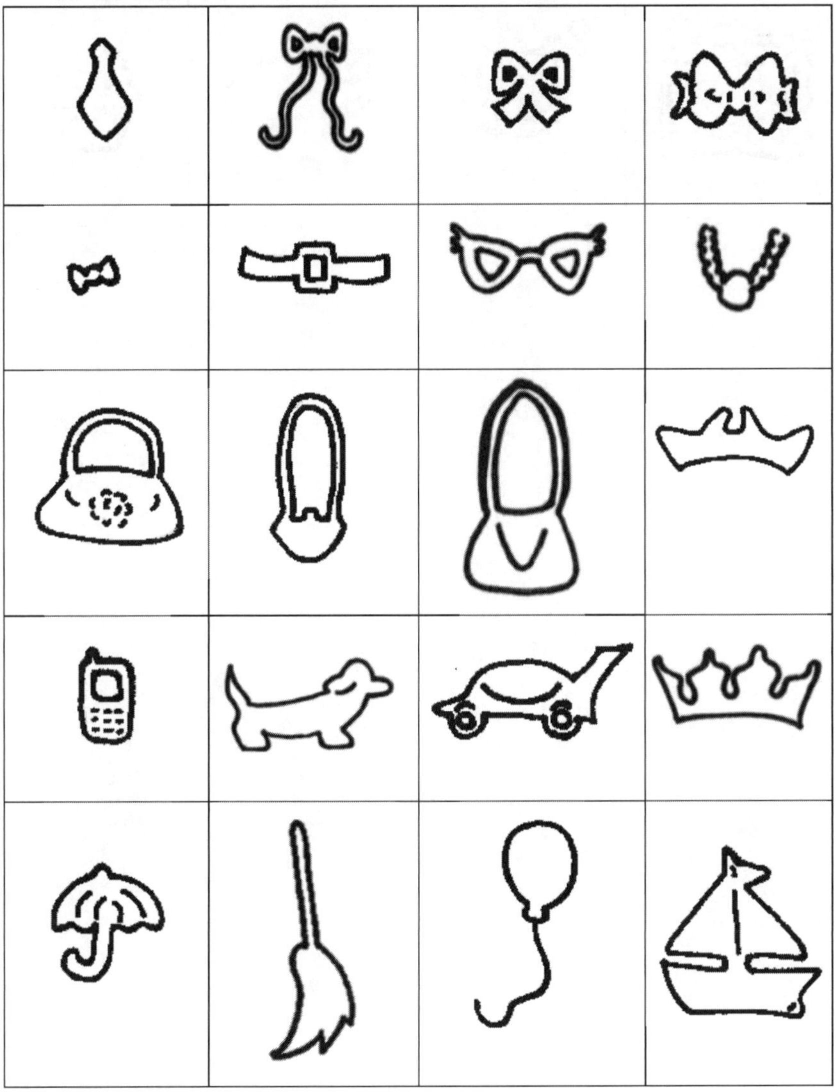

204 *Therapeutic Games and Guided Imagery*

Figure A42.4 Clothes and Accessories—(continued)

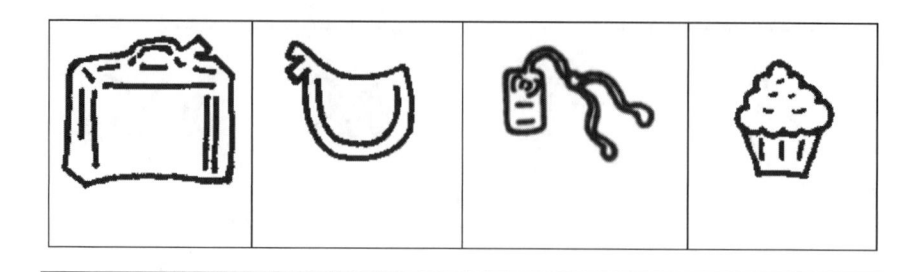

A43
My Favorite Things
Marilyn Hotchko-Scott

Items Needed

One set of different colored pawns; one set of blue, yellow, red, and green question cards (six each, containing four questions each) (see figure A43.1); one color game wheel; one die

Target Population

Children ages 6 to 12 who are survivors of child abuse, or children with divorced parents.

Purpose

To help build rapport

To build feelings of safety for client in a therapeutic environment

To assist children in connecting with one another in a group setting

To encourage the child and parent or guardian to spend quality time together in family therapy

Procedure

Each player will pick one pawn to use on the game board. Each player will then place his or her pawn at the starting point on the color wheel. The first player will roll the die on the game board, and move the pawn the same number of spaces. The player will then be asked a question from the question card corresponding to the color space he or she landed on. After answering the question, the second player will repeat this procedure. The game may continue for five or more rounds, lasting about ten minutes. All players will be awarded with a special sticker for their participation.

Function in Assessment and Treatment

Assessment

This game is a good ice-breaker to get acquainted with the child or other participants in the group. The game is used to bring about more in-depth discussions regarding behaviors, feelings, or emotions surrounding his or her current situation by allowing the child to express his or her likes and dislikes about the topics.

Treatment

Throughout the game, children are able to express what they consider to be their favorite things. Since this game has no "right" or "wrong" answers, children are reassured that it is fine to have differences among group members. Encouragement of open expression helps build a sense of safety. This exercise may also lead to discussions about group cohesion through exploration of similarities among the answers or about group diversity through differences.

Modifications:

1. One-on-one: Use specific questions to get more information from a client regarding family life.
2. Group setting: Help the client find something in common with another client in the group.
3. Parent/child setting: Help the parent understand his or her child's likes, favorite things, and reasons behind the liking.

Figure A43.1 "My Favorite Things" Game Cards

Blue Cards	Yellow Cards	Green Cards	Red Cards
1. What is your favorite TV show? 2. What is your favorite cartoon show? 3. Who is your favorite actor/actress? 4. Who is your favorite cartoon or comic character?	1. Who is/was your favorite teacher? 2. What is/was your favorite school subject? 3. What is your favorite sport? 4. Who is your favorite sports figure?	1. What ice-cream flavor do you like the most? 2. What kind of cookies do you like the most? 3. What is your favorite breakfast drink? 4. What color in Kool-Aid do you like the most?	1. What is your favorite outfit? 2. What is your favorite Halloween or dress-up costume? 3. What do your favorite shoes look like? 4. Where is your favorite hiding place?
1. When is your favorite day of the week? 2. When is your favorite month of the year? 3. Which is your favorite holiday? 4. When is your favorite time of the year (Spring, Summer, Fall, Winter)?	1. When is your favorite time of the day? 2. Do you like breakfast, lunch, or dinner? 3. What is your favorite cereal? 4. What is in your favorite meal?	1. What do you like to do during recess? 2. Who do you like to play with among your schoolmates? 3. What is your favorite school lunch? 4. Where is your favorite place when you are with your friends?	1. What is your favorite toy? 2. What is your favorite music video? 3. What is your favorite video game? 4. What is your favorite musical instrument?
1. What is your favorite color? 2. What is your favorite pastime? 3. What do you like about yourself? 4. Who do you like to spend the most time with?	1. What is the name of your best friend? 2. What is the best characteristic of a hero? 3. Who can be a superhero? 4. What kind of super powers would you have if you were a superhero?	1. Where is your favorite place in your home? 2. Where is your favorite place to spend time alone? 3. What household chores would you like to do at home? 4. What kind of house would you like to have (one-story; multi-stories)?	1. What is your favorite activity at the park? 2. What is your favorite activity with your mom? 3. What is your favorite activity with your dad? 4. If you play in the snow, what games would you like to play?

Figure A43.1 "My Favorite Things" Game Cards—(continued)

Blue Cards	Yellow Cards	Green Cards	Red Cards
1. What is your favorite game? 2. What is your favorite thing to do after school? 3. What is your favorite hobby? 4. Name two people you would like to spend a day with.	1. What is your favorite story book? 2. What is your favorite memory? 3. Whose nickname do you like the most? 4. Who was your favorite character in a school play?	1. Where is your favorite vacation place? 2. What would you like to do during a vacation? 3. What do you enjoy doing with your family? 4. What do you enjoy doing with your friends?	1. What do you like to do when you visit your grandparents? 2. What activity do you like at the beach? 3. Who is your favorite uncle? 4. Who is your favorite aunt?
1. What is your favorite fruit? 2. What is your favorite vegetable? 3. What is your favorite snack? 4. What is your favorite dessert?	1. What is your favorite gift you ever received? 2. What is your favorite item in your bedroom? 3. What is the best gift you received for your birthday? 4. What is a favorite way to spend your evening?	1. What do you like to do on weekends? 2. What do you like to do during the summer? 3. What do you like to do during Christmas break? 4. Who do you like to visit during a long holiday?	1. What is the name of your brother (or a favorite male friend)? 2. What is the name of your sister (or a favorite female friend)? 3. What kind of exercises do you like to do? 4. What is your favorite Bible story?
1. What is your favorite zoo animal? 2. What is your favorite kind of pet? 3. What is a name you like for a pet? 4. What animals do you like to play with?	1. What is your favorite movie? 2. What popular TV star would you like to visit? 3. Who is your favorite singer? 4. What is your favorite song?	1. What do you like best about your mother? 2. What do you like best about your father? 3. What career or profession would you want to work in? 4. If you would turn into someone else, who would this person be?	1. What is your favorite fast food restaurant? 2. What is your favorite form of transportation? 3. What is your favorite kind of car? 4. Who will be a part of your dream future?

A44
Name It . . . Word It . . . Style It!
Jasmine Walls

Items Needed

Alpha beads; regular beads; necklace rods; pieces of string (should be long enough to wrap around the wrist and to tie)

Target Population

Adolescents 13 to 17 with expressive language disorder

Can be used with individuals, partners, or groups

Purpose

To break the ice

To encourage use of positive language and speech

To strengthen ability to convey meaningful expression of emotions or feelings to others

To enhance understanding of differing perspectives

To increase comprehension of other's expression

To encourage group cooperation and social interaction

Procedure

Each participant should be provided with a piece of string or necklace rod, and alpha beads.

Using the alpha beads, instruct each individual to choose a positive, encouraging word or phrase to place on their string. Emphasize creativity in their design (see figures A44.1 and A44.2).

Other words that may be used are: strong, caring, lovable, accomplishment, motivation.

The participants should be given five minutes to create their design. Once they have finished, each participant must share the word or phrase they chose with the group, and use it in a positive sentence. They should also explain any details, designs, colors, and so on they chose to use and why.

210 *Therapeutic Games and Guided Imagery*

Figure A44.1 Example 1

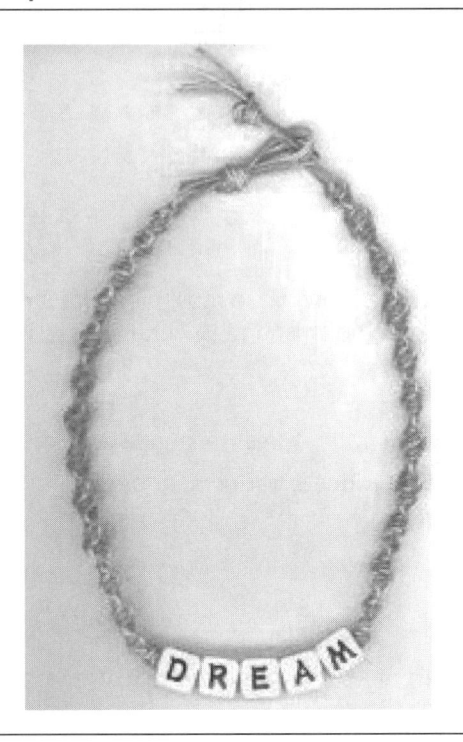

Figure A44.2 Example 2

Follow up with discussion questions that address feelings participants may have had, how their word or phrase relates to them, how they feel when they think of this word, and so on. Individuals may also discuss any differences they had between their accessory and what aspects they like about another participant's creation. Group discussion should also incorporate the provision of synonyms and antonyms of the words or phrases chosen by the participants, to provide context for word use and to increase vocabulary.

Function in Assessment and Treatment

Assessment

This game can provide the facilitator with insight into individuals who struggle to find appropriate words during discussion and can provide those individuals with appropriate options through vocabulary building. It assesses the prevalence of the use of specific words or phrases due to a lack of applicable vocabulary and understanding of word usage.

Treatment

This game helps clients creatively use positive words to emphasize appropriate language skills, allowing its participants to strengthen their ability to use positive language in discussion and during peer interaction. This discussion can create a safe place for self-disclosure, guiding participants toward greater understanding of their perceived situations and connecting personal emotions. Identified struggles or issues may be further addressed in future group or individual sessions.

Personal development comes from within, from self-growth. You can change yourself, lasting change comes from self-development. Personal development is a matter of wanting to change, wanting to be better and getting past self-sabotage. Powerful affirmations can form part of your self-development program. Include a daily affirmation in your personal development plan.

Power comes from believing in your own self. Self-belief is unstoppable. A powerful affirmation for self-belief can unlock that power. Your self-belief is your strength. Just believe in yourself and you will do more that you ever believed you were capable of. An affirmation of self-belief can transform your life forever.

Self-improvement power comes from within. Self-power is unstoppable. A powerful affirmation can unlock that self-empowerment, and empower you to do more that you ever believed you were capable of. An affirmation for self-empowerment can remind you of your personal capability, of your power to cope, to survive and win and come through smiling.

Figure A44.3

Positive Daily Affirmation for Development
Every day I look for new ideas, because new ideas stretch my mind, and it never goes back to its original limit.
Today, I am going to listen. Really listen to what people are saying. I am going to listen to what their clothes are saying, what their voice is saying, what their posture is saying, and especially what they are not saying.
Today I am going to reflect back to everyone what I think they are saying, until I show them that I understand what they are really saying.
Our future is determined by our thoughts, and thoughts are easily changed.
If only you can give of your best today, you can do it for the rest of your life.
People overestimate the changes possible in a week, and underestimate the changes possible in a year.
The positive change you want in your life will not be finished today, but it can start today.
Think about how to make the watch work for you rather than worrying about how the watch works.
Listening is more than not talking.
Today is a great day for investing. Today I am investing in myself, in my body, my mind, my spirit.
Today I will not try to change anybody but myself.
Being certain isn't the same as being right.
Success consists of learning from failure after failure without loss of enthusiasm.
I can learn something from everyone I meet.

Figure A44.4

Positive Daily Affirmation for Self-Belief

I am really quite remarkable once I start believing in myself.

What I can or cannot do is not about my real capability. It is about what I believe about myself. And I believe I have the power to do anything today.

Circumstances do not make us who we are, they only let us find out for ourselves who we really are.

I welcome my weaknesses. Strength grows out of weakness.

I am a loving, special, talented human being, and nothing can change that.

Today I choose to live unconditionally.

Self-respect is doing the right thing even when no one is around to notice.

It's not our abilities or talents or upbringing that determines what we are, it's what we choose to do with them.

Repeating the affirmation leads to belief. Believing that there is a way out creates the way out.

Nothing can stop me from being the best.

I deserve to be happy and successful.

I believe I have something to contribute to the world.

I know what I need to do, and I have the will to do it.

Figure A44.5

Positive Affirmation for Empowerment

I think of my life like paper rolling out of a printer. Today I am going to write some powerful sentences.

Today is another chance to empower myself by doing something I have never tried.

I recognize and accept my talents, skills, abilities, and faults. They are all equally powerful in their own way.

Every human being has four things in varying measures: confidence, love, independence, imagination. These give me my power to choose.

All the breaks I need in life are waiting there right now inside my imagination. And I have power to make them real.

I can because I think I can.

The more they try to pressure me, the more I bounce back. I do it just to annoy them and that empowers me to come back faster and stronger than ever.

There is no such thing as bad weather, only the wrong clothes. I have the power to change.

Blaming someone else is just the same as giving away my power to fix it.

It doesn't matter how long we have had a problem, fixing it once is all it takes.

If I don't like how things are, I empower myself to change them!

Every difficult task is a chance to learn about my own power.

Adversity just makes me stronger. The experience teaches and shapes me, and I feel strangely empowered.

I am unique and special; there has never been anyone else exactly like me. I use each new day to flex my power.

The most valuable thing in my career is my failures. Every failure gives me the power to know myself better.

I will not let what I can't do stop me from doing what I can do.

If you can dream it, you can do it.

I have the power to turn any setback to my advantage.

Power is neutral. It is how you choose to use it, and how you choose to allow others to use theirs that matters.

A45
Overcoming Shame Game
Allison Marek

Items Needed

Markers, crayons, or oil pastels; blank sheet of paper (8½" × 11", any neutral color); four items that have four different tactile sensations (examples: a rock, a piece of soft fabric, sandpaper, Play-Doh); tape or glue

Target Population

Adolescents seeking to overcome shame, low self-esteem, and other issues common in survivors of sexual abuse

Individually or in a group of four to five adolescents

Purpose

To help adolescents recognize and discuss feelings of shame

To assist in identification of self-defeating thinking patterns

To teach the concept of visualization in order to build resilience and the ability to overcome obstacles

Procedure

This game can be utilized when addressing any obstacle a client may be experiencing. If the issue being addressed is about shame, the therapist should discuss the meaning of shame with specific examples prior to the start of this activity.

Ask the clients to tell you about a time that they felt shame. Next, ask them to choose one of the four objects that best represents the source of shame (e.g., a rock, a piece of soft fabric, sandpaper, and Play-Doh). If they do not feel these objects represent their shame, ask them to envision an object that might be a better representation and describe the image. Ask the clients how they feel as they either explore or envision their object or image. Ask how the object reminds the client of something or someone.

Next, take out the drawing materials and the paper. Explain that this is an opportunity to work through the feelings of shame. Ask the clients to draw, trace, or attach the object that represents the shame onto the paper. Then encourage the clients to find a way to overcome, work through, or transform the object that represents their shame. For example, the clients may choose to make the object into something totally different (e.g., turning a rock into a friendly face), draw a soothing environment around the object, or create a path around the object.

Function in Assessment and Treatment

Assessment

Researcher Dr. Brené Brown (2004) defines shame as the "intensely painful feeling or experience of believing we are flawed and therefore unworthy of acceptance and belonging" (15). Children and adolescents often feel shame associated with their experiences of sexual abuse. This exercise can be useful in assessing a child's ability to think abstractly about the concept of shame. The use of this exercise can help in assessing the child's current (and future) coping strategies and the child's level of self-efficacy. It is also important to explore the different ways the child might have already overcome his or her shame.

Treatment

This exercise can be used with children who are facing an internal or external struggle. It provides a concrete way of dealing with the problem through the unique creation of artwork. The word *shame* may be defined differently according to the client's cultural background. Possible therapeutic questions include:

1. You said you felt _____ at the beginning of this session. How are you feeling now?
2. What is a way that you could _____ (use strategy depicted) in real life? What would that look like? (Encourage the client to add a few things on the drawing or artwork just created.)

3. Have you ever felt this way before? When did this happen in the recent past?
4. Now if you would transform your ___ feeling into something positive, what would you do or say?

A46
Peer Influence Exercise
Sergio Cruz

Items Needed

Cause and Effect Board (see Figure A46.1); Action/Behavior and Consequence cards (figure A46.2); markers, colored pencils, crayons

Target Population

Adolescents with behavioral problems in school or with peers

Intended for use with individuals

Purpose

To assess functioning and decision-making patterns

To emphasize acknowledgment, recognition, and identification of consequences of specific behaviors and actions

To aid clients in identifying and recognizing peer influence

To promote the discussion, analysis, and encouragement or discouragement of behavior

To encourage development of healthy boundaries and relationships

Procedure

To begin, ask the adolescent to write or draw something that represents his or her self-image on a full index card. The client can reference unique characteristics, which could include a drawing of a person, objects, words, sentences, and so on. After the adolescent has finished, place the card on the board in the "client" slot. After that, have the adolescent draw or write characteristics of a close friend. When finished, place the card on the "peer" slot.

Next, ask the adolescent to think of some actions or behaviors (i.e. play sports, study, play video games, sell drugs, destroy property, steal, use drugs, etc.) that he has engaged in with a friend or that he has in common with a friend, and select three of the "action/behavior" cards. The client will place each card in a space along the "actions/behaviors" row on the board. Again, have the client consider the possible consequences that could result from these actions/behaviors and choose three appropriate "consequence" cards. You may provide blank index cards for the client to create his or her own cards for either category if the other cards do not apply. Remind the client that some of the actions or behaviors could have the same consequence and he or she may choose to replicate a "consequence" if necessary.

Once the board is complete, process the activity with the adolescent. Ask him or her to tell you about each of the choices made and discuss what feelings the client experienced, and how the experience affected his or her perspective on these choices. Discuss the presence of natural consequences and how to account for them when making decisions.

If the adolescent has chosen all positive actions/behaviors and consequences, discuss the impact of negative selections. You may select and place a new set of negative actions/behaviors on the board and ask the adolescent to choose the consequences. Again, process with the adolescent and help the child identify peer influence and how he or she can resist negative influence and embrace positive influence. Use this opportunity to teach the client about healthy boundaries and healthy relationships.

Function in Assessment and Treatment

Assessment

This exercise provides insight into the adolescent's ability to assess actions, behaviors, and potential consequences. It also aids the adolescent and the professional in conceptualizing the client's thought process and patterns of behavior, as well as assessing the cognitive functioning of the adolescent.

Note: Although establishing relationships with emotional dysregulation and behavioral issues can be difficult, adolescents are still susceptible to peer pressure as they explore their personal identities and roles. This can be used as a support tool but should not be a replacement for treatment for possible trauma or other acute mental disorders.

Treatment

It is essential for adolescents to develop the skills necessary for adulthood. This exercise can help the adolescent develop important skills and is a good introduction to the development of healthy boundaries and healthy relationships. The professional can also teach the adolescent problem-solving techniques that will encourage him or her to resist negative influences and make positive, appropriate decisions. The adolescent is encouraged to acknowledge and recognize that there are consequences to actions and behaviors, and he or she should be able to identify the difference between positive and negative peer influence and personal behavior.

Figure A46.1 Cause and Effect Board

(approx. 14" x 22" or half of a 28" x 22")

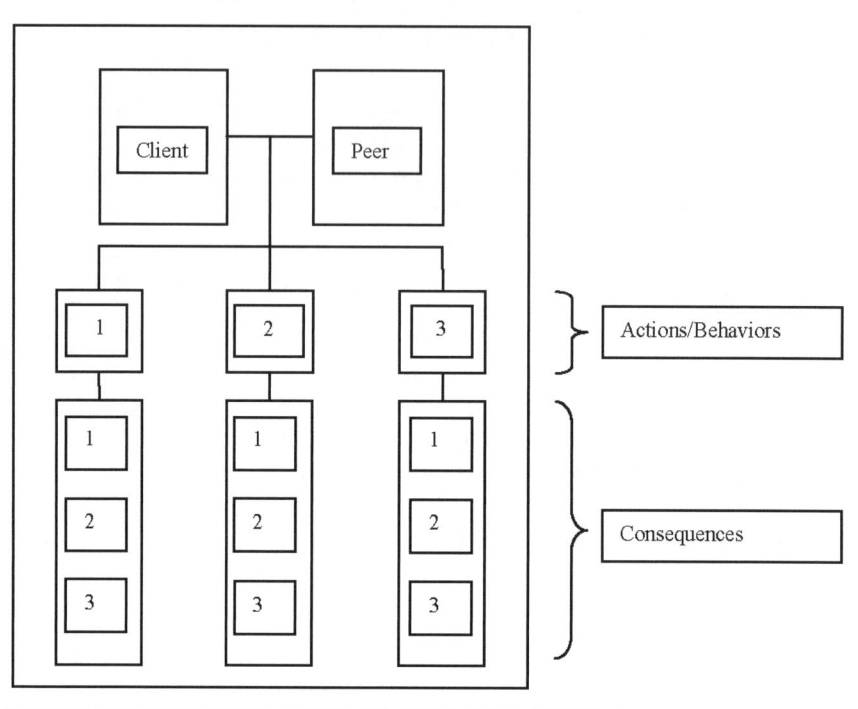

Figure A46.2 "Action/Behavior and Consequences" Cards

(half of an index card)

"Action/Behavior" cards (half of an index card)

| Fighting | Volunteering | Bullying |

"Consequences" cards (another half)

| I will hurt someone | I will feel happy | Mom will be upset |

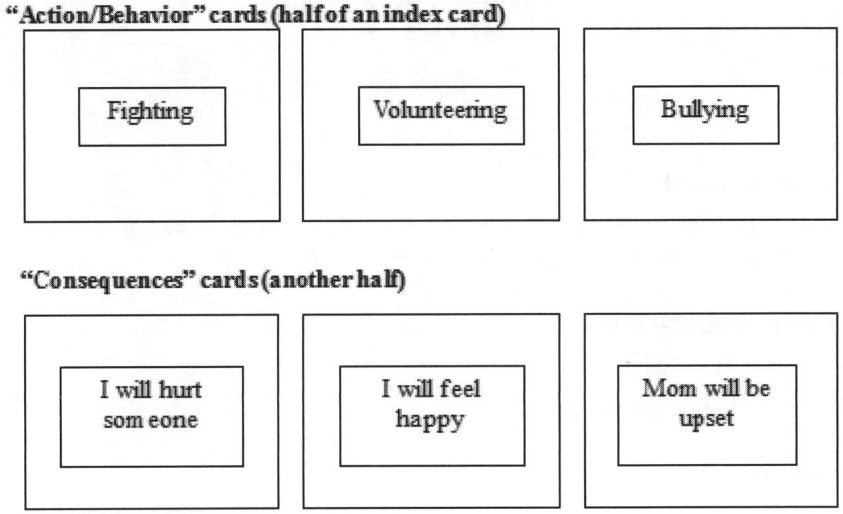

A47
Power List
Anny Ma

Items Needed

House template (see figure A47.1); Power List cards (see figure A47.2); drawing utensils (colored pencils, markers, pens)

Target Population

Children 6+ who have experienced homelessness

Individual or group use

Purpose

To build rapport

To help children identify their strengths and empower them

To share thoughts, feelings, and experiences

Procedure

Prepare the Power List cards, ensuring that each category is represented by a different color card (e.g., Empowerment-green, Problem Identification-blue, etc.). Have the participants sit in a circle with the Power List cards in the middle. Provide each participant with the house template and inform them what each category is. Each participant will take a turn picking a card from the top of one of the six respective Power List piles. Each time the client responds to the card, he or she may color over one straight line on the house. To ensure that clients get an opportunity to respond to each type of question, ask the clients to complete the line using the color of the card they selected. They must answer one question from each category before revisiting a category for the second time. The exercise is complete when the clients have colored over every line on their house.

After completing the activity, ask the participants to draw or color the empty spaces of their house. Have each participant present a completed "home" to the group. Encourage clients to share about the contents they drew or words they added. Additionally, therapeutic questions should be related to possible solutions such as:

1. When you responded to the cards, what thoughts came to your mind? When you were completing your house, what was in your mind?
2. Which part of this game was difficult for you and how did you respond to this difficulty?
3. Tell me a strength that you use or see in this game that is also required for you to solve problems.

Create a new Power List if the game is to be played again with the same group of children or if you would like to focus on other issues.

Function in Assessment and Treatment

Assessment

This activity assesses children's needs and strengths. It helps explore thoughts and feelings about themselves and the systems that have affected their daily lives, such as family and school. Once the difficulties have been identified, interventions would be designed and provided accordingly. Allowing the clients to color and add to their house provides an opportunity for creative expression and may provide insight into the clients' desires and expectations of their home.

Treatment

Through this game, children will be empowered to focus on their strengths and understand their thoughts and feelings. "Building" a house through participation symbolizes hope and home-like feeling. It empowers the clients to believe that lack of a physical home does not diminish their strengths and abilities. The Power List cards foster open expression of thoughts, feelings, and experiences, aiding in the establishment of comfort with the clients' current situation.

Figure A47.1 Home Template

Figure A47.2 Power List

Empowerment	Tell us one of your strengths and briefly describe how it helped you in the past.
	Name one favorite character, such as a superhero, and describe one thing you have in common with this character.
	Tell yourself, "I am a great person."
	Share one thing you did that you think is a great job.
	Share one experience when you helped others to solve their problem.
	Recall one compliment you received and describe how you felt.
	State one thing that can give you hope and explain how you can get it.
	Describe one exciting thing or event that you are looking forward to.
	Name one thing that makes you smile.
	Complete the sentence: I am proud of myself because. . .
Problem Identification	Discuss one incident that bothered you the most and how you dealt with it.
	Describe an embarrassing incident and how you handled it.
	Describe one thing that is bothering someone in your family now.
	If you encounter a problem or difficulty, whom do you go to?
	If you encounter a problem or difficulty, what is the first step you would do?
	Have you ever learned from your problem? Explain how.
	Describe one issue that both you and your peers experience.
	Describe a conflict you have with your parents or caregivers.
Emotions	Identify a positive feeling you had in the past week. How do you know it was a good feeling?
	Identify and discuss a difficult feeling you had in the past week.
	What do you do when you have positive feelings?
	What do you do when you have difficult feelings?
	Name a person you can share positive feelings with. How does this person usually respond to you when you are happy?
	Name a person you can share difficult feelings with. How does this person usually respond to you when you are upset?
	Describe one incident that made you feel positive.
	Describe one incident that made you feel sad.

Figure A47.2 Power List—(continued)

	What have you done to feel positive?
	What could we do to help you feel more positive?
Identity Formation	Describe your race, ethnic background, or culture.
	Describe one thing that makes you feel different from your classmates or friends.
	Describe one feeling about your friends with the same cultural background.
	How do you feel about being with people with a different cultural background?
	Tell us one thing about you that is uniquely different from others.
	Name one thing you would like to change about yourself.
	What changes can make your life better?
	Name one thing you agree on with your parents/caregivers.
	Describe how you feel about your family.
Living Environment and Security	How long do you think you will live/stay at your current place?
	Where do you consider your home to be? Describe it.
	Describe one thing in your current living environment.
	Do you feel safe where you are living/staying?
	Name a place that makes you feel safe.
	Name a person who can make you feel safe. What does this person do or say to make you feel safe?
	What could be done to make you feel safer?
	When you feel scared, what do you usually do?
School Life	What is the best grade you received at school?
	What is your favorite subject at school and why?
	Name a person whom you think can help you with your homework.
	What can you do to improve your grades?
	What do you think others can do to help you improve your grades?
	Name a friend in your school and describe one nice thing about this person.
	Share your experiences about your school in general.
	Share your experiences about your classmates in general.
	Share your experiences about your teachers in general.

A48
Practice Your Limits
Susan Kulbeth

Items Needed

One poster board, 30 note cards to prepare for the (situation, secret, and question) cards (see figures A48.1 and A48.2), chips, a die, rewards (optional)

Target Population

Females, age eight to twelve, in a group setting

Suitable for girls of all socioeconomic backgrounds

The game is not intended to discuss sexual orientation issues

Purpose

To promote discussion and self-evaluation among group members, and to aid in assessment of self-concept and esteem related to boundary issues in girls who have been sexually abused by a relative or another significant adult.

Procedure

Prepare three piles of cards (see examples) and write the instructions on a poster board. In clockwise order, each player rolls the die to get a number, reads its corresponding category from the poster, and then follows the directions for that number. To encourage participation, each player may receive the corresponding number of chips.

The instructions for each category are as follows:

Make sure you announce that all scenarios and situations are make-up cases for discussion only. The game is over when one player has 35 points or chips, or when the discussions addressed some therapeutic contents to facilitate further discussions. At the end of the game, have the children count their chips. The person with the highest number of chips may pick the first reward (rewards such as a journal, key chain, or lip gloss). The other numbers follow in order from most to least. If there is a tie, the die may be rolled again to determine that the higher number will choose first.

Figure A48.1 Examples of Situation and Secret Cards

Situation Cards	Secret Cards
A friend told me this: *"My older sister and her husband are staying with me until they find a place to live. While my sister and mom were out, my brother-in-law, Tom, whom I have always liked, puts his arm around me on the couch while watching TV. He does this often and it feels good that he likes me—only this time his hand dropped down and touched my breast and he did not move it right away. After Tom left for work, I told my sister what happened. She accused me of being jealous of her and asked that I shouldn't have sat with him in the first place. I hate her."* What would I respond to this friend?	Christopher, the cutest boy in school, kissed you today in front of your locker after you picked up your restroom pass. You felt butterflies in your stomach. Though it was quite exciting, it made you somewhat nervous. You didn't go to the restroom but ran back to your classroom. Should you tell anyone about it? What would you tell this person?
My neighbor friend told me this: *"My mom's new boyfriend was staying with us last evening while my mom went to work. We kind of got along well but he came to my room and started cuddling with me. I didn't want him to think that I don't like him but I wasn't really comfortable with him sitting too close on my bed. I told him to leave. I was scared and didn't know if I did it right. I didn't say a word when I saw my mom in the morning. What should I do?"* What would I possibly say to this friend?	You noticed that your best friend is upset. When you ask her about it, she begins to cry and says that her dad comes into her room at night. You really don't know for sure what that may mean. She wouldn't tell you exactly what happened but made you promise not to tell anyone. How would you handle this secret? What would you say to your mom if she asked how everything had been with you and your best friend?
A female friend told me about this: *"My best friend asked me to spend the night with her. I usually have fun when we are together but I really didn't feel like going this time and told her no. She said she would invite someone else if I didn't come. I went. Now I am kind of regretting it. Am I doing it wrong?"* What would I respond to this friend?	Uncle Mark and his kids were staying with your family for the weekend. There is only one bathroom in the house. When you knocked to see if someone was using the bathroom, you heard him saying *"Come on in. I'm in the shower but the curtain is closed. Just use it quickly."* You went in but while you were using the toilet, he opened the curtain and asked if you had ever seen a naked man before. As you were running out of the bathroom, he yelled down the hall that he was only kidding. He later told you not to fuss about it. Should you tell an adult and how?

Figure A48.1 Examples of Situation and Secret Cards—(continued)

A teenage told me about this: *My boyfriend kissed me several times in the past week. He came to my house yesterday and tried to touch my breasts; that made me feel mixed up and I didn't know how to refuse him. I finally told him stop but he told me he loves me and it's okay. When I insisted that it was not okay with me, he finally stopped. I felt torn and don't know what to do now. He must think that I am too conservative. What should I do?* What would I say to this person?	Your best friend found a book about sex from her older sister's drawer and showed it to you. The two of you read it with interest. After reading a section on masturbation, you and your friend decided to try it on your own bodies. It felt alright but made you feel nervous at the same time. You stopped and didn't want to talk about it. Should you tell someone about your feeling? What was it that you should or should not tell?
A 12-year-old male told me this: *"I went to a party Sunday night thinking it was a birthday party. It ended with alcohol tasting and my best friend offered me a toast. I felt that I shouldn't drink but everyone was watching. I didn't want to embarrass my friend and drank a little. I made a funny face after a sip but my friend was laughing very loudly and making fun of me. I felt absolutely embarrassed. What should I tell him now?"* What would I advise?	Your aunt and cousins were visiting from another town. The adults went to dinner and left your older brother and cousin at home with you. While you were home alone with these two boys, they expose themselves to you. You ran to your room and locked the door. They called your name through the door for a minute but then went to watch TV. You stayed in your room for the whole time until the adults came home. What should you tell or not tell? How would you tell if you decided to tell your mom?
A 14-year-old female told me this: *"My boyfriend tried to kiss me in front of his friends. I told him no and really didn't want to be with him any longer. I've been going out with him for two weeks although I've known him for a year. I didn't like the way he acted when it came to being sexual with me. I didn't want to hurt his feelings but what could I say to him about me not wanting to be his girlfriend anymore?"* What would I respond to her?	A classmate missed school for a week. Everyone in your class talked about her being sexual to boys. When she came back, she told you that she was sexually molested by her dad and the police came to take her away for a few days. She told you not to tell anyone about it because everything was alright now for she told the police that she was just kidding. She told you not to come to her house and you should keep this a secret. What would you do next?
Add other situation here	Add another secret here

Function in Assessment and Treatment

Assessment

This game can be used in an individual session to learn about a child's self-concept through dialogue about situations relating to boundaries. It can also provide insight into the child's perception of boundary violation, and the possibility that the female child kept it a secret because she did not realize it was not her fault.

Treatment

This game can be used to identify concrete strategies for coping with boundary issues. The therapist can ask follow-up questions based on the answers or emotional responses of the group members toward the answers from the scenarios. It also provides an opportunity to explore negative thinking patterns about self-blame. After these patterns are identified and reactions discussed, the therapist and group members can discuss how to use their awareness of these negative patterns for future reference in setting and maintaining healthy boundaries.

Figure A48.2 Examples of Question Cards

Name a time when it is hard to maintain boundaries with your friends or family.	How do you know when you should set a physical boundary from your boyfriend?
Name a personal boundary.	Name a personal limit.
When is it unacceptable for someone to cross your boundaries?	What can you say to keep someone from crossing your personal boundaries?
Who should you tell when your secret is making you upset?	Where would you go when you want to have a quiet time for yourself?
What would be a first step to set limits for yourself?	When do you know you need to set limits for yourself?
Who would agree with you about setting limits?	How do you feel when someone broke into your boundary without asking?
What would you do when you were told that someone's boundary had been violated?	Who should know if you are getting into trouble?
How do you tell your parents about your personal problems?	What is a secret?
Ask a question about boundary setting.	Ask a question about setting limits.
Ask a question about secrets.	Ask a question about abuse.
Ask any question about being healthy.	Ask any question about friendship.

A49
Puppet Communications
Monit Cheung

Items Needed

Finger puppets or animal puppets (lion, lamb, angel, bird, pig, and other animals with hands and feet)

Target Population

Children, adolescents, and adults who need to use a medium to project feelings

Children who are suspected of being sexually abused

Individual therapy

Purpose

Build rapport and decrease defensiveness

Assist in safe disclosure and identification of secrets

Use drama to build self-esteem

Discuss conflict

Procedure

Invite the client to talk using the puppets as the means of communication. There are a number of ways in which puppets can be used to elicit a different type of information or response. You may start with the client acting out a drama-like session using puppets to role play the skits provided in the appendix. You then respond to each of the client's skits. The client can respond to you or guess what the puppet is trying to do in the skit (see figure A49.1 for suggestions).

Function in Assessment and Treatment

Assessment

A puppet is a means of communication using a third person to assist with the assessment process. Clients feel safe to talk about difficult experiences or feelings by projecting them through the puppets. This allows you to gather more information about the client's history and current situation. It also assists in clarifying with the client for the purpose of the interaction and the nature of the helping relationship.

Treatment

Indirect communication through the puppets encourages clients to talk about issues that may have been "off limits" but still preserving a safe distance. Using puppets as a way to communicate can build trust between the therapist and client, and illustrate to the client that the therapist is there to listen and help the client deal with uncomfortable feelings.

Assuming the client chooses "Rabbit" and the therapist chooses "Lion" as the puppet

Note: Change the puppet's gender in the skit before asking the client to role play, when appropriate.

Figure A49.1 Appendix: Puppet Skits

Free Association	Rabbit said, "Who are you?"	I am ___. What comes to your mind when you see Rabbit? What is special about Rabbit?
Break Defenses	Rabbit said, "I'm not feeling well."	Do you know what made him or her feel this way?
Reflect Feelings	Rabbit said, "My name is Lex. I have a story to tell. Once upon a time (story content) . . . and I feel relieved."	Have you ever felt this way before? Do you have this feeling now?
Validate Feelings	Lex asked, "Can you do something to make me feel better?"	What did you do to make Lex believe I can help?
Label Feelings	Rabbit said, "I have a problem."	Do you know what Rabbit would say to his best friend Lion about this problem?
Find a Helper	The bad guys are gone now and Lion is here to help.	Lion told Rabbit, "It's okay to feel overwhelmed but you must talk about it to feel better. We are here to help."
Disclose Secrets	I am here with a friend, Rabbit, who is a good listener. Rabbit said, "Hello! I am here to listen."	Rabbit is listening. You are now feeling better because you will tell me what's been bothering you.
Encourage Expression	Here is Rabbit who is willing to share a secret with you.	How about you ask Rabbit about what's going on? Lion wants to hear about it.
Reflect Motives	Rabbit asked, "Tell me what you want."	I want to ask you what you want. Lion, what would Rabbit tell you about ___ (client)?
Identify Wants	You're the teacher now. Can you teach Rabbit what he can get from seeing a counselor?	I am the teacher and Lion is the counselor now. Lion, you are good at listening. Lion now asked you, "What do you want to get from a counselor?"
Empower the Client	Here is Rabbit; he is going to tell his people that it is important to be brave.	Can you tell me what "brave" means to you? Have you ever done something brave?
Highlight Strengths	Rabbit has solved his problem.	Lion said, "I like how you did it. I can do it too." Take Lion and repeat what he just said.
Analyze Conflict	Rabbit said, "I don't like it!" Lion said: "I like it!"	How does it feel to have a conflict? It's okay to have mixed feelings. Tell me more about it. Let's work on it together.

A50
Puzzle Pieces
Antonella Lazzaro

Items Needed

One puzzle stencil for each child (figure A50.1 for young children for easy cutting; figure A50.2 for adolescents); one sheet of colored construction paper; scissors; crayons, colored pencils, or markers

Target Population

Children or adolescents that are experiencing anxiety, or have been diagnosed with adjustment disorder, ADHD, or autism

Procedure

This exercise begins with a focus on "happy thoughts." Encourage the child to recall memories, people, places, or things that made him or her feel happy and relaxed. When the child has recalled his or her "happy thought," have the child draw a picture about this "happy thought" using the stencil (face down so the lines are not visible) and as many colors as he or she wishes. Encourage the client to fill in the entire stencil and leave no empty spaces. When the child is finished, ask him or her to tell a story about the drawing.

After telling the story, the child cuts the puzzle out according to the stencil. Ask the child to put the pieces together against a piece of construction paper. Once the puzzle pieces are formed as a whole, remove one piece of the puzzle, exposing the construction paper beneath it. At this point, observe the child's reaction to this maneuver. Ask the child how this missing piece affects the rest of his or her "happy thought" and how it may make things different. Encourage the child to use coloring utensils to represent a place he or she would like to go in place of the absent puzzle piece. Inform the child that he or she does not have to draw the same thing in its place, but that it is possible that he or she could draw something different or leave it untouched. Then, encourage the child to explain what may have led him or her to make that choice. Be sure to validate constructive choices and feelings.

Wrap up the exercise by presenting the child with the puzzle piece that was previously removed and explain that while some things in life may change or disappear, a piece of it will always remain (with a happy thought). Suggest that the child carry this piece as a reminder for when times are tough and when he or she may feel overwhelmed while making decisions.

Function in Assessment and Treatment

Assessment

This is an assessment tool utilizing the concept of cognitive restructuring. As the child experiences a happy memory being altered or changed, the child is encouraged to articulate his or her feelings and to explore alternatives to putting the puzzle (or "happy thought") back together. The child is presented with an opportunity to experience abrupt change and test his or her coping mechanisms in a safe environment.

Treatment

This exercise can be therapeutic in the sense that children and adolescents may not have the natural inclination to express their feelings. This activity facilitates creativity without being too rigid or conforming. By presenting the child with a missing puzzle piece, this allows for free association. The child can then free associate something through the missing piece.

Therapeutic questions may include:

1. What title would you give to your first drawing? What title would you give to the second? Tell me what is in it.
2. Identify the way you felt when the puzzle was first completed and then again after it was finished.
3. Did you learn something about yourself from this?
4. How does thinking of this happy thought help you in the future?
5. What would you do with this puzzle, or a piece of the puzzle, if you were to give it to someone special? What would you say?

Figure A50.1 Puzzle Stencil for Children

238 *Therapeutic Games and Guided Imagery*

Figure A50.2 Puzzle Stencil for Adolescents

A51
Rainbow Questions
Diana Scroggins

Items Needed

Approximately 20 3" × 5" note cards; game card sheets (see figure A51.1); prize

Target Population

Adolescents, ages 13 to 18, who identify as GLBTQ (gay, lesbian, bisexual, transgender, queer/questioning)

Intended for use with groups of two to five participants

Purpose

To build rapport and encourage discussion and openness

To create a sense of community among adolescents

To initiate exploration of identity and self

Procedure

Each game card sheet contains a rainbow drawing on one side (or a more colorful version of a similar image) and, on the other side, a quote regarding identity and sexual orientation from famous and notable people, along with relevant therapeutic questions. The object of the game is to get rid of all of the cards in your hand by answering the question on each card. A small prize or privilege may be awarded to entice all adolescents to participate.

To begin, think of a number from one to ten and have the players try to guess what the number is; whoever is closest to your number will begin the game. Play will continue in a clockwise direction. Each participant is dealt three cards. On their turn, players must either choose to answer the question on one of the cards they were dealt or they may draw cards from the remaining deck until they draw a question they would like to answer (maximum of two draws). Players can discard their cards only when they have answered the question on that card. After each player's turn, encourage all players to share their answers with the group as well.

Rainbow cards (see figure A51.2) allow players to "steal" another participant's card and answer the question on the "stolen" card. Rainbow cards may be excluded from the deck if time or place demands it.

Function in Assessment and Treatment

Assessment

This game may be used to assess adolescents' comfort level with discussing GLBTQ issues. It can also be used to assess issues of self-esteem, identity, and social support.

Treatment

This game allows GLBTQ-identified adolescents to share their experiences with others who may have similar experiences and gain peer support and encouragement. It provides a safe environment in which they can freely express emotions that they may not be able to express in other situations.

Figure A51.1 Quote/Question Cards

Quote	Question(s)
"Every gay and lesbian person who has been lucky enough to survive the turmoil of growing up is a survivor. Survivors always have an obligation to those who will face the same challenges."—Bob Paris	In what ways are you a survivor? Do you agree that survivors have an obligation to give back? Who has helped you? What do you do (or might you do in the future) to give back?
"Never be bullied into silence. Never allow yourself to be made a victim. Accept no one's definition of your life; define yourself."—Harvey Fierstein	How do you define yourself? How do you protect yourself from being bullied?
"Deep down, my mom had long suspected I was gay . . . Much of her anger and hurt came from her sense of betrayal that she was the last to be told."—Chastity Bono	Who have you come out to? What were their reactions?
"Everybody's journey is individual. If you fall in love with a boy, you fall in love with a boy. The fact that many Americans consider it a disease says more about them than it does about homosexuality."—James Baldwin	How has your journey been unique? Share one unique aspect of your life (or your family life).
"Labels are for filing. Labels are for clothing. Labels are not for people."—Martina Navratilova	What labels have people given you? Do you agree with them? What labels do you embrace, and which ones do you reject? Do you agree that labels are not for people?
"I just wish more of my fellow queers would come out sometimes. It's nice out here, you know?"—Elton John	What is nice about being out? If you're not out, what do you imagine would be nice about being out? What's not nice about being out?
"One of the first things I think young people, especially nowadays, should learn is how to see for yourself and listen for yourself and think for yourself."—Malcom X	How do you think for yourself and form your own opinions? Whose opinions matter to you?
"Sometimes I feel discriminated against, but it does not make me angry. It merely astonishes me. How can they deny themselves the pleasure of my company? It's beyond me."—Zora Neale Hurston	Has anyone ever discriminated against you because of your orientation? What did they miss out on because of that discrimination?

Figure A51.1 Quote/Question Cards—(continued)

"Homosexuality is a discovery, not a choice or a sin."—Vangie Jones	How did you "discover" your homosexuality (or bisexuality, or transgenderism)? What kind of discovery is it?
"No matter how far in or out of the closet you are, you still have a next step."—Unknown	What is your next step? What is keeping you from doing it?
"While many minority groups are the target for prejudice . . . and discrimination . . . in our society, few persons face this hostility without the support and acceptance of their family as do many gay, lesbian, and bisexual youth."—Virginia Uribe and Karen Harbeck	In what ways has your family been supportive? In what ways have they not? If you have not come out to your family, how do you imagine they may or may not be supportive?
"There came a time when the risk to remain tight in the bud was more painful than the risk it took to blossom."—Anaïs Nin	What risks did you take when you came out? What risks did you face by staying in the closet?
"Gay friendships often create an alternative to family, a link more compelling than blood."—David Bergman	Who are some of your closest GLBTQ friends? What makes these relationships different or stronger than other friendships?
"It is always the same: once you are liberated, you are forced to ask who you are."—Jean Baudrillard	How did your image change after you came out? What kind of change made you feel liberated/free?
"Before you criticize queens, fairies, or someone who acts 'too queer,' consider where we'd be without them."—Kenneth Hanes	Who do you consider some of the most influential GLBTQ people? Which GLBTQ people have touched your life, directly or indirectly? In what way?

Figure A51.2 Rainbow Image for Game Cards

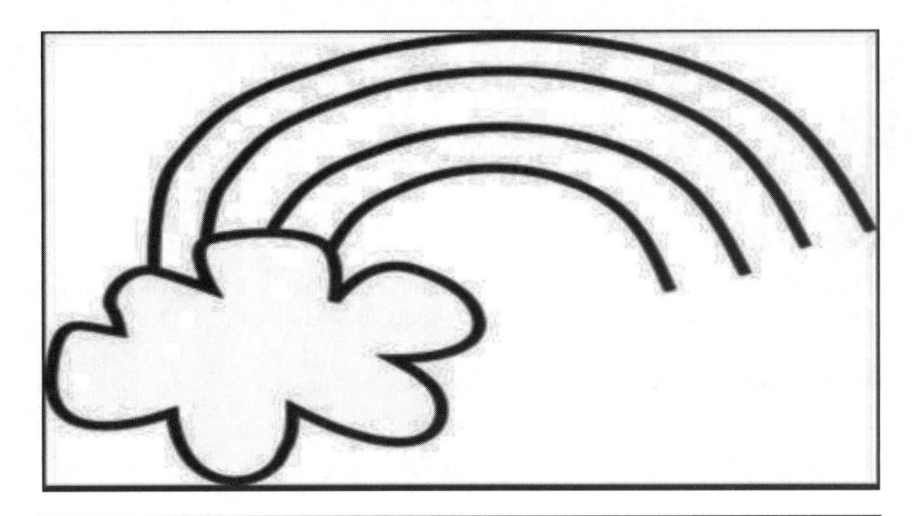

A52
Safe House, Safe Space
Ashleigh Scinta

Items Needed

This game requires two to three large pieces of blank paper, markers or crayons, and about ten small stuffed animals or small plastic dolls.

Target Population

Children who have witnessed domestic violence

Children who have been victims of sexual abuse or other forms of child maltreatment

Siblings of children who have experienced abuse or other forms of trauma

Purpose

Process fears and anxieties related to the exposure to various types of trauma

Assist children to develop a safety plan

Identify safe people and places

Develop healthy coping strategies

Help children to feel empowered and safe

Procedure

Ask the child to select the crayons or markers that he or she would like to use to draw his or her house. Instruct the child to draw a picture of his or her house on a piece of paper. Instruct the child to draw security measures that they would like to have to keep themselves safe in their home; these can be concrete tools or imaginary figures (e.g., guard dog, lock/key, fence, moat, dragon, etc.).

Ask the child to look at the stuffed animals or dolls, and identify a role for each (e.g., family members, friends, or other people who would come to their home). Ask the child to place those who are allowed to enter the house on top of the "house" drawing, and then place those who are not allowed to enter the house outside of the security measures.

Process with the child who these people are. Discuss steps with the child in how to stay safe from individuals who have caused them harm. If this individual no longer has access to the child, discuss what has kept this person away (e.g., how protective orders work, what is a jail, who is a protector, etc.). Talk about the caregiving roles of some of the individuals on the "stay in" list. Role play what to say to show appreciation of these protective or caring individuals.

Ask the child to select markers or crayons to draw a room where he or she feels the safest in the house on a second sheet of paper. Ask the child what this room is (e.g., bedroom, game room, living room, etc.). Instruct the child to draw all the things that make him or her feel safe and happy inside this room (e.g., stuffed animals, favorite toys, family pets, or specific feelings).

Ask the child to describe how these items in or outside of the room can help them feel safe. Ask the child when he or she feels anxious and what he or she usually does to feel safe or calm. Discuss and validate these strategies. Suggest additional coping strategies. Facilitate the discussion with the child and the caregiver about these strategies.

Function in Assessment and Treatment

Assessment

This game aims, particularly with children who have witnessed domestic violence and victims of child maltreatment, to reduce anxiety and fear related to trauma. The game explores people, spaces and places, and strategies to decrease anxiety and fear, and increase feelings of safety and control. Additionally, it identifies people who make the child feel unsafe and strategies or information to allay the child's concerns about these individuals.

Treatment

This game helps children to deal with feelings of fear and anxiety related to traumatic experiences. It also helps them to develop healthy coping strategies to enhance a sense of safety and control over their environment. It provides them with an opportunity to share their experiences, identify the individuals who have evoked feelings of fear and anxiety, and appreciate the individuals who help them alleviate these feelings. It also helps them develop safety plans, healthy coping strategies, and safe places and spaces to combat the negative feelings associated with the trauma. This game can help facilitate discussions with caregivers to enhance their understanding and enlist their support in creating safe environments for the child.

Therapeutic questions may include:

1. Who is allowed inside the house? What would you say to this person to thank him or her for being nice to you?
2. Who is not allowed inside the house?
   a. What has happened that makes you want to keep this person out?
   b. How do you feel about this person?
   c. What types of feelings do you have when you are or were around this person?
3. What room do you feel the safest in your house? Tell me more about this room.
4. What would you like to have in this room to help you feel calm, safe, or happy?
5. What is a bad feeling? Anxious? Scared? Upset? Tell me more about it.
6. Who would you talk to if you felt scared, anxious, or upset?
   a. What would you tell this person about your safety plan and safe place?
   b. How could this person help you feel safer?
   c. What would you do to feel happier?

A53
Sharing Your Heart
Casey Williams Hedges

Items Needed

Markers; pencils; scissors; magazine clippings; "Sharing Your Heart" stencil (figure A53.1)

Target Population

Youth in child protective service (CPS) custody

Youth who have been abused or neglected

Youth receiving treatment for issues concerning their self-image

Purpose

To encourage appropriate self-disclosure and trust building

To identify self-image, or perception of self-image defined by others

To recognize differences between the two viewpoints

To assess client functioning

Procedure

Give the "Sharing Your Heart" sheet (figure A53.1) to the client, and ask him or her to cut out the stencil along the edges. Fold the heart along the two dotted lines. Once folded, the two outside flaps should cover the heart to form one heart.

Provide a variety of markers, magazines, and crayons for the client to decorate the heart. First, close the flaps and ask the client to decorate the outside of the heart with a theme such as "How other people view me." Encourage the client to determine how to decorate the heart by using magazine parts to make a collage, drawing pictures, or writing words. To encourage communication after decorating the front of the heart, ask follow-up questions such as:

1. How was it to identify different views about you from other people?
2. How do you feel about how this part of your heart looks?

3. What views do people have of you that make you feel good about yourself? What about those views that make you not feel good?
4. Choose one item to represent the way you want others to view you. What does it mean to you?

Once these questions have been answered and processed, continue on to the next part of the activity. Ask the client to open the flaps and decorate the inside of the heart with the theme: "How I view myself." To encourage self-disclosure, follow-up questions may include:

1. How does it feel to find things to represent yourself?
2. How do you like the way the inside of your heart looks?
3. Pretending you were looking at this heart, but didn't know anything about the person who created it, what would you say to this person about your impression?
4. If you could choose only one item to represent you, which item would it be? What does this item mean?
5. Was there anything not on this heart that you now wish you could have included?

To help the client connect the relationship between both sides of the heart, the following discussion questions may be used:

1. Looking at the outside of the heart, how do you feel about what it says about you? How do you feel about the inside?
2. Name one similarity and one difference between the inside and the outside of your heart.
3. What is the most important item you placed on the outside of your heart? The inside?
4. Was it easier to create one side over the other? If so, which one and why?
5. Which side was more difficult for you to talk about?
6. After completing this activity, what did you discover about yourself that you had not noticed before?

Function in Assessment and Treatment
Assessment
This activity can be used to explore a range of issues experienced by children in child protective service custody, since they are often experiencing very tumultuous transitions. Often, the removal from home into placements

results in a skewed self-image and negative perceptions from society and peers. By providing the client the opportunity to explore both of these angles, the client will gain a better understanding of his or her identity within the context of the current situation.

Treatment

Clients could engage in an exchange of ideas by sharing their creations. The session can serve as an arena in which clients are able to develop trust as they share sensitive materials. When using this activity with younger clients, the therapist may assess self-image and areas that may need support. For adolescent clients, this activity provides an opportunity to self-identify and assess feelings about their identity and current situation. This may also help them gauge their readiness for a more independent life. By incorporating the creative expression of decorating the hearts with the verbal observations, the session will foster a sense of self and self-worth.

250 *Therapeutic Games and Guided Imagery*

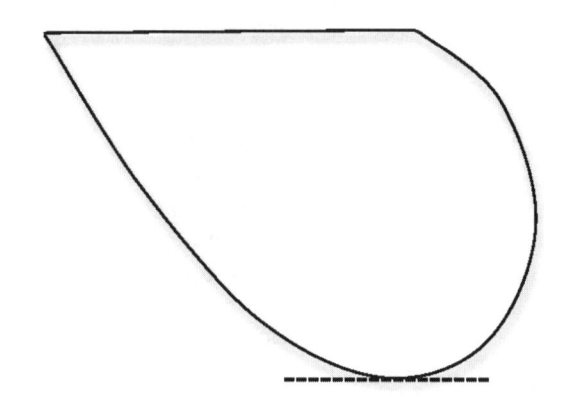

Figure A53.1 "Sharing Your Heart" Stencils

Figure A53.1 "Sharing Your Heart" Stencils—(continued)

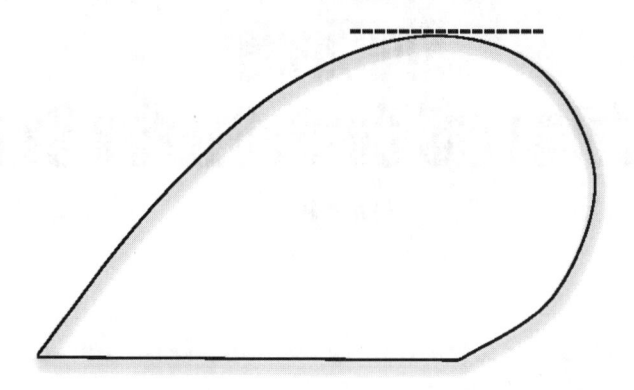

A54
SimCircle
(Simulation and Circle-Building Game)
Agnes Ho

Items Needed

Different colors of construction paper; scissors; poster with rules (figure A54.2); cards with instructions (figure A54.3)

Target Population

Children or adolescents who have behavioral or conduct disorders

Intended for use with groups

Purpose

To serve as an ice-breaker

To identify participants' strengths

To understand and assess participants' willingness and resistance towards rules and instructions

To promote self-directed thinking about following rules and instructions

Procedure

Prior to the session, cut out varying sizes of circles from the construction paper so that every participant has one circle. You may also choose to have each participant cut out a circle at the beginning of the session. The circles should be placed in a large ring and an instruction card should be placed face down on each circle.

To play the game, have the participants stand on the outside of the circle, or in front of a circle and instruction card (figure A54.1). Before playing, introduce the rules of the game (figure A54.2) and inform players that once the music begins, they will walk around the circle until the music stops. Once the music stops, everyone must find a circle to stand on. When everyone has found a circle, participants will read the instruction card on the circle (figure A54.3), replace it (face down), and complete the required action until the music begins again. Continue this process for as many rounds as desired.

Figure A54.1 Participants Standing in Circle

To intensify the game, you may also remove one circle at a time, making the game more competitive. The player who does not find a circle, when the music stops, will be out of the game but serve as an observer until the next round. Each time when the music stops, a circle will be removed. The game ends when only one circle remains. Follow-up discussion questions may include:

1. What made you choose a particular circle?
2. Which circle was the hardest to stand on? Explain.
3. Which circle did you like the best? Explain.
4. How did you feel when you were outside the circle?
5. Were the rules easy to follow? Explain.
6. What rules did you like? What rules did you dislike?
7. Were there any rules that you did not want to follow or chose not to follow?

Function in Assessment and Treatment

Assessment

Through fun, interactive instructions, this activity encourages the participants to follow specific rules. The facilitator observes individuals' reactions and willingness or resistance to following the rules and instructions, in order to gauge all participants' strengths, potential for improvement, and progress throughout the game. It is important to be aware that an individual's response to rules and instructions may differ between engaging them in a group setting vs. an individual session. Responses to the discussion questions may also provide insight into this individual's perceptions of rules.

Treatment

This activity applies a strengths perspective to help the participants realize their ability to obey rules and instructions. By playing the game, the players may become more comfortable following instructions, and subconsciously develop self-directed thoughts towards obeying rules. The use of a group setting may also encourage increased participation and self-directed thinking as the players observe peer participation in the game. Therapeutic questions may include:

1. How do you feel about rules?
2. What makes you follow rules?
3. What would make you choose not to follow rules?
4. What are some "everyday" rules that you like or don't like?

5. What would you do when you are given rules that you don't like? How would you feel if you must obey them?
6. What are some of the consequences of not following the rules?
7. How do you feel when you have to face consequences?
8. How have other people (parents, teaches, friends, etc.) reacted or felt when you did not follow their rules?
9. Who do you talk to when you are upset or in trouble for not following the rules?

Figure A54.2 Rules of the Game

RULES

1. You must follow all of the rules on this poster.
2. When the music stops you must find a circle to stand on.
3. You must read the instruction card on the circle.
4. You must leave each card face down on the circle after you have read it.
5. After you read the card, follow the instructions on the card and continue the instructed action until the music starts again.
6. Do not push others.
7. Be polite.
8. ENJOY!!

Figure A54.3 Instruction Cards

Stand on one leg	Stand on one leg with one hand on top of your head	Stand on one leg with both hands on top of your head	Stand on right leg and jump up and down	Stand on left leg and jump up and down
Close one eye	Clap your hands	Keep smiling	Sit down and then stand up	Sing a song
Stay in the circle and receive a piece of candy!	Say "hello" continuously	Tell everyone your name	Jump inside the circle	Tap your right foot and then your left foot
Put your left hand on your right ear and put your right hand on your nose	Put your right hand on your left ear and put your left hand on your nose	Put a book on top of your head	Make a funny face	Open and shut your mouth

A55
Smiling Face
Lai-man Ada Yip

Items Needed

Jumping frogs (fold them or buy them) (see figure A55.1); handmade pool (see figure A55.2); different colors of smiling faces (red, orange, yellow, green, blue, purple, white, etc.) (see figure A55.3); crayons; colored pencils; question cards (figure A55.4); coping cards (figures A55.5 to A55.7)

Target Population

Children or adolescents with issues in controlling anger

Can be used individually or in small groups (two to three members)

Purpose

To encourage the expression of feelings

To help identify feelings other than anger

To provide clients with options for anger management, including the use of visual materials.

Procedure

Give each participant a jumping frog. Show participants how to tap the frog to make it jump. Ask participants to take turns making the frog "jump" into the handmade pool.

Clinician will watch to see whose frog jumps into the pool first, second, and so on. This will determine who goes first, second and so on. In an individual session, the therapist and client will both "jump" the frog into the pool or let the client go first. The client will select a question card and answer the questions on that card while the other participants, and therapist, listen to the answer (figure A55.4). The next participant will also select a card and answer the questions. This will continue until each member has answered a card. Have the frogs "jump" into the pool again, shuffle the cards, and repeat the process. Once each participant has answered two or three questions, ask the group to use three "coping cards" to talk about other ways to manage anger. Follow the instructions on "coping cards" accordingly. Each participant will have a smiling face with a favorite scene in it. Ask participants to share their "happy" scenes and talk about how the color and scene make them feel.

Encourage participants to think about the smiling face whenever they feel angry, or are faced by a scenario or an environment which causes them to feel they are about to lose control of their anger.

Function in Assessment and Treatment

Assessment

This game helps assess what children and adolescents have done to control their anger. Debrief with the children about whether their anger control strategy is appropriate or not. Explore feelings by asking the clients to contribute questions to add to the question cards.

Treatment

This game helps children and adolescents to control anger by using visual materials, including colors and a safe scene or place. It helps them to explore the meanings of their feelings as well as to find appropriate ways to express how they feel when they are angry. Participants can practice the use of the smiling face to control anger during the part when feelings are shared. It provides an opportunity for them to use the smiling face for maintaining self-control.

This game can be modified to address other emotions such as stress management, frustration, or depression.

Figure A55.1 Jumping Frog

Figure A55.2 Handmade Pool

262 *Therapeutic Games and Guided Imagery*

Figure A55.3 Smiling Face

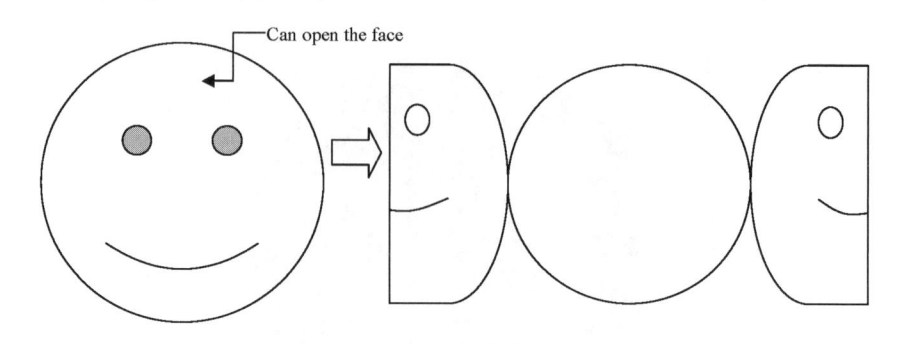

Figure A55.4 Question Cards

1. How would you respond when someone made you feel uncomfortable?

2. How do people you know usually act when they are angry?

3. What would you say when you start feeling angry?

4. What would you think about when you are angry?

5. What music would you listen to when you are angry?

6. Who would you talk to when you are angry?

7. Share one event/issue/experience that made you angry.

Figure A55.5 Card 1

Card 1

1. What is your favorite color?
2. How does the color make you feel when you are angry?

Pick up your favorite color smiling face

Figure A55.6 Card 2

Card 2

1. What is your favorite scene/place?
2. How does the scene/place make you feel when you start to feel angry?

Draw your favorite scene/place inside the smiling face

Figure A55.7 Card 3

Card 3

1. Share one past experience that you got into anger.
2. What did you do to control your anger?
3. Look at the smiling face with the scene/place inside.
4. How would this scene make you feel if you are angry?
5. What did you learn from other players?

A56
Snapshots for Moods
Ada Cheung

Items Needed

A piece of paper with a piece of photo film (figure A56.1); pens, pencils, crayons, or markers

Target Population

Children age five and up, adolescents and adults, with mood swings

Individuals or groups of four to six; including their family members in family therapy

Purpose

To assess the client's current mood

To identify significant memories and the emotions associated with the memories

To identify coping strategies

Procedure

Explain that memories are parts of our lives, and our previous experiences have significant ways of impacting our thoughts and actions in certain situations. Present the client with the photo film paper. Encourage the client to imagine that he or she has a camera inside his or her head. Ask the client to draw four images that frequently pop up in his or her head. Encourage the client to take time to complete the four images, then discuss and explore each of the images with the client. Remind them that there is no right or wrong image, and encourage the client to draw the first few things that come to his or her mind. Put a date on the drawing and ask the client to determine a theme for it.

Function in Assessment and Treatment

Assessment

This exercise helps assess the client's current mood. The images that come to mind at the moment tend to reflect how the client is feeling at the moment or bad memories that affect his or her daily life. It helps the client talk about the people in these images and the feelings associated with his or her thoughts. This exercise also provides an opportunity for the client to reflect and visualize his or her current mood through images or words.

Treatment

This exercise helps clients express feelings and thoughts associated with their past issues, experiences, and events. The use of a date on it helps the clients process different thoughts disclosed in a later session that is associated with the same memory. It will help clients understand the importance of focusing on the positive aspects in life. Clients can later be educated how to change their "frame" of mind and reprocess the past from a more positive angle.

Figure A56.1 Photo Film Paper

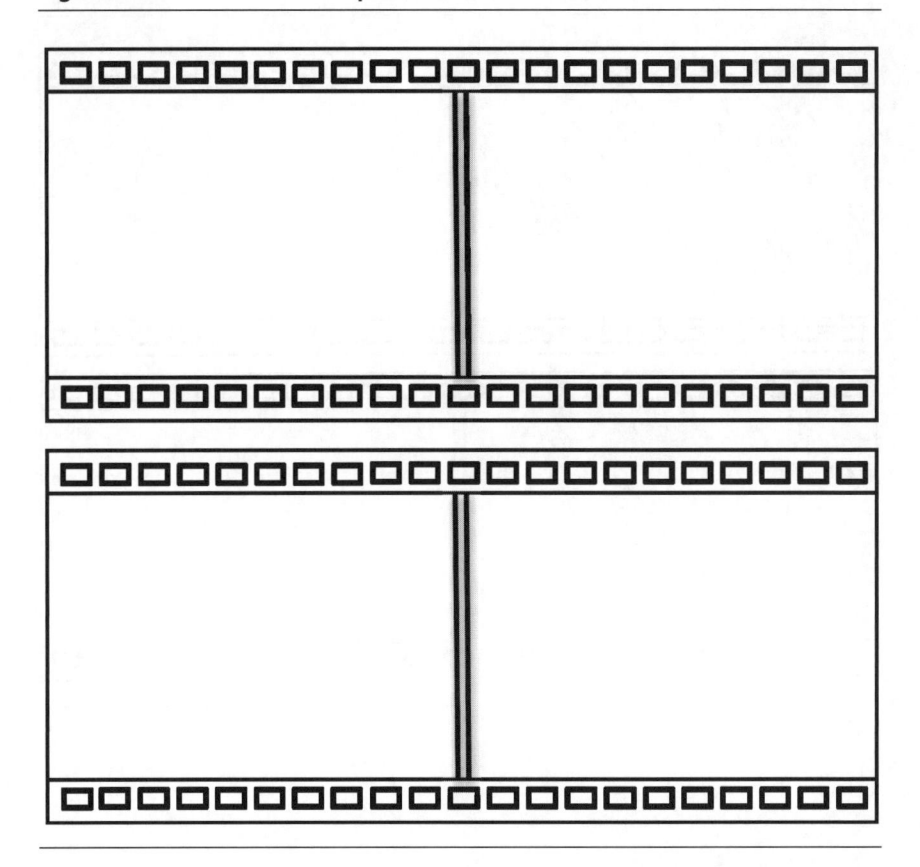

Figure A56.2 Example: Negative Feelings

Figure A56.3 Example: Positive Aspects of Family Life

A57
Strength Flower
Ada Cheung

Items Needed

A piece of paper with the Strength Flower (figure A57.1); pens, pencils, crayons, or markers

Target Population

Adolescent or adult who has low self-esteem and poor self-image

This exercise is designed for a group of six to eight people who have been in contact with each other for at least three to four times. Groups can be comprised of family members or non-related individuals who share something in common. It can also be used in a school or community setting with classmates or members of a sport team.

Purpose

To appreciate own strengths and the strengths of others

To help the participants find appropriate ways to accept compliments

Procedure

Explain to the group that everyone has his or her own strengths and everyone is special. Often, people overlook their strengths or focus only on weaknesses. When this happens, they tend to experience lower self-esteem and poor self-image. Also, it may be hard for them to accept compliments. By identifying both weaknesses and strengths, clients can help improve self-esteem and self-image. Recognizing strengths of others can help clients build empathy skills and practice how to accept compliments from others.

Have the group members sit in a circle. Present each member with a piece of paper (figure A57.1). First, ask each client to put his or her name inside the circle. Then ask each client to pass the paper to the right. In one minute's time, ask each member to draw a petal next to the circle which will eventually form a flower, and write a positive word inside the petal to describe the strength of that group member whose name is written inside the circle. If the member wants to describe two or more strengths, he or she can add as many petals as desired. Advise the group to write any compliment anyone would like to hear even though they do not know this person well. After drawing and writing, pass the paper to the right until each member receives his or her own flower back. Then ask each member to add one more petal and write a self-assessed strength on it. You will invite each member to choose one strength and take turns to read it aloud.

Function in Assessment and Treatment

Assessment

This exercise helps the therapist to observe how clients use the strengths of others to become their own, and how they receive and use positive words in this process. During the assessing process, it is important to encourage each client to contribute to building group bonding and focus on the strengths and uniqueness of other members.

Treatment

This exercise helps clients process how hard it has been for them to respond to compliments and explores their typical reactions to greetings and compliments such as "How are you" or "You look beautiful today." Clients are encouraged to talk about their feelings toward being praised, with a focus on their good qualities that can be used to deal with adversity. Clients are recommended to keep this Strength Flower and look at it when they have self-doubts or are feeling negative about themselves.

Members may practice alternative ways to accept compliments during this exercise. The therapist may pair up the participants and ask them to take turns to read one strength from the other person's flower and the other person then practices from one of these responses for each compliment:

"Thank you very much."

"I noticed this strength too."

"I like to hear you saying this to me."

"I am proud of having this strength."

"I am happy to hear this."

"I think you have this strength too."

"I feel happy about it."

"I will work hard to maintain this good quality."

"My friends told me this too."

"I appreciate it."

"This is a nice compliment."

"I like it very much."

274 *Therapeutic Games and Guided Imagery*

Figure A57.1 Strength Flower

Figure A57.2 Example of Strength Flower

A58
Visualizing
Kelly Holmes

Items Needed

One pre-cut circle of poster board (or construction paper) with another circle drawn in the middle (namely, "Making Changes"; see figure A58.1); an array of different types of magazines; scissors; glue; digital camera

Note: If clients have previously exhibited any dangerous behaviors, do not provide scissors.

Target Population

Adolescents struggling with addiction, such as substance abuse and eating disorders

Suitable for individual and group work

Purpose

To help adolescents identify problem areas and create a positive outlook

To assist the client in addressing changes and improvements that can be made

To create goals for a healthy future

To teach problem identification and solution-building

Procedure

Prepare this activity beforehand. Cut out images and words from the Internet or magazines associated with addiction problems. Provide various types of magazines for the clients to use as well.

Step 1. You may use the pre-cut circle or a blank sheet of paper and ask each client to draw a circle in the middle to begin. Ask clients to relax and focus on the inner circle of the "Making Change" poster. Have them think about the standards society holds and the consequences of not meeting these standards. Ask them to think specifically about the consequences of not following a healthy lifestyle. Then ask each client to arrange the pre-cut words and images in the inner circle to represent current problems and the corresponding negative consequences. Do not glue them yet (see figure A58.2). Ask each client to look at the newly created poster board as a whole and discuss what images come to mind when looking at this small circle that is crowded with expectations, problems, and consequences.

Step 2. Take a digital photo and then ask the client to tear the clippings into smaller pieces and glue everything onto the inner circle. The entire circle should be filled with colors and pieces, void of any negative images. Add more cut-up pieces if needed. This step allows the client to release negative emotions and recharge energy (see figure A58.3).

Step 3. Ask the clients to cut or tear out pictures from magazines that represent positive aspects in life (now and in the future), such as people and things that make them happy or proud. When this task is done, ask them to visualize how these positive aspects can be obtained and maintained. Finally, glue these clippings to the outer circle or place some on the inner circle to represent solutions to the previously discussed issues or problems (see figure A58.4). Ask each client to take a look at the entire creation and address feelings, thoughts, and solutions (see figure A58.5 for examples).

Function in Assessment and Treatment

Assessment

This exercise allows clients to compare positive and negative aspects of their lives, and to visualize how their choices have impacted them. Some images, such as a picture of an anorexic woman or a drug addict, may help them connect current issues with possible consequences. The images or words the clients choose can be used in discussion to process troubling feelings and thoughts. Discussion questions may include:

- How do these images make you feel?
- What advice would you give someone about changing negative feelings to positive ones? How do you feel about changing these behaviors?
- Do you think the "feeling" words will change after you have worked on the behaviors shown in these pictures?
- What do you think will happen if you don't make these changes?
- How do the positive pictures and words make you feel? How do you conquer the negative words or behaviors?

Treatment

Start this exercise only after rapport has been established and clients are ready to discuss their problems. Before this exercise is used, simple exercises such as word association or making a collage about "self-image" can be introduced to process feelings about self-esteem. This visualizing exercise can be done in an individual or group session, but the group impact may be stronger. If you can still see negative words or pictures on the collage once the client has completed the exercise, keep it in the office until the client can make a collage that is filled with positive words or pictures. You can bring out the collage at each additional meeting and ask the client to adjust the visualizing images towards improvements and changes. The client can paste these clippings on top of any negative ones. The goal is for the client to eventually cover all of the negative behaviors with positive, healthy ones. This will allow the client to see recent progress and will then reinforce a full recovery. The client can keep a digital photo of the final product as a reminder of positive changes.

Figure A58.1 Making Changes

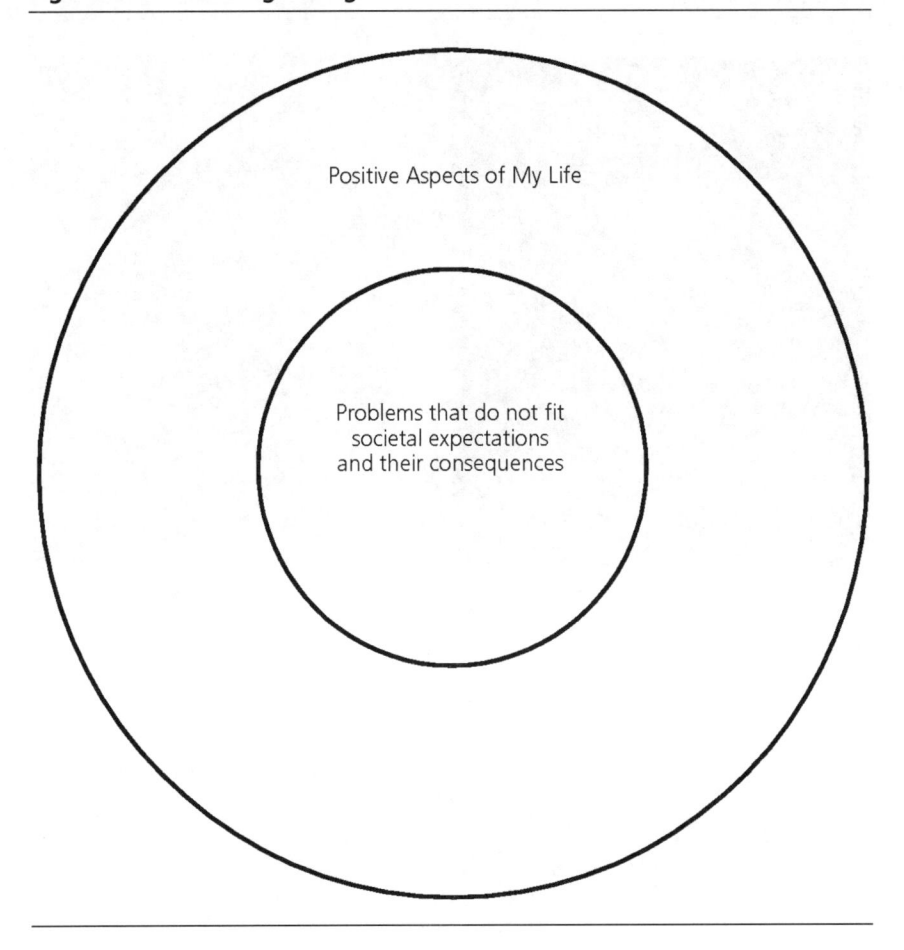

280 *Therapeutic Games and Guided Imagery*

Figure A58.2 Step 1

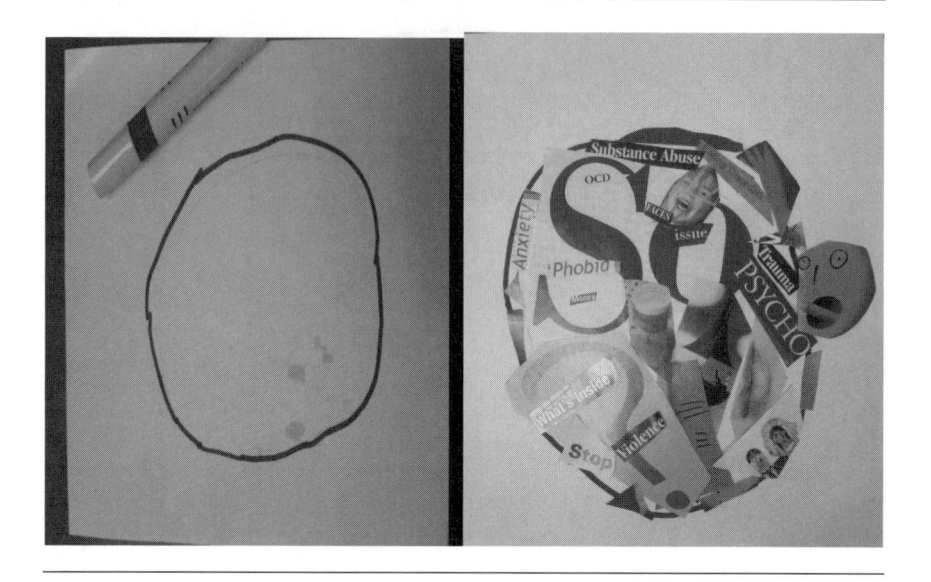

Figure A58.3 Step 2

Figure A58.4 Step 3

Figure A58.5 Examples

A59
Where Is the Bird?
Monit Cheung

Items Needed

One sheet of white paper for each person; cut out each bird from figure A59.1; a ballpoint pen; colored markers; crayons; masking tape (or glue)

Target Population

Clients with anxiety related to therapy

Nonverbal clients and children ages two to six

Children or adolescents who have recently moved to a new house or school

Can be used individually or in a group

Purpose

To provide an ice-breaker

To help clients talk about their issues in a non-threatening way

To empower clients to choose a topic for discussion

Procedure

Give one bird and a sheet of paper to each client. Ask the clients to paste the bird on the paper provided. Ask them to draw a dwelling place for the bird. Provide an opportunity for each client to share the meaning of this place. If it is a house or cage, ask if there is an entrance or door. Then ask them to add anything else and to provide a title for the drawing to reflect the content, which may be used later as a topic for further discussion. An additional step can be done if the bird is taped on the paper—ask the clients to move the bird to another place on the drawing and then ask what happened to the bird and what the bird may say. Discuss the symbolic meaning of each item on the drawing. For example, a bird may mean freedom, and a cage may mean confinement. Do not interpret for the clients but encourage them to discuss what they see and how they feel about a new environment.

Function in Assessment and Treatment

Assessment

This exercise provides a chance for the client to feel comfortable about working with a therapist for the first time. It is a brief modality to identify topics of interest for future discussions. It also helps assess the client's level of anxiety or discomfort. This free association exercise can lead to discussions about freedom, choices, feelings, problem-solving, help-seeking, moving, and adjustment to a new environment.

Treatment

You may help the clients to process the drawing with these questions:

- Where is the bird?
- Does this place (e.g., a cage) have an entrance (exit)?
- What kind of entertainment can be provided for the bird?
- What would the bird say in this environment?
- What is in the surrounding (e.g., people, nature, additional birds)?

Therapeutic questions may include:

- If you were this bird, what would you do or say?
- What is inside or outside of this place?
- How do you define freedom?
- How do you feel about this environment? Do you think the bird would like it? What can you add to this place to make sure the bird would like to stay?
- If this bird is in trouble, who can be a helper?

286 *Therapeutic Games and Guided Imagery*

Figure A59.1 Birds

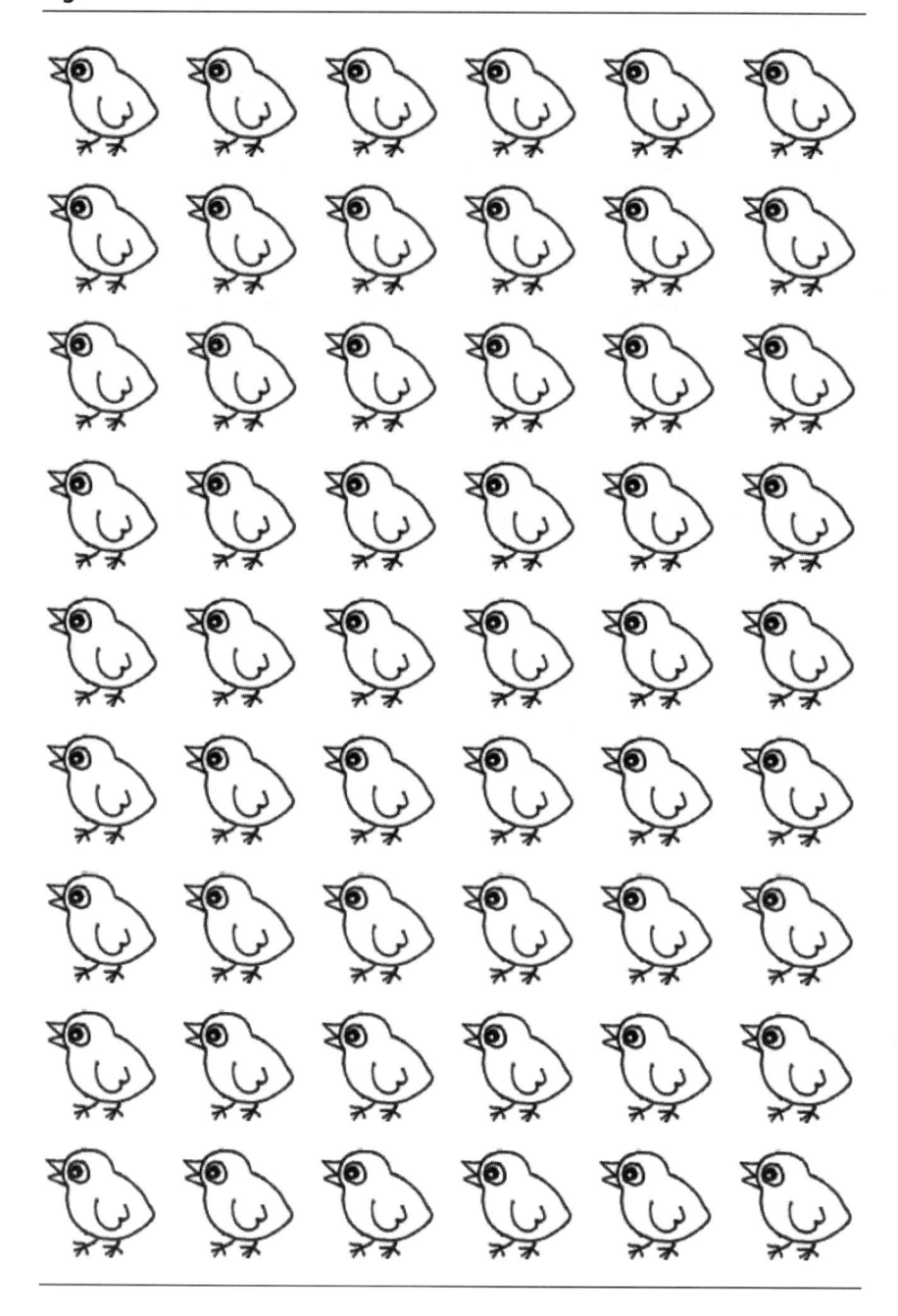

A59 – Where Is the Bird? **287**

Figure A59.2 Example

A60
Working Through Secrets
Noa Ben Yehuda

Items Needed

Ten to 12 small random items (suggested items include stuffed animal, baby doll, flashlight, kaleidoscope, lock and key, sunglasses, rubber ball with spikes, Play-Doh, plastic knife, scissors, glue, empty picture frame, box of tissue, magic wand, treasure box, cell phone, dry-erase board); two pieces of circle-shaped white paper; pen or marker

Target Population

Adolescents (ages 14 and older) and adults presenting depressive symptoms

Individual therapy with clients from all cultures and socioeconomic backgrounds

Purpose

To assess the client's depressive symptoms and perception of the future

To help the client verbalize feelings and thoughts about a secret and its effect on his or her life

To help the client visualize an option for change

To shift client's focus from past to future

To help clients develop problem-solving skills

Procedure

Although this activity is about secrets, the client should be informed that the focus is not the secret itself but rather *working through* the secret and to emphasize future thoughts and behaviors. Do not ask direct questions about what the secret is.

Part 1:

Lay the items in front of the client and ask the client to choose three items that:

1. Represent the secret
2. Represent how this secret makes him or her feel or behave
3. Represent how life would look without the secret

If the client has any difficulties choosing the items this way, they may choose any three items that make them think about the secret or something related to it.

Next, discuss the client's choices using the following therapeutic questions:

Item one:

1. Which qualities about the item resemble your secret?
2. If you could give a title to the story of your secret, what would it be?

Item two:

1. How does this item reflect your feelings or behavior?
2. How do these feelings or behaviors affect your life?
3. Would you like to change the effect they have on your life?

Item three:

1. What made you choose this item to represent your life without the secret?
2. What does your life without the secret look like?
3. How would you feel or act?
4. Who is in this life with you?

Part 2:

Ask the client to take a piece of the circle-shaped paper and write in the middle, "My Present Life." Next, ask the client to divide the circle into three portions, according to how much each item affects his or her current life, so the bigger the effect, the bigger the portion.

When the client is done, give him or her the second circle and ask them to write in the middle, "My Future Life."

Ask the client to divide the circle to portions again, but this time, according to the effect he or she *wishes* each item would have on his or her future life.

Discuss this activity with the client using the following therapeutic questions:
1. What are the differences between the "present" circle and the "future" circle?
2. How can you make this change happen?
3. If you could fill each section of the "future life" circle with something new, what would you fill it with?

Function in Assessment and Treatment

Assessment

This activity provides context for you to understand the effect the secret has on your client's life, to assess the client's potential depressive symptoms and his or her ability to perceive change for a better future.

Treatment

The activity helps the client to verbalize feelings and thoughts about the secret itself, without full disclosure. It also gives the client an opportunity to identify and process other stressful factors related to the secret while providing a safe environment in which the client is able to reimagine his or her future, set goals for creating such a future, and develop problem-solving skills.

This game can be modified to address a more applicable issue facing the client, such as a "difficult memory" or "past event," rather than a "secret."

Part B
Guided Imagery

B1
A Walk in Someone Else's Shoes
Chloe Walker

Use this guided imagery with older children who are struggling to cope with divorce. This activity will help them understand what aspects of divorce they can and cannot control. This process utilizes breathing control techniques used in yoga practice. Children will feel empowered and confident in their ability to exercise control over their state of mind when it comes to a difficult situation, such as their parents' divorce, when they consciously think about control over their "prana" (the energy that encompasses the mind and body through breath). It will help the children to process feelings of powerlessness over others when they begin to see the divorce through the eyes of their parents or siblings.

Script

Close your eyes. Take a long, deep breath in. Feel the air fill up your lungs. Exhale and let out a big "sigh." Continue to take long, deep breaths in and out. Pay attention to how the air feels moving through your lungs, your throat, and out of your mouth. Good.

Now take a sharp breath in and exhale quickly. Pay attention to how your body reacts.

Return to long, slow breaths and continue breathing slowly.

Today I would like you to think about a situation that has happened recently that made you feel frustrated. In this exercise, we will focus on controlling your breath and your body. When you control your breath, your mind will also automatically follow.

Take a moment to think of a situation that made you sad, angry, confused, or frustrated. Continue to breathe while you think about this situation. If someone else's words or actions caused some emotion, think about whether or not you have control over those words or actions. Don't forget to take this controllable breath while you think about this situation! If you were to get a "do-over" in this particular situation, would you have been able to change the outcome? What could you have done differently? What would you not be able to do? What could you do to control your emotions?

Now, let's take a walk in someone else's shoes. Think about the other person who has been involved in this situation. Take another deep breath in and out. What was this person doing when you felt upset about this situation? What did this person's facial expressions look like? Keep your eyes closed, but make the facial expression that you saw when it happened. Mouth the words that were said or act out what happened with your body movements. (pause) Good. Think about how your body just told you to relax, to gain control. Take another deep breath in and think about what that person might have been thinking when it happened. Take the breath out and think about what emotions might this person have felt. Take another deep breath and think "I can control my own thoughts."

Let's think about a sibling or a friend who is in a similar situation. Do your deep breathing with them. What have they been thinking, feeling, and doing? (pause for a minute) Could you observe their reactions? Good. Your body told you to relax, to gain control. Take another deep breath in and think about what your sibling or friend might have been thinking when it happened. Take a breath out and think about what emotions they might have felt. Take another deep breath and think "I can control my own thoughts."

Now, you understand that it is important to know that you are in control of your own thoughts and emotions. Take two more long, deep breaths—in and out. Roll your shoulders back slowly. Wiggle your fingers. Slowly open your eyes.

Application

This guided imagery is designed to make children think about their parents' divorce from different perspectives. It also helps teach them that they cannot control the actions of others but only the way they react to them. The following are suggested process questions:

1. What situation did you think about?
2. If you could imagine the situation exactly the way you wanted it to be, how would you imagine it?
3. Did you notice any change in your breathing during this exercise?
4. Whose shoes did you walk in?
5. What do you think that person felt like during your interaction when you were calm and relaxed?
6. If you were to tell the persons in this exercise how their words or actions have made you feel, what would you say? What would they feel?

B2
Bullying Role Reversal
Jolanna Jenae' Watson

The purpose of this guided imagery practice is to use the technique of role reversal to guide perpetrators of bullying in becoming aware of their hurtful actions. It is intended to allow the perpetrators to become the victim in a safe therapeutic environment. The bullies will then analyze how their behaviors have affected others and see how outsiders react to their bullying behaviors. The goal of the role reversal is to increase empathy with the victim so that the bully or potential perpetrator can come to realize how others may perceive the bully's behaviors as negative emotions and actions. The ultimate goal is to increase self-directed actions for eliminating the bullying behaviors.

Script

Sit back comfortably in your chair. Clear your thoughts as we count backwards starting with 5, 4, 3, 2, and 1. Close your eyes. Relax. Now take a deep breath as you let any anger or anxiety leave your body. Feel relaxed as you breathe in, breathe out, breathe in—and breathe out. Breathe slowly with a relaxation feeling. As you take a deep breath in, let your lungs expand; as you take a deep breath out, feel the calmness over your entire body. Good!

Now you are entering a situation as if you were a small lonesome child. Imagine that you were this person walking home from school—you live a short distance away. You're anticipating a delicious dinner, hoping there's something good, wishing for your favorite dish. You hear your belly growling and the growing hunger begins to formulate some pain in your head and tummy. This feeling causes you to move even faster to get home. You didn't eat lunch because the bully, who teases you along with his friends, took your lunch money again. You start feeling sad and embarrassed because earlier this morning they called you names again and had other kids joining in chanting whatever they could think of to hurt you. You used to have some friends but now they join the bully to tease you and beat you up. Earlier today, they joined in with the bully in a game of name calling and spitting. The spit that hits your face made you feel so helpless and desperate. You wonder what you have done wrong to make them hate you so much when all you did was just sit down and attempt to stay out of their way. You are still walking and about to turn at a corner of the street. Quickly you remember that the bully lives close around this corner. You walk carefully across the street to avoid any contact with this bully. You are still trying to hide ever since the last beating two days ago. Your right arm is still sore, but fortunately your left eye is not as swollen as it was. Your fear of this bully is growing stronger and you begin to move even faster as your heart races with some pounding beats. You hope that you will make it home in one piece.

You are running really fast and finally reach home, but you begin to slow your pace as you enter your back door. You once had a smiley face, now you don't even have friends. You want to unleash your anger and stop the abuse. Who can help you? Ask yourself again, who will that be? Think about it when you are breathing in and out deeply.

Now you are back to your own self—you are not a bullying victim but have been labeled as a bully who teases others and beats them up. Keep your eyes closed and step back to feel your own body. Think about yourself. Feel the anger inside of you spread all over your face. You are so angry that you become a bully, but you're not sure why. You wonder in your mind, "Did someone step on my toes? Did I dislike my classmate's shirt so much that I even hate the person in it? How agitating! Why did I do the name calling game? Why did I tease someone in front of others?" As you laughed at others, you also felt that anger was growing inside of you and you were not sure why. You noticed that people surrounding you began shaking their heads in disappointment. Your teacher was upset at your behavior.

Now, as you are examining your future, you tell yourself to calm down. You know you can change your behavior. Relax. Repeat after me, "Calm down; it's ok!" Repeat or silently repeat it, "Calm down, it's ok!" Repeat, "I care and deserve a hug." "I care and deserve a hug." Put your arms around yourself, hug yourself. Hug tight, tighter and tighter! Take a deep breath and when you let it out, begin to feel a sense of relief. You have changed to a person with empathy, feeling how others may feel. A new sense of calmness and love is surrounding you. Your teachers and your family smile in approval and offer you hugs and congratulations.

Imagine a bully coming along and sticking his tongue out at your family members or your best friends. You don't have to be upset because you can stay calm and let the bully know that it's not cool to hurt other people's feelings. You are now good at bullying prevention. You decide to start with yourself. You shout loud and proud that you will not be a bully! Repeat after me, "I am no longer a bully!" You will treat people the way you want to be treated. You will respect people the way you want to be respected, no matter what their differences are. Weak, small, wearing a shirt you dislike—all of these should not be reasons to bully. After all, we are all different and you want to be treated nicely and treat others with integrity. Repeat after me, "I do not hurt others to feel strong." Good! Repeat after me, "I do not hurt others to make myself feel stronger." Now open your eyes and feel strong. Repeat after me, "I am not a bully!"

Application

This application should be used for children and adolescents labeled as "bullies." It is formulated based on incidents reported about them being disruptive and disrespectful to their peers. The content can be adjusted based on the complaints relating to fighting, teasing, or other bullying behaviors. Engage the client in an individual session and explain that the purpose of this guided imagery is to help him or her become more empathic toward other people's feelings. The client must be able to relax in a comfortable therapeutic setting with the goal of changing negative behaviors. Before this guided imagery, conduct a preliminary assessment: (1) make a list of problems at home and in school; (2) describe reasons for having angry feelings toward others; and (3) describe feelings of being labeled "bully" and how bullying may affect the client's family and social life. After the imagery exercise, ask the client to describe feelings of being a bullying victim, speak about what the client could do to help someone who is being bullied, and commit time to make behavioral changes to prevent bullying.

B3
Children in Military Families
Monique McWilliams Wall and Monit Cheung

This guided exercise is a supplementary tool that can be used by clinicians working with children and adolescents who frequently relocate with their military families. This exercise's purpose is to provide a comfort zone during the counseling process when clients are dealing with painful memories from any unpleasant experiences during their frequently relocating history. It can be prerecorded and accompanied by soothing background music. This exercise aims to help clients relax and process positive thoughts. The main goal is to help them learn how to open their emotional doors and become aware of factors in their external environment that they may possibly have control over. Simultaneously, this exercise will also guide the client to recognize that there are thoughts and ideas within their reach and possibly control.

Script

Gently close your eyes and take three deep big breaths. One, in and out; two, in and out; and three, in and out. Imagine you are sitting under a tree, thinking through some of the things you have gone through in the past few months, or past few years while relocating from one home to another home. Packing, moving, unpacking, moving again; going to a new environment and preparing for another new day of school, and another new home. Imagine you are meeting a group of new schoolmates, new teachers, strangers on campus, new neighbors; everyone and everything is new.

Imagine even after all these moves and with all these changes, you are still calm and relaxed!

With your mind relaxed, think about something that represents "nice." What do you see in your thoughts? How does it feel to think about something nice? Who has been nice to you when you needed help or when you felt lonely? What feeling do you feel on your forehead? What can you do to let go of your worries? When thinking about something that is nice and positive, how does that make your entire body feel at this moment? Remember, even with all these thoughts flowing through your mind, you are still calm and relaxed!

Now imagine that all the changes that came with moving to a new place are finally settled. Think about the thoughts and worries that revolve around these changes and find words to represent these thoughts and worries. Imagine these words leaving your mouth without any sound, but yet you feel comfortable not speaking. Imagine these worry words leaving your body through your hands and feet, allowing you to feel calm and relaxed. You are ready for your next day of school. . . . You may not be able to control your family's frequent moving, but you can accept the changes and let go of all the worries surrounding it.

As you are thinking about your family, know that it is very important for you to stay relaxed and calm. Your calmness will help others to relax, too. Remember, you are calm and relaxed!

When you are ready to come back, start wiggling your fingers, shaking your hands (pause), and stretching your arms. Now you will feel the relaxation and will be able to move your body in whatever way you please. (pause) Now gently open your eyes, be aware of the peaceful feelings within you. This is how it feels to be calm and relaxed!

Application

This exercise allows children and adolescents to release their worry through an emotional outlet with guidance on how to recognize and feel inner peace. Furthermore, it helps them to understand that it is not only healthy but also relaxing to "let the worry off their chest" instead of bottling it up inside. Before engaging the client in this exercise, you should assess the client's comfort level with another simple breathing exercise for the purpose of checking whether this exercise would be appropriate for this client. Start with the client closing their eyes for a few seconds and learning how to do deep breathing. Pay attention to the level of relaxation in the client's eyes and forehead before, during, and after the exercise. Ask the client how he or she felt at the moment, and how he or she would rate his or her own level of stress (anxiety, nervousness, etc.) while deep breathing. The client can try this guided imagery and then share something about his or her family. Therapeutic questions may include:

1. We often feel that we are not able to talk about our feelings because our parents don't have time to listen. Do you agree with this statement? (If agree: Please share this "not talking about my feeling" experience; If disagree: Please tell me what your parents do to help you talk about your feelings.)
2. Now, please show me what you do to let out a sign of relief. How do you feel after showing this to me?
3. What are some of the nicest memories about your family you could share with me? How can these memories help you when you are lonely (sad, not happy, etc.)?

B4
Coping with the Aftereffects of Physical Abuse
Debbie Kumar-Misir

Use with children who are survivors of physical abuse. Either use it at a face-to-face session or pre-record this piece added with background music if used in a home environment. This exercise may be used as often as once a week to ensure the child has proper time to process the information and deal with residual feelings.

Prior to the exercise, dim the lights and have the child sit in a comfortable position.

Script

Welcome to your feelings. We are going to go on a voyage. This is a place that you have traveled to before. When you take the voyage this time, you will come back rested and peaceful. First you will need to close your eyes. Lean back against your chair and get as comfortable as you possibly can. I am going to ask you some questions while you are traveling but you do not need to answer these questions out loud. Instead, answer the questions to yourself, in your mind. Now, I am going to count to ten. I want you to breathe in from when I count from 1 to 5, and breathe out when I count from 6 to 10. Okay, breathe in: 1, 2, 3, 4, 5. Now breathe out: 6, 7, 8, 9, 10. Great. Let's do that one more time. Breathe in: 1, 2, 3, 4, 5. Wonderful. Now breathe out: 6, 7, 8, 9, and 10.

Now I want you to really focus on listening to me while you take a trip through your body. Let's start at your mouth. Imagine that you jump into your mouth, landing on your soft tongue. You walk towards the back of your mouth and slide down your tongue into your throat. What does it look like as you slide down? Is it dark or light? Does it hurt or does it feel good? You keep sliding down your throat, all the way down, just like a water slide. When you reach the bottom you splash into your stomach. Stand up and look around. What do you see? How do you feel? Go to the spot in your stomach that causes you the most pain. I want you to really think about that spot and the pain there. What does the pain feel like? What is causing this pain? Feel the pain.

Now, let's make that pain go away. How can you make that pain leave your stomach? Try rubbing the pain. Acknowledge that it is there and how it feels. Tell yourself that you want to feel better. Feel the pain getting better. You feel relieved as the pain slowly leaves your body. What else can you do to help your pain go away? How will you do this? Will it be easy for you to get rid of your pain? Right now your pain in your stomach is becoming less painful, less noticeable. Your pain is almost gone now. Now imagine that the inside of your stomach is a water park, full of organ-shaped slides. Hear the rushing water. You want to stay with your pain a little longer so the two of you go walking, taking in the sights. You see children laughing and having fun as they splash around in the water. You imagine the bright sun is shining down on you, making it a warm day. You take your pain on a slide and as you feel the rush, and the cool water against your skin, you laugh with your pain. Next, you take your pain to the top of the longest waterslide and you tell your pain good-bye as you let it down the slide by itself, slowly fading out of sight. How do you feel? Enjoy this feeling. Your pain is out of sight and out of mind.

Before you leave the park, you find one more slide and as you glide down, you feel relaxed and free. At the bottom of the slide, you see and hear all of the happy, laughing people, and you wave good-bye. The warmth of the sun is against your skin and you close your eyes. When you open them, you are back in your stomach. You begin your journey back home, back up the long tunnel of your throat. Does it look any different than it did before? When you reach your mouth, sit on your tongue. Enjoy the way you feel in this moment. Remember that whenever you have bad feelings again, you can send them away and replace them with good ones. You can do it. You just did it. You will always be able to do this. You did a wonderful job of getting rid of that pain and making yourself feel better. I want you to remember how happy you feel and come back on this voyage anytime you need to.

Now I am going to count to ten again. I want you to breathe in on numbers 1 to 5, and breathe out on numbers 6 to 10. Okay, breathe in: 1, 2, 3, 4, 5. Now breathe out: 6, 7, 8, 9, and 10. Great. Let's do that one more time. Breathe in: 1, 2, 3, 4, 5. Wonderful. Now breathe out: 6, 7, 8, 9, and 10. Try to remain relaxed and when you are ready you can open your eyes.

Application

Conduct this exercise in a calm and relaxing environment after establishing rapport with the child. This will enable the child to relax and fully participate in the exercise. Following the exercise, assess the child's comfort level in discussing his or her feelings after the exercise. If the child seems comfortable, facilitate a discussion about the child's current feelings and experience during the exercise. If the child appears uncomfortable sharing his or her feelings, utilize another activity that will allow the child to express his or her feelings nonverbally, such as taking a deep breath or standing up with hands extending up to the ceiling to symbolize relaxation. To assess the child's progress, complete this exercise several times over several sessions and record responses and reactions after the exercise. This will give insight into the child's ability to address the residual feelings and ways to release them.

B5
Everyone Is Important
Maria Cano

Use with young people who are depressed and do not see a purpose in life. This exercise can be used in individual or group therapy to assist with the expression of feelings including hopelessness and frustration. It particularly helps teenagers to identify and understand the importance of the numerous roles they play in life, and how each of these roles will continue to serve a purpose for them and those around them.

Script

Sit in a comfortable position.

Okay, let's begin with closing your eyes and breathing in and out slowly. Repeat the breathing, in and out, clearing your mind. You are feeling relaxed. Imagine you have no worries, nothing bothers you, and you are able to handle everything that comes your way.

Okay, now imagine the roles of every important person in your life. Think about what makes each of these persons important, unique, and special. Imagine the importance of being a sibling and how important you are to your sister or brother. You are the one he or she can talk to about problems. You are able to help your sibling, offer support, and can help show them the way. Next imagine the importance of being a student. Imagine yourself using your education in the future to help other people, to teach them, to heal them, or to assist them with their day-to-day lives. Think about the talents you have that can benefit others. Next think about being a friend. Think about how people share secrets with you and ask you to help solve problems that they find difficult. Think about how many times you have been there for your friends when they have needed you or when they felt lonely or alone. Think about how you showed you cared.

Now, imagine the future to when you become a parent. Think about how important you will be to your children. Imagine how you will take care of your family, how you will provide for them and keep them safe. Think about how you will show your children that they are loved and wanted. Picture the activities you look forward to doing with them.

You can be anything you want in life. Your dreams are not real just in your imagination; they are real if you make them real. You can be a parent, sibling, student, friend, doctor, or teacher. There is a purpose for you in life. You can be whatever you want to be. Don't ever forget you are important! The best is yet to come!

Now open your eyes. Look at yourself in the mirror and see the person who makes a difference in the lives of others. Smile and always remember how important you are.

Application

The main purpose of this exercise is to reinforce what a person sees as the important and purposeful aspects in life. Sometimes it is hard to comprehend the importance of the role we play in the world and in the lives of others. This exercise builds upon the roles that we have now, and helps us visualize the impact that we may have in future roles. The following therapeutic questions can be used to follow up this exercise:

1. What does the word *important* mean to you?
2. Who are the important people in your life? What makes them important?
3. What do you want to be when you grow up?
4. How will you accomplish your goals?
5. How do you make people feel important?
6. Who makes you feel important?
7. Who is your best friend? What qualities do you look for in a best friend?

B6
Fighting the Feeling of Anger
Marilyn Hotchko-Scott

Use with children and adolescents ages 6 to 14 who have experienced danger and distress, and have acted on those feelings through physical aggression. This exercise allows the client to experience tension in a safe environment, and learn how to decrease that tension through distress tolerance and by increasing self-regulation. When we learn how to relax our bodies and minds, the result is a decrease in emotional distress that may manifest itself in inappropriate physical behavior.

Script

Please come in, sit down, and lean back in your chair. Make yourself comfortable. To begin this exercise, think about which part of the body reacts first when you become angry, angry enough to fight. Let's try a few simple ways to move tension to relaxation. When you are relaxed, don't forget to take a deep breath out. Let's start.

Take a deep breath in. Hold it and exhale. Now, tighten the muscles around your forehead, then close your eyes really tight. Make them tighter. Feel the warmth of the blood rushing to your face. Hold it . . . hold it . . . and relax. Take a deep breath out. Now, tighten the muscles of your cheeks, the muscles around your mouth, and the muscles of your chin. Make them tighter. Hold it . . . hold it . . . and relax. Take a deep breath out. Let all the anger, frustration, and tension drain from your face. Take another deep breath . . . hold it . . . hold it . . . and exhale. Take your time to enjoy this feeling of relaxation. You are very relaxed and calm. Relaxed and calm.

Now, stretch out your arms. Make two fists, and then tighten the muscles in your fingers. Feel the tightness . . . hold it . . . hold it . . . and relax. Take a deep breath out. Let your arms slowly drift to your sides. Feel the relaxation. Now stretch out your arms again. Tighten the muscles in your wrists, in your lower arms, in your upper arms . . . hold it . . . hold it . . . and let go, just let it go. Take a deep breath out. Let your arms drift back to your sides. Stop for a second and notice the calming feeling of relaxation in your fingers, your hands, your wrists, your lower arms, and your upper arms. Let your arms go completely limp. Give in to that wonderful feeling of relaxation. You are very relaxed, very calm; relaxed and calm.

Now, arch your back towards the back of the chair and raise your chest. Tighten the muscles in your chest, your stomach, your back, and your neck. Hold it . . . hold it . . . take a deep breath out. Now, let go of your anger, your tension, your sense of frustration . . . just let it go. Notice your muscles relaxing. Take time to really feel, and enjoy, the relaxation in your chest, your stomach, your neck, and all over your back. All of your muscles feel nicely relaxed.

Now . . . breathe in through your nose, slowly and deeply. Breathe the air down into your abdomen first, then your chest, and your throat. Hold it . . . hold it . . . and slowly breathe it out through your nose. Feel the relaxation. Breathe in . . . tense up . . . hold it . . . hold it . . . breathe out . . . relax.

Now, imagine you are at the top of a mountain or on the front bow of a large boat, and a cool breeze brushes against your face, and through your hair . . . and now you are free . . . free from the tension . . . free from your frustrations . . . free from all anxieties and anger . . . Take time to breathe out anything you don't want; stretch your body, focus on your surroundings. Breathe in . . . tense up . . . hold it . . . hold it . . . breathe out . . . relax.

You are now ready to continue your day . . . free . . . relaxed . . . calm . . . focused . . . and attentive.

Application

This relaxation and tension release exercise can be used to help clients learn self-regulation of the body and mind. With some practice, it may also help clients decrease negative emotions that may have led them to use physical violence as a way of dealing with these uncomfortable feelings. After completing the exercise, discuss the following questions:

1. How do you feel right now?
2. Did this exercise help you release some built-up anger or frustrations?
3. What usually happens when you feel angry or frustrated?
4. Did the peaceful images, such as imagining the cool breeze against your face, help to bring a calming sensation to your body?
5. How might this exercise help you work through some built-up anger or frustrations in the future?
6. Do you think that with some practice you may be able to control your angry feelings in the future? How would it help you refrain from being angry or fighting?

B7
Finding Hope
Laura Welch

This guided imagery targets adolescents in juvenile detention centers, but can be used with any juvenile experiencing feelings of hopelessness about the future. This exercise is unique because it allows the clients to actually see and touch some objects during the exercise. They can also choose to open or close their eyes when processing the questions associated with these objects. It uses concrete objects for visualization, and can be used with groups or individuals. This exercise focuses on concentration and awareness, and helps the youth to visualize their success and to begin thinking about their future. The creation of small goals gives the client a realistic way to start changing current patterns of behavior without feeling overwhelmed. This guided imagery leaves the client in control, thereby allowing the youth to create their own goals. The script can be shortened (by eliminating the second paragraph for each object), especially for clients who cannot concentrate for more than five minutes.

Script

You have four items in front of you: a house, a book, a dollar bill, and an empty glass jar. These items represent different areas of your life: past, present, and future.

First, pick up the house. The house represents love and family. Hold it in your hands (pause). Feel the weight of the house in your hands. Now picture your family in this house. What thoughts, feelings, or images come to mind? Good. Now, think about your family and what they mean to you. Do you feel love from them? Remember a time when you felt that a family member had a strong love for you (pause). Try to remember how they spoke to you and how they looked at you. How did they make you feel? Think about the way they physically expressed their love for you. Good. Now, think about your family again. How do you get along with your family? What do you do together for fun? How did you show them you loved them? Do you wish you were closer to them? Think of how you can make your relationships with them stronger. Imagine what it would be like to spend more time together, or talk on the phone once a week, or maybe even give more hugs and kisses (pause). Great.

308 *Therapeutic Games and Guided Imagery*

[Keeping this house in mind, think about everything your family brought to your life. Happiness. Sadness. Fun. Excitement. Love. Stress. Let those feelings sink in. Now imagine what you want your family to be like in the future. What would their personalities be like? (pause) Imagine how you will interact with them and what things you will do together. Great. What will you do to keep your family happy? How will you make your home a happy, loving home? Now imagine that you write these goals down on a piece of paper. Crumple it up. Picture yourself putting the crumpled-up piece of paper in the empty glass jar. The glass jar will keep your family dream safe. (pause)]

You can put the house down. Great job.

Now, pick up the book in front of you. The book represents your education. Hold the book in your hands. Flip through the pages of the book. How do you feel when you hold the book? When you think about school, what does it make you think of? How does it make you feel? Good. Now, think of three things you like about school (pause). Now, think of three things you do not like about school. What is your favorite class? Why? Remind yourself of what you enjoyed about that class. Remember how you felt during this class. Now recall a time when you were excited to go to school. Try to remember how that excitement felt and how it made you act. How did you feel and act differently when you did not want to go to school? Picture yourself in class with the book you are holding. Imagine you are taking notes and listening to your teacher. Picture the classroom and look around at the other students. Pick a classmate you want to be like. What do you like about him or her? Great.

[Feel this book; decide what you must do to get good grades on all of your assignments. Remind yourself that you can make good grades. Tell yourself that you are capable. Great. Now, think of a goal you want to reach in school. How will you reach this goal? What do you need to change or continue that will help you reach your goal? Good. Now, imagine that you write this goal on a piece of paper, just like you did with the house (pause). Crumple it up. Picture yourself putting that piece of paper in the jar with the other one. Both goals are safe.]

You can put the book down. Good job.

Now pick up the dollar bill. Look closely at the details on the dollar. Feel both sides of the bill. How does it smell? Is it crisp or wilted? This dollar bill represents your finances. Think about your life at home. Does your family live comfortably or is money tight? Remember a time when you did not have enough money for something you wanted or needed. Think about how this made you feel. Did it make you think negatively about yourself? Now, try to think about what would have been different if you had had enough money. Would you have felt differently about yourself or your family? What would change if you had less money? Now consider how you would feel if you had all the money you could ask for. Picture the different ways you would spend your money. What would be the first thing you buy? Imagine how little stress you would feel if you did not have to worry about money (pause). Great.

[With this dollar bill in your hand, now think about how you would feel to live on a few dollars each day. What things would be different? What would be the same? Would you work? Would you still have fun? Now think about your future. Imagine that you live comfortably: you do not have unlimited amounts of money, but you do not struggle to pay the bills. How would you spend your money? How would you feel when you spend that money? Imagine the confidence and power you will feel as you stand at the cash register and pay, knowing that you have enough in your bank account. Is this how you want to feel when you spend your money? Choose a financial goal for your future. How will you achieve this goal? Decide the role your education will play in your finances. Think about how you will combine this goal with your educational goal. Now imagine you write this goal down on a piece of paper and crumple it up. Picture yourself placing this goal in the jar with the other two.]

You can put the dollar bill down. Great work.

Now, look at your glass jar. It is full of your goals. It holds the keys to your future. Pick it up. Look at your goals, safe inside the jar. Remind yourself that you are in charge of your life. You are the one who creates your goals. You are the one who chooses how you will reach them. You are the one who makes your decisions. You are the one who will keep yourself on track. Great job! Now picture yourself putting the glass jar in your pocket. You will take this glass jar with you everywhere you go. Your goals are safe, and are always with you. When you reach one of your goals, remember to create another one. The more effort you give, the better the results. You can create and change your future. It is in your hands.

You can now put the jar on the table. Excellent!

Applications

In a juvenile detention setting, this exercise may be best when used during group sessions. Other settings may benefit either in individual therapy or with groups. After completing the exercise, ask clients if they could share any of their goals, action plans, or other thoughts they had during the session. The disclosure they provide may give more insight into struggles they may be having with school, life at home, and so on. The therapist then asks the clients if they feel confident in their ability to reach their goals, and follows up about the clients' perceived ability by asking "What can you do to make this happen?" or "How do you know you cannot do it?" If treatment with an individual is ongoing, this exercise can be used on a regular basis to continue goal-setting that is realistically attainable. This discussion can still be used if a client is not comfortable sharing specific details. The items used (house, book, dollar bill, and glass jar) can be substituted by other items such as a ball if the client is an athlete, or an item to represent sobriety if the client is a substance abuser. For practice purposes, the therapist may also focus on only one item at a time. Another item can be added in subsequent sessions when the client feels comfortable with the current items.

B8
Float Away
Kayla Cooper

The purpose of this exercise is to help physically disabled clients to relax, and to promote a self-image that does not focus on their physical disability and the inherent restraints they experience. This exercise can also help clients release negative feelings associated with the limitations resulting from having a physical disability. Engaging in activities such as pushing one's child on a swing, riding the rides at an amusement park, walking along the beach, or going camping may be difficult or impossible, which may cause feelings of sadness, anger, loneliness, or isolation. Many relaxation exercises focus on the entire body and may include stretches and movements of individual body parts. This activity would not be applicable or appropriate for clients with a physical disability. This exercise emphasizes the areas that the client has full control over, including focus on breathing and how to monitor the client's body tension.

Script

Find a place where you can sit comfortably. If you can, feel free to lie down, flat on your back. When you are ready, close your eyes (pause). Take a deep breath. Inhale deeply and slowly count to 3 as you breathe out. 1 . . . 2 . . . 3. Good. Let's take another deep breath. Inhale deeply and slowly count to 5 as you breathe out. 1 . . . 2 . . . 3 . . . 4 . . . 5. Let your body relax. Imagine you are outside in a big open meadow, relaxing, and lying or sitting, in the freshly cut green grass. Your eyes are closed but you can see the tall patches of grass swaying in the cool breeze. The flowers of the meadow are in full bloom, displaying every color of the rainbow. The grass underneath you feels cool against your skin, while the sun above you warms your face. You can hear the wind rustling through the trees that surround you. A few leaves swirl around you before landing in the grass nearby. You can feel butterflies flutter softly by your face.

Next, imagine a place that you would like to go. Maybe this is a place that you cannot easily get to. Can you see this special place?

In the distance, you hear the wind. At first it moves softly, swaying the trees, the grass, and the flowers. Suddenly the wind picks up and you feel the cool breeze wash over your body (pause). Let the wind gently lift you off the ground. Relax your body and allow all of your weight to be held by the wind as it gently carries you away from the meadow (pause). Don't be afraid. The wind is gentle and safe. Relax and enjoy the feeling as it carries you to that special place you want to go. You hear birds chirping to one another as they fly alongside you. The butterflies are also flying alongside you watching over your journey. You can hear the water moving along a stream beneath you.

The wind carries you higher and higher over the treetops, over the meadow, and up into the sky. Stretch your arms and reach way up to the sky. The open blue sky is bright and welcoming as you float through it (pause). How are you feeling? Do you feel free? Remember, do not be afraid. The wind is gentle and safe. Take this opportunity to allow all of your negative feelings to surface and give them to the wind. As the wind carries you toward your special place, it will blow all of these feelings into the sky, far, far away from you (pause).

Take a deep breath. Slowly count to 3 as you breathe out. 1 . . . 2 . . . 3 (pause). Good, how does that feel? Think of happiness, joy, peace, and excitement. All of these positive feelings wash over you as the wind carries you closer to your special place (pause). Do you see it up ahead? You're almost there (pause). Is anyone there waiting for you? Let's take one more deep breath. Inhale and slowly count to 3 as you breathe out. 1 . . . 2 . . . 3. As you get closer, the wind gently glides you closer to the ground. The birds are still at your side. The butterflies flutter around you. The leaves are blowing softly in the wind, as it gently places you into the soft, green grass. You have safely made it to your special place (pause). Enjoy this place, stay here as long as you would like (pause). When you are ready, slowly open your eyes.

Application

This exercise can be used for any age and the script can be modified in a number of ways to best fit the client's needs. If the client has a specific place or activity in mind, the therapist can incorporate the details of this place or activity into the script. The script can be extended or shortened to be age-appropriate. If possible, engaging in this exercise outdoors may enhance the client's ability to visualize a nature scene. Music can also be used in the background and modified to match the particular scenario used.

B9
Freeing Feelings
Jenna Halseth

Use this exercise with children between the ages of 6 and 12 suffering from guilt or experiencing difficulty with other unresolved issues. Feeling guilty can be an especially confusing emotion for children because their cognitive functioning has not yet completely developed. Guilt is a complex emotion that includes a mixture of many emotions, and therefore children are challenged to grasp this feeling while they are still increasing awareness of their basic emotions, such as happy, sad, or angry. Children lack the full capability to understand the process of how to handle a guilty conscience, and they may be unaware that they need to release this feeling in order to feel completely satisfied again. This exercise helps children let go of these complex feelings and experience a sense of relief. Ideally, with some follow-up questions, this action of letting go can be translated into the other areas of the child's life where emotional release is needed.

Script

This is an exercise to help you relax. Please find a comfortable position in your chair. Relax your hands on your thighs or release your arms entirely so they hang loosely down toward the floor. Next, slowly close your eyes and relax all the muscles in your face. Clench your jaw tightly, and then relax. Open your mouth widely, hold it, then relax your jaw again.

Now I want you to imagine a beautiful natural setting. It could be the beach, the forest, the mountains; whatever you prefer. Once you have it in mind, just imagine and enjoy the beauty of this scenery. Somewhere in your imagination you see green plants, blue water, and white clouds. You feel the puffy clouds floating above you. Now, experience the clean, pure air with all your senses; smell it, hear it, breathe it in and out and feel comfortable with it. Touch something around you . . . maybe the sand on the beach, the mossy forest floor or the rugged mountain side. Just revel in the beauty of what's around you, and think about how exquisite and relaxing it is.

But wait! What's that? The sound of chirping birds enters your ears. After some searching, you see a giant cage full of birds hanging on a tree. You wonder how this has happened, how this is possible in such a beautiful location. These poor, trapped birds against the gorgeous, natural background just don't make sense. You realize that you must free these birds. You start running toward the cage, but it seems to be moving further away from you. It feels like you might never get there!

Once you finally reach the cage, you fumble with the latch for a bit. You get the gate open and the birds fly away with happiness, as if each of them is saying "thank you" to you for their freedom.

Once the birds are gone, you absorb the great feeling of relief. You know you have achieved a satisfying feeling and want to have this feeling again and again.

You feel so relaxed while holding on to this thought. You are about to come back to reality and want to enjoy a more open and free reality. In your mind, count backward from 5 . . . Now, 5, 4, 3, 2, 1. When you are ready, open your eyes. You are still relaxed.

Application

After the exercise, process the client's feelings through therapeutic questions such as:

1. How do you feel now after the exercise?
2. What does letting go of something in your life mean to you?
3. If there is one issue taking all your attention away from an otherwise beautiful life, how do you deal with it?
4. What could you do to get some release?
5. When was the last time you had a chance to talk to someone you trust about something that's been bothering you?

B10
From Yellow School Bus to White City Bus
Elizabeth Owsley

This exercise is designed to assist students with disabilities between the ages of 17 and 22. It was originally designed for the residents of Lake Jackson in Texas, who are at the stage of aging out of the school system under special education (primarily those in a "self-contained," life-skills classroom). The transition for a student with disability from a school service setting to a community-based instruction (CBI or "real world") can be particularly challenging, stressful, and intimidating from a mental and emotional standpoint. As students experience service system changes, they will need guidance in making a smooth transition. This exercise would be useful especially when they encounter situations where learning how to do things may feel differently than their expectations.

This imagery activity is designed for use in an individual setting, particularly with students in their last two years of school, but it can be modified to fit a group setting. The script can be modified based on the environment the students will encounter.

*Under Federal Law 20 U.S.C. § 1412, students have the option under special education law to stay in school until or through age 22.

Script

This is an imagery journey preparing you to think about your bus journey. This journey is taking you to your school bus and will also show you a new bus that will be taking you to your new job. Close your eyes and stay focused. You may remain silent and think about the questions and your answers throughout this journey, while continuing to imagine that you are relaxed.

Imagine we are walking outside to where the bus drops you off. Think about the color of the bus. Yes, it is yellow. Do you see another color bus? Yes—there is *a white bus with a blue strip on it*. You are on the right track! Let's focus on the yellow bus first. Every day you go to school by riding this yellow school bus. Imagine who else is riding with you. Who do you see riding with you on the bus? Yes, several classmates that you know by name. Think about their names. Good. The bus driver picks you up at your homes and you travel to your high school. It is wonderful that you know your route and who is riding with you every day on the yellow bus.

Imagine we are going to take a walk over and take a tour of the *white bus with the blue strip across the front*. This is the bus that will be taking you to your new job. Let's walk around the white bus to see and think about the differences. The bus has a large sign above the driver; does the yellow bus have anything like this? (pause) There are two doors on the white bus for the walk-on passengers and another one for wheelchair riders. Is that the same or is it different on the *yellow* bus? There are a lot of pictures on the *white* bus, including a flag covering the side of the bus or something else; is that the same or different? What is on the flag? (pause) You have now walked and observed the outside of this white bus. You begin to feel comfortable with this new bus.

Let's see what's in the white bus before we actually ride on it. Imagine we are entering the white bus. We have two stair steps before getting onto the bus. We first see the handrail on the right of the stair steps to help people get on. Is this the same or different than the yellow bus? (pause) We then see a silver box that is clear with a slot on top—it has money in it. This box collects the money paying for the bus trip that you will take from the bus stop to your place of employment. You drop the money in the box and tell the driver where you wish to go. Do you pay to ride the school bus? Do you have to tell the bus driver where you want to go every morning? (pause) Directly behind the driver you see two reserved spaces for wheelchairs. Do you remember the yellow school bus having a space like this?

You continue to walk into the bus and see that there is only enough room for 14 people to sit on the bus with seat belts. Let's take a seat on the bus. These seats are blue in color, made for two people. There is a seat belt for you to strap into. Do you have a seat belt on the school bus? (pause). The seats are low enough so that you can see where we are going without straining to see over the seats; can you do that on a school bus? (pause). If you look above the window, there is a white cord (or bell). You have to pull (or press) that when you want to get off the bus. When you pull the cord (or ring the bell) the driver will be notified by a light on their dashboard and a red light sign that says "stop requested." The driver will know you want to get off when you arrive near your workplace. You are aware of what is inside and begin to feel very comfortable with this new bus.

The next time we will actually take a riding tour of our city by one of the bus routes offered. Remember, you feel very comfortable with this new bus. For now, relax and open your eyes.

Application

This guided imagery is intended to begin guiding students with disabilities into understanding that although life will change, they are still capable of doing many things, such as riding a bus, because they have been doing it during their school careers. These students will face differences and similarities when learning to adjust to their new environment, and in time, they will learn how to be comfortable with it. Throughout this counseling session, it is important to remember that the abilities of each student (language, mobile abilities, and cognitive abilities) may have direct influence on the student's readiness to work on this transition process.

Process some feeling questions after the exercise:

1. What feelings did you have as we described both buses?
2. We sometimes can feel anxious about a new environment, such as riding on a different bus or getting a new job. What can you do to help yourself be more comfortable when taking the new transportation to your new job?
3. Tell me what you like about the new bus or new environment. What do you dislike?

B11
Go to My Country
Cristal Atilano

This guided imagery is for Mexican children (or other children) who have moved away from their native country to the United States. *It can be modified to include vocabularies representing the child's native home.* This exercise aims to help newly migrated children visualize and reconnect to a self-selected "safe place" to control anxiety and enhance resilience, particularly when they experience separation anxiety or attachment issues due to immigration. The first part is a relaxation component in which the children, individually or in a group, will learn to relax through a deep breathing exercise. It will continue to the guided imagery component of using the children's native language and culture to create a mental trip to this special "safe place." If the English version is preferred or to be added after the native language is used, it should contain some of these vocabularies—folk music, people, family, food, and food market—to represent their home country and culture.

Script

Let's begin by getting comfortable in your seat. Try to place your feet flat on the floor and rest your hands lightly on your thighs. Good. Now you are going to close your eyes and begin deep breathing. Remember to breathe in slowly and deeply as if you are smelling a flower; . . . inhale . . . and then blow the air out . . . exhale. Again . . . inhale . . . exhale. As you exhale, feel the tension of your body releasing . . . relax . . . one more time . . . inhale . . . and exhale . . . good job!

(Begin the Spanish version for Mexican children. If preferred to use English, use the translated version)

Spanish Version

Ok, ahora sigue con los ojos cerrados. Quiero que te imagines ese lugar en México en donde te sentías cómodo, relajado y seguro. Puede ser un lugar real o imaginario, pero debe ser un lugar especial donde tú te sientas seguro. En este lugar tú te sientes relajado, íntegro, y sereno. Recuerda que este lugar es lo que tú quieras que sea. Mira a tu alrededor del lugar especial y seguro. Toma en cuenta las diferentes que te rodean . . . el mariachi . . . la gente . . . la comida . . . el mercado. Pon atención a todos los detalles de lo que ves; este es tu propio lugar seguro y especial. El olor está presente, respira profundamente y huele los delicioso aromas a tu alrededor . . . los tacos . . . los churros . . . las gorditas . . . las flores . . . la lluvia, los aromas de tu lugar especial y seguro. Siente la textura de tu lugar seguro y especial. La brisa fresca y agradable durante el día . . . o los rayos del sol sobre tu piel. Los sonidos son muy agradables . . . la música del mariachi . . . la risa de la gente . . . la brisa en la plaza. Eso es fenomenal. Tú puedes elegir cualquier persona o cualquier cosa para que sea parte de tu lugar seguro y especial. Tú tienes el control. Todo lo que hay en tu lugar seguro y especial te hace sentir relajado, seguro y cómodo.

Observa y siente las cosas diferentes tu alrededor, como los colores, los olores, las texturas, y los sonidos. Experimenta tu lugar seguro y especial. Nadie más que tú tiene el control sobre este lugar. En este lugar te sientes seguro, relajado y feliz. Este sitio te ayuda a sentirte renovado con la ayuda de la serenidad y la maravillosa imagen de tu lugar especial. Este lugar siempre estará aquí para cuando tú lo necesites.

Ha llegado la hora de salir de tu lugar especial y seguro. Mira a tu alrededor una vez más y recuerda este lugar. Recuerda lo que ves, lo que hueles, lo que sientes, y lo que escuchas. Recuerda que este lugar es tuyo y que tú puedes regresar aquí cuando tú así lo necesites. Estás relajado y tú sabes que estás seguro. Ahora vas a regresar a esta habitación al escuchar las letras del alfabeto de la Q a la Z. Inhala profundamente . . . Q . . . R . . . S . . . exhala . . . Y y Z; ahora abre los ojos. Al mirar a tu alrededor te sientes relajado, seguro, y feliz. ¡Te sientes muy bien!

English Version

Ok, now keep your eyes closed. In your head, I want you to picture yourself in that place in your home country (Mexico) where you would feel comfortable, relaxed, safe, and secure. It can be a place that is real or imagined. This can be your special safe place based on your memory of a good place. In this place you feel the soothing relaxation of wholeness and serenity. Remember this place is whatever you want it to be. Look around in your special safe place. Observe the different things around you . . . the *mariachi* (folk music) . . . the *gente* (people) . . . *la comida* (food) . . . *el mercado* (food market). Be aware of the details in whatever you see; this is your very own special safe place. The smell is present, the food—*tacos* . . . *churros* . . . *gorditas* . . . ; inhale the delicious smells from this special safe place. Feel the texture of your special safe place. The nice cool breeze during the day . . . at the plaza . . . or the sunbeams against your skin. The sound is very pleasant—the *mariachi* playing . . . the *familia* (family) laughing . . . the breeze in the plaza. That's great. You can choose anybody and anything to be part of this special safe place in your memory. You are in control. Everything in your special safe place is to make you feel relaxed, safe, and at ease.

Observe the different things around you like the colors, the smell, the textures, and the sounds. Feel your special safe place. This place belongs to you and nobody but you has control over it. In this place you feel safe, secure, relaxed, and happy. This place helps you feel new with the help of the serenity and the wonderful image of your place. This place will always be here when you need it.

It is now time to step out of your special safe place. Look around one more time and keep this place in mind. Remember how it looks . . . smells . . . feels . . . and sounds. Remember this place is yours and you can come back to it again when you need to. You are relaxed and you know you are safe. You are now coming back to this room as you hear the alphabets from Q to Z. Let's breathe in . . . Q . . . R . . . S . . . breathe out . . . T . . . U . . . V . . . breathe in . . . W . . . X . . . breathe out . . . Y and Z; now . . . open your eyes. As you look around, you feel relaxed, safe, secure, and happy. You feel great!

Application

This guided imagery exercise can be used as a therapeutic intervention to help immigrant children process feelings and thoughts about their migration and new home. It assists children in their ability to relax and to imagine a safe place from their memory of their country of origin. Giving the children an opportunity of a personal selection is valuable for them to find the best parts to re-create in their future home. Some native vocabularies can be used to process how the native environment has been helpful for them and what they could do to create a similar environment in the new country.

After the exercise, use these suggested therapeutic questions to process:

1. Tell me which part of this exercise was most relaxing (helpful).
2. Share with me about the culture in this special safe place (such as music, people, food, language, etc.).
3. How did it feel for you to create your special safe place? Which part in this place came from memory of your home country?
4. What would you share with someone (such as your parents) about the soothing effect of this special safe place?

B12
Glistening Stream and Body Image
Ivy E. Crank

This exercise is designed for adolescent females who are struggling with body image. Participants are presented with a choice and then are encouraged to stay in the moment as active observers of their own sensory experiences. This exercise is best used once rapport has been established with the client and should be followed by process questions.

Script

Close your eyes gently and take a slow deep breath in through your nose and out through your mouth. Imagine that you are standing by a quiet, isolated road. Ahead of you is a thick forest filled with dark green fir and spruce trees. As you walk forward through the field towards the forest, you pause for a moment to look to either side of you, but it seems that no one is there. You see a sign, which reads, "No trespassing," and your heart beats a little faster. But as you look again towards the forest, you feel driven to go further. Your pace quickens as you pass through the field, and your feet feel light. You smile as you feel the warm sun shine on your hair, and you wonder what you might find in this forest. As you enter you notice the way the sun passes through the trees and the shade on the mossy forest floor. Your legs brush against plants and undergrowth as you make your own path, and you wonder how many others have passed here before you. Your path gently rises, and on the hillside in front of you there are wild blueberry plants and small wildflowers in white, blue, and yellow. Every now and then you notice a small animal scurrying by, and as you breathe in deeply through your nose you smell the fragrant evergreens. You stop walking for a moment, and you see that all around you is forest. You forget the risk you took to be in this place and you feel safe and peaceful in this moment.

You continue walking and soon come to a stream unlike any you have ever seen before. Amber-colored water glistens in the sunlight as it passes slowly over large rocks spread throughout the stream. You walk closer until your feet are at the edge of the wet rocks, and again you notice the sun on your hair and that your back begins to feel warm. You notice your reflection in the water as you lean closer, and watch as your form shifts with every ripple. Focus upon this moment and how you feel as you watch your shape, ever-changing and adapting to the stream. Then, as the light reflects upon the golden water, your eyelids droop and you take a slow, deep breath.

Something about the sparkling water and the sense of solitude reminds you of winter, and you smile softly to yourself thinking of family and friends over winter holidays. You imagine for a just a moment that you are a snowman built by some children who left you in this spot to stand on your own. You stand strong, supporting your head, body, and two long arms that stick straight out to the side. You think that the afternoon feels lovely as the sun shines upon you. But the warmth causes you to feel as though you are melting. Your head melts first, and then your right arm slowly melts, followed by your left. Then a little at a time, the rest of your body melts until all that is left of you is a puddle that slowly flows into the sparkling stream by which you once stood. As you drift away you feel a sense of peace and connectedness. As part of the stream you feel free to move without any limitations, without worries of what others might think. Letting go of yourself and all of your fears, you feel strength both physically and emotionally.

Keep your eyes closed as you take a deep breath and slowly return to the road where you began. As you slowly open your eyes, remember the strength you felt when you observed and connected to your surroundings. Remember today's journey and the freedom you gave yourself to explore.

Application

Immediately follow the exercise with process questions to explore the adolescent's feelings, relationships, identity, and connections. Viewing her reflection in the stream offers the client a more fluid perspective on the self and her appearance and prompts feelings of relaxation rather than anxiety. Although this exercise is designed for adolescent females, it can be modified for any age group and also used with men or boys. This exercise may also be adapted for clients who are not familiar with snow, due to geographic reasons, or whose culture does not practice winter holidays. Clients can return to this exercise as appropriate and may be given a gold-colored gem as a reminder of the strength and peace they felt during the exercise from the sparkling stream. The following questions are suggested:

1. What fears came to mind when you first saw the "No trespassing" sign? What do these two words mean to you? In what ways do others set limits on your behaviors? How can these limits be helpful to you? And harmful? How do you know when to take risks?

2. How easy or difficult was it to stay in the moment and focus on your surroundings? If you found yourself distracted by outside thoughts, what was coming to mind for you?

3. Tell me about the image you saw in the water. How was your reflection different from the way you usually see yourself? How did you feel as you looked at your reflection?

4. What was it like being the snowman? In what ways did the snowman's experience of being built, and left to stand alone, remind you of your own life growing up? How did you feel about melting and letting go? What prevents you from letting go and relaxing in your everyday life?

5. What similarities connect you to others? How do you think others perceive you? How do others' perceptions impact what you say and do? What are some things that you would like to do if you didn't have to worry about what other people thought? How can letting go bring you feelings of strength?

6. How can this exercise help you rethink concerns about the way you look? What specific actions can you take to feel more peaceful?

Suggested Music

"American Beauty—Plastic Bag Theme" by London Music Works, which was featured on the album *The Film Music of Thomas Newman*.

B13
Healing Parent-Teen Conflict
Ruprekha Baruah

The goal of this exercise is to reduce frustration and stress related to memories of troublesome family situations between teenagers and their parents. It provides teenagers and their parents with a technique to aid in reducing their stress levels, and assists them with insight into their relationships and their respective roles to promote positive interactions.

The facilitator begins the exercise by dimming the lights and instructing participants to sit or lie down in a comfortable posture. Proceed by preparing the accompanying recording or beginning to read the script.

Script

This is an exercise to help you relax and to calm your thoughts in order to feel happy, content, and strong in your body, mind, and spirit. It provides a window to increase your inner strength that allows you to explore physical sensations, thoughts, and feelings as you experience them in the present moment. As you tune out the mental chatter in your head, you will use your mind to change the sensations into positive ones towards a situation that has made you feel stressed or frustrated. As you achieve your goal of concentration, you will be able to do this anytime and anywhere to feel calm and peaceful again. Let go of any anxiety and mental discomfort. As you participate in this exercise, take what is meaningful to you and leave the rest.

Begin by taking a deep refreshing breath through your nose, and hold it for a few seconds (1, 2, and 3). Now, breathe it all out through your lips. Take in another refreshing breath, hold it (1, 2, and 3) and now let it all out. Notice that with each breath you take in and out, you are getting more and more comfortable.

As you relax and concentrate on your breathing, remember that any conflict with your family member is now being dismissed. You have gained insight that can increase your ability to disregard any distracting thoughts. You have developed power that can restore energy to replace negative comments with something positive. Think about a nice smile, a good day, or a relaxing walk with your family member—you feel comfortable. Notice how you are able to let go of negative thoughts and feelings. What was in the past can be left behind. What you disliked can be changed because of your positive attitude toward life. You are positive about your ability to build a better relationship. Next time, you can talk without frustration, feel positive without distractions; anything that is unpleasant can be breathed out.

Keep taking refreshing breaths and think positively. Are you ready to talk more about your feelings? (pause) As I count down from 3 to 1, you will take three long, refreshing breaths. 3 . . . 2 . . . 1, and now slowly open your eyes.

Application

This exercise may be used with both teenagers and their parents on a weekly basis to reduce the stress and frustration derived from negative family interactions. To track progress, the facilitator may ask participants to keep a weekly journal noting any incidences of successful resolution of family conflicts. The journal will be used during future individual or family sessions.

B14
Helping Children Sleep after a Parent Has Been Incarcerated
Nicole Willis

This guided imagery exercise is intended for use with children who are experiencing problems sleeping after a parent has been incarcerated. This exercise should be used at bedtime to help the child fall asleep, or when the child awakes during the night. Many young children experience difficulty coping with parent-child separation, and those who are used to a bedtime routine with their parent, such as being "tucked-in," experience problems sleeping after a disruption in this routine. The incarcerated parent should pre-record this relaxation technique and include soft background music. The use of the parent's voice will comfort the child at bedtime and will allow the child to feel that the parent is near and the parent is safe. In this script, you may use the child's nickname and dad's voice.

Script

Hey, "sweetie" (insert nickname), it's mom. I see that you are having trouble sleeping. Just listen to mommy's voice, honey, and everything is going to be all right. Just lie back in bed and put your head on the pillow. That's right. Feel how fluffy the pillow is against your cheek. Do you have your favorite teddy next to you? Hug the teddy bear really close. Imagine you are lying down in my arms and I am holding you close. Do you have all the covers pulled up? Mommy wants you to be nice and cozy.

Now, close your eyes. That's right. Relax your arms around the teddy bear. Now, let's take three deep breaths together, on the count of three. Ready? One . . . two . . . three (take three deep breaths). Very good. Your legs and shoulders are feeling heavier. Your toes and fingers feel relaxed. Let's take three more deep breaths together, on the count of three. Ready? One . . . two . . . three (take three deep breaths). I want you to imagine that I'm right there next to you. It's quiet all around you and all you hear is my voice. Imagine the moonlight peeking through the curtains. Your eyelids feel heavier and you are in a safe place. Mommy's feeling sleepy, too.

Now, with your eyes closed, I want you to imagine that mommy is in a different place but not too far from here. You can see mommy is in a nice, comfortable bed, going to sleep just like you are. Mommy's bed looks a lot like yours, with big, fluffy, white pillows and warm blankets. You can see me in a quiet room with the moonlight peeking in the window. You see that mommy is falling asleep and she is safe.

Do you remember the picture you drew for me when ____ (insert a specific example)? Imagine now that you can see the picture on the wall next to where mommy is sleeping. As I feel my eyelids getting heavier, I am thinking of you and how much fun we have together. Now, as you are falling asleep, remember how much mommy loves you. You are almost asleep now. Just keep listening to the music and drift off to sweet dreams.

Application

The caseworker should work with the incarcerated parent to record the tape. However, the caseworker should gather some of the following information from the parent, before the script and music are recorded, in order to better personalize the tape: (1) the child's nickname, (2) any specific stuffed animals or toys the child likes to sleep with, (3) any memorable occasions of quality time that the parent and child spent together. If the child does not have a bedtime comfort toy, the caseworker should ask the parent to create one and put it in the script. The caseworker and the caretaker should discuss the use of the recording during a therapeutic session. The caretaker will be responsible for setting up the recording near the child's bed. The child should be encouraged to play the tape when he or she cannot get to sleep or when the child wakes up in the middle of the night. The child's caretaker should keep track of the frequency with which the child plays the recording after their parent's incarceration. This will help track the child's progress.

B15
I Am Strong, Confident, and Powerful!
Jenaia Leffel

The repetition of the title "I am strong, confident and powerful!" helps clients achieve a state of empowerment. It will not only empower the clients to overcome their insecurities but also allow them to feel more relaxed about voicing their feelings, needs, and opinions. It will help them become encouraged about the choices and control they have over their own bodies. This exercise will guide clients towards change and the process of evolving mentally in order to prepare them in dealing with life stressors. It will also enable them to provide peace to their own environment and well-being.

This exercise is useful for children, age ten and above, and to adults who have low self-esteem or feel as though their environment is too chaotic. In an uncluttered room, ask the client to sit comfortably in a chair or couch.

Script

Sit comfortably with your arms resting on your lap. Close your eyes and concentrate on my voice. When you hear "repeat after me," you may repeat the phrase aloud or silently. Keep your eyes closed. Take a deep breath. Exhale for five slow counts. 5 . . . 4 . . . 3 . . . 2 . . . 1 . . . Good. Repeat after me: "I am strong!" (Client repeats). "I am confident!" (Client repeats). "I will speak my mind calmly and respect others while doing so." (Client repeats). "I am mentally powerful." (Client repeats). "Please give me time and space to organize my thoughts." (Client repeats). "I will prevail!" (Client repeats). Take a deep breath. Exhale for five slow counts. 5 . . . 4 . . . 3 . . . 2 . . . 1 . . . Good. Repeat after me: "I am strong!" (Client repeats). "I am confident!" (Client repeats). "I will speak my mind calmly and respect others while doing so." (Client repeats). "I am mentally powerful." (Client repeats). "Please give me time and space to organize my thoughts." (Client repeats). "I will prevail!" (Client repeats). Take a deep breath and exhale at your own pace. Now, relax your body.

(Repeat as many times as client needs or requires).

Application

This exercise is available for use when discussing feelings of low self-esteem or for those who have a chaotic home life or environment. The exercise is used to encourage the client by suggesting the message "stick up for yourself" in a situation in which the client would normally retreat. You can provide positive affirmations for the client to repeat when he or she feels a need to relax and do guided imagery at his or her own pace.

Follow up with therapeutic questions. Here are some examples:

1. When you hear the words "strong and confident," how do you feel?
2. Tell me about the situation(s) that came to your mind during this exercise.
3. Tell me about other phrases or words you would like to incorporate to tailor this exercise specifically for you.
4. What feelings or insight did you gain from this exercise? Explain them.

B16
Laughing Yoga
Monit Cheung

Laughing yoga is also called "laughter yoga." It is a relaxation method without language requirements. You don't have to think about why you are laughing. Laughing itself, with or without a reason or trigger, increases oxygen intake and stimulates the brain to release natural relaxation chemicals in the body such as endorphins and serotonins. These natural hormones within the body can help us reduce fatigue, relax muscles, strengthen our immune system, increase our ability to fight illness, and reduce the high cortisol level that causes chronic fatigue. Laughing as a movement is also considered an "internal jogging" for our least moved internal organs. Since the body does not differentiate a real laugh from a fake laugh, laughing yoga eventually helps us produce real happy moods that can be contagious to those surrounding us. When everyone is happy, you become happier. When you are happy, you tend to breathe naturally without stress and you influence others to feel happy, too.

Script

This is an easy exercise to relax. No matter how busy you are, spare about one or two minutes' time per day to laugh or smile, with or without a reason. In this exercise, we will laugh. Laugh as hard and as much as you can. You don't have to think about a reason to laugh. You don't have to recall a comedy or a joke to laugh. Simply repeat after me. Ok?

He, he—he, he, he. [He, he—he, he, he.]

Ha, ha—ha, ha, ha. [Ha, ha—ha, ha, ha.]

He, he—he, he, he. [He, he—he, he, he.]

Ha, ha—ha, ha, ha. [Ha, ha—ha, ha, ha.]

Who, who—who, who, who. [Who, who—who, who, who.]

Me, me—me, me, me. [Me, me—me, me, me.]

Hee, hee—he, he, he. [Hee, hee—he, he, he.]

Hee, hee. [Hee, hee.]

Haa, haa. [Haa, haa.]

Hee, ha, he, he, he. [Hee, ha, he, he, he.]

Haa, ha, ha, ha, ha. [Haa, ha, ha, ha, ha.]

Hee, ha. [Hee, ha.]

Haa, he. [Haa, he.]

Ha—Ha. [Ha—Ha.]

Ha, ha, ha. [Ha, ha, ha.]

He, he, he, he. [He, he, he, he.]

Ha, ha, ha, ha. [Ha, ha, ha, ha.]

Hee, hee—hee, hee, hee. [Hee, hee—hee, hee, hee.]

Haa, haa—ha, ha, ha. [Haa, haa—ha, ha, ha.]

Hee, haa—hee, hee, ha. [Hee, haa—hee, hee, ha.]

He—Ha. [He—ha.]

He, he, he, he, he. [He, he, he, he, he.]

Ha, ha, ha, ha, ha. [Ha, ha, ha, ha, ha.]

Ha, ha. [Ha, ha.]

He, he. [He, he.]

Deep breathing. In—1, 2, 3, 4, and out.

Ha, ha. [Ha, ha.]

Bye, bye. [Bye, bye.]

Application

Clients can practice this exercise freely without thinking about what patterns of he-ha to use. Other sounds or words may be used to continue or replace the "he" and the "ha," such as letters of the alphabet, used as: "A, a, a, a, a" or "B, b, b, b, b." Immigrants who are learning English as their second language can replace the he-ha in the original script with sounds from alphabets, numbers, or simple words that they recently learned to create their laughing yoga in a form that they can memorize without stress.

B17
My Family Tree
Joy Welch

This exercise helps adopted children, from ages 5 to 11, to learn how to become actively involved in exploring self-concepts in relation to their birth and adoptive families. Begin by asking the children to share what they want other group members to know about themselves, their families, and their adoption experience. Tell them that if they are not comfortable sharing personal information in a group setting, they can listen to how others share first and then participate in this individualized exercise that focuses on their thinking and thoughts. In this exercise, imagination is used to help us relax. Follow the instructions, or simply sit quietly and listen.

Script

We are going to learn a little more about ourselves today. First, let's see if we can all get comfortable. Lie down on your mat, or sit comfortably. You may close your eyes if you like, or leave them open. Let's take a slow deep breath and fill up our body with air. Good. Now let's push that air out through our mouths. Ok, good. Again, a slow big breath, and now, push that air slowly out. Very good.

Now let's imagine that you see a beautiful . . . tree! We are going to imitate this tree to relax.

Allow your feet to act like the roots in this tree. Waggle your toes as fast as you can—like the roots are quickly growing. Your solid roots are planted deep into the warm brown earth. Good. Now let's focus on the trunk of this tree. It's brown, and the bark is hard and solid. You're strong. Now, slowly s-t-r-e-t-c-h your arms out like the branches of the tree. They're long and curved upward. Good. See how tall you can become by stretching your arms up, up, and up. Good. On the tips of your long branch-like arms, you see the green soft leaves. Wiggle your fingers and move your arms up and down, right and left, like leaves blowing in the wind. Good. What a beautiful tree!

Feel how strong you are, from your roots all the way to the top of your leafy branches. Sense how the trunk of your tree feels solid. Imagine the curved branches reaching toward the blue sky, and the leaves blowing softly in the breeze. Picture fluffy clouds in the sky above you. Feel the warm sun shining on the branches that makes you feel safe and warm. Nature is taking care of you, and you feel loved and cared for. You feel relaxed because you know more about yourself. You feel strong, peaceful and alive. You know you belong.

All of your parts make you feel like a strong, tall, and growing tree. Without your roots, you would not have grown into the beautiful tree you are. Without your trunk, you would not be the strong tree you are. And without your branches and leaves, you would not be complete. You are like the tree. Your birth family is like your roots. They cannot make you who you are, but they are part of who you are. They have given you the roots so you can grow. Your adoptive parents are like your branches. They do not make you who you are, but they help to shape you. The leaves are your own expression of who you are. They may not all be the same size, shape, or color, but their appearance is what makes you stand out. The tree, whose foundation begins with its roots, takes shape through its branches. And from both, the leaves unfold and give the tree its own unique beauty.

Can you see your tree? Can you see the different parts? Can you see that each part is needed? Can you see that your tree is unique? Can you see that you are growing and thriving to be your very own tree? And you are whole, and beautiful.

Now that you see how you, your birth parents, and your adoptive parents are all connected, and you feel the sun shining its beautiful warm rays and feel the breeze blowing through your branches, you begin to realize how warm and loving you are in your heart. You feel so loved! You are unique and amazing. Always remember this and keep this special feeling in your heart at all times. There is no one else like you. You are a very important part of the universe and no one can do exactly what you do, in the way you do it.

Now when you are ready, you can open your eyes and slowly begin to stand on your own two feet. It was a wonderful journey. You are who you are. Say, "I am ME!"

Application

This exercise can be done individually or in a group. It helps children develop and support a positive outlook on their adoption. Adopted children often struggle to understand, appreciate, and accept the duality inherent in adoption and the love that contributed to their birth family's decision. The imagery of the tree emphasizes the connections and contributions of both families, and encourages adopted children to embrace the uniqueness of their birth and adoptive families. It instills strength in the clients by reminding them that they are a product of two families with love and support surrounding them. In a group setting, this exercise provides the clients with a supportive peer group who can relate to the different aspects and experiences that adopted children and their families encounter.

B18
My Favorite Thing
Juan C. Macias

Use this relaxation exercise with clients who suffer from concentration problems or attention deficits such as ADD/ADHD. It may be used with individuals and groups, children, adolescents, or adults. Prior to the use of this imagery, assess the client's ability to follow directions and the capability to sit still for a couple of minutes. Next, have the client identify his or her favorite object (such as a specific toy), which will be the focus during this exercise to help the client to maintain interest and concentration. If the client does not choose an item or if the item is not suitable for this exercise, ask him or her to imagine a person or choose a ball to represent the client's all-round personality. "Ball" will be used as an example which may be replaced by another item from the client's choices. This exercise can be done either with or without music.

Script

Get into a comfortable position. Take a slow deep breath in through your nose. Now slowly release it through your mouth. Relax your whole body. Close your eyes and clear your mind. Take another slow deep breath, in—through your nose, hold it, and now slowly breathe out through your mouth. Feel the relaxation throughout your body as you breath out. Keep breathing slowly, in . . . and out.

Now, picture the item you chose at the beginning. What is it? What is in this item that can make you relaxed? Imagine how it may feel to hold it, touch it. Take a slow deep breath in and release your breath out through your mouth. Feel your body relax as you focus on the "ball." Now, in your mind, slowly spell out "ball": B-A-L-L. Remember, you are still slowly breathing in and out, in and out. Focus. Nothing else is in your mind now except the "ball" and my voice. You feel relaxed and have a single focus. Take in a slow deep breath and let it out slowly.

Now, continue to focus on the "ball" as you slowly open your eyes. Breathe in and out. Now whenever you need to focus you can close your eyes and think about your favorite thing, spelling it out (pause for the spelling). Remain calm and relaxed. Maintain this image until you are fully focused.

Application

A shorter version (e.g., only the first paragraph) can be used to provide an easy starting point when working with clients who have trouble focusing. Then gradually include a second paragraph to it until the client can concentrate on the entire exercise. This activity may be practiced and rehearsed by the client to learn how to concentrate and focus on a particular item, such as a ball, for a short period of time before going back to an assigned task. This exercise allows the facilitator to observe the client's behavior and gauge the client's attention span. The client can continue to use this exercise to relax when needed after he or she has become comfortable and confident in his or her ability to visualize and maintain focus.

B19
Pain Management
Ashleigh Scinta

This is a relaxation technique to prepare children and adolescents for medical treatment. It is appropriate for patients undergoing treatment requiring mild sedation before or after treatment. This exercise will help patients relax by diverting them from the unsettling hospital environment and reducing the anxiety caused by the procedure. The patient can drift to an imaginary place to escape the pain of the procedure. Prior to the use of this exercise, it is imperative to consult with the child's doctor to ensure that the exercise is appropriate to meet the child's needs.

Ideally, the child should be seated or lying down in a comfortable position, based on the type of treatment or the procedure the child will have.

Script

Gently close your eyes and take three deep big breaths. One . . . Two . . . Three. Good!

Picture a boat in your mind that you have been on before, or you could use an imaginary boat if you like. Imagine that you are on the boat.

You can feel the gentle sway of the water beneath the boat and the warm sun shining on your face. Look around you. Your boat is in the middle of a calm lake. The lake is a bright green color and the rays of the sun are reflecting on the surface like diamonds.

On your boat, you find a magic bag full of colorful seashells. You pick up the first seashell. It is bright blue. It feels warm and smooth in your hands. This seashell is very special; when you tell it your secrets or concerns, your secrets and concerns will go in this seashell. However, as soon as you drop the seashell in the water, your secrets and concerns disappear. Now you have these special seashells in your mind that can take away any problems, worries, or upsetting situations. No matter how big or small these problems may be, the special seashells are here to listen to you.

Whenever you feel anxious or concerned, you can share these feelings with your special seashells. These feelings will go in a special seashell. Remember, as soon as you drop the seashell in the water, your feelings of anxiety will be washed away and leave you with the calm feeling that you are in full control.

Now, picture yourself holding a special seashell close to your mouth so that you can tell your secrets to it. It has a color that calms your feelings. In your mind, silently tell the seashell whatever you want to say. No one else will know what you tell to your special seashell—only you and your special seashell! As you say your words, they go in your special seashell and the seashell takes these problems away from you. Now, tell your special seashell about your concerns or problems silently . . . (pause)

Good. Picture yourself reaching over the side of your boat and dropping your special seashell into the bright sparkling water in the lake. As your special seashell enters the water, you see all your concerns disappear! As the concerns disappear, you feel yourself letting go of your fears, anxieties, and problems. The special seashell has made those feelings disappear! It's your will power. Just like magic!

After dropping the special seashell in the water, you sit back in your boat and feel a sense of happiness and peacefulness. You feel relaxed from the top of your head to the tips of your toes. Feel it right now. Pay attention to how it feels.

You can imagine your boat and special seashells whenever you wish to make any upsetting thoughts and feelings go away or whenever you want to feel calm and at ease. Your special seashells will always be waiting for you. It's your will power. Just like magic!

You can always look for your own real special seashell. It can be a friend, a drawing, or a real seashell you picked up on a beach. You know that it has special power because it is your will power. Next time when you find a seashell, paint it or draw pictures on it. You can even design your own seashell on a piece of paper and keep it. This seashell will be your special one. Keep this special seashell by your bed or place it on your desk. It will always be there to listen to you.

You feel calm and relaxed! You are back to this room and you have a strong power within you. Now gently open your eyes and be aware of the peaceful feelings within you.

Application

If the child is afraid of water, the content can change to a place that the child would like to visit. After the child has gained some experience with this exercise, the seashell can be replaced with a soft item such as a marshmallow. You may add a few relaxation exercises, such as "Hold your marshmallow and slightly squeeze it. Feel the softness and relaxation." "Imagine the marshmallow comes in many different shapes. Here is a rabbit just like the candies you see in your Easter basket." After the content design is done, record it for the child to take home. Ask the parent to observe the child as he or she listens to the recording and to pay attention to the level of relaxation in the child's eyes and forehead before, during, and after the exercise. This exercise assesses the client's ability to relax, records how long it may take for the child to enter a relaxed state, and determines its appropriateness before continuation.

B20
Petals Overcoming Trauma
Monica Ortiz-Holtkamp

This therapeutic exercise can be used with children and adolescents who are survivors of child sexual abuse or other traumas. Survivors of trauma, especially involving child sexual abuse, often feel anxious about unfamiliar places and new friends. They also have trouble expressing emotions and feelings. This exercise should be used after rapport has been established with a client. Before beginning the guided imagery, ask the client to think about any bad feelings he or she has experienced and what qualities he or she had to overcome related to these bad feelings. Have the client draw a flower with five petals and label each petal with a negative feeling that he or she struggles with and also a strength that he or she uses to cope with these feelings. This flower will be used during the guided imagery. Background music may be included and pre-selected with the client to avoid any unintended trigger of negative emotions.

Script

Have you ever felt afraid of a new place or uncomfortable around new friends? That's normal; that is called the journey to growing up. Let's begin our journey! Take a moment to relax and breathe in some fresh air. You may keep your eyes open or you may close them. Now, think of a place that makes you feel calm, happy, and safe—this will be your special place. Take a deep breath, in . . . out. Good.

Imagine you are in your special place. As you look around and take in the sights and sounds, you see a flower. This flower has five petals just like your drawing. Each petal represents a fear or a bad feeling you have. Let's take another deep breath. These fears are familiar to you but you know you have the strength to counter them. Remember the flower you drew and each of the positive, powerful qualities you mentioned. Together we will work through these fears. Take a deep breath. You are doing great!

Now, when you're ready, imagine holding the flower in your hand. Look at each petal and think about the fears and strengths you have. Now, let's pluck the first petal. Can you think of another way to fight your fear? What about courage? Yes, you have courage! Let's pluck another one. What new methods can you think of to use when experiencing negative feelings? How about your support system? Yes, you have a support system including your family, teachers, and friends! Are you ready to pluck another petal? Yes, let's pluck the third petal. Now try to think of a way to cope with discomfort in new situations or environments. Have you tried using your internal power to bring something special to the situation? You have it—you can do it! Let's pluck the fourth petal. Think about a way you can fight feelings of despair. Sometimes all you need is a good night of sleep to feel refreshed in the morning. You can do it! Now, let's pluck the final petal. Can you think of a strength that can help you face any of your fears head on? Remind yourself that your strengths and actions can influence any situation or feeling and turn it into something positive and different. When you feel overwhelmed, remember this exercise! Your strengths can make these problems go away.

Now imagine that you take all of the plucked petals in your hand and let them fly away with the wind. 1, 2, 3, they're gone! Take a deep breath. Let's take another deep breath, in . . . out. Allow your body to relax as you leave all the bad images behind you. Now it is time for you to plant seeds of happiness for new beginnings.

You are strong and brave for fighting against these uncomfortable feelings and fears. Now they are released and they are no longer your problems.

Application

This exercise allows the client to feel in control through choosing his or her own special place. The therapist can customize this script in a way to make the client feel safe, and to draw on any positive qualities that the client has mentioned in previous sessions. The details of the exercise may be modified through substitution of an image other than the flower, which may be something the client connects with, or something the client would like to get rid of. It is important to process feelings and thoughts upon completion of this exercise. Therapeutic questions may include:

1. How did you feel when you were able to pluck these bad feelings out?
2. How did this exercise help you feel better and safe?
3. What would you like to add to the list of your strengths and good qualities?

B21
Practice Makes Perfect
Patrick Leung

Traveling with a Taoist means that you look at the world from a different angle. A Taoist is a Chinese philosopher who travels around the world to discuss life issues with people, particularly those with emotional disturbances. This guided journey is a story that discusses life, using wood as a material to explain that nothing comes out perfectly if you do not practice.

Script

This is a story about an elderly person who makes wheels for carts in ancient time.

One day an old man met a Taoist. The old man asked the Taoist "What are you reading?" The Taoist said, "I'm reading a book." The old man said immediately, "Well, listen, this book has no use at all." The Taoist was upset and thought, "Why, these books are written so beautifully; they transform simple words into knowledge. These books have taught me so much and even inspired me to write my own." Without waiting for the Taoist to say anything further, the old man said, "Well, let me tell you how I experienced my life, therefore you will then understand what I am saying." He continued, "I have been making wheels. Look at this piece of wood—it's not round at all. When I make a wheel, I use my knife to cut it and make it round. I can cut it so fast that I save time and energy. However, because I cut it fast, I cannot see how the angle goes. After the first few fast cuts, I must slow it down, cutting it slowly until it is round. I don't use the same force or speed in every cut because I want to make it round. Now, you see, it is spinning very slowly. I may cut it fast sometimes and then cut it very slowly other times. When it spins, it has the right timing and right angle. See, I make nice wheels. This is how I have done it in my lifetime.

The Taoist asked, "How can you pass your skill to your son?" The old man said, "I cannot transmit what I learned to my children or other people, because what I learned is what I know. I'm seventy years old and I'm still cutting wheels but I cannot give the entirety of my knowledge to anyone. I can only provide instruction—knowledge will be obtained through experience" The Taoist then said, "Let me write down each procedure of making a wheel and ask my students to come to observe after they read it." Yes, what we have read may not be useful at all, but without this first step, life is not easy. If you learn it yourself, it may take forever to understand the steps. Once you observe, you incorporate what you have already learned. Don't throw away your books too soon or too fast. Wait until you observe and add your practice to your learning.

This is the end of the story. The moral of this story is that only when you observe and practice what you've learned will you have that knowledge for a lifetime. Integrate your book knowledge with direct experience, with your practice and a good attitude in your application, and then create something that is most relevant and useful to you. Everyone is unique—learning is the first step and you can add to it and create your own skill as you go along. Learn first, then create what is most useful to you; add what is most relevant and the new knowledge, skill, and attitude are yours.

Application

A Taoist is a Chinese philosopher and the moral of his story is applicable to every culture. Several metaphors are used in this guided journey with the Taoist, including the book, wood, spin, wheel, and student. He is good at using the theory of relativity—a theory about no absolute answers. In his Taoist theory, people can see the same thing from different angles and then find different meanings from this same thing. When a client is emotionally disturbed by a life challenge or cannot concentrate on studying because of life stressors, you can help him or her to find an answer by looking at the challenge from a different angle, from a different person's view, or from a different time reference. The Taoist's story from the ancient time tells us that learning is timeless and without boundaries. The essence of this story is "learning is not a one-size-fits-all book" and we should write our own practice journal after learning from books. Life is meaningful if we believe in writing our own journey.

B22
Release Angry Feelings
Lai-man Ada Yip

Children usually have difficulty managing their emotions when they get angry. They tend to yell, scream, and may even hurt themselves or others. These inappropriate responses often impact those around them or bring about negative consequences. Therefore, it is important to provide children with anger management strategies. The goal of this exercise is to provide guiding actions and steps to help children decrease angry feelings and replace the negative behaviors with positive, appropriate ones.

Script

This is an exercise for you to express your emotions and angry feelings. Find a comfortable place where you have enough space to stretch your body. Now close your eyes. Raise your arms to shoulder height. Imagine that you are holding a piece of paper. Transfer all of your angry feelings onto this piece of paper. Now, use all of the energy from your body to tear it. Tear it now! Good job. It's easy, isn't it? Put down your hands slowly.

Now raise your arms up again to shoulder height. Imagine that you are holding a stack of paper. Transfer all your angry feelings on this stack of paper. Use all of the energy from your body to tear them. Tear them now! Now, transfer all your energy to your fingers. Tear the stack of paper into small pieces. You can do it! Excellent! Put down your hands slowly after you are done.

Still have angry feeling? Toss it away! Picture yourself rolling a piece of paper into a ball. Transfer all of your angry feelings into this paper ball. Hold it tightly. Use all of the energy from your body to toss it away. Toss it now! Toss it far, far, away so that it does not hurt anyone or anything. Good job.

Try it once again. Imagine that you transfer all your angry feelings into many paper balls. Imagine that they are heavy. Hold them tightly. Use all of the energy from your body to toss them away. Keep tossing them until they are all gone. Toss them far, far, and away! Excellent!

Relax your body now. Shake your fingers, arms, and shoulders to relax your muscles. Take a deep breath. Exhale. Let fresh air in and replace the air inside your body. Take another deep breath. Exhale. You are now very calm and relaxed. The paper and paper balls take away your anger. Your angry feelings are now gone, far away from you.

Now, recall a moment that you felt happy. When was it? Where was it? Who was there? What made you happy? Take a deep breath again. Exhale. You are now feeling calm, relaxed, and happy. Open your eyes slowly. You are now ready to go back to your life.

Application

This exercise can be adapted for people of all age groups who want to release their angry feelings. The action of tearing the paper and tossing the paper ball(s) can be modified with other less aggressive and harmless actions. Ask the client for suggestions before the exercise. Here are some suggested therapeutic questions for discussion after the exercise:

1. How did you feel when you tore the paper? When you tossed the paper ball?
2. On a scale of 1 to 10, 10 being the angriest and 1 being the least angry, how would you rate you level of anger now? (This question can also be asked before the exercise to provide a point of comparison.)
3. On a scale of 1 to 10, 10 being the most helpful and 1 being the least helpful, how would you rate this exercise in terms of helping you release your angry feelings?
4. What other items can you imagine during this exercise to help you release your anger? What are some other ways for you to release your emotions?
5. Can you see yourself using this exercise next time you are feeling angry? Just close your eyes and imagine that you have dealt with the emotions and you are fine. Can you do it now for a minute? Close your eyes and relax. Good.

B23
Releasing the Emotional Burden of Trauma
Rachel Barajas

Use this guided imagery with adolescents and adults who have a history of trauma, specifically any event in which the clients have felt at fault. The exercise encourages the clients to let go of the painful feelings and allows them to experience joy and happiness instead. The beginning of the script aids the clients with relaxation and to become accustomed to your voice. Speak slowly and remind the clients to continue breathing if you notice they are becoming tense or holding their breath. Encourage them to relax and focus on their breathing.

Script

Get in a comfortable position, sitting or lying down on your back. Now close your eyes, but if you feel more comfortable leaving them open, that is okay. First, focus on your breath. Take a deep breath in for five counts, feeling the air fill your lungs, and expanding your belly and rib cage. Now slowly exhale for five counts and release all of the air out of your lungs (pause). Continue focusing on your breath, but now also focus your awareness on your right arm, starting from your fingers, all the way up to your shoulder. Release any tension you may feel in your right arm (pause). Now do the same for your left arm by letting go of any tension throughout your entire arm (pause). While remaining aware of your arms, become conscious of your torso, feeling the air fill your lungs and then leave it, your chest and belly rising and falling.

Focus your attention on your neck, head, and face. Allow your face to soften, letting gravity pull the tension from your muscles and the tightness slowly melting away. You are now aware of your entire upper body. Good (pause). Now without losing this awareness, slowly become aware of each part of your lower body. Wiggle your toes, point and flex your feet, and then move onto your legs. As you become aware of your legs, notice if they feel tight or relaxed. Stretch them out, wiggle them, and let gravity pull the tension from them if they are tight. Appreciate your legs for taking you places throughout your day and allow them to relax in this moment. Good.

Continue your breathing, take air deep into your lungs and exhale it all out. Make peace with each breath you take and feel gratitude for your lungs. Now bring your awareness to yourself as a whole. Be conscious of yourself as a presence, as occupying space, as part of creation. Be aware of your life's path so far, leaving the details aside, and be aware that only your path exists. Now be aware of yourself as a being with a future. Recognize that you have no real boundaries, that you are not limited by the past, and that you do not have to be affected by the opinions of those around you. You cannot control others; you can only control your reaction to the circumstances in your life.

Now, remember the experience of feeling pain or sadness in your life. Focus specifically on one painful incident and how you felt when that incident occurred. Were you scared? Sad? Anxious? Feel that emotion again, deep inside you. Really let that emotion gain strength, just for a moment (pause). Good effort. Now focus on letting go of the feelings associated with that experience or incident. Give yourself the freedom to let that weight and heaviness go. Ask yourself if holding on to these emotions is negatively affecting your well-being in life. If so, let it go. These painful feelings do not have to influence your life. If they are dragging you down, keeping you in a negative place, or preventing you from living your happiest life, then release them. You do not have to bear this burden forever.

Now, imagine you are holding a big balloon with a long string. Picture yourself using the string to tie up any feelings of guilt, shame, worry, sadness, or anxiety. Now, imagine you are releasing the balloon into the sky. Allow it to drift off, disappearing into the distance. The heavy burden of emotion is now far away. The experience you had is still with you, but those overwhelming feelings are now floating off to another place, a place where it is not your responsibility to carry them. Now imagine a second balloon, even bigger than the first. Imagine that whatever you tie to this balloon will come into your life. Tie feelings of hope, happiness, gratitude, love, and compassion to this balloon. Now send this balloon out into the universe and it will send all these great things back your way. Think about how the positive things you want in life will be brought to you by this big, wonderful balloon.

Continue to breathe deeply, in and out, for five counts. (pause) Now imagine standing under a warm, clear waterfall, with water pouring over you from the top of your head down to your feet. (pause) Can you feel it? (pause) Let the water purify your body and wash out any negative thoughts and energy you may be carrying. The water is cleansing you of any remaining unpleasant feelings.

Now, take one very deep inhale. Try to fill your entire body, from your toes to your belly button and all the way up to your neck, with air. Now exhale! Push every drop of air out from your body. Take one more, big inhale, the biggest breath you have ever taken in your entire life! Hold it for just a second, and now as you exhale, sigh loudly and stick your tongue out, making whatever noise you want. Good work!! Now open your eyes.

Application

The intent of this exercise is to allow clients to free themselves from the burden of any painful emotions they may be carrying related to a traumatic experience. The goal is not to block out past experiences or ask for total removal of the painful memory, but rather to focus on the emotional aspects instead of the negative side of the trauma. Debrief these feelings with the client and focus on the positive learning from this exercise. Once a client has completed the exercise, you may ask if the client would like to participate in a balloon exercise that would require them to tie or write words on the balloons and release them into the air. After the exercise, ask the client:

1. What negative words did you attach to the first balloon? What positive words did you attach to the second balloon?
2. What does that word (that represents your feeling or emotion) mean to you? In what ways does it affect your life?
3. What did it feel like to release the first balloon? What did it feel like when you released the second balloon?
4. What is one positive aspect about this balloon experience? What did you learn from it?

B24
Rice Therapy
Monit Cheung

This touch therapy activity for immigrant families incorporates the idea of sand-tray therapy along with a structured play therapy technique. It targets children 3–12 who have experienced acculturation gaps with their parents. It provides a concrete channel for the clients to connect feelings about cultural diversity. It is also an assessment tool to test concentration power and eye-hand coordination. Prepare a plastic bin (approximately 4" deep and 15" × 12" wide) and put white rice grains in it. Use three transparent containers to hold three types of rice (purple, brown, and red).

Script

This is an activity that requires your full attention. First, look at your hands. Stretch your fingers and wiggle them. Feel your energy flowing inside each finger. Join your right-hand fingers with your left-hand fingers—just like praying. Squeeze them and then release. Do this three more times. Squeeze, release; Squeeze, release; Squeeze, and release. Good! Feel the relaxation in each finger as you separate your hands. Now, place both your palms on top of the rice inside the tray in front of you. What feeling do you have? It may feel like you are transferring your energy into the rice grains. It may feel like you are staying in touch with your culture, your family, your language, or something else. Feel how good it is to be able to do something with your hands that may transfer feelings, thoughts or experiences.

Now, use your right hand to pick up some rice grains and place them on your left palm. Feel the grains against the skin of your palm. Now, count to ___ (use child's age) while putting them back to the tray. Ready? One, two, three, keep counting if you would like to continue (pause). Put all the rice grains back into the tray. How do you feel about putting the rice back into the tray? Relax. Placing any leftover rice back in the tray is part of this exercise. It's your experience.

Now, you are going to add more rice to the tray. First, choose the color you like. Add the entire container of this color to the tray and mix them. Mix them well. They are now mixed. How do you feel about the process of mixing? How do you feel about seeing them mixed? Relax.

Now, add another container of rice to the tray. What color is it? How does it relate to you? Mix them well. They are now mixed. How do you feel about mixed colors? Relax.

Finally, add the last container of rice to the tray. What color is it? Do you want to mix them this time? Do whatever is best for you. Relax.

Application

After mixing the rice, the client will share the process about mixing the colors. If each grain of rice represents a person, check how the client may have felt to think about the mixed culture in this society. Since this exercise requires the client to follow instructions, it also helps the client to process how the instruction may make them think. It also serves as a means to encourage the client to take a new perspective when talking with someone from a different culture.

B25
Safe Driving for Teens
Monit Cheung

Teenage years represent a stage of transition. Teens want to show that they have the greatest abilities to develop their own self when experiencing this transition journey from dependence to independence. However, teens also take risks while showing their abilities because the hormonal changes in their body can affect how they think and act. According to the Centers for Disease Control and Prevention (CDC, 2012), "motor vehicle crashes are the leading cause of death for U.S. teens." These accidents occur not only because they lack driving experience, but also because they are driving with peers who may influence them to take risks. According to the CDC (2012), the death rate among male teens is twice that of female teens. This may indicate that many young males lack concentration skills and can be easily distracted by their surroundings.

This exercise aims to provide an environment for teens (14–18) to prepare their driving journey.

Script

Relax and think about how you are a young person—a responsible and energetic individual who is successful in making friends. Now, think deeply about this situation. Imagine you are about to hit the road. You are with your close friends who are talking loud and singing rock 'n' roll. You start your car and announce, "Seat belts on!" Yes, it is important to you and your passengers.

You say to yourself, *focus. Concentrate.* You continue to drive safely like a professional and enter the freeway. You obey the law and follow the speed limit.

A sports car is zooming next to you as fast as lightning strikes. You press on your accelerator and want to race after it. Your friends are giggling and laughing as if to say, "Go faster. Zoom, zoom, zoom!" A few words come to your mind—*obey the law*. You react quickly and say to yourself, "Slow down. Slow down." You know that the other driver is not thinking about the danger of racing, but you are. Yes, you are on the right track.

Your friends take out some bottles of beer and want to twist them open. A word pops to your mind—*responsibility*. You say, "Stop! Wait until we get there." Yes, you are on the right track. Yes, you are a responsible driver. Your friend asks, "What's wrong with you today?" Two words come to your mind—*no argument*. You smile and answer, "Nothing!" Yes, you are on the right track. You focus and concentrate on your driving. You smile and feel the relaxation. You have the will power to determine what's right to do and not to do. You are yourself, and you won't argue. You know you do not need the heated argument. Yes, you are on the right track.

You continue your journey. You are tired but you take a deep breath, one . . . , two . . . , and three, slowly exhaling. You are relaxed and alert. You are not risking your life or your friends' lives for anything dangerous. You are not driving for excitement because you are a responsible person. You are not driving to show off because you have high self-esteem. You drive with full responsibility. Yes, you are on the right track. You arrive safely.

Now your mind is crystal clear as you prepare for your actual journey. Some words come to your mind—*Focus. Concentrate. Be responsible*. You are ready to hit the road.

Application

This exercise is designed for pre-adolescents who need to learn to be responsible drivers. Parents may present some of the fatal statistics reported by the CDC (see website in the reference). It is important for the new driver to know the three main factors that result in teen involvement in car crashes—risk taking, driving with peers, and newly licensed drivers. As a preventive measure, teens should participate in the design of this exercise by adding more scenarios or replacing the italicized words in the script with other encouraging words that are more personal to them. These words will become their reminders as they begin to drive and experience stimulation and distractions that can cause them to take risks on the road.

Further Reading

Centers for Disease Control and Prevention. (CDC, 2012). Teen drivers: Fact sheet. Retrieved from http://www.cdc.gov/motorvehiclesafety/teen_drivers/teendrivers_factsheet.html.

B26
Sandbox Play
Ashante Montero

This exercise was created for children who may have experienced sexual abuse. Many children fear discussing what has happened to them, especially with someone they perceive as a stranger. This exercise helps the clinician build trust and rapport with the child, while instilling a sense of comfort and safety during the therapy session. It will allow the child to relax, and eventually discuss the abuse. This exercise requires a sandbox and several small toys, or objects, which will be placed in the sandbox. The client does not need to use imagery because the sandbox is a real object that can be seen and touched. If a sandbox is not available, you may substitute it with a dish box filled with rice. If you use the prerecorded instruction, remind the client that sand is used in the script.

Script

This is a guided exercise. I would like for you to follow me to do several things in the next five minutes. First, there is a sandbox in front of you. If you feel comfortable, I would like for you to place your hands in the sandbox. Good! Now I want you to take a really deep breath in and then let it all out. Let's take another deep . . . breath in and let it out. One more deep breathing—breathe in and let it out. Very good!

Now, I want you to feel the sand on your hands. Move your hands around the top of the sand . . . really feel the sand touching your palms. Now grab a handful of sand and squeeze it really tightly in your hands. Feel the sensation of the sand in your fists. Now release the sand back into the box. Nice! Grab the sand with your hands again and squeeze . . . now release the sand back into the box.

Next, bury your hands underneath the sand and let the sand completely cover your hands. Notice how the sand feels. Is it cold or warm? Notice the sensation of the sand between your fingers. Lift your hands from underneath the sand and place them back on top of the sand. Let's do that one more time. Bury your hands in the sand and cover them completely. Feel the sensation of the sand surrounding your hands. Breathe in and breathe out . . . Breathe in and breathe out. As your hands rest in the sandbox, relax your arms so that they feel like soft spaghetti. It feels so good to be relaxed.

Good! Now that you are relaxed, I want to know more about you. I am going to ask you some questions. The toys right here may help you to answer the questions. You can write the answers in the sand if you'd like. If you do not understand the question or if it makes you feel uncomfortable, place both your hands on the sand, and I will try to help you. But remember to breathe in and breathe out slowly.

Wonderful! Can you tell me your name? You can spell it in the sand in the best way you know how. Great! This is a safe place. Do you know what safe means? It means no one in this room will hurt you. Can you spell *safe* in the sand? Awesome! Now think about what makes you feel safe. Is there anyone who you feel safe with? Do you feel safe at school? What do you like about school? Do you have any friends at school? What do you like to do for fun? Who do you live with? Can you tell me about things you do with them? How do you feel around them? What makes you feel happy? Let's think about that right now so that you feel happy.

Very good! Now you can take your hands out of the sandbox and wash them at the sink. I want to thank you for telling me a little bit about you today. I hope you felt safe here with me today. This will always be a safe place for you.

Application

Creating a safe environment is essential for working with children who have, or may have, been abused. Often children are more comfortable with nonverbal communication, especially when they are young. Using the sandbox to encourage communication allows the therapist to build rapport with the client and provides an easy avenue for emotional expression. After the exercise, ask the client the following questions:

1. What did you like about what we did today?
2. Were there any parts of this exercise you did not like? If so, what were they?
3. What is your favorite toy or object? What made it special for you?
4. What is your least favorite toy or object? What did it remind you of?
5. Is there anything else you would like to tell me about yourself?

B27
Secret Password
Monit Cheung

This exercise aims to help young children develop concentration skills while helping parents train their children to increase self-control and reduce temper tantrums. First, work with the child to determine a secret password that will be used to gain self-control. The child will determine the secret password so that he or she will view this word as a self-control mechanism. The child will give this password to his or her parents to use as a reminder when the child loses self-control. Second, decide upon a movement or body language to use in response to this secret password. This will allow any emotional outburst to be transformed into something peaceful and help prevent a temper tantrum from the child. In this script, "monkey" is the secret password, and "touch my nose" is the body language for the child to use. If you read from this script instead of using the prerecorded CD, these two keys may be changed according to the client's preferences to increase a sense of ownership.

Script

Think about a secret password: "monkey," yes, it is "monkey." What is the meaning of this word? It means self-control. Yes, it means self-control. What does "monkey" do to help you relax? It is funny. Yes, it is funny. You like it because . . . because it is a good choice, right? And it is funny. Next time when you hear the word "monkey," you know it is your password to self-control. You know it is your secret password to stop a problem, to stop a temper tantrum, to stop a bad mood, and even to feel happier. It is your password to a better world. If you hear this word next time, simply reply with "touch my nose." Yes, when you hear your password, from someone else or from yourself, you will touch your nose. Touch it with one finger . . . now two fingers . . . now three fingers. Hold it. Now, take a deep breath in . . . and out . . . in . . . and out. Good! Your reply means you are relaxing. Good job! Now, try it one more time: "monkey." Touch your nose with one finger, two fingers, and three fingers. Breathe in . . . and out . . . in . . . and out. Excellent!

Application

Remind the child that he or she determines this password and will use it when feeling upset or mad. In a therapeutic session, the child simply follows you, says the password aloud, and then responds through body language. You can encourage the child to silently reply when parents are saying this password to remind him or her to regain self-control. This dynamic exercise will help the child to relax and be in control of their thoughts and actions. It will also send a signal to the parents that the child is trying to control an angry outburst or a temper tantrum. Although this exercise is designed for a very young child, it can be modified for older children to use as a reminder when they face anxiety or want to concentrate on a task. It is a short guided imagery for practice purposes and the relaxation thought will become automatic after practicing for a few times.

B28
Sleep Tight
Karen R. Greenberg

This exercise is designed for children and adolescents who have nightmares. Clients who are prone to nightmares may have difficulties falling asleep, staying asleep, and waking from sleep. They may experience anxiety about the process of going to sleep, particularly when it involves being left in a darkened room and the client has feelings of insecurity. Nightmares may be associated with trauma, lack of security, fear, recent change, or other negative experiences.

The progressive relaxation techniques and imagery used in this exercise are intended to reduce or eliminate the negative aspects of going to sleep and replace them with a sense of tranquility and security. It is suggested that this prerecorded tape be used nightly for ten minutes immediately before bedtime.

Recommended Music: artist, Deep Sky Divers, album, *Highlands and Skylands*, track, "Beyond the Hills," 2002.

Script

Find a comfortable position, either sitting or lying down. Make sure your arms and legs are not crossed. Close your eyes, not tightly, but make sure they are completely closed. You are going to count aloud 1, 2, 3, and take deep breaths each time, breathing in through the nose and out through the mouth. Let's begin. One . . . breathe in through the nose, breathe out through the mouth. (pause) Two . . . breathe in through the nose, breathe out through the mouth. (pause) Three . . . breathe in through the nose, breathe out through the mouth.

Now, let's begin to stretch the muscles in your body. Let's go from head to toe. First, slowly turn your head to one side and hold it there as you count to five: 1, 2, 3, 4, 5. Next, slowly turn your head to the other side and hold it there as you count to five again: 1, 2, 3, 4, 5. Finally, look up at the ceiling, down at the floor, and straight ahead. Relax. Now lift your shoulders. One shoulder up, hold it, and put it back down. Other shoulder up, hold it, and put it back down. Now, put your arms out straight and make two fists. Squeeze your fists tightly and then open. Now you are going to do it two more times. Ready. Squeeze, hold it, open. Squeeze, hold it, open. Now shake them out.

Now focus on your feet. Curl your toes, hold it, open. Now you are going to do it two more times. Curl, hold it, open. And again, curl, hold it, open. It feels as if a weight has now been lifted from your body.

You are now ready to go on a special journey. Imagine you are lying on a soft bed floating just above the ground through a friendly animal park. It is a beautiful day. The sun is shining brightly and you can feel its warmth on your face. The gentle wind is blowing through your hair. Suddenly, a snow white rabbit with floppy ears and a large puffy tail appears out of nowhere and hops onto your bed. He looks at you with big kind eyes as you reach out to pet him. You never knew a rabbit could be that soft. He decides to go along on the journey with you for companionship.

As you float along, you see what looks like a large fluffy ball of cotton lying on the grass ahead of you. As you get closer, the little ball moves. It stands up on four wobbly legs and lifts its head to sniff the air. You realize it is not a ball of cotton, but a little lamb with a curly coat of wool. You reach out and manage to run your fingers through its soft curls as your floating bed moves on.

Look to the right and you will see a deer coming out from between the trees. His shiny brown coat with white spots lets you know that this is a young deer whose parents must be nearby. He puts his head down to nibble the grass to let his parents know that he is gaining his independence by learning to feed himself.

As your journey continues, a black pony comes trotting by and then slows down to keep pace with the floating bed as she curiously eyes you and the rabbit. She greets you with a "neigh" and continues on her way.

As you watch her pass, you feel a spray of water on your head. Startled, you look up in the sky, but there is not a cloud in sight. To the left is a large pond. In the pond is an elephant bathing and squirting water from his large trunk into the air.

Then, a sudden wind lifts your floating bed, moving you along until you find yourself eye to eye with a baby giraffe. She sticks out her tongue and licks your face with a loving kiss as your journey through the animal park comes to an end.

As you travel on into the setting sun, you see a familiar house in the distance. A smile crosses your face as you think about your experiences with the animals. As you get closer to the house the bed dips down, and the rabbit, with a shake of his tail, jumps off and scurries across the grass. The bed slowly floats through an open window and comes to rest back in the room where your journey began.

Now that your special journey has ended, you suddenly realize how relaxed you are.

When I count down to one, you may open your eyes and think about your happy journey or, if you choose, you may keep your eyes closed and sleep peacefully through the night.

I will now begin the countdown: 5 (pause), 4 (pause), 3 (pause), 2 (pause), 1.

Application

It is important that children and adolescents who suffer from nightmares be taught how to relax in order to reduce their anxiety and be able to sleep peacefully through the night. To introduce this therapeutic tool, the therapist should meet with both the parent and client to discuss appropriate use. Following that discussion, the therapist and client will utilize this exercise in a session at which the parent may be present but depending upon the age and consent of the client. Processing with the client, the therapist would ask questions such as:

1. On a scale of 1 to 3, how much do you feel the muscle exercises helped you to relax? 1 = Not at all, 2 = Somewhat, 3 = Very much
2. What feelings did you have when the sun warmed your face? When the wind blew through your hair? When the elephant sprayed you with water?
3. Name the animal that made you feel the happiest and tell me about it.
4. What was it about this journey that made it special for you?
5. In what ways do you feel remembering your journey at bedtime can help you sleep better?

Nightly usage of this exercise at bedtime after its introduction for the first week will be most helpful to the child or adolescent. Thereafter, use of the exercise two to three times per week for the next three to four weeks would be appropriate. Following that, the exercise should continue to be used as needed or per therapist's suggestion. As needed, the parent may cue the child or adolescent by simply saying something such as, "Take your bedtime journey."

B29
Stay Focused
Patrick Leung

This is a Taoist story that can be used as a guided journey for the clients to see themselves travel to a different world. The Taoist is a Chinese philosopher who travels to many places to advise people to relax and listen to their hearts. When reading this story, encourage the listeners to imagine that they are traveling to ancient China. They can keep their eyes open or closed. The purpose of this journey is to identify our limitations and address how we can go beyond these limitations and focus on our tasks. Every detail in the story represents or symbolizes a distraction in our lives. Our solution is to observe our limitations and stay focused. Through the lens of this ancient story, we are able to understand the inherent similarities across cultures.

Script

Let's travel to Asia together. Here we see a Taoist, who is a wise man in China, telling a story.

One day the Taoist sees two archers who are good friends but also competitors to each other. These archers are very competent and skilled at shooting targets with a bow and arrows. The archers are playfully arguing back and forth about who is the best, so they say, "Well, let's see who is the best!" One archer says, "Why don't we place a bet?" He puts down his silver coins, "I'll put in one thousand silver coins." The other archer counters and says, "Ok, I also put in one thousand silver coins for one of us who can hit the target ten times in a row. I bet I can win." They are both very confident and they start to shoot. They each hit the target ten times in a row. So they agree to another round, and this time they decide to make the wager a little bigger. "Let's play with one thousand gold coins. Gold is more precious than silver," one of the archers says. They agree and they start to shoot. This time, both are only able to hit the target seven out of ten times—still no winner. They become frustrated and more serious, so one shouts out, "Let's gamble our lives." The Taoist continued to watch but this time neither of the archers could hit the target. They both failed and still there was no winner.

What does the Taoist want you to learn from this story? He suggests that even if you have the skills, you must have both your target and your equipment to be successful. You are knowledgeable because of what you have learned and the time you have taken to practice. However, if your concentration strays from the task at hand, you will not be successful. In the story, both of the archers had the talent and skills necessary to win, but they could not perform well because they were focused on their pride. Winning and raising the stakes became more important than the art of archery, and this distraction became their downfall. Take this story with you, and when you are working on a task, remind yourself that you will do well only if you concentrate on what you are doing. There will always be many internal and external distractions. Your success is dependent on your ability to put aside these distractions and refocus your energy towards the task at hand.

Application

You may use this exercise to analyze and discuss the different metaphors used in this story—the competition, the bow and arrows, the silver and gold coins, the lives of two people, and their pride. What are the connections between these metaphors and the target? Does the target represent a life goal? Can the target represent something different for each person, place, or time? How do we know we have been distracted and cannot perform well? How can we make the distractions smaller and less influential to us? How can we concentrate when there are so many distractions in our surroundings? Who will tell us about what to do with our lives? What is concentration? How can we stay focused? These open-ended questions will allow the client to process and connect the relevance of these metaphors to actual life experiences.

B30
The Journey Home
Allison Marek

Many treatment centers and therapists in private practice have begun incorporating equine assisted psychotherapy (EAP) when working with children and adolescents who are survivors of abuse. The use of horses in therapeutic work has proven to be a successful treatment for many types of mental health conditions, and also helps clients who are coping with grief and loss, life transitions, and trauma. This guided imagery is suitable for use during the termination phase of equine-assisted therapy.

Script

To begin, lie down on your back and gently close your eyes. Breathe in (1, 2, 3) and out (1, 2, 3). Breathe deeply into your diaphragm (1, 2, 3) and out (1, 2, 3). That's it. If your lower back is arched and tense, bend your knees so your whole back sinks into the floor. Allow the earth to hold you. Kick your legs, shake your arms, do whatever you need to do, but do it gently to stay grounded. Remember that you have all of the tools you need to keep yourself safe and present in your body. Promise yourself that throughout this exercise you will use these tools whenever you need to.

Imagine yourself standing in a field. What do you see? What do you hear? How does the air feel? Visualize a herd of horses. In the herd, you see one of the horses that you have connected with during your time here. What does the horse look like? What is the horse doing? Is the horse with any friends? Breathe (1, 2, 3). Notice how your body feels. When you are ready, approach the horse. Be very aware of your surroundings. When you reach the horse, how does it greet you? How do you greet the horse? How does the horse's coat feel? Is it soft and shiny? Is it muddy? How does the horse smell?

Imagine the horse leading you to the forest where you and the horse first met a few months ago. When you first arrived here, the forest was dark. You told him things that you never told anyone and light began to peek through the trees. When you fed him and groomed him, you learned to feed and nurture yourself, too, and the forest transformed from brown and dry to green and lush. What else have you and the horse done in the forest? In what other ways has this forest changed?

The horse tells you, "You have everything you need to live the life you want." You take a deep breath, mount the horse, and imagine what you want your life to be like when you return home. Home is more than your house—it's your family, your school, your friends. Hear the horse's message again: "You have everything you need to live the life you want." When you are ready, you give the horse a little kick. You move through the field . . . past the herd . . . beyond the barn and the mountains. The horse completely trusts you. You are a leader. You have the power over your destiny. Be aware of how you feel. Remember, feelings aren't good or bad. They are just feelings. Give in to these feelings. Feel the horse moving with you, in touch with your feelings, and supporting you on your journey.

You have finally returned back to the field. Some things may be exactly the same and others may be different; just as some things within you have remained the same, and others have changed. Take a deep breath, and when you are ready, dismount your horse. Feel your feet planted on the ground. Look into the eye of the horse. Hear his message: "I honor the work you've done. I honor the journey you have taken." As the horse turns and canters away, back to the herd, you are filled with love, confidence, and gratitude. You are grounded in who you are, and no matter what may happen in your environment, you will take care of your mind, body, and spirit. You are back now.

Application

If a client has worked with one specific horse, you may wish to use the horse's name in the script. For clients with more energy, or who may be in need of more energy, this exercise can be completed using movement. For example, clients may wish to "gallop" about the space in order to anchor in the feeling that arises in response to that image. Allowing clients to make their own decisions regarding their environment is very important, as this exercise emphasizes independence from the therapeutic setting and from the equine and human therapists. After this exercise, invite the client to draw or write about their experience to help remind them of what they have gained through treatment, and more specifically, this exercise. Therapeutic questions may include:

1. What feelings did you experience during this exercise?
2. In what ways have you remained the same since entering treatment? In what ways are you different? In what ways did the forest relate to your growth?
3. During this exercise, how did you feel when you were with the horse? Were you able to remember what it was like working with the horse? How will you carry this feeling(s) with you when you leave here?

4. How did you feel as you came closer to your home? What are you excited or happy about? Do you have any feelings of fear, sadness, or anger? If so, where do these feelings come from? How do you make them go away?

Suggested Background Sound Effects

Country Stables. Artist, Nature Sounds; album, *Relaxing Sounds of Nature for Relaxation, Meditation, Deep Sleep and Spa*.

Horse, Ride, Dirt, Gallop 1 Sound Effect. Artist: Pro Sound Effects Suite; album: *Pro Sound Effects Suite*, vol. 31, *Amphibians, Horses and Insects*.

Further Reading

Bachi, K., Terkel, J., & Teichman, M. (2012). Equine-facilitated psychotherapy for at-risk adolescents: The influence on self-image, self-control and trust. *Clinical Child Psychology and Psychiatry, 17*(2), 298–312.

B31
Trilingual Relaxation Journey
Monit Cheung, Elena Delavega, Wenjun June Zhu

This relaxation exercise focuses on understanding the importance of concentration in a culturally different or new environment. If the clients do not understand all three languages, encourage them to appreciate how much effort it may take to relax when the environment is not familiar to them. Even when the clients know all three languages used in this exercise, they should focus on their relaxation without thinking about what the background means or does not mean to them. This exercise is especially helpful for adolescents, particularly those who are (or if their parents are) new immigrants, to understand and appreciate the difficulties in learning a foreign language.

Script

Let's relax with this trilingual journey. It is not important to understand all three languages used in this exercise; the main purpose of this exercise is to listen and to imagine that you are traveling to three different environments. One or two of these environments are unfamiliar to you, but try to relax and appreciate the language that you do not thoroughly understand.

Let's relax and have fun.

Now, imagine that you are traveling to three different places. You are first greeted by a group of American children. They ask you to relax and be happy. Please follow them to do this relaxation exercise:

Breathe in, deep in, deep out, and out. Breathe in again, deep in, deep out, and out.

Breathe naturally. In your mind, in your heart, count from one to ten—one, two, three, four, five, six, seven, eight, nine and ten. Count backward—ten, nine, eight, seven, six, five, four, three, two, and one. Very good!

One more time: one, two, three, four, five, six, seven, eight, nine and ten. Backward—ten, nine, eight, seven, six, five, four, three, two, and one. Excellent!

The children say "hello" to you with a big smile. Each of them gives you a fruit you like. Is it an apple, an orange, a banana, a pineapple, a mango, a gigantic watermelon, or something else? You say, "Thank you. Thank you very much!" You are relaxed and happy.

Now you meet a group of Chinese children. They ask you to relax and be happy. Please follow them to do this relaxation exercise, same as what you just did:

深深地吸一口氣，慢慢地呼出來，全部呼出來。再深深地吸一口氣，慢慢地呼出來，全部呼出來。

自然地呼吸。在你的腦海中，在你的心裡，從1數到10──1，2，3，4，5，6，7，8，9，10。倒數一次──10，9，8，7，6，5，4，3，2，1。非常好！

再一次：1，2，3，4，5，6，7，8，9，10。倒數──10，9，8，7，6，5，4，3，2，1。太棒了！

孩子們微笑著對你說"你好"。每個孩子都給了你一個你愛吃的水果。它是一個蘋果、一個橘子、一根香蕉、一個菠蘿、一個芒果、一個巨大的西瓜，還是別的水果？你說"謝謝。非常感謝！"你很放鬆，而且很快樂。

Now you meet a group of Mexican children. They ask you to relax and be happy. Please follow them to do this relaxation exercise, same as you did before with the Chinese children:

Inhale profundamente. Ahora, exhale despacio. Inhale muy profundamente de nuevo, y exhale muy lentamente otra vez.

Respire naturalmente. En su mente y en su corazón, cuente del uno al diez—uno, dos, tres, cuatro, cinco, seis, siete, ocho, nueve, y diez. Cuente hacia atrás—diez, nueve, ocho, siete, seis, cinco, cuatro, tres, dos, y uno. ¡Muy bien!

Una vez más: uno, dos, tres, cuatro, cinco, seis, siete, ocho, nueve, y diez. Hacia atrás—diez, nueve, ocho, siete, seis, cinco, cuatro, tres, dos, y uno. ¡Excelente!

Los niños le dicen "hola" a usted con una gran sonrisa. Cada uno de ellos le da una fruta que a usted le gusta. ¿Es una manzana, una naranja, un plátano, una piña, un mango, una enorme sandía, o alguna otra fruta? Usted dice: "Gracias. ¡Muchas gracias!" Usted se siente relajado y feliz.

Application

You may first rehearse with your clients using the language most familiar to them. Then use this exercise in many different languages you know (or pre-recorded) and ask the clients to repeat the same relaxation scene each time even though they do not fully understand the language in the background. The purpose of listening to different languages is for them to appreciate the struggles some of us are experiencing when we are living in an environment that is culturally different from our place of origin. When they feel comfortable enough to relax, even when they are hearing or experiencing something different, they will start to appreciate the existence of different cultures surrounding us. Therapeutic questions may include:

1. How do you deal with stress when you are talking with people who do not understand you?
2. What would you do if you did not understand your friends, your teachers, or your parents?
3. If your parents were not fluent in English, how would you feel about talking with them in English? How would you react to them if they did not understand you?
4. If your friends are new immigrants to this country, how would they adjust to this new place? Who would understand or listen to them?

Jornada de Relajación Trilingüe
Elena Delavega, Monit Cheung, Wenjun June Zhu

Con este ejercicio de relajación se trata de comprender la importancia de la concentración en un ambiente extraño o una cultura nueva. Si los clientes no entienden alguno o varios de los tres idiomas, esto los ayudará a apreciar el enorme esfuerzo que puede tomar relajarse cuando el entorno no le es familiar a uno. Aunque los clientes conozcan los tres idiomas que se utilizan en este ejercicio, se les instruye para que se concentren en relajarse, sin pensar en el significado de las palabras que escuchan a su alrededor. Este ejercicio es útil para que los jóvenes aprecien las dificultades que presenta el aprendizaje de una lengua extranjera, sobre todo si ellos o sus padres son inmigrantes recientes.

Guion

Vamos a relajarnos con esta jornada trilingüe. No es importante que usted entienda los tres idiomas utilizados en este ejercicio, el objetivo más importante de este ejercicio es el de escuchar e imaginar que va a viajar a tres ambientes distintos—uno o dos de estos ambientes no son familiares para usted, y usted está tratando de relajarse y apreciar las lenguas que usted no entiende completamente.

Vamos a relajarnos y pasarla bien.

Ahora, imagine que usted está viajando a diferentes lugares. Primero le recibe un grupo de niños mexicanos. Le piden a usted que se relaje y se ponga contento. Los niños le hacen las siguientes indicaciones para ayudarlo a relajarse:

Inhale profundamente. Ahora, exhale despacio. Inhale muy profundamente de nuevo, y exhale muy lentamente otra vez.

Respire naturalmente. En su mente y en su corazón, cuente del uno al diez—uno, dos, tres, cuatro, cinco, seis, siete, ocho, nueve, y diez. Cuente hacia atrás—diez, nueve, ocho, siete, seis, cinco, cuatro, tres, dos, y uno. ¡Muy bien!

Una vez más: uno, dos, tres, cuatro, cinco, seis, siete, ocho, nueve, y diez. Hacia atrás—diez, nueve, ocho, siete, seis, cinco, cuatro, tres, dos, y uno. ¡Excelente!

Los niños le dicen "hola" a usted con una gran sonrisa. Cada uno de ellos le da una fruta que a usted le gusta. ¿Es una manzana, una naranja, un plátano, una piña, un mango, una enorme sandía, o alguna otra fruta? Usted dice: "Gracias. ¡Muchas gracias!" Usted se siente relajado y feliz.

Ahora se encuentra usted con un grupo de niños estadounidenses. Le piden a usted que se relaje y se ponga contento. Le hacen las mismas indicaciones que los otros niños para ayudarlo a relajarse:

> Breathe in, deep in, deep out, and out. Breathe in again, deep in, deep out, and out.

Breathe naturally. In your mind, in your heart, count from one to ten—one, two, three, four, five, six, seven, eight, nine and ten. Count backward—ten, nine, eight, seven, six, five, four, three, two, and one. Good!

One more time: one, two, three, four, five, six, seven, eight, nine and ten. Backward—ten, nine, eight, seven, six, five, four, three, two, and one. Excellent!

The children say "hello" to you with a big smile. Each of them gives you a fruit you like. Is it an apple, an orange, a banana, a pineapple, a mango, a gigantic watermelon, or something else? You say, "Thank you. Thank you very much!" You are relaxed and happy.

Ahora se encuentra usted con un grupo de niños chinos. Le piden a usted que se relaje y se ponga contento. Le hacen las mismas indicaciones que los otros niños para ayudarlo a relajarse:

深深地吸一口氣，慢慢地呼出來，全部呼出來。再深深地吸一口氣，慢慢地呼出來，全部呼出來。

自然地呼吸。在你的腦海中，在你的心裡，從1數到10——1，2，3，4，5，6，7，8，9，10。倒數一次——10，9，8，7，6，5，4，3，2，1。非常好！

再一次：1，2，3，4，5，6，7，8，9，10。倒數——10，9，8，7，6，5，4，3，2，1。太棒了！

孩子們微笑著對你說"你好"。每個孩子都給了你一個你愛吃的水果。它是一個蘋果、一個橘子、一根香蕉、一個菠蘿、一個芒果、一個巨大的西瓜，還是別的水果？你說"謝謝。非常感謝！"你很放鬆，而且很快樂。

Aplicaciones

Usted puede practicar con sus clientes primero en el idioma que les sea más familiar a ellos. A continuación, utilice este ejercicio en diferentes idiomas que usted conozca (o pregrabados) y pida a sus clientes que escuchen la misma escena de relajación en un idioma diferente cada vez, aunque no entiendan las palabras de ese idioma. El propósito de escuchar diferentes idiomas es el que sus clientes logren apreciar el esfuerzo que algunas personas tienen que hacer cuando viven en un ambiente que es culturalmente diferente a su lugar de origen. Cuando sus clientes se sientan lo suficientemente cómodos como para relajarse a pesar de que están escuchando o experimentando algo diferente, van a empezar a apreciar la existencia de las diversas culturas que nos rodean. Las preguntas terapéuticas que usted hará a sus clientes pueden incluir las siguientes:

1. ¿Cómo lidia con el estrés cuando está hablando con personas que no le entienden?
2. ¿Qué haría si no pudiera comprender a sus amigos, sus profesores, o a sus padres?
3. Si sus padres no hablaran con fluidez en inglés, ¿cómo se sentiría usted al tratar de hablar con ellos en inglés? ¿Cómo reaccionaría usted si ellos no le entendieran?
4. Si sus amigos son inmigrantes recientes a este país, ¿cómo se están adaptando a este nuevo lugar? ¿Quién los entiende o los escucha?

三種語言的鬆馳旅程
朱文君，張錦芳，伊蓮娜
Wenjun June Zhu, Monit Cheung, Elena Delavega

這項放鬆練習旨在理解在陌生或全新的環境中，集中注意力的重要性。假使你不能完全懂得這三種語言，也可以體會到在陌生環境中放鬆身心的不易。即使懂得在這項練習中所使用的三種語言，也請專注於放鬆的過程，而不必太注重背後的聲音和環境。這項練習有助青少年體會到學習外語的困難，使其更能明白作為新移民的父母所經歷的難處。

練習引導

讓我們利用三種不同的語言去享受這個輕鬆的旅程。在練習過程中能否完全聽懂這三種語言並不重要；最重要的是聆聽，並且想像你正在這三種不同的環境中旅行——其中的一種或兩種環境對於你來說可能並不熟悉，但請嘗試享受這種你不能完全聽懂的語言，並在這個過程中放鬆身心，了解自己。

讓我們放鬆並享受這種樂趣。

現在，想像你來到三個不同的地方。首先，你遇到一群中國小朋友向你打招呼。他們用中文告訴你要放鬆並且快樂起來。請跟著他們做放鬆練習：

深深地吸一口氣，慢慢地呼出來，全部呼出來。再深深地吸一口氣，慢慢地呼出來，全部呼出來。

自然地呼吸。在你的腦海中，在你的心裡，從1數到10——1，2，3，4，5，6，7，8，9，10。倒數一次——10，9，8，7，6，5，4，3，2，1。非常好！

再一次：1，2，3，4，5，6，7，8，9，10。倒數——10，9，8，7，6，5，4，3，2，1。太棒了！

孩子們微笑著對你說"你好"。每個孩子都給了你一個你愛吃的水果。它是一個蘋果、一個橘子、一根香蕉、一個菠蘿、一個芒果、一個巨大的西瓜、還是別的水果？你說"謝謝。非常感謝！"你很放鬆，而且很快樂。

現在，你遇到一群美國小朋友向你打招呼。他們用英語告訴你要放鬆並且快樂起來。請用剛做過的放鬆練習跟著他們一起做：

Breathe in, deep in, deep out, and out. Breathe in again, deep in, deep out, and out.

Breathe naturally. In your mind, in your heart, count from one to ten—one, two, three, four, five, six, seven, eight, nine and ten. Count backward—ten, nine, eight, seven, six, five, four, three, two, and one. Good!

One more time: one, two, three, four, five, six, seven, eight, nine and ten. Backward—ten, nine, eight, seven, six, five, four, three, two, and one. Excellent!

The children say "hello" to you with a big smile. Each of them gives you a fruit you like. Is it an apple, an orange, a banana, a pineapple, a mango, a gigantic watermelon, or something else? You say, "Thank you. Thank you very much!" You are relaxed and happy.

現在，你遇到一群墨西哥小朋友向你打招呼。他們用西班牙文告訴你要放鬆並且快樂起來。請用剛做過的放鬆練習跟著他們一起做：

Inhale profundamente. Ahora, exhale despacio. Inhale muy profundamente de nuevo, y exhale muy lentamente otra vez.

Respire naturalmente. En su mente y en su corazón, cuente del uno al diez—uno, dos, tres, cuatro, cinco, seis, siete, ocho, nueve, y diez. Cuente hacia atrás—diez, nueve, ocho, siete, seis, cinco, cuatro, tres, dos, y uno. ¡Muy bien!

Una vez más: uno, dos, tres, cuatro, cinco, seis, siete, ocho, nueve, y diez. Hacia atrás—diez, nueve, ocho, siete, seis, cinco, cuatro, tres, dos, y uno. ¡Excelente!

Los niños le dicen "hola" a usted con una gran sonrisa. Cada uno de ellos le da una fruta que a usted le gusta. ¿Es una manzana, una naranja, un plátano, una piña, un mango, una enorme sandía, o alguna otra fruta? Usted dice: "Gracias. ¡Muchas gracias!" Usted se siente relajado y feliz.

臨床應用

你首先可以用孩子和家長最熟悉的語言。然後在練習中使用其它多種語言（可用錄製的版本），儘管他們不能完全理解背景中的語言，也請他們重複放鬆的練習。讓他們知道聽不同語言的目的，是在於學習適應生活，也可明白在與祖國文化不同的環境中會遇到的困難。當他們在聽到或者經歷著不同的事物時，也能夠感到舒適和放鬆，他們就會開始習慣並享受身邊存在的不同文化。治療問題可包括：

1. 當與你交談的人不能理解你的話時，你如何處理心中的不快？
2. 如果你聽不懂你的朋友、老師或者父母的話時，你會做什麼？
3. 如果你父母的英語不流利，當他們和你用英語交談時，他們感覺如何？如果他們不能理解你的話，你會有什麼反應？
4. 如果你的朋友是這個國家的新移民，他們會如何適應這裡的新環境？誰會理解他們或者傾聽他們？

B32
Under the Sea
Sandra L. Williams

This guided imagery exercise can be used for groups of children age 7 to 12. The exercise helps children who are victims of emotional and physical abuse. The exercise has two parts. The first is a relaxation exercise that will offer a way for children to relax, feel more at peace, and find tranquility and calmness through deep breathing. The second part is a guided imagery exercise involving a magic boat ride underneath the sea. This will help the children to release tension and anxiety when settling into the new adoptive home. Soft and soothing ocean music enhances the imagery.

Tell the children that they can open their eyes at any time during this exercise, especially when they begin having unpleasant thoughts.

Note: Modify this exercise for children with hydrophobia symptoms by shortening the magic boat ride time, then increasing it gradually each time you use the exercise if you use it as a desensitization exercise.

Note: Be aware of the use of the word *Magic* that may not be suitable for some children who have religious or cultural beliefs that do not allow them to perform or believe in magic.

Ask clients to clear their minds of what has happened and focus on the here and now.

Suggested sound as the background of this exercise:

> Tranquil Moments Advanced Therapy Sounds: developed by Dr. Jeffrey Thompson, who practiced at the Center for Neuroacoustic Research. On the sound device the therapy sound is found under the category RELAX-OCEAN: The ocean surf provides a calm rhythm that helps create a relaxing oceanside environment. Manual information: Merrimack, New Hampshire, USA 03054, 1800-846-3000, Brookstone.com.

Script

(Start ocean music) Take your shoes off, sit with your back softly against the chair. Close your eyes. Taking deep breaths, breathe in through your nose and out through your mouth, now begin, breath in through your nose, out through your mouth, breath in through your nose, out through your mouth, last one, breathe in, breathe out. You're doing great. Now raise your arms above your head. Stretch, stretch long. Now relax your arms at your sides. Now you are going to move your shoulders forward and backwards three times, now forward, backwards, forward, backwards, one more, forward, backwards. Now relax. Keeping your eyes closed, place your hands flat on your legs, close and open your hands three times, ready, close, open, close, open, one more, close, open. Relax your hands at your sides. Now you will raise and lower your right leg three times, ready, up, down, up, down, one more, up, down. Now raise your left leg three times, ready, up, down, up, down, one more, up, down. Keeping your eyes closed, now take a deep breath, breathing in through your nose and out through your mouth. Now you are ready to take a journey.

Imagine that you're in a big magic boat. You're feeling the excitement of going on a journey. The boat is taking you magically on a very special, very safe journey to the beautiful sea and beneath. As you look around, you see the bluey green sea; the water is calm and still. The weather is warm against your body. Seabirds are flying very gracefully over your head.

The magic boat is now going to take you on a magical ride under the sea. You see many beautiful sea animals that live and play here. You see mermaids, sea horses, octopuses, stingrays, and many fishes of all shapes and sizes. They are a sight to see. Here under the sea, in this beautiful and peaceful place, you make friends with these friendly sea animals. The coral reefs are colorful and shiny. You watch the sea animals go in and out of the coral reefs, some sliding through holes, and others lying on the rocks, the same color as the rocks. As you watch the sea animals play, you notice the bubbles and ripples they make.

You feel calm and peaceful as the magical boat surfaces from the sea. You once again feel the warm sun rays on your body and see the sea birds flying above your head. You can feel this calmness and peacefulness in your daily life. You can take a journey on this magic boat anytime. The journey is your safe place for new beginnings. You can take this journey to help you feel safe in your new home and ask for help if you need it. Continue to feel calm and peaceful, and when you are ready, you can now open your eyes.

Application

Use this exercise to help clients relax and find inner peace and calmness in adjusting to a new home environment. The purpose of this exercise is to help children find a safe place when they feel tension and anxiety. Clients can then talk or write about their journey as part of the therapeutic exercise.

Therapeutic questions:
1. How do you feel now after coming back from this relaxation journey?
2. If you wanted to tell your adoptive family about this journey, what would you tell them?
3. How has this journey helped you to adjust to your new (adoptive) home?
4. What feelings or emotions did you have once you reached your journey?

B33
Willing to Seek Help
Carol A. Leung

Mental illness is a stigma, especially among immigrants who did not encounter mental health issues before their immigration. Many families are reluctant to seek help, thinking that problem disclosure indicates they are having many weaknesses within the family. When children are referred to see a school counselor or principal, they may feel ashamed and may have the thought of how their peers may tease them or how their parents may react to their misbehavior or academic challenges. When you notice that your child client is not willing to open up, you may divert his or her attention to something non-threatening such as a relaxation exercise like this one. For example, you may say, "Let's do a relaxation exercise together to get rid of anxiety or discomfort."

This exercise aims to relax the client and find a means to talk about problem-solving and help-seeking. It can be used as an ice-breaker in any therapeutic process. Prepare four plastic bottles of water and a big transparent container before starting.

Script

I'd like us to relax and do this exercise together so that we can get rid of any unwanted thoughts and will be able to concentrate within the next 20 to 30 minutes on something important to you. You know what brought you here today, right? You don't have to give me any answer in this exercise. Just relax, listen, think about your answers in your mind, and follow the instructions if you can. First, close your eyes if you can. Relax by taking three quick breaths—*one*, *two*, and *three*. Good! You are much more relaxed. Now you may open your eyes. Take a deep breath. Excellent!

Use your right hand to grasp a bottle of water. Hold on to it and look at it. What does it remind you of? A clear mind? A crystal ball? A good friend? Now, with your left hand, pick up another bottle of water. Hold both bottles up toward the ceiling, holding them as high as you can. Think about if you must hold these bottles up for a whole day, how would your body feel? Would your body want to rest? What would you do and say? Holding it for a while isn't too bad, right? It's like reaching out to someone who helps you immediately to solve your problem. However, holding it for a whole day would be tiring. It's like no one is listening—no one cares. Now put these bottles down and think about how relaxed you are feeling without any burden. Holding a problem within you for a long time can be a burden—a burden that you would like to get rid of, to share with someone, someone you can trust.

Do not hold on to something that may trouble you. Instead, look at any problem like you are facing a crystal ball or passing a clear water bottle to someone who can offer help. I'm this someone. Now, are you ready to talk? Yes, I'm ready to listen.

Application

Encourage the client to talk about something that no one seems to care or believe. This exercise is a stepping-stone to empower the client to disclose a secret, to reach out for support, and to talk about a concern or issue. Provide an opportunity for the client to share a feeling about holding the bottle very high for a few minutes so that he or she can talk about how it may symbolize a burden. If the client does not seem to get the meaning of it, you may ask the client to hold two bottles with one hand and gradually let his or her arm drift and see how this action may be different. Many clients try to handle many things at the same time and feel frustrated. Through holding two bottles they could then see how not juggling between the two hands may add more burden to your arms. It feels like having a problem but not being able to resolve it unless you reach out for help.

Therapeutic questions may include:

1. If the bottle on your right hand represents a specific feeling you are having right now, what would it be?
2. If the bottle on your left hand symbolizes a solution, what would you see? How do you know the problem is resolved?
3. Let's imagine that these two bottles measure the effect of a specific feeling you have experienced over time; pour out the water into this container to indicate how much release you have achieved so far.

B34
Working through Trauma
Noa Ben Yehuda

This semi-structured guided imagery is designed for adolescents who are dealing with memories of traumatic events and may feel powerless and passive. It is meant to provide the client a sense of control over the events in his or her life. It transforms the traumatic event into something more concrete, and as a result, more manageable and approachable. This exercise also focuses the client's ability to create a better future through self-competence and resilience.

Script

Today we will go on a journey. This journey is meant to explore those things that happened to you in the past and that are affecting your thoughts and feelings in the present. The journey might involve some parts that feel unpleasant to you. It may trigger some memories or thoughts you would rather not think about. Remember that you are in a safe place and that you will be safe on your journey. You are in control of the journey—you can decide where to go and what to do.

Ready? Let's start. . .

Sit comfortably with both your legs touching the floor. Rest your arms in your lap. Close your eyes and take a deep breath. Breathe deeply and slowly: as you breathe in, relax your body and clear your mind. As you exhale, release your stress, tension, and anxiety. Inhale, 1, 2, 3 . . . Exhale, 1, 2, 3 . . . Inhale, 1, 2, 3 . . . Exhale, 1, 2, 3 . . .

Picture yourself in a place where you feel safe. It can be a real place you have been to, or an imagined place you go to in your mind. It can be a room, a house, or some place in nature like a beach, lake, or forest. Whatever you choose, picture everything that surrounds you, what you see, what you hear, what you smell, and what you feel. You are sitting in your safe place, feeling secure and confident. Nothing in your safe place is threatening you. It is familiar and comfortable. Everything around you is calm and relaxing. You feel your legs touching the ground and you feel grounded and strong.

Now think about yourself opening a door to another place. Allow yourself to think about a traumatic memory. While you are thinking of that memory, remember you are in a safe place. Feel your legs touching the ground. You are safe here. Take a deep breath.

Picture this memory. What happens in the memory? How does it make your body feel? What emotions are you experiencing?

Now think about taking this bad memory out of your head and putting it inside of a container. What does this container look like? What shape and size does it have? What color? Can you see through it? What is the container made of? Is it open or closed? If it is closed, can you open it?

Now take this container and imagine yourself placing it to where you feel the pain the most. Put your hand on this part of your body. Allow the warmth of your hand to reach this container and fill it with love and forgiveness. Tell this place on your body: "it is ok . . . it is ok . . ." Feel this container shrink a little with the touch of your hand . . . feel it become a little bit smaller each time you say, "it is ok . . ."

Keep your hand on this part of your body, imagine yourself opening a door, and leaving this place to return back to your life. Before entering back into your life, take a moment and look at it from a distance. You see all the people in your life, see all the things you want to do, and all of your dreams and desires. You feel strong and capable to face any challenge the world may give you . . . let this feeling fill you up and start walking . . . Imagine yourself walking the path of your life, strong and confident, your hand still radiates warmth, transforming the container holding your traumatic memory, making it smaller and smaller . . . You are walking this path and seeing familiar faces and places . . . if at any time you feel your memory starting to hurt again, with your hand on your container say, "it is ok . . ."

You keep on walking, and in the distance you see your dreams and hopes for the future. They are waiting for you at the end of the road. You know you can get there. You feel confident and secure. You know you have a way of coping with what hurts. You know you are ok.

Now move your hand and put it back to its original position, in your lap. You can still feel its warmth and energy surrounding the container in your body. You know that whenever you need it, this energy is available to you. All you need to do is put your hand on that part of your body and think positively, "It's ok now."

When you feel ready, you can open your eyes.

Application

This exercise helps the client to transform a traumatic event. The memories associated with it, from something vague and unmanageable, become something that can be contained, with its relevance decreasing over time. This provides the client with a context that makes the trauma more approachable, thus allowing the client to work through his or her traumatic memories.

The image of the traumatic event (the container) can be used in other follow-up activities to further process the traumatic experience and to create a greater sense of control and competency. Additional "hands on" exercises can give the container a physical shape through drawing, sculpting, or creating a collage, allowing the client to engage in other therapeutic exercises, such as talking to the object, moving it, or even throwing it around, as a means of expressing negative feelings and releasing negative energy.

B35
Yes or No
Monit Cheung

Post-traumatic stress disorder (PTSD) is a common psychological issue facing many veterans. PTSD symptoms affecting veterans include constant stressful thoughts, repeated nightmares, flashbacks of traumatic experiences in the killing field, tremor with muscle cramps, unpleasant connections to the war, harsh training and extreme alertness experienced during wartime, and negative feelings toward changes experienced after deployment. These veterans need to receive positive feedback from others to help them deal with these strong emotions. This kind of interaction allows them to discover or rediscover their strengths, to appreciate and notice their family members' physical and psychological changes, and to learn to put their body at ease with built-in positive thoughts. Replacing negative and traumatic thoughts with something positive is a suggestion in this exercise so that the client can feel more secure and that their life is manageable.

This is not an ordinary guided imagery exercise because it does not require clients to close their eyes. It provides visualization through something concrete, which the client (or the therapist) has designed. Concrete visualization tools may be a happy face posted on a tongue depressor to represent "yes," and a face with big eyes and an open mouth, posted on another tongue depressor to represent "no" (see figure 1 below).

Script

Take a deep breath. Remember we are here today to relax. Feel relaxed in this safe place for you. You have two answers on your hands, "yes" or "no," which can also represent your feelings—happy or questionable. You will hear a series of questions, phrases, or words after this introduction. When you hear these questions, phrases, or words, simply hold up your answer and say aloud or silently a word or feeling that comes to your mind. If you are not sure if your answer is "yes" or "no," you may hold up both or do nothing. For example, when you hear "Are you ready?" you may hold up the "yes" answer and say "yes" or "I am" or "happy" or "okay"; or you may hold up the "no" answer and say "sure" or "not sure" or "sad" or "move on." In your mind, try to think positively when you answer because being positive is a great starting point. Another example, when you hear "Are you tired?"

you may hold up the "no" answer and open up your mouth as wide as possible to let go of the unwanted pressure from your body; or you may hold up the "yes" answer and say "too tired" or "too tired, but I am fine" to maintain your positive posture. When you hear a single word, try to relax and hold up "yes" if you can relax and "no" when are unable to relax. Try to enjoy a few minutes of relaxation.

Are you ready? (wait for a response)

Now, a series of words and questions are coming.

How are you?

Birds

Sky

Blue

Swimming

Are you strong?

Excellent

I am strong.

Camping

Relaxing

Can you relax?

Take a deep breath—one . . . two . . . three.

Are you all right?

Happy

Sad

Feelings

Are you tired?

Yes

No

Are you a nice person?

How do feel when you are relaxed?

Relaxation

Joy to the world

My family

Are you ready to talk more?

Beautiful

Okay

Fine

Feel the power of relaxation

Are you positive?

Open your eyes if closed

How are you?

Application

This exercise can be used as an ice-breaker during an educational seminar with the veterans to empower them to feel positive about their future prospects. It can be used to work with groups who are depressed about their future as a means to boost up their spirit. After the instruction, if the clients prefer to close their eyes to complete this exercise, encourage them to think about safe, happy, positive feelings while their eyes are closed. They do not have to actually hold up the answers if they prefer not to, but can still say "yes" or "no" aloud or silently think about the words that come to mind. If they feel disturbed by any of the words, they should ask to stop by simply saying "stop" and addressing the feelings(s) with the therapist. In a group setting, encourage them to simply open their eyes or stop engaging and wait until the group is done with this exercise to share feelings.

Figure 1 Concrete Visualization Tool

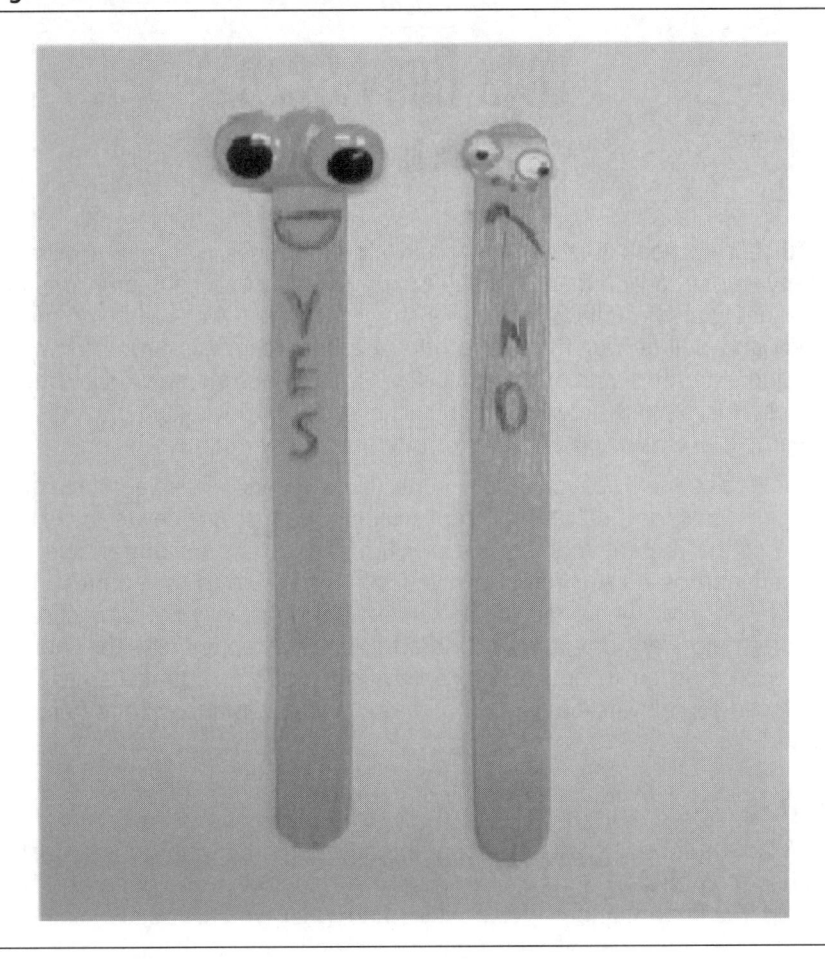

B36
Yoga Body Scan
Tira Burford

With busy schedules and unexpected life challenges, we may experience many emotional and mental health issues. This may include depression, anxiety, grief, or the effects of trauma that may affect the well-being of our body and pollute our mind. We often experience physical symptoms and tension manifestations that are directly related to our mental and emotional states. This exercise provides an opportunity to introduce yoga practices and breathing exercises to help relieve those physical symptoms.

Explain the benefits of yoga movements to the clients: "There are three guiding principles for the client to keep in mind. The first is to invite the experience of the present moment. At any time, if you are uncomfortable or if something doesn't feel right, give yourself permission to take a break. Secondly, you have the power of choice. Feel free to modify these practices as you feel necessary, or you may choose to skip any step entirely. The choice is yours. Last, listen to and be guided by your body. This practice has been designed to cultivate body-mind harmony and acceptance of the here and now."

Script

Let's do a full body scan when you're ready. Begin by lying on your mat or sit back comfortably. Simply allow your breath to flow in and out of the body freely. You may stay here for a while, and when you are ready, take your attention to the toes of your right foot. Continue breathing as you allow your attention to move from your toes to your entire foot, then to your calf and knee. As you begin to move your attention up your body, you may become aware of sensations residing in the area you are attending to. Focus on your breathing and feel the support of the ground beneath you.

When you are ready, take your attention to your thigh, then the hip, spending a minute or two in each area of the body. Repeat this exercise on the left side of your lower body, starting with the toes and moving up towards the calf, knee, the thigh and the hip. Breathing freely, focus your awareness on your back and your shoulders, being mindful of how it feels to reside in your body. On your next breath, move your attention to your fingertips, then the wrists, the arms, the back of the neck. As you exhale, you may feel the body melt further into the ground beneath you.

Stay with your breath, now allowing awareness of your jaw, your chin, the roof of your mouth, the nostrils, and then the eye socket, the space between your brow, the back of the head, and the top of the head. Allow your breath and awareness to nourish your body as you take full and deep breaths into the complete body. You may even say to yourself, "I am all right, right now." And as you allow this deep sense of ease, I invite you to stay here as long as you like. When you're ready, slowly roll to your right side and gently push yourself up to a sitting position.

Now, your body is completely scanned with nurture and comfort. May you have peace and harmony.

Application

This body scan practice is intended to empower clients on their path to healing and recovery. After introducing breathing exercises, you may use this body scan as a tool for the clients to self-regulate body movements and provide nurturing thoughts for their minds. As the client becomes more comfortable with the exercise, he or she may choose to spend more time on problem areas or introduce new areas of the body for focus.

Final Words: Solution-Focused Interventions

Variety, diversity, and context are the three main themes in this book to represent the practice of working with diverse populations. Children and adolescents represent diversity because of their multiple needs in their ever-changing developmental processes. The games and guided imagery exercises are designed to help clients prepare for their therapeutic moments and guide them to discover personal techniques of self-relaxation. They could also use the variety of given expressive means to disclose their concerns and realize that other possible solutions exist. Additional therapeutic questions may be included as needed to further explore clients' strengths and potential resources towards resolving their issues while remembering to consider the context of where the clients are and how the clients perceive their issues. It is expected that a brief practice modality will be used to identify the best possible alternative so that the clients can proceed with changes and find ways to satisfy their unmet needs.

After each exercise, therapeutic questions are included to guide clients in reaching their goal of discovering solutions. The following list summarizes possible questions or comments to be utilized during a therapeutic session that focuses on specific outcomes in assessment, finding coping methods, exploring feelings, locating formal and informal resources, setting up future goals, finding insight through miracle questions, examining past successes, picturing a problem-resolved scene, measuring expected outcomes or treatment goals with scaling questions, identifying client strengths, and focusing on closure. Finally, a list of items for a mini-toolbox is also suggested to help professionals prepare for sessions outside of a traditional office session, such as a home or school visit. These items are especially useful to connect clients with concrete examples when speaking about their strengths and possible solutions.

Assessment

1. Describe the best mood you had at home in the past week.
2. How does this issue make a difference in the meaning of your life?
3. How has this problem motivated you to seek help?
4. If I were to spend a day in your house, what would I see?
5. If the fear (you mentioned before) becomes a reality, what would be the worst that could happen? How would you have handled it?
6. If you were to confront a person you have conflict with, what would you say to this person?

7. If you could choose any song as "your song," a song best representing you, what would it be? What is it about this song that you can relate to?
8. If your current coping skills are working "just fine," help me understand how you have resolved the problem described by you (or by your parents or teachers)?
9. Pretend you could be anyone or anything you want to be; who or what would you choose? What made you choose this particular person or thing?
10. Reminisce on a good day you had in the past month. What made it a good day?
11. Suppose your mother (father) was here, what would she (he) say about your behavior at home?
12. Thinking about your typical day, what takes up most of your time?
13. What activities do you like to do during the day?
14. What are some things you can do to resolve this problem that you have not yet tried?
15. What are the things that are missing in your life? How could you get them?
16. What can you do to make sure that you can complete the task assigned to you?
17. What comes to your mind when you hear "mom and dad"? "Hope"? "Happiness"? (add other words that are related to the complaint)
18. What do you hope to gain from our sessions, specifically related to your issue?
19. What do you like the most about your home (or school) life?
20. What does a small change look like compared to a larger one?
21. What happened during the time you were happy?
22. What is considered a great success?
23. What needs to happen in order for you to feel successful?
24. What skills can you use to calm yourself when your parents are mad at you?
25. What would be some things that you would like to do if this issue did not affect your life?
26. What would you draw on this paper that represents who you want to be?

27. What would you give to a family member you are not fond of?
28. What would you say are some important things in life? What could you absolutely not live without?
29. Where do you want to go when you have this feeling?
30. When a particular characteristic about yourself is the solution of your biggest problem, who could help you see it? What would this person say?
31. When are you the happiest? Who are you with?
32. When do you notice yourself getting stressed out? How do you deal with stress?
33. When you feel that something is missing, how do you know it is not there for you?
34. When you look in the mirror, what do you see in yourself? What do you like about yourself? What would you like to change?
35. Who else noticed it (this symptom described by you)?
36. Who told you that you have a problem? How did this person know?

Differences in Solutions or Coping Methods

37. Do you feel that your current coping method has been working for you? How would you apply the same method to situations that are more intense?
38. Do you think you will feel different after this meeting?
39. How do you deal with sad news?
40. How do you know you need solutions to your problem?
41. How old will you be when you stop thinking of yourself as a "child" (or a "foster child")? What has to happen or change for you to not consider yourself a "child"?
42. How soon could this issue be resolved?
43. How would you tell a person if you want to refuse what this person offers?
44. How will things be different when this problem is resolved or less severe?
45. How will you know that our session is successful? What changes would have to happen?
46. If nothing is done towards correcting this concern, how do you know there will be changes for you?

47. If someone took advice from you and got better, what advice might you have given? What would this person have said to you?
48. If your deceased relatives could see how you are living your life now, what would they see? What would they say to you?
49. If you reach your desired level, what will be different?
50. If your problem is acting as a barrier to your solution, what needs to be done to resolve this problem?
51. Since leaving your parents (foster parents, etc.), what has been the most noticeable difference in your life?
52. Suppose there is a fly on the wall in your classroom; what would this fly see about your work on a typical school day?
53. Think of a problem you encountered in the past. What did you do to overcome this problem?
54. What are some hobbies you wish you could have spent more time on?
55. What are some signals that indicate a problem is being resolved?
56. What are some things you do to alleviate or eliminate the stress?
57. What are some things you have done to keep yourself motivated?
58. What are some ways in which you were able to change (the situation)?
59. What can make today better than yesterday? What could make tomorrow better than today?
60. What can you do differently today to move to a better place?
61. What coping mechanisms do you apply to lessen the intensity of a situation?
62. What could be used to divert your attention away from the problem?
63. What could you do to make yourself feel proud more often?
64. What could you dream (or think) about that can bring you hope?
65. What difference would it make in your life if you have achieved a higher level of happiness?
66. What does your parent see in you that is different from your own perspective?
67. What have you done this week to improve your situation in school?
68. What kind of change could make a difference for you?

69. What made you realize that something needed to be done?
70. What makes you feel better about yourself after you shared this situation with me?
71. What questions have I not asked you that are important to you?
72. What would you like to see yourself doing differently between now and next time we meet?
73. Which part of your life thus far should not change?
74. Whose advice sounded good to you? What is good about it?

Feelings

75. Based on your current mood, pick an animal to best represent you. What does this animal represent?
76. How are you feeling now after you talked about what you've learned in the past week?
77. How do you feel about other people's perception of you?
78. How do you feel about yourself? What would you change to make yourself feel better?
79. How does that person's perception affect you (or make you feel)?
80. How would you change that feeling (reaction)?
81. How would you feel if you could take a step towards that goal?
82. If people noticed this problem, how would they feel?
83. What are you feeling right now about this issue?
84. What color can describe your feelings best? What color reminds you of happiness (or another positive feeling)?
85. What do you do when you are angry (sad, etc.)? How does it differ from when you are happy (excited, etc.)?
86. What do you need to hear from others in order to feel better?
87. What does being happy look like to you?
88. What feelings connect you to this individual you just mentioned?

Formal Help and Informal Support

89. How can therapy help you reexamine your issue?
90. How can this help you when times get tough (or tougher)?
91. How can we help you fulfill what is missing?

92. How can you make this a helpful experience?
93. How can your parents (teachers, social worker) help you stay on track?
94. How could your close friends or family members help you (even if you don't ask)?
95. I feel a sense of discomfort. What can we do to make you feel comfortable?
96. If our counseling sessions have restored your hope, how do you know? Elaborate on what you have done.
97. If you had a choice, would you come to this session? Tell me more.
98. If you had a family member or friend in your position, what would you tell or advise them to do?
99. If your parent/girlfriend/boyfriend were sitting in this (empty) chair right now, what would you say to her/him?
100. Imagine a place that would inspire hope. What would it look like?
101. Is there anybody in your family that you enjoy spending time with?
102. Is there anyone close to you and that you can trust when you have a problem?
103. Is there someone whom you like or admire?
104. Think of a person you can get ahold of when you need help. Who comes to your mind?
105. What advice would you give to your family when they hear sad news?
106. What can I do to help you gain more out of therapy?
107. What could your family do to help you through this difficult time?
108. What in our sessions that have helped you did you find that is not helpful?
109. What do I need to know from you to help you feel better?
110. What encouraged you to share this confidential (private) information with me today?
111. What has been keeping you away from your family (friends, foster family, etc.)?
112. What have you done to make your parents (teachers, etc.) to believe that you can be better (achieve your goal)?
113. What is one thing, in your opinion, that will help you get better?

Final Words: Solution-Focused Interventions **393**

114. What kind of relationships would you like to have with your parents?
115. What life lessons did you learn that have helped you cope with this issue?
116. What things would you like to hear from your mom or dad?
117. What things would you need before you could accomplish that?
118. What traits embody health to you?
119. What would a trusted friend say that is helpful to you?
120. What would your friends see from outside of the problem?
121. What would your parents have to do to earn your trust?
122. What would your teachers say that you like to hear?
123. Who can you think of when we talk about these successful traits (stories, etc.)?
124. Who can you work with that can help you achieve your goal? How?
125. Who do you feel most connected to? What is in that connection?
126. Who do you talk to when you're upset?
127. Who encourages you to pursue your life goal?
128. Who in your life do you feel safe being with?
129. Who in your life understands you and stands next to you for what you are going through?
130. Who would you tell first when you have good news?
131. Who, from your experience, has offered you the most help?
132. Whose opinion matters the most to you? What is it that matters?
133. You mentioned that you have a supportive person in your life. What does that person see in you?

Goal/Future

134. Help me understand what you would like to get from therapy.
135. How can our work be helpful to make this goal a reality for you?
136. How confident do you feel about working toward your goal?
137. How do you help yourself to cope with sadness (specific feeling)?
138. How do you know when you have reached your goal?
139. How do you see your life in the next year? How about in two or three years?

394 *Therapeutic Games and Guided Imagery*

140. How do your future goals influence your present (profile)?
141. How will you go about achieving your goals? What do you see yourself doing first?
142. How would you handle the situation differently next time?
143. How would you handle the situation if you were in charge of it?
144. How would you like your life to be different when you have finished your "work" here?
145. If someone close to you were to ask if there were any other issues you wanted to work on, what would be your answer?
146. If this is your goal, what will you do next week to help you move closer to meet it?
147. If this was someone else's issue, what suggestions would you have for them?
148. If you can overcome this issue today, what will that say to your grandchildren in the future?
149. If you could draw a picture of the day you achieve your goal, what would it look like?
150. Predict what your tomorrow or future will look like. What would you like to see?
151. What are some positive consequences that would happen as a result of going through this counseling process?
152. What are the things we have been doing here that have helped you get closer to reaching your goal?
153. What are your life goals after treatment?
154. What color would represent you best in a rainbow? What is its meaning for your future?
155. What do you think will happen if things get better? What will happen after that?
156. What has kept you from giving up?
157. What is the first goal you would like to see achieved?
158. What needs to happen that can take you to the next level of success?
159. What plans do you have to avoid this issue from happening again?
160. What will happen when you start to realize you have more hope in your life?
161. What will you do next month to help you meet your goal?

162. What would be your idea of a great day at school?
163. What would happen next if today were our last session?
164. What would happen if you did not do anything towards achieving your goal?
165. What would help you step up and try this approach?
166. What would it mean to you to solve this issue?
167. What would you be willing to do to resolve this issue?
168. What would you like to see happen over the next three sessions so that this is worth your time?
169. What would you use or do if you were to experience this problem (emotion) again?
170. Where do you want to be when you are sad (angry, frustrated, etc.)?
171. Where is your safe place? What's in it that you consider it safe?
172. Which of these traits do you feel you have or do not have?
173. Who do you see as your role model? What qualities does this person possess that are desirable to you?
174. Who is another person in your life to ask for help when needed?
175. Who would you share your life goals with?
176. Who would you tell first when you reached your goal?

Miracle and Solution

177. Close your eyes and imagine your problem is now gone. What do you see?
178. How can your "now" help you in the future?
179. How would life be different without this problem?
180. What would your parents be like tomorrow if they were to change to what you want them to be?
181. If a genie granted you three wishes and the general rules apply (not to repeat the same wish, no more new wishes, no harm to self or others), what would the first wish be?
182. If a miracle occurred to totally resolve your problem, what would you notice that was different?
183. If this change were to happen, what would you have done to take you to that point?
184. If you could be a cartoon character, who would you be? What attributes does this character have that relates to you?

185. If you could change anything about your life, what would it be? In your family? At school?
186. If you could change one thing about this situation, what would it be?
187. If you could have a big party, who would you invite? What would it be like?
188. If you could have one wish come true, what would it be? How would it change your life (or your problem)?
189. If you could have the "perfect" life, describe what it would be like.
190. If you could picture yourself without any worries or concerns, what would your week be like?
191. If you could plan your day in any way you would like to, what would that day be like?
192. If you had an invisibility cloak that you could wear for a day, where would you go and what would you see?
193. If you had more hope, how would it change the situation or problem you are facing?
194. If you knew you had a short time left in life, how would you spend it?
195. If you successfully resolved your difficulties, who would be the first person to notice this change?
196. If you were granted three wishes, what would you wish for first? How would this wish be different if you were president of the United States?
197. If you woke up tomorrow but saw that things didn't change in the way you wanted them to, what would you do?
198. If you woke up tomorrow and were completely "normal," what part of your life would have changed?
199. If you woke up tomorrow morning and everything was the way you wanted it to be, what would that look like?
200. If your problem was becoming less of a problem, what would be the first sign of this for you?
201. Let's say you can make three wishes for your parents and family; what would they be?
202. Pretend your name and your achievement were listed on the Internet (in the dictionary or history book); what would it say about you?

203. Say there was a miracle one day that there would be no more hurting. What do you suppose would be different for you?
204. Suppose that you walk through this door and all issues had been resolved, what would be one thing you wanted to tell your parents?
205. Suppose that you were asked to pick one day to relive again in which everything was going great. Describe that day for me.
206. What advice would a genie give you after your wish had come to life?
207. What can you do now to make your parents feel proud of you?
208. What can you take from this session that helps you through the next week?
209. What could you do to give yourself more hope when times are difficult?
210. What could you do to help you from repeating this same problem?
211. What miracle would be needed to make you become more motivated to work on your next goal?
212. What solution do you need to better yourself?
213. What would be the first thing you would tell me if you had overcome your situation by the next session?
214. What would you or things be like at school tomorrow if everything became the way you wanted it to be?
215. Which strength of yours could help you maintain this "miracle" (positive change)?
216. Which part of this change would you like to start with if you have the support you need?
217. Who would you notice first if you made a first change in your life? What would this person say about you?
218. Who would you like to be with when this problem is totally resolved?
219. Who would you like to see in your perfect world?
220. You just walked through a miracle door and saw your best friend there; what would your best friend say about you that would make you very happy?

Past/Similar Issues Resolved

221. Has there been a time you felt very happy (or possessed a positive attribute you wish to have)? What did you do during that time?

222. Have you ever overcome a similar difficulty in the past? How did you manage that?
223. How can your past help you now?
224. How did you cope with change?
225. How did you get through tough situations?
226. How did you manage to do this in the past?
227. How has problem-solving in the past helped you in this situation?
228. How have you been dealing with the issue before now?
229. How have you managed to survive without much support from your family?
230. How have you tried to tackle this particular goal before?
231. If you could change something in the past, what would it be?
232. In this situation you've described, what worked well?
233. Is there anyone you know who had experienced this problem in the past? How did this person resolve the problem?
234. Name a thing or two from your past that helped you solve a problem.
235. Name three things you like or would change about your past experiences.
236. Tell me about a time in the past before this problem existed. What was life like then?
237. Tell me about a time that you were able to accomplish something. What did you accomplish? Who was involved?
238. Tell me about a time when you were able to adjust to a new environment.
239. Tell me about a time you overcame a bad habit. How did you do it?
240. Think of a time when you needed help; who was there to help you?
241. Was there a time in your past when you could have encountered a problem but you did not?
242. What are one positive and one negative thing you have to say about our sessions?
243. What have you learned from earlier efforts or this episode?
244. What helped you know this was a better week?
245. What played a role in your decision?
246. What progress did you see in yourself in the past two weeks?

247. What was one successful thing that happened this past week?
248. What were some clues that helped you avoid the problem (the situation)?
249. What were you doing differently on a good day as compared to a bad day?
250. When was the first time you hoped that this problem would not come back?
251. When was the last time someone said something good about you? Describe that moment.
252. When was the last time you felt proud of yourself?
253. When you resolved this problem in the past, how quickly did you realize that the problem was gone?
254. Who has been able to resolve this similar issue?
255. Who was involved when you could do this in the past?

Resolved Scene

256. How can your parents tell that things are getting better? What would be a first sign they would notice?
257. How will you know that you have been resolving the issue?
258. How would your best friend deal with this problem if it were his (or her) problem?
259. How would your relationship be different if this problem were not present?
260. How would you want a person to describe you?
261. If you could use all the resources available to you, what could help you the most to keep this problem from reoccurring?
262. Imagine that you were your mom or dad for a moment. What would you do to help your son or daughter?
263. Imagine your mother or father is sitting in this (empty) chair. What would she or he say to you?
264. Let's go back two weeks; what would be one thing you would change about our sessions?
265. Let's suppose you get to the next step tomorrow. What's the smallest sign that will tell you that things are improving?
266. Look into the mirror. How would you see the reflection differently if the problem disappeared?

400 *Therapeutic Games and Guided Imagery*

267. Tell me one person you can think of now that has been helping you resolve this problem. How would this person respond if you could leave this problem forever?
268. Think about a similar situation that you resolved differently. At what point did you realize you had control over (the problem)?
269. Was there ever a time when you did not have (this problem)?
270. What about your life makes you believe that this problem can go away?
271. What advantages has "being a child" given you?
272. What has changed about you since the first time we met?
273. What has changed so that you feel you need a little help in solving the issue?
274. What have you already tried that is helpful to you?
275. What is one difference you could tell immediately when your problem disappeared?
276. What represents a perfect world to you?
277. What would you recommend to another person going through the same issue?
278. Who was helping you with your other problems prior to this recent conflict? How can this person help you this time?

Scaling Techniques to Evaluate and Empower

279. How did you come up with this score (on a scale of 1 to 10 with 10 being the best)?
280. How would you know that the level of the positive attribute you wish to have has increased in your life (by a score of 1 higher on the scale of 0 to 10)?
281. How would you know that you have achieved the score you wish to have?
282. How would you know you will get a perfect 10 regarding something you wish to have in yourself?
283. If 0 = no stress and 10 = stressed, where are you now? What can you do to go down one number?
284. Imagine a scale from 1 to 10. Ten represents how you want things to be when the problem is fixed and one is the opposite. What number are you on that scale right now?

285. Let's set some goals. What goals would you like to target? On a scale from 1 to 10 with 10 being most likely, how likely are you to meet your goals?
286. On a scale of 0 to 10 with 10 being excellent efforts being done and 0 being no effort being done, how would you rate yourself in the past few days?
287. On a scale of 0 to 10 where 10 = your very best, where are you now?
288. On a scale of 1 to 10, 1 being far from ready, and 10 being totally ready, at what rating would you be okay ending our sessions?
289. On a scale of 1 to 10, 1 being the worst possible day and 10 being the best day of your life, how would you describe your day? What can you do to raise that number?
290. On a scale of 1 to 10, how beneficial do you believe our time is together?
291. On a scale of 1 to 10, how confident are you that your problem can be solved?
292. On a scale of 1 to 10, how would you rate your participation in school? If I asked your teacher, would she give me the same answer?
293. On a scale of 1 to 10, how would your teachers rate your learning motivation?
294. On a scale of 1 to 10 (where 10 is full of hope), how much hope do you have? Even with little hope, how do you know it?
295. On a scale of 1 to 10 with 10 being the happiest, how do you feel about your relationship?
296. What rating would you give yourself on a scale of 10 to 0, where 10 = ready to jump in and work towards this goal and 0 = not at all ready?
297. What would you do differently at the next step? How will you (or your parents) be able to tell?
298. What would your mom or dad tell you about moving up the scale?
299. Who would give you a 10 for your effort without calculating the results?

Strength and Positivity

300. How can you use your personal strengths to overcome this issue?
301. How did you find the strength to go back to school or work after this incident?

302. How do you cope when things are difficult?
303. How do you find the courage to face your enemies?
304. How do you think other people see you or perceive your strengths?
305. How do you turn a negative situation into a positive one?
306. How would others respond when asked about what they appreciate about you?
307. How would your best friends describe in one word something positive about you?
308. I have heard you talk about things about yourself that you do not like; let's focus on something positive. Tell me about your good qualities.
309. If you could become a leader at something, what would you want to lead?
310. If you could use your strengths to do anything, what would you do?
311. In what ways can you positively surprise your parents (teachers, friends, classmates, etc.)?
312. It is not easy making such good grades in math (or a subject of high grade/achievement). How did you do it?
313. Recall three accomplishments (successes) you have achieved. Describe the most important one.
314. Tell me three things that you are good at.
315. Tell me about the things that really excite you, like subjects in school, hobbies, or social causes.
316. Think of a peer in your class that you do not like. Can you tell me one thing that you do like about this person? (Remember you do not have to like this person, but you can still like some of the things about him or her).
317. Think of a positive way this situation has impacted your life. What is it?
318. What about this person (you are most connected to) that you like the most?
319. What are some positive things that people say about you, and how does it make you feel?
320. What are some positive things that your parents (teachers) would say about you?
321. What are some things that a person with a high level of positive attribute that you wish to possess is different from a person who has a low level of that attribute?

322. What are some things that make you happy or smile?
323. What do you feel you are good at that you can teach a younger person?
324. What do you like to do for fun? How can this fun become your power for bettering your school work (or resolving your problem)?
325. What gave you the strength to come here today?
326. What has helped you gain strength in past difficult times?
327. What have been some of the happiest moments in your life?
328. What have you done to attain your positive attribute?
329. What helps you stay positive?
330. What is one character trait you wish to possess? What is unique about that trait? How can you obtain it?
331. What is one good thing about being different from others?
332. What is one helpful thing this person could say to you if he or she were still here?
333. What is one item that reminds you of hope?
334. What is one of your strengths? What is one of your weaknesses? How can you turn your weakness into strength?
335. What is one positive thing you can think about when you begin to feel that you have no hope in resolving this issue?
336. What is one positive thing you would like to do when you turn 20 (30, 40, etc.)?
337. What is one positive trait about you that would help you resolve this problem?
338. What is one thing that you can do this week to get one step closer to attaining your goal (solving your problem)?
339. What is one thing you did since our last session that required a lot of courage?
340. What is one thing you like about yourself that you want others to notice?
341. What is something positive that will result from this change? How will this change impact your life?
342. What is something you have done very well?
343. What is your best childhood memory? Tell me one good thing in this memory.
344. What is your greatest accomplishment in school? How did it make you feel?

345. What is your one strength that others find as a challenge?
346. What would that supportive person in your life say are your strengths?
347. Where would you go if you have success stories to share?
348. When you think of hope, what do you imagine?
349. Who has a positive attitude you wish to possess? What has that person done to attain the high level of positivity?

Termination and Closure
350. Five years from now, what will be some of the changes you can share with your closest friend?
351. Now you are ready to say good-bye to me, think of a word (or some words) of advice for someone who might have the similar problem you had before. What would you say to this person?
352. Say three times, "I made it" (or any words the client wants to express to close the session).
353. Since this is our last session, what would you like to say to show that your (therapeutic) work has come to a closure?
354. Tell me one word that represents "completion" for you.
355. Ten years from now, what would be an achievement for you to feel proud of?
356. Your parents will come in next; pick one thing you've done successfully to share with them. Before they come in, think what would be unique about this sharing. How would you like them to respond after your sharing?

Portable Therapeutic Toolbox: An Example

Obtain objects in miniaturized form that are suitable for age 3+

Portable Items	Purpose
Alphabets and numbers	Counting, hand-eye coordination
Ball (small)	Stress reduction, attention, focus
Bell (or something that makes sound)	Attention, focus
Car or truck (small)	Moving
Crayons (3–5 colors)	Colors, drawing
Dice and token chips	Game, numbers
Digital camera (toy)	Memory, photos
Fabrics (different colors and patterns)	Feeling expression, touching, connections
Family or house pictures	Family, memory
*Gloves (two different sharp colors such as green and orange)	For thought stopping or do/don't choices
Hand or finger puppets	Communication
Hand sanitizer	Cleaning hands before starting
Magic wand	Solution-focused questions
Markers (2–3 colors)	Colors, drawing
Microphone (toy)	Talking, communication
Mirror (unbreakable)	Time out, facial expressions
Notebook (small)	Writing, homework
Pen or pencil and papers	Drawing
Poker cards or flash cards	Game, storytelling
Puzzles (small and easy to solve)	Solution
Rice or sand (in a small transparent container)	Concentration, counting
Rope (short)	For magic and solutions
Stickers	Rewards
Stop sign	Thought stopping
Timer	Timing, reminder
Toy gun and soldiers	War, struggles, storytelling

*Help young children differentiate between good and bad, right and wrong, etc.

References

Abdoli, S., Rahzani, K., Safaie, M., & Sattari, A. (2012). A randomized control trial: The effect of guided imagery with tape and perceived happy memory on chronic tension type headache. *Scandinavian Journal of Caring Sciences, 26*(2), 254–261.

Andersson, E. K., & Moss, T. P. (2011). Imagery and implementation intention: A randomised controlled trial of interventions to increase exercise behavior in the general population. *Psychology of Sport and Exercise, 12*(2), 63–70.

Apóstolo, J., & Kolcaba, K. (2009). The effects of guided imagery on comfort, depression, anxiety, and stress of psychiatric inpatients with depressive disorders. *Archives of Psychiatric Nursing, 23*(6), 403–411.

Baile, W. F., De Panfilis, L., Tanzi, S., Moroni, M., Walters, R., & Biasco, G. (2012). Using sociodrama and psychodrama to teach communication in end-of-life care. *Journal of Palliative Medicine, 15*(9), 1006–1010.

Bell, R. J., Skinner, C. H., & Halbrook, M. K. (2011). Solution-focused guided imagery as an intervention for golfers with the yips. *Journal of Imagery Research in Sport and Physical Activity, 6*(1).

Body Language. (2012). In *Merriam-Webster Online Dictionary*. Retrieved from http://www.merriam-webster.com/dictionary/body%20language.

Borg, J. (2011). *Body language: How to know what's really being said.* Harlow, England: Pearson Prentice Hall Life.

Brown, B. (2007). *I thought it was just me (but it isn't): Tellinng the truth about perfectionism, inadequacy, and power.* New York: Gotham Books.

Centers for Disease Control and Prevention. (CDC, 2012). Teen drivers: Fact sheet. Retrieved from http://www.cdc.gov/motorvehiclesafety/teen_drivers/teendrivers_factsheet.html.

Cohen, G. D. (2000). Two new intergenerational interventions for Alzheimer's disease patients and families. *American Journal of Alzheimer's Disease, 15*(3), 137–142.

Cohen, G., Firth, K., Biddle, S., Lewis, M., & Simmens, S. (2009). The first therapeutic game specifically designed and evaluated for Alzheimer's disease. *American Journal of Alzheimer's Disease and Other Dementias, 23*(6), 540–551.

Council on Social Work Education. (2008). *Educational Policy and Accreditation Standards*. Retrieved from http://www.cswe.org/File.aspx?id=13780.

Duncan, L. R., Hall, C. R., Wilson, P. M., & Rodgers, W. M. (2012). The use of a mental imagery intervention to enhance integrated regulation for exercise among women commencing an exercise program. *Motivation and Emotion, 36*(4), 452–464.

Eryilmaz, A. (2012). A model for subjective well-being in adolescence: Need satisfaction and reasons for living. *Social Indicators Research, 107*(3), 561–574.

Fisher, R. W. (2007). The effect of guided mental imagery on the intrinsic reading motivation of fourth and fifth grade students. *Dissertation Abstracts International Section A, 68*(3–A), 930.

Gibbons, G., & Jones, T. (2003). Kinship care: Health profiles of grandparents raising their grandchildren. *Journal of Family Social Work, 7*(1), 1–14.

Gonzales, E., Ledesma, R., McAllister, D., Perry, S., Dyer, C., & Maye, J. (2010). Effects of guided imagery on postoperative outcomes in patients undergoing same-day surgical procedures: A randomized, single-blind study. *AANA Journal, 78*(3), 181–188.

Harvey, V., & Retter, K. (2002). Variations by gender between children and adolescents on the four basic psychological needs. *International Journal of Reality Therapy, 21*(2), 33–36.

Hernández-Guzmán, L., González, S., & López, F. (2002). Effect of guided imagery on children's social performance. *Behavioral and Cognitive Psychotherapy, 30*(4), 471–483.

Jaffe, A. (2003). Ritual, storytelling and play: A therapeutic board game. *Dissertation Abstracts International, 64*(5–B), 2390.

Jain, S., McMahon, G., Hasen, P., Kozub, M., Porter, V., King, R., & Guarneri, E. (2012). Healing touch with guided imagery for PTSD in returning active duty military: A randomized controlled trial. *Military Medicine, 177*(9), 1015–1021.

Khandaker, M. (2009). Designing effective video games to support the social-emotional development of teenagers with autism spectrum disorders. *Annual Review of Cybertherapy and Telemedicine, 7*, 37–39.

Kim, B., Newton, R., Sachs, M., Giacobbi, P., & Glutting, J. (2011). The effect of guided relaxation and exercise imagery on self-reported leisure-time exercise behaviors in older adults. *Journal of Aging and Physical Activity, 19*(2), 137–146.

Kramer, E. S. (2010). *Healing factors in guided affective imagery: A qualitative meta-analysis.* (Union Institute and University). *ProQuest Dissertations and Theses,* 381. Retrieved from http://search.proquest.com.ezproxy.lib.uh.edu/docview/787904384?accountid=7107.

Kwekkeboom, K., Huseby-Moore, K., & Ward, S. (1998). Imaging ability and effective use of guided imagery. *Research in Nursing and Health, 21*(3), 189–198.

La Roche, M., Batista, C., & D'Angelo, E. (2011). A content analysis of guided imagery scripts: A strategy for the development of cultural adaptations. *Journal of Clinical Psychology, 67*(1), 45–57.

La Roche, M., D'Angelo, E., Gualdron, L., & Leavell, J. (2006). Culturally sensitive guided imagery for allocentric Latinos: A pilot study. *Psychotherapy: Theory, Research, Practice, Training, 43*(4), 555–560.

Leversen, I., Danielsen, A., Birkeland, M., & Samdal, O. (2012). Basic psychological need satisfaction in leisure activities and adolescents' life satisfaction. *Journal of Youth and Adolescence, 41*(12), 1588–1599.

Li, W. H. C., Chung, J. O. K., & Ho, E. K. Y. (2011). The effectiveness of therapeutic play, using virtual reality computer games, in promoting the psychological well-being of children hospitalized with cancer. *Journal of Clinical Nursing, 20*(15/16), 2135–2143.

Lin, M., Hsu, M., Chang, H., Hsu, Y., Chou, M., & Crawford, P. (2010). Pivotal moments and changes in the Bonny method of guided imagery and music for patients with depression. *Journal of Clinical Nursing, 19*(7–8), 1139–1148.

Louie, S. (2004). The effects of guided imagery relaxation in people with COPD. *Occupational Therapy International, 11*(3), 145–159.

Mazza, E. (2007). Review of "Therapeutic games and guided imagery: Tools for mental health and school professionals working with children, adolescents, and their families." *Social Work Education, 26*(3), 321–322.

McLean, C. (2008). How the mind/body connection can empower children during painful procedures in hospital. *Australian Journal of Clinical Hypnotherapy and Hypnosis, 29*(1), 23–27.

Meadows, A. (2000). The validity and reliability of the guided imagery and music responsiveness scale. *Journal of the Association for Music and Imagery, 7*, 8–33.

Menzies, V., & Kim, S. (2008). Relaxation and guided imagery in Hispanic persons diagnosed with fibromyalgia: A pilot study. *Family and Community Health: The Journal of Health Promotion and Maintenance, 31*(3), 204–212.

Misurell, J., Springer, C., & Tryon, W. (2011). Game-based cognitive-behavioral therapy (GB-CBT) group program for children who have experienced sexual abuse: A preliminary investigation. *Journal of Child Sexual Abuse, 20*(1), 14–36.

Mooradian, J. K., Cross, S. L., & Stutzky, G. R. (2006). Across generations: Culture, history, and policy in the social ecology of American Indian grandparents parenting their grandchildren. *Journal of Family Social Work, 10*(4), 81–101.

Muller, B. J. (2011). Guided imagery and music: A survey of current practices. *Dissertation Abstracts International Section A, 71*, 38–43.

Omizo, M. M., Omizo, S. A, & Kitaoka, S. K. (1998). Guided affective and cognitive imagery to enhance self-esteem among Hawaiian children. *Journal of Multicultural Counseling and Development, 26*(1), 52.

Paralinguistic Cues. (2009). In *Mosby's Medical Dictionary, 8th Edition*. Retrieved from http://medical-dictionary.thefreedictionary.com/paralinguistic+cues.

Peck, H. L., Bray, M. A., & Kehle, T. J. (2003). Relaxation and guided imagery: A school-based intervention for children with asthma. *Psychology in the Schools, 40*(6), 657–675.

Phillips, S., & Zhao, J. (2010). The relationship between witnessing arrests and elevated symptoms of posttraumatic stress: Findings from a national study of children involved in the child welfare system. *Children and Youth Services Review, 32*(10), 1246–1254.

Rabin, C., Blechman, E., & Milton, M. (1984). A multiple baseline study of the Marriage Contract Game's effects on problem solving and affective behavior. *Child and Family Behavior Therapy, 6*(2), 45–60.

Review of "Therapeutic games and guided imagery: Tools for mental health and school professionals working with children, adolescents, and their families." (2006). *Family Therapy, 33*(2), 119–120.

Robson, M. (2008). The driver whose heart was full of sand: Leigh's story—a play therapy case study of a bereaved child. *British Journal of Guidance and Counselling, 36*(1), 71–80.

Russell, E. B. (2009). Review of "Therapeutic games and guided imagery: Tools for mental health and school professionals working with children, adolescents, and their families." *The Family Journal, 17*(4), 375–376.

Saice, R. (2007). Review of "Therapeutic games and guided imagery: Tools for mental health and school professionals working with children, adolescents, and their families." *School Social Work Journal, 32*(1), 93–94.

Short, A. E. (1991). The role of guided imagery and music in diagnosing physical illness or trauma. *Music Therapy, 10*(1), 22–45.

Sklare, G. B., Sabella, R. A., & Petrosko, J. M. (2003). A preliminary study of the effects of group solution-focused guided imagery on recurring individual problems. *Journal for Specialists in Group Work, 28*(4), 370–381.

Springer, C., & Misurell, J. (2010). Game-based cognitive-behavioral therapy (GB-CBT): An innovative group treatment program for children who have been sexually abused. *Journal of Child and Adolescent Trauma, 3*(3), 163–180.

Staples, J., Abdel Atti, J., & Gordon, J. (2011). Mind-body skills groups for posttraumatic stress disorder and depression symptoms in Palestinian children and adolescents in Gaza. *International Journal of Stress Management, 18*(3), 246–262.

Stokes, E. (2008). Profiles used in teaching and research for developing multimedia games for pupils on the autism spectrum (AS). *International Journal on Disability and Human Development, 7*(1), 39–47.

Streng, I. (2008). Using therapeutic board games to promote child mental health. *Journal of Public Mental Health, 7*(4), 4–16.

Swank, J. (2008). The use of games: A therapeutic tool with children and families. *International Journal of Play Therapy, 17*(2), 154–167.

Tsai, S. (2004). Audio-visual relaxation training for anxiety, sleep, and relaxation among Chinese adults with cardiac disease. *Research in Nursing and Health, 27*(6), 458–468.

Weigensberg, M., Lane, C., Winners, O., Wright, T., Nguyen-Rodriguez, S., Goran, M., & Spruijt-Metz, D. (2009). Acute effects of stress reduction interactive guided imagery on salivary cortisol in overweight Latino adolescents. *Journal of Alternative and Complementary Medicine, 15*(3), 297–303.

Wiener, L., Battles, H., Mamalian, C., & Zadeh, S. (2011). ShopTalk: A pilot study of the feasibility and utility of a therapeutic board game for youth living with cancer. *Supportive Care in Cancer, 19*(7), 1049–1054.

Wilkinson, N., Ang, R., & Goh, D. (2008). Online video game therapy for mental health concerns: A review. *International Journal of Social Psychiatry, 54*(4), 370–382.

Wuang, Y., Chiang, C., Su, C., & Wang, C. (2011). Effectiveness of virtual reality using Wii gaming technology in children with Down syndrome. *Research in Developmental Disabilities, 32*(1), 312–321.

Contributors

Cristal Atilano, MSW, is a graduate of the University of Houston. She has worked with children and adolescents in a variety of settings. Currently she is working as a program manager for a youth leadership program in the Mayor's Anti-Gang Office in Houston, Texas.

Kim Ba, LMSW, is a graduate of the University of Houston Social Work program. She has internship experiences at the Star of Hope Transitional Living Center and the Michael E. DeBakey VA Medical Center. She obtained her license as a licensed master social worker in Texas, moved to Fort Bragg, North Carolina, and is working toward a clinical license in social work. Her areas of interest include mental health, gerontology, and military social work. Ba is an "Army wife" who sees herself as a bridge to link military experiences to clinical social work.

Rachel E. Barajas is a first-generation college graduate. She received her bachelor of arts from the University of Texas at Austin and her master's degree in social work from the University of Houston Graduate College of Social Work. Barajas applies her clinical skills in all sorts of life situations.

Ruprekha "Roopa" Baruah, LMSW, is a magna cum laude graduate from the University of Houston Graduate College of Social Work, where she also serves as a field instructor for graduate students. She has served over 14 years in the Department of Family & Protective Services, Child Protective Division in various capacities. Baruah's areas of expertise include crisis intervention, conflict resolution, and resource coordination. She ascribes to a trauma-informed approach in working with youths transitioning out of the foster care system.

John Betancourt, MSW, LCDC, has worked with adolescents and adults with substance abuse disorders in treatment centers and the Miami-Dade County Drug Court. He has also worked for the Research Triangle Institute on the National Survey on Drug Use and Health. He is interested in clinical practice with Latinos.

Tira Burford, LMSW, is a practicing, licensed social worker and registered yoga teacher. She specializes in complex trauma treatment, mindfulness, and yoga for the mental health community. Tira obtained her master's degree in social work from the Graduate College of Social Work at the University of Houston. Burford infuses yogic practices into psychotherapy with her bachelor of science in psychology and background in creative arts. This allows for a more holistic approach to client mental health care. She enjoys sharing the benefits of utilizing yoga and relaxation for self-care, and sees it as an adjunct to psychotherapeutic modalities.

Maria Cano, MSW, is a social worker at Child Advocates, Houston. She is an active advocate on behalf of children and their families.

Ada Cheung, PhD, LCSW, is an adjunct faculty teaching in the Graduate College of Social Work at the University of Houston. She works at the IntraCare Adult Intensive Outpatient Program as a psychotherapist treating patients with mental illness, personality disorder, and chemical dependency. Cheung also has her own private practice at IntraCare Behavioral Health Clinic, seeing patients aged seven and up, and provides individual, couple, and family therapy. She has been serving at IntraCare Medical Hospital for seven years, and is also affiliated with the Behavioral Hospital of Bellaire.

Rachel Wai-Yi Cheung works as an illustrator in different educational institutes and publishing companies in Hong Kong.

Kayla Cooper was born in 1985 and was diagnosed with neuroblastoma at 15 months of age, which left her paralyzed and confined to a wheelchair. In 2006 she gave birth to her daughter and decided it was time to make some changes in order to provide a better life for her. She enrolled at the University of Houston-Downtown and graduated with a bachelor of science in sociology with a minor in psychology. She graduated with a master's degree in social work at the University of Houston. Cooper is now a renal social worker at Sohum-Southeast Houston Dialysis, working towards strengthening her social work skills and raising her now six-year-old daughter.

Ivy Elizabeth Crank, LMSW, currently provides individual substance abuse counseling and case management services at Behavioral Health Group in Gretna, Louisiana. She received her master's degree in social work with a clinical concentration from the University of Houston in 2012. As an intern at Texas Children's Hospital's Employee Assistance Program, Crank utilized a variety of therapeutic approaches in working with individuals, couples, and families. She also facilitated individual and group therapy at Odyssey House Texas, Inc., a residential substance abuse treatment facility for adolescents. She received a bachelor of arts in psychology with minors in political science and criminal justice studies from Elon University in 2009. Crank currently lives in New Orleans with her fiancé and plans to begin supervision toward the LCSW license for independent clinical practice.

Sergio Cruz, LCSW, earned his master's degree from the University of Houston Graduate College of Social Work and a bachelor's degree from the University of Texas at El Paso. Cruz has over four years of experience working with children, adolescents, and adults in residential and outpatient settings. His training and experience includes assessment and treatment of individuals and families that have experienced trauma. Cruz has a wide scope of practice experience with a variety of mental health concerns and problems of everyday living, including depressive disorders, anxiety, relational problems, grief, adjustment issues, and life stressors.

Elena Delavega, PhD, MSW is an assistant professor of social work at the University of Memphis, where she teaches social welfare policy analysis and human behavior in the social environment. Her research interests are focused on sustainable economic development which includes ways to alleviate poverty, wages, the relationship between education and capital, capital transformations, and immigration. Delavega has 17 refereed and non-refereed publications and abstracts, including articles in such academic journals as the *Journal of Ethnic and Cultural Diversity in Social Work* and the *Journal of Policy Practice*. In addition, she has presented 21 juried and invited papers at various state and national conferences. Delavega has served on a number of committees, boards, and councils dealing with immigration, social work, and Alzheimer's disease. She is fully bilingual in Spanish and English.

Jennifer Lynn Edwards is an MSW intern who graduated magna cum laude from the University of Houston with a bachelor's degree in psychology in 2008. She worked at the Menninger Clinic from 2008 to 2012.

Karen R. Greenberg, LMSW, has a bachelor of science degree in human development and family studies and a master's degree in social work with a specialization in health disparities from the University of Houston. She also has a mediation certificate. She was born and raised in South Florida and presently resides in Houston, Texas, where she works full-time for a private company and part-time as a psychotherapist for a nonprofit organization. Previous experience includes working as an early intervention specialist with young children and families. In her leisure time, she enjoys volunteering with an animal rescue organization.

Jenna Halseth, MSW, is a social worker in Houston, Texas. She received her undergraduate education from the University of California, Santa Barbara, where she studied French and global studies. She received her master's degree in social work from the University of Houston. Her social work interests are child welfare and refugee/immigrant assistance.

Casey Williams Hedges, LCSW, obtained her bachelor's degree in social work from the University of Texas at Austin in 2006 and graduated with her master's degree in social work from the University of Houston in 2007. She has been working in the medical field at Children's Memorial Hermann Hospital–Texas Medical Center in Houston for six years. Hedges specializes in work with childhood trauma, at-risk children, grief and bereavement, substance abuse, and pregnancy-related issues. Her experience includes case management, assessment, treatment planning, therapeutic support, counseling, support group facilitation, and referral to community resources.

Caroline Hendrix has an interest in working with youth, providing psychoeducational information about dating violence at the National Dating Abuse

Helpline. She has expanded her understanding of adolescent challenges by working with diverse populations, including homeless youth and youth with eating disorders and anxiety/mood disorders. She completed her master's degree in social work at the Graduate College of Social Work, University of Houston. Currently, Hendrix is assisting families with special needs children. Her ultimate goal is to promote resilience within underserved populations in order to enhance all people's daily lives.

Agnes Oi-Yee Ho, LMSW, is a social worker at Rice University. She provides counseling and consultations on mental health and administrative issues for faculty, staff, students, and student family members. She has had many years of experience working in child abuse and domestic violence prevention programs in Texas and establishing partnerships and collaborations to support families' health and well-being. She also has experience working with diverse Asian populations. Her practice expertise has been related to families with adolescents who are experiencing social, academic, familial, and behavioral difficulties.

Kelly Holmes, LMSW, is a child and family psychotherapist in Houston. Her primary focus is working with children and adolescents who have been traumatized by physical, sexual, and verbal abuse and also specializes in working with those suffering from substance abuse and eating disorders as well as their families.

Regenia G. Kerr is currently working for Baytown Communities in school settings, specializing as a case manager for at-risk students on a junior high campus. She was born and raised in Huntsville, Alabama. The NASA program and the Redstone Arsenal were and still are major industries that influence the diversity of Huntsville and the surrounding areas. Since much of NASA transferred to Houston in 1965, she relocated to Houston and has made it her home for the past 45 years. She received her master's degree in social work at the University of Houston.

Susan Kulbeth, LMSW, is the program and clinical services director for the Hill Country Children's Advocacy Center in Burnet, Texas. She provides therapeutic services for children and their non-offending family members as well as ongoing workshops focused on parenting children who have experienced trauma.

Debbie Kumar-Misir, LMSW, is a well-being specialist at Child Protective Services in Texas. Her past positions with the agency include program director for investigations, on-the-job training supervisor, development disabilities specialist, and family-based safety services and investigations worker. She received her bachelor's degree in social work from the University of Windsor, Canada and her master's degree in social work from the Graduate College of Social Work at the University of Houston.

Karen Mei-Lin Lau, M. Soc. Sc. (EP), PC Ed., PC Psy, BASW, DipSW, is a registered educational psychologist and a registered social worker in Hong Kong. She received her master's degree in social science (educational psychologist) and has been working in different social settings for more than 13 years. She works with children, youth, elderly, families, community, teachers, and supervises educational psychologist trainees. Currently, Lau is an educational psychologist at the Boys' and Girls' Clubs Association of Hong Kong.

Antonella Lazzaro, LMSW, received her master's degree in social work from the University of Houston Graduate College of Social Work. She received her bachelor's degree of social work with a minor in sociology from Meredith College in Raleigh, North Carolina. Lazzaro has gained experience from both her academic work and a variety of field placement settings. In these settings, Lazzaro has engaged in social work practice with at-risk youth in a therapeutic foster care program, the homeless in a transitional living facility, and youth and adults in an outpatient mental health clinic.

Jenaia Leffel, MSW, is a social worker in Houston. She received her master's degree in social work from the University of Houston and her bachelor's degree of science from Middle Tennessee State University with a major in psychology and minors in criminal justice and life-span development. She specializes in clinical practice to help and educate children and has helped animal rescue organizations in the Houston area.

Carol A. Leung, BA, LMSW, is currently a doctoral student at the Luskin School of Public Affairs, Department of Social Welfare, at the University of California, Los Angeles. She has been practicing clinical social work as a psychotherapist in New York City at Flushing Hospital Mental Health Clinic, primarily providing counseling to the Chinese immigrant population. Carol received her MSSW from the University of Texas at Austin. Carol's research interests are related to mental health stigma and suicide among people with severe and persistent mental illnesses. Her prior work experiences at Adult Protective Services and AdoptUSkids have prepared her for further research with older adults and adoptive youth.

Patrick Leung, PhD, is a professor and director of the Office for International Social Work Education and former doctoral program director at the University of Houston, Graduate College of Social Work. He teaches program evaluation, research methodology, survey design, and doctoral-level multivariate statistics. His research areas include cultural sensitivity training, Asian mental health issues, children and families, immigrant issues, domestic violence, and gerontology. Leung received his PhD, MSW, MA (public administration), and BSSW from Ohio State University. He is coauthor of two books, entitled *Child Protection Training and Evaluation*, and *Multicultural Practice and Evaluation: A Case Approach to Evidence-Based Practice*.

Anny Kit-Ying Ma, LMSW, is a social worker at the VA Medical Center in Houston, Texas. She is passionate about promoting positive change for children and families with diverse backgrounds. Her professional experiences include disaster planning and recovery services, homelessness prevention and rehousing programs, child development and welfare, family education and planning, nonprofit development, and fund-raising as well as management and supervision. Ma's critical and creative thinking has allowed her to effectively and efficiently assist persons in need and manage social service programs. Her goal is to use her continued efforts to seek innovative solutions for human needs and social issues.

Juan Carlos Macias, MSW, graduated from the University of Houston Graduate College of Social Work as an advanced standing student and obtained a certificate in health disparities in 2012. He is originally from Compton, California, and attended California State University, Long Beach, before transferring to Prairie View A&M University, where he graduated summa cum laude with his bachelor's degree in social work. Macias's areas of interest include juveniles at risk for delinquency and health disparities among immigrant minority youth.

Allison Marek, LMSW, is a psychotherapist at Lone Star Behavioral Health, where she utilizes equine assisted psychotherapy in her work with adults with chronic, severe mental illness. Her other practice areas include adolescents and their families, addictions, and trauma. She is currently pursuing certification in Brené Brown's The Daring Way method. She is a graduate of the University of Houston Graduate College of Social Work.

Yuliana Alvarez Medina, LMSW, a native of Bogota, Colombia, is an alumnus of the University of Houston Graduate College of Social Work. She has experiences working with female survivors of domestic violence and sexual assault, school social work, and in a rehabilitation program for adolescents. Her passion is contributing to the achievement of social and economic justice in this society by working with minorities groups and underrepresented communities such as the Hispanic or Latino population.

Misty Miller, LMSW, received her master's degree in social work in 2007 from the University of Houston. She is a native and proud Houstonian of Costa Rican descent. Prior to earning her master's, she worked with bilingual children, adolescents, and their families struggling with mental illness. Since then, she has served her community on a macro level through promoting the mission of the United Way of Greater Houston by connecting people to services and impacting lives through the 2-1-1 Texas United Way Helpline, and more recently connecting the community to affordable health care for all at Legacy Community Health Services.

Ophelia Mok, LMSW, graduated from the University of Texas at Austin with a bachelor's degree in social work. She worked as a child protection worker in

Travis County for several years before returning to school to pursue a master's degree. She completed her master's degree in social work at the University of Houston. Mok is a social worker working with children and families affected by abuse and neglect at Child Advocates of Fort Bend in Rosenberg, Texas.

Ashante "Bree" Montero, MSW, received her master's degree from the University of Houston and her bachelor's degree in social work from the University of Texas in Austin. She is passionate about social justice issues, especially concerning children and families. She concentrates on counseling services for families with children who have experienced trauma. Montero is also interested in providing bilingual services to Spanish-speaking clients.

Tuan Nguyen, LMSW, earned a bachelor's degree in psychology and social behavior from the University of California, Irvine, and a master's degree in social work from the University of Houston. As a son of Vietnamese refugees, Nguyen has a deep interest in understanding the challenges refugees and recent immigrants face and the impact of culture on the mental health and development of youth. Nguyen has worked as a therapist and youth program coordinator for a nonprofit agency in Houston, and is currently working at an urban university in Houston.

Monica Ortiz-Holtkamp, MSW, earned her master's degree in social work from the University of Houston Graduate College of Social Work. She specializes in clinical practice and is interested in working with children and adolescents with anxiety.

Elizabeth Owsley, BSW, is attending the University of Houston Graduate School of Social Work, pursuing her master of social work degree with a focus of working with the disability population.

Shaneka Postell, BSW, MSW, graduated from Prairie View A&M University for her undergraduate work and the University of Houston Graduate College of Social Work for her graduate studies. She is interested in working with children and adolescents and has created innovative interventions that help children express their emotions.

Benjamin Pratt earned his bachelor's degree in anthropology from Brigham Young University and master's degree in social work from the University of Houston. He has worked clinically with adolescents at Baylor College of Medicine in Houston and at multiple private residential treatment facilities throughout northern Utah. Currently, Pratt is the assistant chief of social work service at the George E. Wahlen Department of Veteran Affairs Hospital in Salt Lake City, Utah. Pratt currently resides in Salt Lake City with his wife, who is a recreation therapist, and their four children.

Victoria S. Reyes, MSW, earned a master's degree in social work from the University of Houston, Graduate College of Social Work. She works at the Social Work Trauma Education Project with a specialization in trauma focused-cognitive behavioral therapy. Reyes has experience working with children and adolescents in a variety of settings including a child advocacy center, residential treatment center, foster care, and community mental health.

Cornesia Russell, a native East Texan, is passionate in providing support to unprivileged individuals who feel voiceless. She attended the University of Texas in Austin and received a BS in human development and family sciences. Russell then traveled to Houston and obtained her master's degree in social work. She is currently working at Memorial Hermann as an oncology/hematology and general medicine social worker. As a social worker and lover of children, Russell uses creative activities to help children to express and advocate for themselves, and help adults to gain insight on communicating efficiently with their children.

Ashleigh Scinta received her BA in history at the University of Houston and her master's degree in social work at the University of Houston, Graduate College of Social Work with a concentration in macro practice and specialization in *Trabajo Social* (Social Work Practice with Latinos). She is currently a doctoral student in social welfare at the University of California, Los Angeles. Scinta's research interests include culturally responsive prevention and intervention for intimate partner violence, child maltreatment, and reproductive health.

Marilyn Hotchko-Scott is an MSW alumnus of the University of Houston Graduate College of Social Work. She received her undergraduate degree from the University of Houston-Clear Lake. Her specialties include multicultural studies, child welfare, women's issues, domestic violence, and substance abuse. She has provided social services to various populations including women, children, adolescents, seniors, persons with disabilities, and the homeless. Hotchko-Scott has experience in case management with Communities in the Schools-Bay Area, Star of Hope Transitional Living Center-Houston, Bay Area Turning Point, and the Northwest Assistance Ministries Meals on Wheels Program.

Diana Scroggins, LMSW, earned her master's degree in social work from the University of Houston. She currently works with adolescents as a Child Protective Services caseworker. Scroggins also worked with GLBTQ adolescents and with women and families in a domestic violence shelter.

Alicia Michele Thomas, LMSW, is a middle school counselor for YES Prep East End in Houston. She came from Detroit, Michigan, and graduated from the University of Michigan with a degree in communications and sociology, and graduated from the University of Houston with her master's degree in social work. Before being a social worker, she taught kindergarten for three years in Houston, interned at YES Prep West and Brays Oak as a school counselor, and worked as a medical social worker at Memorial Hermann Hospital. Her practice interest is working with adolescents.

Chau Nguyen Todd, LMSW, specializes in both psychotherapy and neurofeedback therapy. As a neurotherapist, she helps clients "train their brains" to improve cognitive functioning. This high-tech and innovative intervention has been effective in treating ADHD, Asperger's, autism, depression, anxiety, oppositional defiance disorder, post-traumatic stress disorder, and bipolar disorder. She holds a bachelor of arts in communications from the University of St. Thomas and a master's degree in social work from the University of Houston. Before she became a social worker, currently at the Houston Women's Center, she served as a television journalist for fifteen years. She was a recipient of an Emmy Award for her work in the documentary "A Return to Vietnam." Her passion to help people grew as she covered life-changing stories up close and personal. She works with individuals, including children, teens, and adults, and volunteers for several nonprofit organizations in Houston.

Mark Trahan, LCSW, is currently a doctoral candidate at the University of Houston, Graduate College of Social Work. He is also an expert in marriage, infidelity, and young adult relationships with training from the Gottman Institute. He has previously worked in adolescent and adult outpatient addiction treatment and served as adjunct professor and a teaching fellow at the University of Houston.

Venus Tsui, PhD, is an assistant professor of social work at the Worden School of Social Service, Our Lady of the Lake University. She has experience teaching undergraduate and graduate social work courses. She has 14 years of cross-cultural clinical and community practice experiences working with children, youth and families, in both Texas and Hong Kong. She has made presentations in workshops and conferences, nationally and internationally, and written articles and book chapters in English and Chinese. Tsui's practice and research interests include intimate partner abuse against men, child welfare issues, marital relationships, mental health of Asian Americans, and provisions of culturally sensitive practice.

Connie Villasmil, LMSW, is a bilingual English-Spanish Licensed Master Social Worker in the state of Texas with over 2,000 hours of LCSW supervision. Villasmil has extensive experience in multigenerational and multicultural counseling services. She has worked as a medical case manager at Memorial Hermann Hospital and as a bilingual psychotherapist at community-based clinics. Villasmil is a strong believer in the eclectic counseling model, integrating psychoanalytical, cognitive-behavioral, and didactic-behavioral approaches to therapy.

Chloe Walker, JD, LMSW, is a family law attorney in Houston. She obtained her law degree and master's in social work at the University of Houston where she interned with Child Protective Services and with the Texas Legislature, focusing on children and family issues. Her interest in child advocacy stems from two years of service with AmeriCorps and from her volunteer work as a court appointed special advocate.

Monique McWilliams Wall, LCSW, is family advocacy treatment manager with the United States Air Force. She worked as a forensic interviewer with the Child Protection Team in Florida, primarily conducting sexual abuse interviews, before moving to New Mexico where she started working for the Air Force in their Family Advocacy program. She and her husband moved to Germany to work at the Family Advocacy program for three years. She moved to Colorado in 2012 and was chosen to be on the Department of Defense Family Advocacy Command Assistance team.

Jasmine Walls graduated from Prairie View A&M University in 2011 with a bachelor's degree in social work. She graduated with her master's degree in social work from the University of Houston Graduate College of Social Work. Walls is involved in the National Association of Social Work and the National Association of Black Social Work. Her current experience in social work includes interning at the Ben Taub Pediatric Mental Health Clinic. Walls's overall career goal is to obtain a challenging career in the social work field that will allow her to use the social work knowledge and skills taught and practiced throughout her educational track.

Micki Washburn is a licensed professional counselor-supervisor and nationally certified counselor who specializes in work with the LGBTQ communities. She is currently a doctoral candidate at the Graduate College of Social Work of the University of Houston. Her research interests include clinical application of the evidence-based practice process and culturally competent practice with diverse communities. Washburn has conducted numerous educational seminars for local businesses and mental health professionals on the topics of gender identity and gender expression. Washburn is also an adjunct instructor at the University of Houston and conducts clinical supervision for LPC interns.

Jolanna Jenae' Watson, MSW, is a social worker in Houston, Texas. She started her career helping children in various ways of protection before entering the field of mental health. Her ultimate goal is to set up her own private practice helping families through counseling and repairing marriages through hope.

Joy Welch, LMSW, is a graduate of the Clinical Practice Concentration in the Graduate College of Social Work at the University of Houston. Welch is a licensed master social worker with independent practice recognition, as well as a licensed child-placing agency administrator. Her areas of expertise are in-patient psychiatric counseling, adoption, birth parent counseling, and adoptive parent counseling. She is the executive director of Angel Adoptions, a licensed child-placing agency.

Laura Welch, MSW, specializes in macro social work with a political specialization through educational preparation from the Graduate College of Social Work at the University of Houston. Her academic focus has been geared towards juvenile advocacy, at-risk youth, minority youth, education, and community development. She is knowledgeable in areas of domestic adoption and trans-racial adoption through experience working with her mother's (Joy Welch) adoption agency. Welch's future interests include political social work and advocacy in urban areas and internationally.

Sandra Lynette Williams, MSW, graduated from the University of Houston with a specialization in clinical social work practice. She received her undergraduate degree in social work from the University of Houston in Clear Lake. Williams plans to explore working with diverse populations within the field of social work. She also plans to obtain her PhD in the future. Williams currently works as a foster care and adoptions coordinator for a child-placing agency in the Houston area.

Nicole Willis, PhD, LMSW, is currently an assistant professor at Texas Southern University, where she teaches courses related to policy, school social work, and international social work and theory. She has over ten years of practice experience with at-risk children, adolescents, and families in educational and mental health in urban settings. Willis's areas of practice interest include program coordination, group work, peer mediation, and parental involvement in public schools.

Noa Ben Yehuda, MSW, has worked with at-risk youth and children in various settings, including residential treatment and counseling centers. She provides therapy to individuals, families, and couples coping with life's difficulties.

Ada Lai-man Yip, LMSW, earned her bachelor's degree in social work at the City University of Hong Kong and is a registered social worker in Hong Kong. She received her master's degree in social work from the University of Houston. Yip has been working with children, youth, and families in school, hospice, and hospital settings. After her MSW study, she worked as a project manager for the Child Welfare Education Project of the University of Houston Graduate College of Social Work, managing grant proposals, child welfare research projects, and administrative responsibilities. Currently, she is a medical social worker helping patients deal with painful medical procedures.

Wenjun "June" Zhu is a research assistant in the Child Welfare Education Project at the University of Houston. Zhu earned her BA from Tianjin Normal University in China and her MA in the Jack J. Valenti School of Communication at the University of Houston. Her research interests include relationship management in charitable organizations, clinical social work practice, child education, and intercultural studies of child welfare policy.

Index

Note: Page numbers followed by "f" refer to figures.

abuse. *See* child abuse victims; sexual abuse, survivors of
Active Feelings game, 12–18
addictions, adolescents struggling with
   Visualizing game, 276–283
adjustment disorder
   Puzzle Pieces game, 235–238
adolescents, xiii, xxi, xxi–xxxvi
   games, 12–18, 25–33, 38–44, 49–57, 95–104, 108–115, 127–150, 186–190, 209–221, 232–243, 252–290
   guided imagery, 298–299, 305–310, 321–325, 334–340, 345–347, 350–351, 356–358, 361–366
adoptive families, children of
   My Family Tree guided imagery, 332–333
anger management
   Back-Off Bingo game, 25–33
   Fighting the Feeling of Anger guided imagery, 305–306
   Giver and Receiver game, 139–143
   How to Tame Your Temper game, 167–173
   King's "Rule-ette" game, 180–185
   Release Angry Feelings guided imagery, 343–344
   Smiling Face game, 258–266
anxiety disorder
   Puzzle Pieces game, 235–238
   A Simple Start game, 6–11
   Where Is the Bird? game, 284–287
attention deficit hyperactivity disorder (ADHD)
   3 in 1 ADHD games, 3–5
   Choose Your Own Adventure game, 68–72
   Focus game, 127–131
   My Favorite Thing guided imagery, 334–335
   Puzzle Pieces game, 235–238
autism, xiii, 235–238

Back-Off Bingo game, 25–33
behavioral problems, adolescents with
   Peer Influence exercise, 218–221
   Simulation and Circle-Building game, 252–257
bipolar disorders, adolescents with
   Choose Your Own Adventure game, 68–72
body image issues
   Glistening Stream and Body Image guided imagery, 321–323
   How I *See* Myself game, 164–166
body language
   Body Speaks game, 42–44
Body Works game, 45–48
Breaking the Ice game, 49–54
bullies
   Bullying Role Reversal guided imagery, 295–297
   Bye-Bye Bullies game, 62–67

child abuse victims
   Cleaning the Dirty Laundry game, 73–76
   Coping with the Aftereffects of Physical Abuse guided imagery, 300–302
   Let's Rebuild game, 186–190
   My Favorite Things game, 205–208
   Under the Sea guided imagery, 372–374
   Sharing Your Heart game, 247–251
child protective service (CPS) study, youth in
   Sharing Your Heart game, 247–251
Children in Military Families guided imagery, 298–299
children of Latino immigrants
   Immigrant Family Tree game, 19–24
Chinese children
   Feeling Faces game, 119–126
   Choose Your Own Adventure game, 68–72
Cleaning the Dirty Laundry game, 73–76
communication, open
   Make Believe or Truth game, 191–195

425

Compliments game, 77–79
concentration problems
　Environmental Mindfulness game, 108–111
　Secret Password guided imagery, 354–355
　A Simple Start game, 6–11
conduct disorders
　Simulation and Circle-Building game, 252–257
Connecting Latino Families game, 80–83
Connections and Relationships game, 84–90
context, xxii–xxiii
contextualized practice, xxiii
coping skills
　Back-Off Bingo game, 25–33
　Safe House, Safe Space game, 244–246
Coping with the Aftereffects of Physical Abuse guided imagery, 300–302
creative modalities, trends in, xxi–xxiii
critical thinking skills
　Choose Your Own Adventure game, 68–72
culture
　games, 38–41, 55–57, 62–67, 80–83, 119–126, 144–146, 196–204
　guided imagery, 318–320, 330–331, 341–342, 348–349, 364–366, 384–385

Dealing with Divorce game, 91–94
death, children or adolescents dealing with
　Giver and Receiver game, 139–143
　Group Drawing game, 151–155
decision-making skills
　Choose Your Own Adventure game, 68–72
　Forum Theater game, 134–136
　Peer Influence exercise, 218–221
depressive symptoms
　Everyone Is Important guided imagery, 303–304
　Working Through Secrets game, 288–290
detained children and adolescents
　Back-Off Bingo game, 25–33
　Finding Hope guided imagery, 307–310

disabilities. *See* physical disabilities, children with
disasters, orphans or survivors of
　Feeling Faces game, 119–126
diversity, xxi–xxii
Divominos game, 95–104
divorce of parents, children dealing with
　Dealing with Divorce game, 91–94
　Divominos game, 95–104
　My Favorite Things game, 205–208
　A Walk in Someone Else's Shoes guided imagery, 293–294
domestic violence
　Safe House, Safe Space game, 244–246
driving, preparing teens for
　Safe Driving for Teens guided imagery, 350–351

eating disorders, adolescents suffering from
　Following Hands and Focusing game, 132–133
　How I *See* Myself game, 164–166
　Visualizing game, 276–283
emotional problems
　Active Feelings game, 12–18
　Family Time game, 112–115
　Graph My Feelings game, 147–150
　Group Drawing game, 151–155
empowerment
　I Am Strong, Confident, and Powerful! guided imagery, 328–329
　Environmental Mindfulness game, 108–111
equine assisted psychotherapy (EAP)
　The Journey Home guided imagery, 361–363
Everyone Is Important guided imagery, 303–304
evidence-based therapeutic practice, xxiv
expressive language disorder
　Name It . . . Word It . . . Style It! game, 209–214

family relationship problems
　Compliments game, 77–79
　Healing Parent-Teen Conflict guided imagery, 324–325
Family Time game, 112–115

fear, children experiencing
  Bye-Bye Bullies game, 62–67
Feeling Beads game, 116–118
feeling cards (Chinese), 122f
Feeling Faces game, 119–126
feelings, expressing
  Family Time game, 112–115
  Graph My Feelings game, 147–150
  Group Drawing game, 151–155
  Make Believe or Truth game, 191–195
  Power List game, 222–226
  Puppet Communications game, 232–234
  Smiling Face game, 258–266
  3 in 1 ADHD games, 3–5
Fighting the Feeling of Anger guided imagery, 305–306
Finding Hope guided imagery, 307–310
Float Away guided imagery, 311–312
focus functioning
  3 in 1 ADHD games, 3–5
Focus game, 127–131
Following Hands and Focusing game, 132–133
foster care homes, children in
  Feeling Beads game, 116–118
Freeing Feelings guided imagery, 313–314
frustration
  Back-Off Bingo game, 25–33

gender identity, 137–138
girls
  Practice Your Limits game, 227–231
Giver and Receiver game, 139–143
GLBTQ (gay, lesbian, bisexual, transgender, queer/questioning) adolescents. *See also* LGBT
  Rainbow Questions game, 239–243
Go to My Country guided imagery, 318–320
goal-directed activities
  3 in 1 ADHD games, 3–5
Glistening Stream and Body Image guided imagery, 321–323
Grandfather's Parcel game, 144–146
Graph My Feelings game, 147–150
grief, children and adolescents dealing with
  Giver and Receiver game, 139–143
  Group Drawing game, 151–155

Group Drawing game, 151–155
guilt
  Freeing Feelings guided imagery, 313–314

Hands Connection game, 156–159
Healing Parent-Teen Conflict guided imagery, 324–325
health issues, xxii, xxi–xxxvi
  games, 34–37, 45–54, 134–136, 160–163, 227–231, 276–283
  guided imagery, 336–338
Helping Children Sleep After a Parent Has Been Incarcerating guided imagery, 326–327
homelessness, children experiencing
  Power List game, 222–226
horses, therapy using
  The Journey Home guided imagery, 361–363
Hospital Visit game, 160–163
hospital visits
  Hospital Visit game, 160–163
  How I *See* Myself game, 164–166
How to Tame Your Temper game, 167–173

I Am Strong, Confident, and Powerful! guided imagery, 328–329
ice breaking
  3 in 1 ADHD games, 3–5
  Breaking the Ice game, 49–54
  Connections and Relationships game, 84–90
  Graph My Feelings game, 147–150
  Hands Connection game, 156–159
  Name It . . . Word It . . . Style It! game, 209–214
  A Simple Start game, 6–11
  Simulation and Circle-Building game, 252–257
  Where Is the Bird? game, 284–287
Imitated for Self-Control game, 174–179
Immigrant Family Tree game, 19–24
impulse control issues
  Following Hands and Focusing game, 132–133
incarcerated parents, children of
  Helping Children Sleep After a Parent Has Been Incarcerating guided imagery, 326–327

428 *Therapeutic Games and Guided Imagery*

King's "Rule-ette" game, 180–185

Latino children of divorced/separated parents
  Connecting Latino Families game, 80–83
Laughing Yoga guided imagery, 330–331
Let's Rebuild game, 186–190
LGBT (lesbian, gay, bisexual or transgender) family members. *See also* GLBTQ
  Building Diverse Communications game, 58–61
life choices
  Forum Theater game, 134–136
loss. *See* death, children or adolescents dealing with
low frustration tolerance
  King's "Rule-ette" game, 180–185
low self-esteem
  Connections and Relationships game, 84–90
  Giver and Receiver game, 139–143
  Grandfather's Parcel game, 144–146
  I Am Strong, Confident, and Powerful! guided imagery, 328–329
  Overcoming Shame game, 215–217
  Puppet Communications game, 232–234
  Strength Flower game, 272–275

Make Believe or Truth game, 191–195
medical procedure. *See* health issues
Mexican children
  Go to My County guided imagery, 318–320
military families
  Children in Military Families guided imagery, 298–299
mood swings
  Snapshots for Moods game, 267–271
multicultural children, adolescents, or adults
  Bi- or Multicultural game, 38–41
  Go to My Country guided imagery, 318–320
  Trilingual Relaxation Journey guided imagery, 364–371
My Family Tree guided imagery, 332–333
My Favorite Thing guided imagery, 334–335
My Favorite Things game, 205–208

negative feelings
  The Dot Exercise game, 105–107
  English and Spanish, xvi f
  English only, xviii f
  no labels, xx f
  A Simple Start game, 6–11
nightmares
  Sleep Tight guided imagery, 356–358
"no," students having difficulty accepting
  How to Tame Your Temper game, 167–173
nonverbal children
  Hands Connection game, 156–159
  Where Is the Bird? game, 284–287

open communication
  Make Believe or Truth game, 191–195
  Overcoming Shame game, 215–217

Pain Management guided imagery, 336–338
parent-child conflicts, 39, 84, 96, 225, 232, 324
  Connections and Relationships game, 84–90
  Healing Parent-Child Conflict, 324–325
participation, encouraging
  Back-Off Bingo game, 25–33
Peer Influence exercise, 218–221
peer problems
  Compliments game, 77–79
  Peer Influence exercise, 218–221
physical aggression
  Fighting the Feeling of Anger guided imagery, 305–306
physical disabilities, children with
  Body Works game, 45–48
  Float Away guided imagery, 311–312
  From Yellow School Bus to White City Bus guided imagery, 315–317
positive feelings
  English and Spanish, xv f
  English only, xvii f
  no labels, xix f
post-traumatic stress disorder (PTSD)
  Yes or No guided imagery, 380–383
Power List game, 222–226
Practice Make Perfect guided imagery, 341–342
Puppet Communications game, 232–234

Rainbow Questions game, 239–243
rapport, building
   3 in 1 ADHD games, 3–5
   Back-Off Bingo game, 25–33
   Focus game, 127–131
   Graph My Feelings game, 147–150
   Make Believe or Truth game, 191–195
   My Fantastic Family game, 196–204
   My Favorite Things game, 205–208
   Power List game, 222–226
   Puppet Communications game, 232–234
   Rainbow Questions game, 239–243
relationships, establishing
   Focus game, 127–131
Release Angry Feelings guided imagery, 343–344
Releasing the Emotional Burden of Trauma guided imagery, 345–347
reticent clients
   How I *See* Myself game, 164–166
runaways
   Grandfather's Parcel game, 144–146

Safe House, Safe Space game, 244–246
safety plans, developing
   Safe House, Safe Space game, 244–246
secondary trauma, children or adolescents dealing with
   Giver and Receiver game, 139–143
seeking help
   Willing to Seek Help guided imagery, 375–376
self-control issues
   Imitated for Self-Control game, 174–179
   Secret Password guided imagery, 354–355
self-esteem. *See* low self-esteem
self-expression problems
   Environmental Mindfulness game, 108–111
self identity, exploring
   Rainbow Questions game, 239–243
self-image issues
   How I *See* Myself game, 164–166
   Sharing Your Heart game, 247–251
   Strength Flower game, 272–275
sentence completion cards (Chinese), 123f
sexual abuse, survivors of
   Let's Rebuild game, 186–190
   Overcoming Shame game, 215–217

Petals Overcoming Trauma guided imagery, 339–340
Puppet Communications game, 232–234
Safe House, Safe Space game, 244–246
Sandbox Play guided imagery, 352–353
shame, overcoming
   Overcoming Shame game, 215–217
Simple Start game, A, 6–11
Simulation and Circle-Building game, 252–257
Sleep Tight guided imagery, 356–358
Smiling Face game, 258–266
Snapshots for Moods game, 267–271
social anxiety
   Connections and Relationships game, 84–90
social skills, lack of
   King's "Rule-ette" game, 180–185
solution-focused interventions, 387–404
special needs, xiii, xxiv, xxx. *See also* attention deficit hyperactivity disorder (ADHD); autism; child abuse victims; impulse control issues; physical disabilities; post-traumatic stress disorder (PTSD); sexual abuse, survivors of; substance abuse; terminal illness, children suffering
Stay Focused guided imagery, 359–360
Strength Flower game, 272–275
strengths, identifying
   Power List game, 222–226
   Strength Flower game, 272–275
substance abuse
   Visualizing game, 276–283

Taoists
   Practice Make Perfect guided imagery, 341–342
   Stay Focused guided imagery, 359–360
temper tantrums. *See* self-control issues
terminal illness, children suffering
   Be Positive game, 34–37
   The Dot Exercise game, 105–107
   The Journey Home guided imagery, 361–363
therapeutic games
   systematic review supporting, xxv–xxxvi

therapeutic toolbox, portable, 405
3 in 1 ADHD games, 3–5
toolbox, portable therapeutic, 405
touch therapy
   Rice Therapy guided imagery, 348–349
traditional families, children/adolescents not represented by
   My Fantastic Family game, 196–204
transgender
   Who Am I? game, 137–138
trauma
   Group Drawing game, 151–155
   Petals Overcoming Trauma guided imagery, 339–340
   Releasing the Emotional Burden of Trauma guided imagery, 345–347
   Safe House, Safe Space game, 244–246
   Working Through Trauma guided imagery, 377–379
trauma, secondary, children or adolescents dealing with
   Giver and Receiver game, 139–143
Trilingual Relaxation Journey guided imagery, 364–371

Under the Sea guided imagery, 372–374

variety and diversity, xxi
violence, domestic. *See also* child abuse victims; sexual abuse, survivors of
   games, 112–115, 186–190, 205–208, 215–217, 227–234, 244–251, 276–283
   guided imagery, 300–302, 339–340, 356–358, 361–363, 272–274

Walk in Someone Else's Shoes, guided imagery, 293–294
Where is the Bird? game, 284–287
Who Am I? game, 137–138
Willing to Seek Help guided imagery, 375–376
Working Through Secrets game, 288–290
Working Through Trauma guided imagery, 377–379

Yes or No guided imagery, 380–383
Yoga Body Scan guided imagery, 384–385

About the Author

Monit Cheung (MA, MSW, PhD, Ohio State University) is professor of social work and chair of the Clinical Practice Concentration in the Graduate College of Social Work at the University of Houston. Cheung is a licensed clinical social worker specializing in family counseling, child and adolescent counseling, and incest survivor treatment. Cheung is a member of numerous boards dealing with child protection and family services. She has taught at the graduate level for 27 years and emphasized the use of a practice-oriented approach to teaching. She is the author of over 600 articles, book chapters, and books including *Child Sexual Abuse* and *Therapeutic Games and Guided Imagery Volume 1: Tools for Mental Health and School Professionals Working with Children, Adolescents, and Their Families*.

To download recordings of the guided imagery techniques in this book, please visit www.lyceumbooks.com/guidedimagery.